THE SHONA PEOPLES

Shona Heritage Series: Volume 1

THE
SHONA PEOPLES

REVISED EDITION

AN ETHNOGRAPHY OF THE CONTEMPORARY
SHONA, WITH SPECIAL REFERENCE TO THEIR
RELIGION

by M.F.C. Bourdillon
D. Phil. (Oxon.)

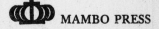 MAMBO PRESS

MAMBO PRESS
P.O. Box 779, Gweru
P. Bag 66002, Kopje,Harare
P. Bag 9213, Gokomere, Masvingo

THE SHONA PEOPLES

1st print 1976
2nd revised edition 1982
3rd revised edition 1987

Cover design by Burford Hurry

ISBN 0 86922 188 4

Printed and published in Zimbabwe
by Mambo Press, Senga Road, Gweru
1987

CONTENTS

INDEX OF MAPS, DIAGRAMS AND ILLUSTRATIONS

PREFACE TO THE THIRD EDITION

While I am delighted that this work is so much in demand as to require the printing of a third edition, it is with some misgivings that I have agreed to produce this edition. One reason is the anomaly that a white man should be writing a text book in Zimbabwe about the Shona. For all my reading and my field research, I certainly do not claim to be an expert on 'Shona culture'. The Shona themselves provide this expertise. I do, however, have a training in social analysis, which involves seeing and unfolding patterns and connections in social life which are not always evident to the actors themselves. And I do have a training in the interpretation of social behaviour, describing it and making it intelligible to observers; and here 'observers' may be complete outsiders or Shona people who are interested in variations over time and place within their own society. In both these areas, expertise is still needed to understand and cope with the changes that are taking place in Shona society.

The second reason for my misgivings is the rapid change taking place in Shona society, and the difficulty in maintaining credibility for the subtitle: *An ethnography of the contemporary Shona...* Since the second edition was prepared, there have been numerous political and administrative changes which have affected the Shona, especially in the rural areas. Most noticeable are the increased facilities in the rural areas: more schools, clinics, better roads, and in some places the growth of administrative and commercial centres. Party political structures have affected institutions of decision-making and of social control. There has been a variety of legislation which either directly or indirectly affects Shona social life. There has been the economic depression, adversely affecting employment opportunities. There have also been two years of severe drought, which must have some social consequences. It is hard to keep abreast of all these changes.

I have introduced minor changes throughout this edition, two areas being worthy of attention.

I have modified what was said in past editions on the position of women. The results of recent research have persuaded me to change my view slightly. In both traditional and contemporary society, the position of women is in need of redress. Anyone wishing to go into this subject is referred to Olivia Muchena's annotated bibliography, listed under 'United Nations' at the end of this volume.

There have been considerable legislative and administrative changes in the conduct of traditional courts in both rural and urban areas. The effects of these changes in practice have not yet been adequately researched from the social point of view. Consequently, I have simply indicated what the changes are, and have changed the tense in my descriptions of traditional proceedings, which form the basis of the new system of primary courts.

I have also added some recent works to the bibliography. I should perhaps draw the attention of more serious researchers to a fuller and more detailed bibliography on the peoples of Zimbabwe which I and Angela Cheater have prepared on the computer of the University of Zimbabwe.

M.F.C. Bourdillon
March, 1985

PREFACE TO THE SECOND EDITION

There is a danger when a man writes about a people he has met and studied, that the objects of the study lose their humanity. The late Professor Sir Edward Evans-Pritchard was very much alive to this danger when he maintained that Social Anthropology should aim to be a humanity rather than a science; it should aim to see and understand the inner man rather than simply to describe outer curiosities. His is the tradition I should like to follow. But on reading my text I find I have often failed. I present at times a dry catalogue of observations on Shona society. So I must make up for the short-comings of the work by emphasizing now that Shona society, from which I count a number of my friends, is made up of men, women and children who are alive and sensitive to the world and the people around them.

When I spent a year and a half in a Shona community in the Mount Darwin district (in 1969 and 1970), two points struck me strongly. One was the hardship of the life of the people: the heat and dust of the country, the poor water supplies during the long dry season, the difficulty of keeping dry in the rains, the poor housing, the constant shortage of money, the frequent shortage of food, the never ending battle with disease. That over the years people become accustomed to the hardships which are part of their life does not mean that they cease to feel them.

The second thing that struck me strongly was the resilience and cheerfulness of the people in the face of hardship. It is true that some were oppressed by the hopelessness of never being able to improve their situation. Some kept their minds off their situation in frivolity, drink and drugs. But the calmness, and even humour, with which people faced, for example, famine after a drought was most striking.

More generally in my studies of the Shona, I have been surprised at how often the Shona themselves are unaware of differences between people from different localities. Since there is a basic cultural and linguistic similarity between all Shona, people from one part of Shona country find themselves readily able to fit into communities elsewhere, often without noticing significant differences in custom and social organization. And here, perhaps, lies a second fault of this book: often I have had to generalize to the extent of obscuring local variations and characteristics, and often I have described one community in detail, perhaps falsely leaving the impression that my description applies to all Shona everywhere. When traditional local variations are reinforced by different reactions to the various changes brought about by nearly a century of white settlement, generalizations about the Shona people as a whole must be taken with caution.

So that more serious readers can discover the localities to which my descriptions primarily refer, and also check on the reliability of my sources, I have thoroughly footnoted the text. Footnotes also enable those who wish to follow up in more detail on points of interest. The system I have used is to cite simply the author and year of the work in the footnotes: the details of the works cited can be found in the bibliography at the end of the book.

The first edition of *Shona Peoples* was published in the early years of the war which led up to the establishment and recognition of an independent Zimbabwe. At that time, the white government still claimed to be in control of the situation. Since then, there have been years of bitter fighting, during which communities and families have been broken up, not only by death and the destruction of property, but also by deep suspicions and fears which destroyed for a time the trust essential for social life.

Respect, at least overtly, for youth with guns replaced traditional deference to the elders of communities. The sufferings of rural people were exacerbated by poor rains in the 1978/9 and 1979/80 seasons, which, together with the impediments the war placed on agriculture, resulted in severe food shortages in 1980. Now there has been a settlement, independence, and reconciliation. Heavy rains in the 1980/81 season promise to produce a good harvest. We hope that the ravages of war will at last be covered over.

Apart from its short term efforts, the war, and the independence which followed, are bound to bring about long term changes to Shona life. The relations between blacks and whites in Zimbabwe have been permanently and radically altered. It is true that blacks are still largely economically dependent on whites, especially for employment; but blacks find it easier now to assert their rights through the political machinery of party and government. Minimum wages have been dramatically raised. Racial discrimination detrimental to blacks is being removed in all spheres of life. Further changes are in the air, involving health services, educational facilities, employment, perhaps even rural land tenure and farming. The precise nature of these changes, and their effects on the social life of the future, are subjects for further studies. Indeed, the effects of the war itself on Shona life have not yet adequately been studied and documented to be incorporated into this edition. A number of references are made to changes that have taken place in the last six years, including some of the consequences of the war, but I cannot guarantee that everything in this edition is fully up to date.

In two chapters, I have made substantial additions and alterations: those on the economy and on urbanization. In the first case, the changes comprise a response to recent research, particularly that of my colleague Angela Cheater, and also to change in perspective on my part. The chapter now reflects a greater emphasis on the inherent coherence and rationality of Shona economic relations than did the corresponding chapter in the first edition. I would like to acknowledge Dr Cheater's help in bringing about the improvements.

The additions to the chapter on urbanization arise largely from recent research. In criticizing the brevity of this chapter in the first edition, Professor Murphree[1] acknowledged the difficulty posed by the absence of available data. The difficulty remains, and more research is needed on Shona urban life. But the shortage of data has been alleviated somewhat by the works of Valerie Moller, Professor Chavunduka, Joan May and Dr Weinrich.

Elsewhere, additions and corrections are relatively minor, usually resulting from publications which have appeared since the first edition went to press. The bibliography contains a number of additions, and I hope contains all the most important works on the Shona in Zimbabwe which have so far been published. Dr Cheater and I, with the help of some students, are in the process of compiling a complete and up to date bibliography on the peoples of Zimbabwe.

One criticism to which I have not responded, refers to my failure to give an account of nationalist politics among the Shona.[2] I concede that the impact of national politics is a pervasive component of the contemporary cultural formation of the Shona, and there are references throughout this volume to the implications of the political environment for Shona life: in land use and agricultural extension work, in the situation of migrant labourers, in the role of chiefs, in the administration of law, in local government, in practices surrounding witchcraft beliefs, in the political roles of spirit mediums, in attitudes to mission churches, in the process of urbanization, and elsewhere. My experience in Korekore country in 1969 and the early 1970s suggested that although there was a strong awareness among the people that the Smith government worked against black interests, there was little explicit consideration of alternative

---

1. Review of *Shona Peoples* by M.W. Murphree in *Zambezia*, vol. 7, no. 1 (1979), pp. 117ff.
2. Cf. review by M.W. Murphree, *loc. cit.*

possibilities. That this impression is not generally true is clear from the strife of the late 1950s in many areas, which concerned support for rival nationalist parties. In Korekore country, the war brought about new possibilities for political action, and consequently a greater political awareness. It is clear that more and more Shona have taken up the nationalist cause against white minority rule, culminating in almost universal support for the guerrilla war. The significance to Shona life of the various political parties and leaders in this process is not so clear. I still maintain that it is virtually impossible to obtain the data necessary for an objective and detailed account of the impact of nationalist politics on Shona life, and further that any attempt to present such an account would stir up in some quarter or another emotional prejudices against the book as a whole. So in this edition, as in the first, the political environments in which the Shona have found themselves appear only as implicit influences on Shona life.

I remain unrepentant about leaving out the Shona in Mozambique. Apart from the paucity of available literature on this group of Shona, the national boundaries which have been in operation for three quarters of a century, have created social and ethnic differences, to the extent that the two groups of people can now be regarded as quite separate. How the different national histories have created social and cultural differences, remains for the time being an interesting speculative question.

I also reject criticisms that my account, particularly in respect of the position of chiefs in Shona society, displays undue bias, reflected in my failure to use government papers and publications.[3] What I am not prepared to do is to use statements of policy as descriptions of practice. Formal policies about, for example, non-interference in the election of chiefs or a non-directive approach to community development or a freedom to choose between legal systems, do not correspond exactly with how the administration operated. This book is concerned to describe how the Shona live, not the ideas and ideals in the minds of policy makers. I remain convinced that I have utilized the sources which provide information on my subject, and have presented this information fairly.

An area of Shona life which deserves mention, although I have not included it in the body of the text, comprises Shona arts, on two fields of which there is a growing body of literature: namely, music and literature.

---

3. Reviews of *Shona Peoples* by R. Howman in *The Rhodesia Herald*, 26th April 1976; and by
   C.J.K. Latham in *Rhodesiana*, vol. 35 (1976), pp. 73f. Cf. my reply in *Rhodesiana*, vol. 36
   (1977), pp. 80f.

The complexity of African drum rhythms is common knowledge. What is unique about Shona music is the development of the *mbira*, comprising metal reeds fixed to a wooden sounding board, and usually inserted into a large gourd resonator. The reeds, which are plucked by fingers and thumbs, are finely tuned, and cover more than three octaves in the larger instruments. It is the most sophisticated of all African musical instruments, and can provide complex rhythms and melodies, especially when a number of instruments are played together. Here I simply refer readers to some of the studies related to this instrument,[4] with the reminder that traditional music provides only one component of the music of the contemporary Shona.

Literature in Shona is clearly not a part of traditional Shona culture; but this literature derives as much from Shona traditions as it does from the Europeans who introduced writing into Shona society, and Shona literature is an integral part of contemporary Shona culture. In this field, I refer readers particularly to the works of Professor Kahari, who explicates the ways in which various writers use fiction to comment on aspects of contemporary Shona life.[5] And one should not ignore other forms of Shona literature, particularly Shona poetry,[6] nor Shona writings in English, which give the reflections of persons who have been fully involved in modern change.[7]

When the first edition of *Shona Peoples* was published, Mambo Press simultaneously produced a pamphlet entitled *Myths about Africans*.[8] In this work, I was deliberately polemical, trying to challenge some of the ways in which white Rhodesians thought about their black countrymen. It is the nature of such a work to provoke both strong support and strong criticism; in this case, even critics conceded that the pamphlet was thought provoking and worth reading, and supporters have suggested that the argument be incorporated into the book on *Shona Peoples*.[9] I am hesitant to do so on two grounds: firstly, the polemical style of the pamphlet contrasts with the more cautious and thoroughly documented approach of the book; secondly, with the passing of white rule, the myths which arose from this rule, and which supported it, have become obsolete. We can expect a

---

4. Tracey 1980; Berliner 1978; Kauffman 1970.
5. Kahari 1972; 1975. See also Krog (ed.) 1966, pp. 97 – 163.
6. Cf. Hodza 1979; also Krog (ed.) 1966, pp. 164 – 210.
7. See Kahari 1980.
8. Bourdillon 1976.
9. E.g., reviews by R. Howman in *The Rhodesia Herald*, 3rd May 1976, and by M.W. Murphree in *Zambezia*, vol. 7, no. 1 (1979), p. 118.

new set of myths to arise, more in conformity with the position of contemporary rulers.

Nevertheless, I maintain that *Myths about Africans* makes a number of important points relevant to the understanding of Shona ethnography. Accordingly, I propose to give in this preface on outline of the argument. If you find this outline too condensed, I refer you to the original pamphlet.

Myths about Africans seeks to expose the prejudice in certain ways in which whites think and speak about their black countrymen. These ideas can be characterized as myths for a number of reasons. Firstly, the ideas, like myths, are seriously believed: although I suggest political influences behind them, I am not concerned to question the good faith of those who hold them. Secondly, these ideas, like myths, are based on partial observations of reality — they are, in fact, usually supported by anecdotal incidents. Thirdly, the ideas are protected from criticism by claiming to provide a generalized view, while admitting any number of specific contrary examples: it is characteristic of myth that it cannot be disproved by empirical observations. Fourthly, like myths, white ideas about blacks supported certain values and norms of white society: in particular, they purported to justify the privileged position of whites in Rhodesian society. And finally, like myths, white ideas about blacks had practical implications in political and economic life.

The first feature in the white myths about black people is an emphasis on the primitive nature of the African past. Focusing on the contrast between the simple technology of African culture, and the sophistication of the European literate tradition and its complicated technology, the myth exaggerates the primitive, even savage, nature of traditional African society. It exaggerates the frequency and effects of ancient tribal wars; tenacious superstitions concerning witchcraft and spiritual powers; horrific magico-religious rites; uncritical subservience to political propaganda and intimidation; the servile status of women; a casual and unproductive approach to agriculture. Against all such exaggerations, readers of this volume will discern the reasonable pragmatism which dominates Shona society, ranging from scepticism about religious practitioners to the development of a viable agricultural economy. Shona traditions can readily be adapted to meet the needs of the modern world.

Associated with an exaggerated belief in the primitive nature of the African past, is the belief of many whites that Great Zimbabwe could not have been built by Africans. Whites saw as a threat to their position the idea that the 'primitive' Bantu were capable, without outside help, of political organization and material skills more sophisticated than those that the nineteenth century settlers found, or chose to find. The privileged position of the whites was justified by the belief that only with their help could the native Bantu do anything constructive. In fact, all professional archaeologists who have worked on the site are agreed that the Zimbabwe Ruins are Bantu in origin.

A further, and to some extent contrary, trend in the white myth is an idealization of the African past. Based on the indubitable importance to traditional African societies of kinship groups and community consensus, the myth denies to Africans an ability to think and act as individuals, claiming that they are always content to go along with the group to which they belong; this aspect of the myth ignores the diversity and the conflicts which have always existed within African societies, and which are clearly evident among blacks today. Also idealized in the myth are the roles of traditional chiefs, headmen and elders, who were assumed to be the leaders and spokesmen of tribal opinion. In this view, people who espoused new ways of life, especially in the cities, or new political mechanisms, could be dismissed as dangerous deviants, or as persons who mindlessly followed popular demagogues.

Progress in African society posed a dilemma to the myths supporting white superiority. On the one hand, traditional African culture was presented as an impediment to progress, encouraging a passive fatalism and idleness which are incompatible with progress. On the other hand, the justification of white rule depended to some extent on the benefits that whites had brought to African life. Accordingly changes to African life, particularly the incorporation of material comforts, are admitted; but they are portrayed as superficial, and blacks are portrayed as being fundamentally tied in thought and in living to their traditional rural homes.

Finally, it is worth noting how little effect on the myths resulted from the scholarly research and the findings of academics. These were deemed to be prejudiced and politically inspired, and many scholars who had done research on African life were deported or prohibited from re-entering the country by the government of the Rhodesian Front. Even when a professional anthropologist was chosen and employed by government to do a piece of research, his conclusions could be readily ignored.[10]

The argument is that stereotypes have been built up about blacks, which provided, and still provide, a balm to any qualms of conscience that whites may feel about the relative statuses of white and black social life, and which were impervious to any evidence which might have exposed

10. Cf. Holleman 1968, pp. 218 — 227.

them. Such stereotypes or myths about outsiders are common in any group of people. In trying to expose white myths about black people, I do not wish particularly to malign the whites of Zimbabwe, not all of whom accept the stereotypes, and many of whom accept them in good faith. Indeed, the stereotypes are supported by not a few blacks, who to some degree have been absorbed into the elitist white society, or who have absorbed ways of thinking of those who held the dominant position in Rhodesian society, or who simply see the partial truths that the myth contains. I should expect parallel stereotypes about backward or intransigent peasants to develop among some of the new ruling class as they increasingly encounter the difficulties inherent in administration. At least an idealization of the traditional past is likely to accompany the overthrow of white rule.

What *Myths about Africans* was intended to convey, and what a careful reader of *Shona Peoples* should see, is the dangerous falsity involved in any stereotype of any group of people. Shona society, like any society, contains people of all types: dreamers and pragmatists, superstitious traditionalists and cynics, conservatives and progressives, socially oriented people and individualists, good people and bad. There is a Shona proverb, *'Murungu munhuwo'*[11]: the message of this book is that the Shona are also people.

A final word: one of the difficulties in trying to describe a contemporary society in rapidly changing times, is that one's work is rapidly overtaken by events. Between preparing the second edition and its publication, I notice that some of the statements on chiefs and primary courts are already out of date, minimum wages have been greatly increased — which changes the economic situation in towns and on commercial farms —, the name Salisbury is due to be changed. There will be others. The reader must make allowances for the time of writing.

M.F.C. Bourdillon
1981

11. 'A white is also a person'.

ACKNOWLEDGEMENTS

I would like to take this opportunity of acknowledging my debt to Stanford Nyakusengwa and the people of Chiruja, the late Renoni Makuni and the people of Diwa, the Fathers of Marymount Mission, and others I met in the Mount Darwin District, for their hospitality, their understanding and patience, and for their help in numerous ways when I was in the field. They provided cheerful and entertaining company in happier times: later in more troubled times, some lost their homes or fields or both, some were tortured, some were imprisoned, some were killed; few escaped the crossfire.

A tribute to Professor Michael Gelfand is in place. The works under his name in my bibliography by no means exhaust the list of Professor Gelfand's publications on the Shona — all the result of spare time activity. Criticisms that professionals in the field may make of some of his works do not outweigh the debt we owe to him for painstakingly recording so many details of Shona culture.

I would like to thank the Society of Jesus for its encouragement and support when I was a member, particularly when I was researching in the field; Julien Hofman, S.J., for the idea of producing this book (my feelings on this point have not always been thankful), and for helpful comments on some sections of it; Fr Michael Hannan, S.J., and Michael Graham-Jolly for reading a first draft of my text and making helpful and encouraging comments on it; also Dr David Beach, Roy Theisen and Christopher Chivanda for their help in sorting out particular sections of it — Mr Chivanda has also greatly assisted me in collecting information; Mrs E. Bourdillon, for help in proof-reading; the Emslie Horniman Anthropological Scholarship Fund and the University of Zimbabwe for contributions towards research expenses. In the preparation of the second edition, I acknowledge help from Angela Cheater, who provided many criticisms of the first edition together with contributions for additions, Professor Chavunduka, Joan May and Mrs Palframan (who helped with the index). There are others who in various ways have been helpful.

Finally, I must thank Mambo Press for publishing this study in their handsome Shona Heritage Series.

M.F.C. Bourdillon
February, 1981

Historical Background

The sources of Shona history

To understand who a people are, we have to look at their past, the history from which they arose. The ever-recurring debate about who built the Great Zimbabwe shows clearly enough how people place their status and prestige on their past, and how many judge the past according to their image of what people now are. This attitude is partly, but only partly true: a man's character to some extent lies in the traditions in which he was brought up and the experiences he has undergone; but anyone can change, especially under the influence of outside pressures. The same applies to a people. When I describe the history of the Shona and their traditional culture, I do this to help understand the Shona people today and how they have adapted to their modern environment. I do not pretend that they have not changed in the last seventy years, still less do I suggest that they should not change.[1]

But before we can look at the history of the Shona, I must say someting about writing the history of a people who left no written documents and the methods used by modern historians.

One important source of information is the archaeological study of the numerous ancient ruins and other relics of past ages scattered around Zimbabwe.[2] Some ruins, such as the Great Zimbabwe and Khami in the south and the hill ruins of Inyanga in the east, are well known; others, such as the excavation site near Bindura or the ruins associated with the famous Mutapa dynasty in the Zambezi Valley and various ancient mining sites, are less spectacular and less well known, but they also provide information about the early Shona. The kind of information, however, that archaeology can yield is very limited in the absence of literary deposits. Styles of building and of pottery dug up from different levels of habitation can tell us something of the large scale movements of peoples. Items introduced from outside, such as beads and porcelain from the Far East, can tell us a little about trading contracts and may also help with dating. The examination of radio-activity in wood deposits can tell us approximately when the wood was cut. By fitting together snippets of information obtained in much arduous and painstaking digging archaeologists are able to build up a surprisingly full picture of the past.

A second source of information is documents from literate visitors to

---

1. There is a danger in some quarters that an over-emphasis on Shona tradition can obscure changes in Shona society. Cf. Bourdillon 1976.
2. The most important works on this field are Summers 1958 and 1969, and Garlake 1973.

the country. The Portuguese first settled in East Africa in the fifteenth century and pursued a policy of conquest and trade with the interior, resulting in dealings with Shona leaders for five centuries. Much of the contact was superficial and the written accounts give an exclusively Portuguese point of view which is not very satisfactory for the understanding of Shona history. In the nineteenth century, Portuguese documentation was supplemented by the accounts of British missionaries, explorers and settlers: while these did not have a Portuguese orientation, they were equally far from providing a Shona history as the Shona themselves saw it and understood it. Nevertheless, written accounts of European contacts with the early Shona fill in some of the huge gaps left by the archaeologists.

A third source of information which has seriously been tapped by historians only in the last two or three decades is oral tradition. Although this is invaluable in that it is the only source that gives us the Shona point of view, it has a number of features which make it unreliable for the elucidation of a factual history.[3]

Firstly, oral traditions are normally recounted only for a specific purpose and survive only as long as people continue to maintain an interest in the subject; a corollary to this is that informants tend to recite only those aspects of their oral tradition which serve their own purpose. Thus when I was collecting detailed information on the history of two chiefdoms in Korekore country, my task was simplified by a dispute over chiefly succession in each chiefdom, to the effect that members of the different houses readily recounted those aspects of their traditional history which supported their own claims to the chiefship; by fitting together the accounts of all the claimants, I was able to obtain a full account of the recent history of the two chiefships. But years later I still came across new items of traditional history recounted by old men and relevant to matters other than chiefly succession. In another chiefdom, the main interest was the status of a dynasty which was once recognised as a chiefship by the government but which now holds the official status only of headman: accounts of the traditional history of the dynasty dealt only with the changing relationships between the chiefs and government administrators although in fact the dynasty appears to have dated from soon after the founding of the Korekore state some five centuries ago. Oral historical traditions tend to

---

3. The use of oral tradition by historians is fully discussed in Vansina 1961. For this reason, I give little credence to Chigwedere's (1980) account of Shona history, which relies primarily on the sayings of spirit mediums.

refer to some contemporary interest and to survive only as long as the contemporary situation arouses interest in them.[4]

Associated with this point is the manipulation of oral traditions to suit a current purpose. People select and recount those items only which suit their particular interest, and even twist and distort them. Thus in one Tavara chiefdom, the clan of the chief and the clan of the most important spirits each gave an opposite view of how the two groups came to live together: each account purported to establish the clan concerned as the first to live in the country and the true owners on the land.[5] It is also possible that certain of the names refer only to symbolic mythical figures, and have no historical base at all.[6]

Another problem in deriving history from oral tradition is that the later tends to telescope history. This applies particularly to genealogies in which unimportant people or unimportant generations tend to get left out, as indeed do persons who are not convenient to the narrator. Thus, for example, in the traditions of a number of Korekore chiefdoms the five centuries from the founding of the Korekore state to the present day are covered in about eight generations of rulers, half of which relate to the British occupation. Telescoping also occurs when two persons of the same name or even two or more persons bearing the same dynastic title become fused into one. The Shona belief in spirit mediumship[6a] emphasizes the process when the historical person becomes confused with a series of mediums of his spirit.

Another common phenomenon in Shona traditional history is that the movements of peoples and wars between them are likely to be recited as the personal histories of their leaders. The story of a conflict between two men is likely in fact to refer to a war or feud between their respective followers. And history becomes reduced to the stories of major lineages giving the false impression that the Shona population has multiplied from a handful of original clans.

Finally, oral traditions tend to refer to particular chiefly dynasties or even to particular commoner lineages with a chiefdom. It is only recently that the disparate Shona groups in Zimbabwe have become united in a na-

---

4. It is interesting to notice that apparent ignorance of, and lack of interest in, traditional history is by no means a new phenomenon among the Shona: it received comment in some groups as early as 1903 (cf. report of A.N.C. North District in National Archives file N3/33/8).

5. See Bourdillon 1972a.

6. David Lan (1983, pp. 167-195) argues that the Korekore legends about Mutota make more sense if understood in terms of mythical symbols than as references to history.

tional consciousness that requires a national history. So even where the reliability of traditions can be checked against other traditions, against written documents and against archaeological findings, they still appear only as pieces of jigsaw puzzle which historians must painstakingly bring together.

Yet in spite of all these limitations, oral tradition has proved to be a remarkably consistent source for historians. The results of collecting and examining such traditions are slowly emerging as a history of the Shona, sometimes tenuous and sometimes well established, but always fascinating, as we trace the growth and fragmentation of various powerful states which exercised widespread influence and which were capable of attracting trade with distant countries. The collection of independent petty chiefdoms, partly subdued by Ndebele, which the European settlers found (or chose to find) in the late nineteenth century, does not truly reflect Shona history.

Shona history to the fifteenth century[7]

The culture now classified as 'Shona' originated from Bantu settlement of the high fertile plateau between the Limpopo and Zambezi rivers, bounded in the east by the drop towards the coast and in the west by Kalahari desert. This country is moister and cooler than the surrounding lowlying country and is free from pests such as the tsetse fly which make the low country less pleasant and less healthy for habitation. The Bantu settlers subsequently found an added advantage: the plateau was rich in minerals with iron, gold and copper easily obtainable from surface mining.

The first known people to inhabit the plateau were bands of stone-age Khoisan hunters ('Bushmen') who left a heritage of rock paintings wherever suitable rock surfaces are to be found. They lived in small mobile camps and ate whatever they could kill or gather. The rock art associated with these hunting bands seems to have died away by the fifteenth century, by which time groups of agricultural and pastoral Bantu-speaking peoples were well settled in the country. It is unlikely that the new settlers violently exterminated the previous inhabitants: bands of hunters are not easily tracked down and eradicated in the hilly and wooded country of the sparsely populated plateau, and the early Bantu are unlikely to have had

---

6a. According to this belief, powerful spirits (usually the spirits of people who were prominent when they were alive) choose a human host who periodically becomes ritually possessed when the spirit wishes to communicate with the living. The host becomes closely associated with the spirit. (See chapters 9 and 10 below).

7. I am deeply indebted to Dr D.N. Beach who has allowed me to see and use his unpublished material. Dr Beach has since modified and published his material in Beach, 1980.

the numbers or the organization necessary for such an operation. The Khoisan hunters may have found that agriculture and stock-raising provided a more secure livelihood than their traditional wanderings. And growing settlements of herders and agriculturalists made a life of hunting and gathering more difficult. Those of the Khoisans who did not move to other lands became absorbed into the new Bantu iron-age cultures and the older stone-age culture died away.

The first Bantu had arrived on the plateau by the end of the second century. Little is known of the first Bantu migration from the north. The people who settled in what is now Zimbabwe appear to have been related to the ancestors of many peoples now established to the south of the Limpopo River, including the Nguni, Sotho, Tsonga, Venda and Chopi peoples. On the Zimbabwean plateau, the early Bantu settled along the watercourses in large villages, where they kept sheep, goats and cattle and farmed millet; and they added to their diet by hunting and gathering. They were also familiar with iron smelting and were able to make iron agricultural implements. It is likely that they washed gold from alluvial deposits and traded gold and ivory with Muslim traders on the coast. Their culture, the early iron-age culture of Zimbabwe, lasted about a thousand years until the ancestors of the present Shona people arrived on the plateau.

The archaeological examination of early settlements shows that during the couple of centuries following the year 1000 a new group of people moved onto the plateau, and the early iron-age peoples were absorbed into a culture cluster which is continuous with the cluster of cultures of the nineteenth century Shona peoples. It is unlikely that these early Shona were known by a common name, but it is likely that the southern group early became known as Karanga, a name which spread to certain other groups after subsequent migrations from the South: the name Shona is of recent origin and was applied to all the Shona-speaking peoples only after the British colonization of the country.

The later Bantu (or early Shona) brought a number of changes: a simpler form of pottery, a greater emphasis on cattle as opposed to other livestock, and improved mining techniques with which they were able during the course of the next nine hundred years to use up most of the surface gold on the plateau.[8] The trade of gold and ivory brought into the interior a few ceramics and large quantities of cloth and beads, and with the

---

8. For an archaeological study of mining in Zimbabwe, see Summers 1969, some of whose findings have been modified by Huffman 1974.

improved economy came larger settlements growing around wealthy men who could gather followings of dependants.

These later iron age peoples formed a number of distinct groups. One, in the south-west, remained somewhat cut off from the rest of the Shona peoples, and formed the basis of the modern Kalanga dialect cluster, whose people are distinct in language and culture from the rest of the Shona-speaking peoples: in more recent times, the Kalanga have been further isolated by the Ndebele settlement in the south of the plateau.[9] There were distinctive groups in other parts of the plateau, but these were later over-shadowed by subsequent migrations which resulted from the development and expansion of the Zimbabwe culture in the south.

The most striking feature of the Zimbabwe culture was the technique of building stone walls from exfoliated granite epitomized by the now famous ruins of the Great Zimbabwe.[10] These are a complex of stone walls which were built from naturally and articifially exfoliated granite during the course of an occupation of the site which lasted perhaps as much as two and a half centuries. The techniques of cutting stone slabs and building walls developed over time as can clearly be seen from the difference between the earliest uncoursed pile-and-wedge building and the finely coursed and dressed walling around the 'Great Enclosure' which was the climax of the building achievements. The massive size of the later buildings clearly shows the ability of their authors to command a large labour force.[11]

There are numerous smaller constructions in the surrounding Shona country, built in the same style as the Great Zimbabwe and in situations which suggest that their purpose was prestige rather than defence, but much smaller in scale to include homesteads housing no more than ten to thirty adults. These lesser zimbabwes suggest that the people of the Great Zimbabwe had widespread influence on the plateau, possibly including some sort of political control over neighbouring peoples. But the control was probably loose and there is no evidence to justify the use of the term 'empire' in connection with the Zimbabwe culture.

The rise of the Zimbabwe culture seems to have been a result of the

---

9. In this study, only occasional reference is made to the Kalanga people.
10. The Bantu origin of.the Zimbabwe Ruins is no longer seriously doubted by archaeologists who have worked on the site in recent years. The most recent and authoritative work on the subject is Garlake 1973. Cf. also Huffman 1972.
11. The wall around the 'Great Zimbabwe' is 240 metres long and at its greatest is five metres thick and nearly ten meters high. It has been estimated to contain 6 400 cubic metres of stonework. There was a clear improvement in building technique during the course of building the wall. (See Garlake 1973, p. 27.)

superior economy of the early Karanga. The site was well suited to the growth of some kind of a state since it was near an alluvial gold field, it had a good supply of water, it was near good grazing areas for cattle, and being on the edge of the plateau, there was a good supply of timber available. The activities of the early Karanga in mining gold and copper enabled their leaders to obtain through trade with Muslims on the coast a wealth of cloth, glass beads and ceramics. Unlike their predecessors, they also emphasised the use of cattle as a means of amassing wealth. Presumably the system of marriage transactions involving the exchange of the child-bearing capacities of women for cattle or services was then in operation, allowing a wealthy man to gather around him a large following of kinsmen and loyal in-laws.[12] The large following no doubt served to increase his wealth through raiding. So some time after the twelfth century, there had emerged at the centre of a growing state a powerful dynasty of rulers who were able to appropriate to themselves much of the trade with the coast and who had sufficient following to build the prominent edifice now known as the Great Zimbabwe.

But the concentration of a large population with a minimum of technology over a long period became too great for the natural resources of the area. Presumably, good farming land became scarce and remote from the residential centre. No doubt the land around the state capital became over-grazed and unfit for cattle, and nearby forests were denuded of timber. The lack of technical knowledge necessary to conserve natural resources inevitably led to the collapse of the state. The Great Zimbabwe had ceased to be a centre for trade with the coast by the middle of the fifteenth century.

Before the Zimbabwe state collapsed, population and political pressures had already pushed groups out to found new dynasties elsewhere on the plateau, sometimes over-flowing onto the surrounding lowlands. Wherever there was available granite, migrant Karanga of importance surrounded their homesteads with the imposing stone walls of the Zimbabwe culture.

The most significant group to move off from Zimbabwe migrated westwards around or shortly before the collapse of the Zimbabwe state towards the middle of the fifteenth century, and created the Torwa state which gave rise to the Khami culture. These people came with their techniques of building in exfoliated granite, but created a new style of architecture. Instead of building massive free standing walls, the Torwa people used their stonework to support prominent rubble platforms on

---

12. This is explained in chapter 2 below.

which to build the living huts of important people. Their stone walls were noted for elaborate and delicate decorations. The Torwa people also introduced a distinctive type of pottery, which they continued to make long after they and their rulers became subject to the powerful Changamire dynasty.

Also by the middle of the fifteenth century, large migrations of Karanga had moved to the northern edge of the plateau and spread east and west to cover all of what is now Korekore country (the name Korekore was applied to these people at some later date). One group travelled under their legendary leader, Mutota, to a land just above the Zambezi escarpment and founded a new state, the ruler of which held the dynastic title Mutapa.[13] Early in the fifteenth century, the Mutapa had spread his influence over the escarpment into the Zambezi Valley and had conducted campaigns to create a loose association of peoples stretching almost as far as the eastern sea coast. The autochthonous Tavara peoples, together with others further up the Zambezi Valley, thus came under the influence of the plateau Shona.

Movements away from the centre of the Mutapa state followed this northerly migration. Some of the autochthonous Tavara fled east and south away from the invading Karanga, moving up out of the Zambezi Valley and settling in the heart of the plateau. Groups of Karanga also hived off southwards.

One significant group from the Mutapa state travelled around the north-east corner of the plateau, settling beyond what are now the eastern highlands of Zimbabwe and subjecting the autochtonous Tonga to the rule of a new state. These people became known as the Barwe and their rulers were significant political figures in later dealings with the Portuguese. An offshoot from the Barwe state travelled eastwards onto the highlands and there founded the Chikanga dynasty of the Manyika peoples.

When the Portuguese arrived on the East African coast in the middle of the fifteenth century, the Mutapa state was just over its peak of power and influence. The Barwe state held strong control over trade routes to the interior. In the south, the new Torwa state was well established and its fame reached the Portuguese.

---

13. The exact full title is disputed: Mwene Mutapa or Mwana Mutapa are both possibilities. The more popular form, Monomotapa, is probably incorrect historically.

Later Shona history

Soon after they arrived on the East African coast, the Portuguese heard tales of the great Mutapa who ruled the land from the Kalahari desert in the west to the Indian Ocean in the east. But when early traders and missionaries reached him, they were disappointed to find what appeared to them as no more than a petty chief living in a kraal of pole and mud huts. The ruler had moved down into the valley and his influence was waning. The successors to the conquering Mutapa, Nyanhehwe, were unable to maintain a hold over widespread subject peoples, and the state of the Mutapa became a loose collection of independent chiefdoms, being forced only occasionally to pay tribute to a particular powerful Mutapa. The Mutapa remained, however, an influential figure, and traders (both Muslim and Portuguese), missionaries and administrators continued to have dealings with his court. The Portuguese even built a small, rough fort near the kraal of the Mutapa in the Zambezi Valley. In later years, the state became disrupted by civil wars as branches of the dynastic family vied for power, sometimes abetted by Portuguese traders and administrators. The conflict was settled in the seventeenth century when Mutapa Mukombwe came to power with the help of the Portuguese. He restored some stability to the state and redistributed the land to loyal subjects. Thereafter the power of the Mutapas declined and the title finally died after the defeat of Chioko, the last of the Mutapas, by the Portuguese in 1917.[14]

As significant for the Portuguese was the Barwe state whose rulers held the dynastic title Makombe. The Barwe occupied the country through which passed the main trade routes from the port at Sena to the interior, and the Portuguese could not avoid continuous dealings with the Makombe. After the Portuguese had defeated the Barwe in battle in 1646, they regarded the Makombe as a subject ruler. After brief missionary activity in the area, a new Makombe required for the accession rituals 'baptismal water' obtained from the Portuguese at Sena, which the Portuguese understood as a sign of his subjection to them. In fact there was no question of religious submission on the part of the Makombes: the 'baptismal water' was associated with traditional succession ceremonies and was drunk by the new ruler only after it had been medicated by a senior spirit medium. The Barwe usually cooperated with the Portuguese: in this way the Makombe acquired powerful allies against neighbouring chiefs, and a

---

14. Cf. Abraham 1959.

11

monopology of guns, simply for allowing the Portuguese to use the trade routes. But in any conflict with the Portuguese, the readiness of the Barwe to attack Portuguese outposts and block the trade routes showed that they retained their autonomy.[15] When the Portuguese tried to exercise their supposed authority over the Barwe in the late nineteenth century, the Barwe showed their resentment of this interference by coming out in two wars against the Portuguese, finally suffering defeat only in 1917.

Meanwhile in the interior, the Torwa state was under stress. By the middle of the seventeenth century it was split by internal strife. Possibly as a result of internal upheavals and population pressures, the capital at Khami was deserted and a new complex was built at Dhlodhlo and Nalatale.

At about the same time a group of Rozvi migrated southwards from the north-east of the plateau, probably fleeing the civil wars of the Mutapa state and also the aftermath of the war between the Barwe and the Portuguese. One group moved south-east to found most of the present Ndau dynasties. A more significant group, attracted by the weakness of Torwa, travelled south-west and set up there the new dynasty of Changamire Mambos. Although the Rozvi take-over coincided roughly with the building of a new capital, it appears that the new rulers utilized the structure of the old Torwa state and recognised many of the old officials, with the result that the new and powerful dynasty was established with a minimum of social upheaval. Aided by a strong military organization, the Changamires controlled a prolonged period of trade with the Portuguese: by this stage alluvial gold was becoming scarce, and the main trade consisted in ivory for cloth, guns and other eastern or European goods.

Presumably under the Changamire rule, the cult of the high god Mwari, which later survived the collapse of the state and the Ndebele invasion, was established in the Matopo Hills.[16] The Rozvi Changamires ruled in the south-west until they were defeated by the invading Ndebele. The dominance of the Rozvi over surrounding chiefly dynasties remains reflected in the instalment ceremonies of many modern Shona chiefs who must have the ritual approval of a member of the Rozvi clan.

Meanwhile, as the population expanded in central Shona country there were numerous movements involving groups of people breaking off from

15. This is described in Isaacman 1973, and is a good example of how the study of oral traditions can correct the picture given by archival documents.
16. See chapter 10 below. The theory that this cult originated in the Great Zimbabwe is unsupported by convincing evidence.

larger chiefdoms. Between chiefdoms and within chiefdoms, intrigues and petty feuds were common. During these unsettled times, many peoples throughout Shona country had taken to building rough stone refuges on the tops of hills and in caves to which people could flee and where they could easily defend themselves against raiders. By the beginning of the nineteenth century the central plateau was becoming settled and most of the modern chiefdoms had been established. By this time, they comprised a hotch-potch of chiefly dynasties with a variety of histories, united by geographical propinquity and a common culture.

A picture of the precolonial period as feuding chaos is not correct. There were networks of trading links, which could only have been possible in a situation of some stability. In the south there is evidence of exchanges of grain from the plateau for cattle from the dry, low country. The ivory trade with the Portuguese continued right into the nineteenth century and people are known to have carried their tusks up to six hundred kilometres to sell them at Sena. Of more interest, perhaps, was a group of enterprising iron workers, the Njanja, who smelted the high class ore from Wedza mountain and traded their products widely in Shona country.[17] Their superior techniques of smelting and working iron produced high quality goods which were valued among surrounding peoples. Neighbouring peoples preferred Njanja hoes to the more local products of inferior iron. Especially prized were Njanja *mbira*, musical instruments comprising perhaps thirty finely tuned iron reeds set on a resonant wooden base and requiring good quality metal and skilled workmanship. The Njanja traded their iron products for cattle and other livestock in areas a couple of hundred kilometres from their home. Their wealth from trade allowed expert smelters and smiths to gather growing communities of apprentices and dependants, who in turn could perform the communal labour necessary for smelting on a large scale. Although militarily they were weak (they never succeeded in taking the mountain which was the source of their ore), they were able to acquire, through trade, wealth in cattle and other livestock.

Before the arrival of the white settlers there were two influential settlements from the Nguni peoples of the south in the early nineteenth century. The first was by the Gaza Nguni who settled on the lower Sabi and the second was the invasion of the Ndebele, both off-shoots from the Zulu state.

The Gaza Nguni were led by Soshangane, the founder of the Gaza state, whose name has subsequently been applied not only to his own

17. Cf. Mackenzie 1975.

13

people but also to neighbouring Ndau and Tsonga peoples. Soshangane's people settled in the far south-east of Shona country and infiltrated surrounding peoples. They have been influential linguistically and culturally in the Ndau peoples, some of whom were incorporated into the Gaza state. Their realm of influence was mainly in what is now Mozambique, overflowing into the south-east corner of Zimbabwe. They did conduct occasional raids for cattle and for wives in that area.

The Ndebele settled in the south-west, conquering the country of the Changamire. They incorporated large numbers of resident Shona into their state; these were considered socially inferior by the Ndebele. The adopted Shona learnt to speak Zulu and even their Shona clan names were translated into Zulu; the language of the Ndebele remains remarkably free of Shona influences. The Ndebele also adopted (in a modified way) the principal religious cult of the local Shona, namely, the cult of the high god Mwari which was fitted into the Ndebele spirit world.

The Ndebele arrived with the powerful military organization developed by the Zulu and were able to conduct occasional raids deep into Shona country, collecting women and cattle from defeated peoples. Nevertheless, these large raids centrally organized by the Ndebele king were infrequent occurrences. On the outskirts of Ndebele country raiding between small Ndebele groups and the neighbouring Shona was mutual. Indeed, by the time the British arrived, there were indications that a number of southern Shona chiefs were coming together in concerted resistance to the Ndebele. Although the Ndebele took over the country of the Changamires, and although they expanded their state into Karanga country, it appears that the Shona who were not incorporated into the Ndebele state were on the whole unaffected by the Ndebele settlement.[18]

So the early colonial view of the Shona as a collection of squabbling petty chiefdoms, subject to the Ndebele state, was clearly false. Shona history shows the rise and fall of a number of larger states, a long history of mining and a history of both internal and external trade. The Shona peoples had for the most part maintained their autonomy against various outside influences.

Partly as a matter of convenience, and partly no doubt deceived by the military inferiority of the Shona to the Ndebele invaders, the early white

18. The relationship between the Shona and the Ndebele is discussed in Beach 1973b where the author points out how accounts of isolated Ndebele raids became exaggerated to the view that the Ndebele were continuously raiding their Shona neighbours. Cf. also Beach 1971.

settlers regarded the Shona as unimportant subjects of the Ndebele king and no attempt was made to obtain from them concessions for mining or trading or settlement. Nevertheless the Shona showed themselves reluctant to accept domination by these new invaders who tried to meddle with their way of life on a scale that no previous immigrant group had done. When the Ndebele rose against the settlers in 1896, the Shona surprised the whites by joining in and maintaining a concerted resistance which lasted months after the Ndebele war had come to an end. It is true that not all Shona joined in the rising, and that some used the war simply to settle internal conflicts, joining the settlers or the rebels as convenience directed; nevertheless, the petty feuding chiefdoms were able to show remarkable unity and resilience when their independence was seriously challenged.[19]

The main rising of 1896 was followed by further lesser risings as British and Portuguese colonizers spread their rule. There was the Mapondera war in the north-east of what is now Zimbabwe around the turn of the century, and as late as 1917 the Barwe and neighbouring Tavara peoples fought against the Portuguese.[20] But eventually the Shona had to bow to superior military strength, and to submit to the laws and taxes imposed by colonial governments.

One early consequence of colonial settlement was the drawing of the boundary between Portuguese East Africa and the British colony of Southern Rhodesia. This boundary was negotiated in Lisbon and London with little regard for the Shona peoples resident in border areas. The boundary sometimes separated related groups of Shona and sometimes even went right through established chiefdoms. Since Portuguese colonial policy differed from British policy, the Shona in Mozambique and in Zimbabwe found themselves subject to different and separate influences. The greater economic growth in Zimbabwe and the greater attention of Zimbabwe settlers in this country to the education of indigenous peoples resulted in growing cultural differences across the frontier. Now many recognise the frontier as being more significant than the traditional boundaries of ancient Shona states.[21] This study deals specifically with the Shona of Zimbabwe.

The two main interests of the early white settlers in Zimbabwe were mining and farming. Although some indigenous peoples were displaced from areas thought to be rich in minerals, they were often given land as

---

19. For an account of the Shona rising, see Ranger 1967.
20. See Ranger 1963.
21. Cf. Bourdillon 1972a, pp. 118f.

15

suitable for farming as the land they had left and they were sometimes allowed to choose their new settlements. Where mining impinged more seriously on Shona life was in the demand for labour: very early on, the administration imposed taxes on the indigenous people in order to force the men to seek cash wages from employment on mines and farms.

Even in farming, the clash between the interests of the settlers and of the indigenous people could have been worse. Where there was a choice, the Shona usually preferred sandy soils, which best suited their staple crops of millet and sorghum: such soils can be very fertile for short periods of a few years, but without very careful treatment and the continuous replacement of organic matter they cannot be used for more than about five years at a stretch.

The settler farmers, on the other hand, preferred the richer and heavier loamy soils which maintained their fertility longer. In some areas, the Shona were left to cultivate the land they had always been using and settler farmers took over unused land. But this did not always happen: sometimes white settlers and indigenous Shona favoured the same land, whether because it received better rainfall, or because both groups recognised its superior fertility, or simply because no other arable land was available. Many Shona were moved off their land to make way for white farmers. Some chiefdoms broke up completely. Others were resettled in less suitable land. Others still, who were not moved, had to make room for displaced groups, causing crowding in land that was left to the Shona.[22] Peoples who have been adversely affected by the apportionment of their land to white farmers maintain today bitter memories which affect their relations with the whites.

In spite of its adverse effect, the colonial settlement of Southern Rhodesia initiated for the Shona an era of material progress and change. The preservation and adaptation of traditional institutions to meet this change is the principal theme of this book.

Contemporary Shona groupings

Now the peoples classified as 'Shona' cover most of Zimbabwe and parts of Mozambique, stretching to the Zambezi River in the North and the Indian Ocean in the east. The derivation of the word 'Shona' is uncertain. It

---

22. For a history of the allocation of land in Rhodesia, see Palmer 1977a. See also Palmer 1968, Roder 1964, pp. 44–51, and Beach 1970.

appears to have been used first by the Ndebele as a derogatory name for the people they had defeated, and particularly the Rozvi. The Shona did not call themselves by this name and at first disliked it; even now they tend rather to classify themselves by their chiefdoms or their dialect groups (Karanga, Manyika, Zezuru, Korekore, etc.), though most accept the designation Shona in contrast to unrelated peoples. The extension of the term to all tribes native to Zimbabwe appears to have been a British innovation.[23]

The currently accepted classification of Shona peoples into the main dialect groups is the result of a lingistic study on the possibility of developing a unified language from the various dialects.[24] The conclusion of the study was that the dialects spoken by the Zezuru in central Shona country, the Korekore in the north, the Karanga and the Kalanga in the south and the Manyika and Ndau in the east are all classifiable as a single linguistic unit: these together with the Barwe-Tonga comprise the peoples at whom we have been looking and whose histories are so interrelated. The Zezuru, the Korekore, the Karanga and the Manyika all speak dialects which can readily be incorporated into a unified language based on the Zezuru dialect. The language of the Ndau peoples is more distinct due possibly to the influence of the Shangaan invaders, and the Kalanga dialect is quite different from the other Shona dialects due no doubt to centuries of separation reinforced by the more recent Ndebele settlement between them and the rest of the Shona peoples. Although these classifications are linguistic, and although the boundaries of the groups classified in this way are not precise, they do reflect the cultural patterns of the Shona peoples and also to some extent their various histories.

The Zezuru peoples of central Shona country comprise a number of independent chiefdoms, united by geographical propinquity, by their common language and culture and also by some of the greater religious cults which spread their influence beyond the boundaries of particular chiefdoms. The current chiefdoms, however, result from numerous migrations over the past few centuries and the Zezuru peoples do not have a common history. Since Harare, Zimbabwe's largest city, is situated in the heart of Zezuru country, industrialization has affected the Zezuru peoples more than peoples in remoter parts of the country, and the central Zezuru are on the whole materially more progressive than surrounding peoples. This has given a certain standing to peoples classified as Zezuru and, especially

23. Cf. von Sicard 1950.
24. Cf. Doke 1931.

17

where the Zezuru and the Korekore meet, peoples traditionally associated with the Korekore may prefer to call themselves Zezuru.[25]

To the north are the Korekore people, descended from the subject chiefdoms of the Mutapas, together with a few more recently settled chiefdoms. To the north-east of them are the Tavara peoples, who were also once incorporated into the Mutapa State. The Tavara were originally the autochthonous people who lived in the Zambezi Valley before the Korekore came down from the plateau, but now the division between Korekore and Tavara corresponds roughly with the boundary between Zimbabwe and Mozambique. There is little cultural difference between the Korekore and the Zezuru, though the Tavara and some others of the valley peoples have a distinctive kinship system which gives less emphasis to the male line than do other Shona systems.

In the south are the Karanga peoples, occupying the area covered by the ancient Zimbabwe State. The contemporary chiefdoms, however, are largely the result of migrations and political alignments in the seventeenth, eighteenth and nineteenth centuries. Although we will refer to distinctive features of Karanga culture, in their religious cults, for example, and in the way they elect a new chief, there is no doubt that it is basically similar to that of the Korekore and Zezuru. Early mission stations in Karanga country brought a more concerted effort at education than other peoples received, and the Karanga are prominent in elite circles today.

Also similar are the Manyika, to the east of Zezuru country, who have distinctive features in their public rituals and in their patterns on kinship. Originally the name Manyika applied only to the people around what is now Mutare, and the extension of the name to neighbouring peoples occurred through the influence of missionary activity and white government administration in the twentieth century. The extension of the name is now accepted by the people themselves, who thereby acknowledge a certain unity between the chiefdoms so designated.

The Ndau peoples to the south-east, some of whom are in Zimbabwe, show marked differences from other Shona groups in their language, in their politico-religious structure (which I shall be mentioning), and no doubt in other ways. Nevertheless, they do have Shona origins, and they are rightly still classified as Shona. The same applies to the Kalanga, who live in the southwest of Zimbabwe and stretch into neighbouring Botswana, and who is some ways align themselves with the Ndebele rather than with the Shona.

---

25. Cf. Bourdillon 1972a, p. 119.

18

The Barwe live for the most part in Mozambique, with a small pocket on the eastern border of Zimbabwe. Although their rulers are associated with Shona history, the Barwe appear to be more strongly associated with the older Tonga peoples, and fall outside the scope of this study.

2

Kinship and Village Organization

Patrilineal kinship

Rural Shona communities, like small, closely knit communities all over the world, are built around their patterns of kinship. How any man or woman behaves towards another depends largely on how they are related. Before outlining these patterns, I should emphasize the point that Shona society is changing. The patterns arose in particular social and economic situations: in the face of growing residential and economic independence on the part of individuals, the relationships described in this chapter have in many cases weakened, and occasionally collapsed altogether.

There are many things that influence people's behaviour. The patterns of thinking and acting that have been instilled into us as children are fundamental to our instinctive patterns of behaviour in adulthood: this area comes broadly under the category of culture. Another important area of influence comprises the material necessities to keep alive. We will see how the Shona patrilineal system works well with a system of settled agriculture, in which access to land is closely related to community identity, and in which ambitious men try to build around themselves a large family of dependent agricultural labourers. As the economic system changes, we can expect to see changes in patterns of kinship behaviour. Employment diminishes dependence on a residential farming community. Residence in the urban centres makes a large family an economic liability instead of an asset. Scattered residence diminishes the emphasis on relations with kin, and makes relations between spouses more significant than they were in the traditional farming communities.

But such changes are always slow. People's kinship behaviour is largely habitual, and is thought of as following ideals and norms which are assumed to be independent of economic convenience, although the economic inconvenience of certain traditional norms may be felt. Breaches of these norms threaten the structure of the society on which people have been brought up to depend. So changes in patterns and ideals of behaviour are slow to follow changes in patterns of residence and in patterns of living. The traditional kinship system of the Shona, which is described in the pages that follow, still governs much of Shona behaviour.

The Shona kinship system is basically patrilineal, which means that kinship through males is stressed over kinship through females. One obvious way in which this expresses itself is in the inheritance of a name. When a Shona man or woman wishes to show respect to another, he or she uses

23

traditional clan[1] names inherited from that person's father (rather similar to English surnames). These names clearly distinguish groups of patrilineal kin who are related through the male line and consequently have the same clan name. A Shona man or woman clearly distinguishes members of his or her patrilineal group from other relatives whose connection is traced through a woman. So the Shona people divide themselves into numerous patrilineal clans each of which has its own clan name *(mutupo):* the clans in turn are divided into sub-clans each with one or more sub-clan names *(zvidao,* in some areas also called *mitupo).* The subclan names are often related to geographical areas suggesting that the subclans originated as local pockets of a particular clan.

Although the clan rarely, if ever, acts as a corporate whole, a major clan or sub-clan is often associated with a particular area or chiefdom, and members of the same clan do acknowledge their kin relationship even when they cannot trace any genealogical connection (which is most often the case). Thus one subsection of a clan or sub-clan may invite representatives from others to attend the installation or funeral ceremonies of an important headman or chief.[2] Further, when two people with no traceable kinship ties meet, they may adopt rules of behaviour towards each other based on any relationship which they know exists between other members of their respective clans. Thus if a Shona woman meets an elderly stranger and discovers that a young man from her clan has married a young girl from his, she can address him as 'father-in-law'. The relationship between individuals is treated as a relationship between the two clans. No two persons from the same sub-clan[3] may marry or have any form of sexual intercourse: this would be regarded as incest even if the persons concerned can trace no blood relationship. So kinship is recognised between members of any sub-clan and they are to some extent regarded as a group even though they never come together in group activity.

The clan name is often the name of some animal, the elephant for example, or the eland or monkey, and usually members of the clan are not allowed to eat the flesh of the animal or at least there is a token taboo on some part of the animal, such as the heart or trunk of an elephant or

---

1. The word 'clan' is perhaps a misnomer. In the Shona context it refers to an amorphous and scattered group of people whose only identity as a group is a common clan name.
2. Holleman 1952a, p. 24.
3. This is normally determined by the clan and sub-clan names a person has inherited, though occasionally two groups from different areas but bearing the same names are said to be unrelated (see, e.g., Holleman 1949, pp. 29f.).

possibly even some inedible part. Most Shona believe that to break this taboo would result in a loss of teeth or some other harm; similar sanctions may support a powerful oath made on the clan name; events involving the animal concerned are sometimes interpreted as signs from ancestral spirits;[4] all of which suggest that the *mitupo* and *zvidao* have religious and symbolic connotations which make them more than simply names. Some writers have seen strong sexual connotations to a number of clan names and suggest that these names arose in connection with the incest taboo[5]: offences against the name are consequently associated with incest, a crime that is believed to be severely punished by the most senior ancestral spirits.

But the mythical or religious significance of the clan emblem should not be over-emphasized. Occasionally names have been changed simply to conceal the identity of a group or to adjust its relations with other groups.[6] The names are most commonly used in a respectful greeting or when one wishes to show gratitude. In the country a wife may praise her husband with his clan names when he presents her with the spoils of a successful hunt; in the towns she may do the same when her husband comes home with a week's provisions after receiving his pay. The words '*mitupo*' and '*zvidao*' are sometimes translated as 'praise names' which aptly describes their normal use.[7]

Descent is traced through the male line for the purposes of membership of clans and sub-clans. For practical purposes, the membership of particular family groups is also traced through the male line. This is important in tracing membership of the different branches of a chiefly family and also for working out one's kinship relationships with other groups. But before discussing this we must look at the kinship structure within the patrilineal group.[8]

In their use of kinship terms (see diagram between pages 28 & 29) people distinguish members of their own patrilineal group only by generation, age and sex, and not according to genealogical distance. Thus the term *baba* (father) can mean a father's brother or any man in the patriclan belonging to the father's generation: a distinction may be made between *baba mukuru* (great father), who is senior to one's father, and *baba mudiki*

---

4. See Sachs 1937; pp. 49, 278f.; Bullock 1951, pp. 48f.
5. Bullock 1931; Roberts 1938.
6. Cf. Stead 1946, p. 5; also Seed 1933, p. 52.
7. This is the translation Garbett uses. See Hodza and Fortune 1979 for their use of praise poetry.
8. For more detailed studies of the Shona kinship see Holleman 1947; Seed 1932, 1933; Stead 1946. For details of etiquette between kin, see Gelfand 1973a. pp. 11-51.

(little father), who is junior, but there is no titular distinction between, for example, father's brother and father's distant cousin (provided they are all in the same clan). Similarly all females in the father's generation and belonging to the same clan are called *vatete* (paternal aunt) no matter how distantly they are related. A man calls the men of his generation *mukoma* or *munun'una* depending on whether they are older or younger than himself, and the same terms are used by women of women.[9] The term *mwana* (sometimes specified as *mwanakomana* for a boy and *mwanasikana* for a girl) applies equally to a child and to any other clan member of one's children's generation. In the generation of a person's grandparents, however, or that of his grandchildren, the kinship terms do not clearly distinguish clan membership. Nevertheless, grouping by patrilineal descent is fundamental to the structure of Shona society and the Shona uphold the close unity of their lineage groups[10] even when they use English kinship terms: thus a man's father's brother's son would take offence were he introduced as a 'cousin', which implies some distance, rather than as a 'brother', which implies a relationship similar to that between sons of the same parents.

Other lineages are also grouped together in the kinship terminology. Thus any male in one's mother's lineage, irrespective of his generation level, is called *sekuru* (grandfather, mother's brother, mother's brother's son, etc): the complementary term, *muzukuru*, is applied to any person descended from a woman of one's own lineage (also to any grandchild). There are also terms applied to men or women of lineages related by marriage. We will consider these relationships later; for the moment it is sufficient to observe that members of the same patrilineage are grouped together in the kinship terminology.

The extension of kinship terms beyond the elementary family (that is, beyond a man, his wife and their children) reflects the common residential pattern of traditional Shona society. It used to be, and often still is, the ambition of a man to gather around him a growing lineage of descendants and dependants, who would act as a corporate body for economic purposes and also as a united body in times of crisis or tension in the community.

---

9. The terms mentioned as applying primarily to members of the lineage also have some applications to parallel relationships outside the lineage. A man's mother's sister's son, for example, is called *mukoma* or *munun'una* whether or not he belongs to the former's lineage.

10. 'Lineage' is used here without precise definition. The size of the group involved depends on a number of circumstances, but is roughly a patrilineal group up to five generations deep.

And so the sons of a family grew up in an extended (rather than elementary) family which included their paternal grandparents, their parents, their father's brothers and their wives, their brothers and sisters and their patrilineal cousins.

In the past a man tended to stay in his father's homestead until the latter's death, when his name and position would be inherited by his younger brother if he was still living in the homestead, or more probably his eldest son. As the extended families grew unwieldy in numbers, and as the heads who held them together died off, the families tended to break up into smaller units which in turn would grow and split. Younger brothers to the heir of a deceased family head were likely to found their own homesteads if they were sufficiently senior and had a sufficiently large number of dependants. Thus a residential group consisted primarily of a patrilineage three to five generations deep under the family head. Although the extended kinship terminology has always applied to a wider group of people, close family ties were normally recognised in practice only between those who lived together.

The old patrilineage of three to five generations of the descendants of one man is still recognised under the name *chizvarwa*.[11] While the head of the group is still alive, it forms the most fundamental family unit, acting together in court cases and other disputes, and acting as a unit in marriage negotiations. Whether the group stays together after his death depends on the size of the group and on the relationships between the sons of the family head; but for ritual purposes the group acts together until all his grandsons are dead or have left the locality.

The spirit of the common ancestor becomes a prominent spirit guardian of the whole group and is frequently honoured with ceremonial millet beer.[12] And whenever he is honoured, the whole group should gather, including women who are married and living away from the group, and even quarrelling factions within the group. The *chizvarwa* has a bull dedicated to the spirit of the common ancestor, to be sacrificed when he shows signs

---

11. For remarks on *chizvarwa* see Holleman 1952a, pp. 24f. The word *mana* signifies a similar family group but appears to have a stronger residential (rather than patrilineal) connotation than *chizvarwa* (see Bernardi 1950, p. 3; Holleman 1952a, p. 387).

12. A full acount of Shona beliefs concerning the spirits of the dead is given later in chapter 9. Briefly, the Shona believe that when a person dies, his spirit is freed and can exert an influence on the world. In the case of senior members of a particular family, their spirits become family guardians: indeed their continued presence is so real to the Shona that they can aptly be called the 'spirit elders' of the community.

of wanting it, and often there is a spirit medium who becomes possessed by the common ancestor when he wishes to speak to his living descendants. So even after his death, the common ancestor keeps the group together.

The ideal system of the past often survives in spite of the numerous influences of change. One of these is social and economic independence encouraged by labour migration in which young men have to fend for themselves without the support of their extended families. Another is the diminishing availability of land which prevents a group dependent on subsistence agriculture from growing too large. A third is the impossibility of the extended family living together in the urban areas: a man has to take a house where he can get one which is rarely anywhere near his father's residence. Nevertheless, in the rural areas the ideal remains of keeping the extended family together, though now young men appear reluctant to live within their parent's homesteads and instead usually set up their own homesteads nearby.

Even prior to modern influences there were variations in residence patterns. A poor man, for example, who was not able to pay bride-price cattle could instead spend his life working for his father-in-law: in such a situation he would leave his own extended family and join his wife's. In some areas (in the Zambezi valley, for example, where the tsetse fly curbed herds of cattle), it was normal procedure for a man to live with and work for his wife's father until his own daughters were married; then he was likely to build his own independent homestead rather than return to his father's home.[13] In this area homesteads were always smaller than in central Shona country where they could grow into nuclear village communities. Apart from these institutionalized variations, it is always possible for a man to live with friends, in-laws or close kin who are not of his patrilineage, whether because of conflict with his own family or because of a particularly close friendship with his new neighbours. In practice not all residential groups conform to the ideal family structure.

One practical result of the extended family system is that should the father of a family be away from home for some time, or should he die, one of his brothers or even a patrilineal cousin can take his place with legal and economic responsibility for his children. Their large extended families help the Shona to care for orphans and widows, also for their old people and such misfits as cripples or idiots, the burden of caring for whom is shared between a large group of close relatives. The extended families also

---

13. Where cattle are scarce a matrilineal marriage system may develop (see Lancaster 1974).

SHONA TERMS OF COGNATIC KINSHIP

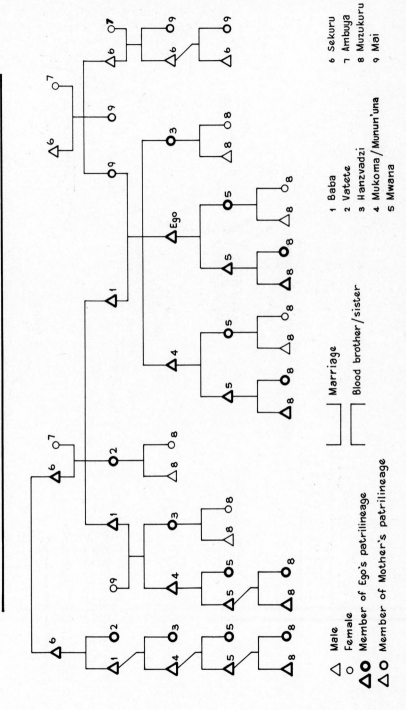

△ Male
○ Female
▲● Member of Ego's patrilineage
▲○ Member of Mother's patrilineage

⌐¬ Marriage
└─┘ Blood brother/sister

1 Baba
2 Vatete
3 Hanzvadzi
4 Mukoma / Mununʼuna
5 Mwana

6 Sekuru
7 Ambuya
8 Muzukuru
9 Mai

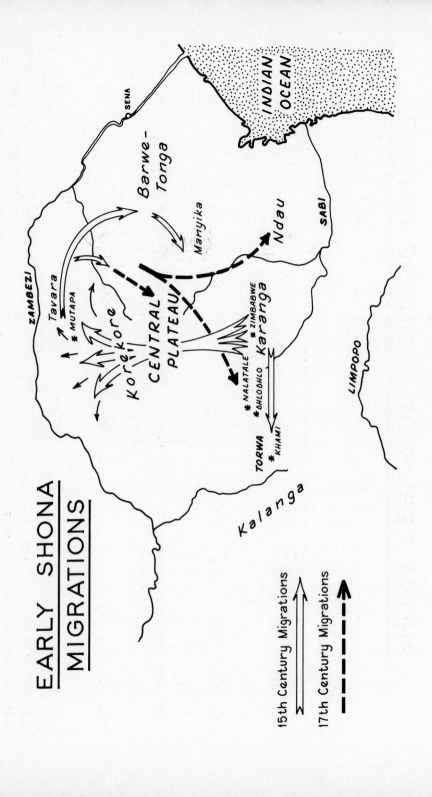

EARLY SHONA
MIGRATIONS

INDIAN OCEAN

SENA

Barwe-Tonga

Manyika

Ndau

SABI

ZAMBEZI

Tavara

MUTAPA

Korekore

CENTRAL PLATEAU

ZIMBABWE

Karanga

NALATALE

DHLODHLO

LIMPOPO

TORWA

KHAMI

Kalanga

15th Century Migrations

17th Century Migrations

provided security in times of trouble and in old age, but to enjoy this security a person must maintain his or her place in the family and accept his or her share of responsibilities.

The extended family system is also relevant in understanding the complex inheritance rules of the Shona. I have said that should a man die his responsibilities towards his children are taken on by a brother or a patrilineal cousin. With responsibility for the children goes the headship of the family, which in traditional society includes control of the family herd of cattle and of the distribution of the property of the deceased. He is also likely to acquire marital rights over widows of the deceased, and authority over the deceased's children, which includes receipt of any bride-price paid at the marriage of the girls. In the inheritance ceremony (which we will discuss later) the inheritor is given the name of the deceased and the deceased's position in the kinship structure, and with the position goes the property. Although the inheritor is supposed to distribute the deceased's personal possessions to his descendants, he does take over the control of family property — particularly the family herd of cattle — which goes with seniority in the family group; and in the extended families of the Shona seniority is inherited by each in turn of one generation before it can be passed on to the next.

In current practice, most property is personal property: wealth obtained through wage labour is likely to exceed the inherited family possessions and even cattle are becoming more associated with personal wealth than with a lineage group. As a result, seniority in a lineage group has less importance and the bulk of a deceased's estate goes to his sons if they are sufficiently old; the eldest son has to take the consequent responsibilities. Nevertheless, the ancient system is still practiced by many, especially if the sons of the deceased have not yet grown up.

The traditional inheritance system remains the practice for succession to important positions such as the chiefship or the headmanship of a village or ward. In most chiefly dynasties, the chiefship was inherited by a number of sons (perhaps three) of the founding ancestor of the dynasty. These sons become the founders of distinct houses, each of which should succeed to the chiefship in turn; in each house seniority likewise alternates between subsections producing the complications which we will consider later. The point to notice at this stage is that the principles of inheritance and succession are both lateral (following a single generation) and lineal (going from father to son).

The fact that the kinship terms of the elementary family are extended to other members within the lineage does not mean that the elementary family is not clearly distinguished from the rest of the lineage. A person clearly distinguishes between his father who begot him and other 'fathers' who have less authority over him and towards whom he has fewer obligations. Obviously one of the problems here is the question of translation: we have no English equivalent of the Shona word *baba* which can apply to men other than one's father, and the same applies to other Shona kinship terms. The close ties binding the extended family together and expressed in the kinship terminology do not obscure the natural divisions within the group.

Perhaps the most important relationship to the Shona is that between father and child. The father has absolute authority over his children and complete responsibility for them. A child 'fears'[14] his father and always displays towards him an attitude of defence and respect. He can take no liberties with his father's property, and should always maintain a respectful posture in the presence of his father, reverently clapping his hands when they meet. Father and children never eat together.[15] The children must either eat separately or wait for their father to finish. In return for obedience and respect, the father is responsible for feeding and clothing his children. He is also held responsible for all their actions and represents them in disputes, and he may pay their debts and fines.

In the past the father was responsible for the marriages of his children, including the payment of bride-price for his sons. As we shall see, the economic independence promoted by wage labour has resulted in sons becoming responsible for their own marriages and in a weakening of paternal authority.[16] Nevertheless, the ideal of distance and authority is maintained: even in sophisticated urban households, the father rarely eats with his children.

After the death of the father, his spirit is believed to continue to provide protection for his children and his grandchildren. Favours are asked of the spirit of the father, and when they are received he is thanked with offerings of snuff or millet beer. Beer should occasionally be brewed for the spirit of one's father simply to honour him. If this is omitted for a long time, the Shona believe that he may ask for beer by causing illness in his descendants: among the Korekore, the strict formality between a father and his

---

14. *Kutya*, 'to fear', is also used to describe the ideal wife's attitude towards her husband and the attitude of a man towards his eldest brother and his father's brothers. Crawford suggests as an alternative translation of the word 'to respect' (1967, p. 149).

15. A man may, however, eat with a baby son or daughter.

16. See Holleman 1952a, p. 259.

children continues in the belief that such a request must be made through grandchildren, and that sickness caused in the child of the spirit can only mean a breakdown of their relationship and anger on the part of the spirit.

The relationship between grandparents and grandchildren is authoritative, but less formal than that between parents and their children. Grandparents are expected to be more tolerant than one's parents, and the relationship with grandparents involves friendship as well as respect.

Brothers and sisters are both ranked according to age, and they are expected to show friendship and loyalty towards each other. The relationship between a brother and sister depends on the position of each within the family. All siblings should pay a certain amount of deference to the eldest brother who may eventually inherit the position of their father, whereas a particularly close relationship exists between a brother and sister whose bride-price has been (or is destined to be) used for his marriage. She, and other sisters to a lesser degree, has a position of special authority over the children of his marriage since it is her marriage that makes their family possible. Her authority over his family is especially evident on his death when a sister is responsible for seeing to a just distribution of his estate. In spite of her authority, and although she may be very strict about behaviour, children do not fear their father's sister *(vatete)* as they do their father.[17] She is an important intermediary between the children and their father when their marriages are being arranged.

The mother and mother's kin

The smallest family unit is the *imba,* or house, which contains a married woman and her children.[18] The relationship between a mother and her child is considered to be extremely close in spite of the fact that the child belongs to different clan and lineage from that of its mother, and sometimes different even from the lineage of the mother's current husband. The mother creates a close bond between her children: it is generally accepted that the bond between half-brothers from the same womb is closer than that between half-brothers by the same father, although in the former case they may not belong to the same patrilineal group.

---

17. In some areas the *vatete* may also be called *baba mukadzi:* female father.
18. *'Imba'* may also mean a larger group of descendants of one woman. The mother-child relationship is described in Gelfand 1969.

The relationship between a daughter and her mother is more formal than that between a son and his mother. The mother has to teach her daughter all her etiquette and her household duties, while the sons receive their traditional education from the men of the family and thus escape the strict authority a mother must exercise over her daughters. This slightly more formal relationship has legal recognition when the girl is married: one cow, the 'cow of motherhood', is supposed to be given by the groom's family to the bride's mother for the propitiation of her ancestors. A woman will often dedicate this cow to the spirit of her mother or her mother's mother, and if the beast has not been paid any trouble in the new family is likely to be interpreted as a demand for the cow by one of these spirits.

At the death of a mother, her spirit is regarded as friendly and protective. Some say that maternal spirit elders are more important than spirits of patrilineal ancestors and that nothing harmful can happen to a person without the consent of his maternal spirits.[19] This is reflected in the exclamation, 'Maiwe', so commonly uttered in distress: it is the spirit of the mother who is supposed to have caused the trouble or at least to have allowed it. Because the mother carried her offspring in her womb, underwent pregnancy and the pains of labour, and nourished and cared for them while they were helpless children, at the death of the mother her spirit demands to be well remembered and honoured. If her children fail in their duties, the spirit is believed to have the same absolute power over them that she had as a mother during their infancy. Maternal spirit elders are so important as custodians of a child's well-being that occasionally a child's father's family waives its legal rights over a sick child in order to allow it to live with its maternal kin who can more readily communicate with its maternal spirits.[20] The maternal spirits of a girl (the spirit of her mother's mother and mother's mother's mother) are particularly associated with her fertility and must be ritually propitiated after the birth of her first child. Should a woman have any problems over fertility or child-bearing, her maternal spirits are presumed to be responsible and must be appeased.

In spite of the influence of maternal spirits, most formal rituals among the Shona are directed to patrilineal spirit elders. Nevertheless, millet beer should be brewed for maternal spirits occasionally, and a woman may keep a cow dedicated to her deceased mother or grandmother. For the sacrifice of this cow, a woman may summon home her own sons and daughters and

19. Kumbirai 1966/7, II (April 1966).
20. Cf. Stead 1946, pp. 17f.

other close relatives related through the female line (coming ultimately from 'the same womb'), but other relatives do not take an active part in the proceedings. Such rituals in honour of maternal spirits are, however, not common[21] and usually only follow a specific request in the form of trouble in the family divined to come from the spirit concerned.[22] Descent through women is recognised by the Shona as involving close but informal relationships with both living and dead.

These relationships concern the physiological fact of motherhood whereas the appropriate kinship term, *mai* ('mother', also now used as a direct translation of 'Mrs'), can be used to address all the women of the lineage of the mother and also of the lineages of other wives of men related as *baba* ('father'). Often it is used with a qualifying adjective: thus *mainini* ('little mother') refers to father's junior wife or mother's younger sister and *maiguru* ('big mother') refers to a woman senior to one's own mother. The formal behaviour towards all such persons resembles the respect and friendliness shown towards one's own mother, but generally the close affection will be lacking.

The relationship of a Shona person towards his or her mother's lineage is quite different from that between members of the same lineage. The women of the mother's lineage are all called *mai* ('mother') and the relationship with these women is typified by the mother-child relationship: one of these women may well replace the mother should she die young. The relationship with men of the mother's lineage is typified in the relationship between a mother's brother and his sister's son, a relationship which plays a prominent role in many ritual and social situations. This relationship is expressed in the complementary terms *sekuru* (mother's brother) and *muzukuru* (sister's son — the uses of these terms are of course extended to include other members of the lineages concerned, so that *sekuru* can be any man of the lineage of any woman who is called *mai* and anyone descended from any woman of one's own lineage is called *muzukuru*; in most areas the terms also apply to grandfather and grandchild respec-

---

21. Many say that only the spirit of the father's father may claim a head of cattle to be dedicated to him (Kumbirai 1964, p. 31).
22. According to Shona belief, family spirit elders usually make their wishes known by making one of their living descendants sick. Thus when any abnormal trouble or illness occurs in a family a diviner should be consulted to determine which spirit is causing the trouble and what it wishes to be done. (See below, chapters 6 and 9)

tively).[23] Unrelated persons can adopt the terms *sekuru* and *muzukuru* towards each other to express a friendly relationship, reflecting the typical relationship between mother's brother and sister's son.

This relationship is cordial and intimate: the Shona refer to it as *ukama hwokutamba* ('a relationship of playing') and anthropologists call it a joking relationship. The sister's son can normally avail himself of anything belonging to his mother's brother without even asking for it, and no action should be taken against him. A sister's son has a degree of freedom and privilege in the homesteads of his mother's brothers which he would never have in the homesteads of senior members of his own lineage.[24] There are, however, limits to this freedom: a man would sue his sister's sons for such crimes as adultery with his wife or serious theft of his property. Some respect is due to the mother's brother, especially on first acquaintance;[25] familiarity develops later, and even then a sister's son should treat his mother's brother with a mixture of deference and equality depending on the circumstances.

From the point of view of the lineage of the mother's brother, a sister's son belongs to another lineage and is not personally involved in any of the rivalries over authority, property, inheritance or any other conflicts that may arise within their own family group. Yet he is a close kinsman with the consequent mutual obligations of loyalty and aid, and is thus in an ideal position to arbitrate in family conflicts. The ties between the families are ideally strengthened by the passage of cattle: the bride-price paid by a man should be used for the marriage of his wife's brother. One marriage makes the other possible. Thus among the Hera a *muzukuru* might jokingly say to younger members of his mother's lineage, 'You are my children because your mother is my "wife". Was she not married with my (i.e., my father's) cattle?' To his maternal relatives the sister's son is *mwana mukati*, which

---

23. Holleman cites the Hera as using *sekuru* and *muzukuru* only when the relationship is through a woman: an agnate of the grandchildren's generation is called *mwana womwana* (a child of a child) (1949, p. 2), an agnate of the grandparents' generation is called *baba mukuru* (great father) (1952a, pp. 36f.) and a deceased patrilineal ancestor is called by the widespread term, *tateguru*. This usage is not common and is not even used by all the Hera.

24. Holleman 1949, pp. 12ff.; Garbett 1963a, p. 164.

25. Boas (1922) in his analysis of the Ndau kinship system places more emphasis on the authoritative position of the mother's brother and claims that the term *sekuru* derives from the fact that a woman is considered a daughter of her lineage: thus any male of a man's mother's lineage has the status of grandparent.

Professor Holleman translates freely as 'a child that somehow belongs "inside" his mother's lineage because it is of the same blood', and a man may declare that he loves his sister's son more than his own.[26]

Depending on local custom, the senior *muzukuru* of a family may be called in to supervise any events which could involve family rivalries, such as the distribution of a deceased man's estate and the installation of a new family head. He also arbitrates in disputes that may arise between father and son. In some areas, this kind of arbitration is extended to dealings with the family spirit elders: the *muzukuru* is master of ceremonies at most rituals performed in honour of the family spirit elders (often following trouble believed to be caused by them) and acts as acolyte should one of them possess a medium; it is thus the *muzukuru* who speaks directly to the spirit elders through the medium, and he usually leads prayers to the spirits on behalf of the family at rituals.[27]

Further light is thrown on how the Shona understand the role of sister's son when we notice that the acolyte of the medium of a powerful 'lion' spirit (which we shall discuss later in chapter eleven) is often called the *muzukuru*. It is he who is primarily responsible for speaking to the spirit and making requests on behalf of the people when the medium is possessed, and for passing on to the people the sayings of the possessed medium.

The role of the senior *muzukuru* to a chief is also significant. He alone can correct the chief if he falls short of what is required of him: Professor Holleman describes a case in which a chief received a severe rebuke in public from his *muzukuru* and said nothing in reply, maintaining a meek silence.[28] Professor Gelfand describes the role of the senior *muzukuru* of another chiefdom: the position is inherited from father to son in a family traditionally descended from a sister of the first chief of the dynasty. He is called the *muzukuru mukuru* (the great *muzukuru*) of the chiefdom, and

---

26. Holleman 1952, pp. 67f. Some of Professor Holleman's remarks appear to be peculiar to the Hera people.
27. Although Professor Gelfand remarks that the *muzukuru* does not say the prayers at ceremonies for the ancestors since this is done by a senior member of the family (1965a, p. 40), elsewhere he gives an example in which the *muzukuru* does address the ancestors to explain the purpose of a sacrifice, with the senior member of the family saying another prayer later (1956a, p. 48). Among the Korekore, the *muzukuru* who officiates makes the most important address to the spirits, though others also address them: for less important rituals, however, the *muzukuru* in charge may be a patrilineal grandchild of the spirit and hence a senior member of the family concerned. Among the Zezuru the *muzukuru* has little significance in common family rituals.
28. Holleman 1958a, pp. 157ff.

his main task is to 'look after' the people. He is well versed in the traditions of the chiefdom, and the chief often invites him to help solve difficult cases at the chief's court. He also claims that at the death of a chief he instructs the acting chief on how to run the chiefdom until a successor is appointed. The *muzukuru* offers prayers to the spirit guardians of the chiefdom and ensures that the traditional days of rest are observed in their honour.[29]

So although kinship traced through men is most prominent in determining residential and economic units and the structure of authority within them, kinship through women is also recognised and plays an important part in the patterns of Shona relationships.

Shona Marriage

Marriage is an institution which now has a variety of forms in Shona society, with respect both to the rites and customs by which the union is achieved and to the nature of the union itself. The processes of marriage vary between the traditional long and elaborate series of negotiations between two families, to a brisk affair between a young man and his girl, over which their respective families have little control. Marriages may result in a number of wives living largely apart from the husband to whom they all defer, or occasionally, a marriage may result in a man and woman equally supporting their shared family life. Bearing in mind such variations, we can look at the traditional ideals and practices of Shona marriage, and see how they relate to traditional family life.

For the traditional Shona, marriage is essentially a contract between two families.[30] Although the choice of spouses is now usually left to the persons concerned (and it seems that the wishes of the couple were normally respected in the past), the negotiations towards marriage normally require participation by senior representatives of each family. Traditionally, the major part of the necessary bride-price[31] was paid from the family cattle herd of the son-in-law into the family herd of the father-in-law, and even now a young man can often expect help from his father and brothers in making bride-price payments, or he might be given his sister's bride-price

---

29. Gelfand 1966b. This account, based largely on the information of the *muzukuru* concerned, probably exaggerates his significance.
30. This aspect is illustrated in Weinrich 1967a. The exact size of the group involved varies.
31. In the absence of an adequate English word, I prefer the technical anthropological term 'bride-price' to the colloquial term 'lobola' which, although in common use in Zimbabwe, is neither English nor Shona.

to pay for his own marriage. In a traditional marriage, when the bride is given in marriage she is initially presented to the head of the family of her husband. Again, after the birth of her first child in her own family homestead, the young wife returns to the home of her father-in-law and spends a few days with a wife of his, moving to her own room only after all the residents have been able to see the baby and bring presents.[32] The dissolution of a marriage also involves the whole family group, and at the early death of one of the spouses, the family of the deceased must provide an acceptable replacement or negotiate the dissolution of the contract.

The fact that marriage is regarded primarily as a family contract by the Shona is further expressed in the relationship terms they use and the patterns of behaviour they adopt. The whole of each family group becomes affined to the whole of the other. Thus a *tezvara* (the-father-in-law of the groom or any male of the bride's family) is *tezvara* to the whole of the groom's family, all of whom should give him the appropriate service and respect. The whole family adopts a new relationship terminology,[33] which is dropped by all if the marriage is dissolved. A man might use the first person when speaking of the marriage of a brother or other close agnate, saying 'we (or I) have married such-and-such a family'. For some purposes, the head of the family of the groom is regarded as the principal *mukuwasha* (normally translated as 'son-in-law') rather than the husband of the bride.[34]

The two lineages thus become related as wife-providers and wife-receivers, a relationship which gives status to the former. Girls given and received in marriage are regarded as daughters of the groups from which they come. Thus a man pays deference to anyone he calls *tezvara* (any male of lineage that gives a wife to his own)[35] and on formal occasions a *tezvara* is often addressed as *baba* ('father'): reciprocally, a man of the wife's lineage can call any of the wife-receiving group *mwana* ('child'). Apart from the forms of address, the wife's family can expect gifts and service from the husband and to a lesser extent from his immediate kin. As we

---

32. See Holleman 1952a, pp. 128f.; Gelfand 1964a, p. 104.
33. An exception is to be found in marriages between affines which would involve a change in existing relationships when for example a widow is inherited by a man in a generation different from that of her late husband.
34. See Holleman 1949, p. 10.
35. This does not necessarily apply to a *tezvara* who is much younger than the man concerned. Nor does it apply to males of lineages who have given wives to the father's or a higher generation: these are *vasekuru* ('mother's brothers').

shall see, the superior position of wife-providers can have political overtones relevant to the chiefship.

From the woman's point of view, the inequality between the two families bound in marriage is reversed.[36] The wife, who remains a member of the wife-providing lineage, has to live among the women of her husband's family and is expected to respect and serve them. The young wife, a newcomer to the group in which she is living, has to do the unpleasant chores around the homestead. Her subordinate position, which is extended to the other women of her lineage, is expressed in the term *vamwene* (owner) which she applies to women of her husband's family. The inequality between the women of the two families is partly explicable in terms of the residence patterns according to which the young wife is an inexperienced foreigner to the group in which she has to live, and partly in terms of the transference of bride-price cattle: the marriage of the *vamwene* theoretically provided the cattle with which the new wife is married.

The inequality between the two families should not be overstressed. Close friendships are sometimes confirmed by an agreement to a marriage either between the children of the friends or between one of the friends and the daughter of the other. This would not be feasible if it were to result in gross inequality between the friends. Nevertheless Shona marriage normally ranks the affinal families sufficiently clearly to restrict the possibility of future marriages between them.

Reciprocal marriage exchanges involving the return of the bride-price cattle usually meet with strong disapproval, although cases of such marriages do occur in some areas when the relationship between the couples concerned is not too close.[37] Most Shona say that a man cannot sit down and respectfully clap his hands to his father-in-law when the latter's brother is seeking to marry the former's sister and honours him as a son-in-law does. The same principle applies to marriages between other affines that would upset the ranking system or introduce contrary norms of behaviour. Thus a man may not marry a girl from a lineage which provided a wife for his father's generation of his own lineage: he calls such a woman *'mai'* ('mother') and is supposed to show her respect incompatible

---

36. See Holleman 1952a, p. 39.
37. Thus the Manyika regard a marriage involving a return of the bride-price cattle as a suitable way of sealing the ties between the two families provided relationships are not thereby too confused (see Stead 1946, pp. 18f). In some parts of Korekore country such marriages are also allowed.

with the intimacy between a man and his wife or her sister.[38] Similarly, a man may not marry a woman classed as 'daughter-in-law' who would be involved in a similar conflict between respect and intimacy. Such marriages are forbidden under the incest taboo although no blood relationship exists between the partners and sexual intercourse between, say, a man and a girl classed as 'daughter-in-law' is treated as a case of incest.

Objections to a marriage between remote affines are often merely matters of formality or personal taste. A woman may, for example, object to being married to a remote affine who is wrongly related to her, simply on the ground that her friends may tease her: in such a case her objections may be overcome if her suitor gives her a token gift to 'drive away her shame', a matter which concerns the couple on the eve of their marriage rather than their respective families.[39] Such objections may also arise during the marriage negotiations in order to obtain more favourable bride price arrangements, after which they are promptly dropped.

Marriages which reinforce existing unions and existing affinal relations are regarded with favour. A satisfactory son-in-law may be given a younger sister of his wife as a second wife with little or no bride-price to be paid. In the old days, after a family head had given a daughter, he had to ask his 'sons-in-law' for permission to negotiate the marriage of other daughters to other families.[40] Even now a man and a girl of similar ages and appropriately related by a previous marriage between their families, may be familiar and intimate with each other: sexual intercourse between them is not strictly allowed outside marriage, but it often takes place and does not worry the elders unduly — no damages would be claimed if the relationship subsequently ended in marriage. From the practical point of view, negotiations between two families which have already contracted one marriage agreement are likely to run smoothly without the suspicion which initially arises in dealings with an unknown family.

But apart form certain facilities in courtship and marriage negotiations, this type of marriage offers no special advantages. Bride-price is not reduced, and some families might prefer to spread the net of affinal relations by marrying their girls to different families. The great majority of

---

38. See Holleman 1952a, p. 54 & n.
39. See Holleman 1952a, p. 58.
40. Holleman 1949, p. 39.

young people marry outside the existing kinship organizations of their families.

I have argued that marriage among the Shona is primarily a contract between groups rather than between individuals. Another way in which Shona marriage is a drawn-out process: there is no clear point at which the couple can say that they are now married whereas they were not married before. To explain this we must look at the normal marriage procedures and payments,[41] that is, in the sense that they are considered the correct ideal, not in the sense that they are always or even usually followed.

Informal courting moves into a private engagement by the exchange of love tokens between the boy and the girl, often passed through a third person. The tokens are small objects of little commercial value, perhaps a small coin from the man and something intimate such as a piece of her underclothing from the girl, providing each partner with a concrete token of their intimacy which can if necessary be produced as evidence in a traditional court. Although sexual intercourse is not strictly allowed at this stage and the girl should certainly not be made pregnant, the exchange of love tokens is often a prelude to sexual intercourse and nowadays does not always indicate intention to marry.[42] Nevertheless, should either party break off the engagement after the exchange without good reason (and a new lover is not considered good reason), the other may sue for damages in a traditional court.

The engagement becomes more formal and public when the suitor approaches the girl's family. The first approaches are made through an intermediary or 'messenger' who is related to neither family and who is an important witness should any dispute subsequently arise. The messenger enters the homestead of the girl and, initially without mentioning the names of the persons concerned, explains the nature of his visit to a responsible member of the family, handing him a token gift such as a hoe, some snuff, or more commonly nowadays a few dollars in cash. This is passed on to the family head, usually the girl's father, who indicates his agreement by accepting the gift. The girl should also show her agreement by touching

---

41. These are described in more detail in Holleman 1952a, pp. 98-147; Gelfand 1973a, pp. 166-179.
42. For a comment on Shona attitudes to sex behaviour, see Gelfand 1967b.

the gift or accepting part of it. From this point the reciprocal terms *muku-washa* and *tezvara* ('son-in-law' and 'father-in-law') are adopted indicating that the affinal relationship has been established, but the prospective groom is still a long way from having full rights over his wife to be: all he can claim at this stage is that the girl is committed to him, which means that he can sue for damages should she commit adultery or should her family start negotiating her marriage to another man.

The messenger makes a second visit with a further gift to 'open the mouth' of the girl's father, that is, to induce him to state the bride-price he wants for his daughter. The bride-price is negotiated by the heads of the two families or their representatives in the presence of the messenger. It has always involved two payments, the first of which is called *rutsambo* and was traditionally some utility article such as a hoe or in some areas a goat, but is now usually a substantial payment in cash: this payment is associated with sexual rights in the woman and is abolished or considerably diminish-ed if the girl has had children prior to the marriage (in the old days it was payable only if the girl was a virgin). In most areas the second payment (*roora*) was a more substantial payment in cattle; now it is usually a second substantial cash payment, often stated in terms of the equivalent in head of cattle thus keeping a symbolic association with the traditional type of pay-ment. *Roora* is associated with rights over children born to the woman.

The substantial payments and my use of the term 'bride-price' do not mean that the wife is bought in a commercial transaction, even though a certain amount of bargaining may be involved.[43] Firstly, the wife is not simply bought as property (as, for example, a slave might be bought and sold): the husband's family have obligations towards the wife and her family beyond the mere payment of bride-price and they may not pass her on to a third family — in case of divorce, officially she must be returned to her kin. Both families have rights and obligations with respect to the woman: the husband's family can complain to the woman's family if she fails to per-form her duties (especially if she does not bear children, in which case the husband can expect a return of the bride-price or a sister of the girl as a se-cond wife at no further cost), and the girl's family should defend her and protect her if she is badly treated.

The fact that the principal payment used to be in cattle gives bride-price religious and symbolic associations. Although it is true that cattle were traditionally the most important form of permanent wealth, to the

---

43. This was pointed out by Bullock as early as 1913 (pp. 21ff.), yet it remains a common myth that the traditional African wife was a mere chattel purchased by her husband.

traditional Shona this wealth was primarily a means of reproducing one's own blood, and a prosperous man was a man with a large and growing family. Further, the bride-price cattle were traditionally paid not simply to the head of the family of the girl, but to the family group, and were normally reserved for the marriage exchanges of the young men in the group. Bride-price payments help to determine status between relatives and affines: a woman's status and that of her children *vis-a-vis* her brothers and their wives and children, depend on the ideal that the bride-price paid for her made their marriages possible, and a man can expect special hospitality from his wife's brother's wife who is married with the cattle he originally paid. The cattle maintain some association with their original owners and have the effect of tying the two groups together: thus sons-in-law must be called in to kill any beast which may be required for ritual or other purposes, and sometimes they have to provide a beast for sacrifice. Just as the wife remains a member of her own kinship group, cattle remain symbolically under the control of the group that provided them.

Among the bride-price cattle is the cow of motherhood which is often consecrated to the bride's deceased matrilineal ancestors, and a bull, which may eventually be dedicated to a paternal ancestor of the bride. When cattle are added to the family herd or taken away from it, the family head should make a formal address to his spirit elders introducing the new cattle or explaining the loss. In some areas cattle were traditionally slaughtered only on ritual occasions[44] (in the past meat could be obtained by hunting the plentiful game), and in others it is said that the family spirits would be displeased if too many cattle from the family herd were sold or slaughtered. Cattle are essential to the continuity of the family group and so become important in the relationship between the living members of the family and the spirit elders, their ancestral guardians. The use of the cattle in marriage exchanges cannot therefore be regarded simply as an economic transaction: there was some opposition when cash payments began to replace the traditional payments in cattle.[45]

A further point on the nature of traditional payments is that they were extended over a number of years, even a lifetime. The groom would be unwilling to make the full payment, even were he able, until he was satisfied that his wife would fulfill all her obligations, and in particular that she would bear a number of children in a lasting marriage. The bride's family too have a vested interest in prolonging the payments since they can

---

44. Holleman 1958a, p. 44; 1958b, p. 64.
45. See Sachs 1937, pp. 50f.; see also Shropshire 1938, pp. 43f.

demand favours in the form of service and gifts as long as the son-in-law remains in debt to them: there is a Shona proverb which says 'A son-in-law is like a fruit tree: one never finishes eating from it.'

At some stage in the negotiations and payments, usually after the payment of *rutsambo*, the father of the girl allows the groom to sleep with his bride when he visits the homestead, and later still the groom is allowed to take her home. The wife must return to her parental home for the birth of her first child, when further ritual payments must be given to her parents by the husband. In particular, he must provide a sacrificial beast with which his wife's family can propitiate her maternal spirits who are responsible for her fertility: these spirits should be honoured and thanked at the birth of each child to ensure the well-being of the woman's family and her continued fertility. In the modern situation, there are often substantial celebrations at the homes of the bride and the groom at which many friends and relatives are invited to partake in the feasting and are expected in return to present the couple with gifts to set up their new home: these celebrations may take place when the wife goes to live with her husband, or perhaps in connection with a church marriage often after the birth of one or more children. Only after the marriage has lasted for many years and has been fruitful in the birth of a number of children are the obligations of the two families mutually fulfilled.

There are other traditional forms of marriage which overcome various difficulties in the normal procedures. One of these is the 'elopement' marriage in which the couple pre-empt some of the lengthy formalities of the normal marriage and eliminate control by their respective family heads: although it goes against the acknowledged ideal, even thirty years ago it was in some areas more common than the regular form and it has probably always been a common form of marriage among the Shona.[46] In an 'elopement' marriage the bride leaves her home usually (though not always) abetted by her prospective spouse, but without the consent of the head of her own family. This action may be taken by the girl in order to avoid an undesirable match or simply to avoid the long delay caused by the full negotiations. The groom may instigate the arrangement and the head of his family may or may not be party to the scheme. Although either family may insist that the union be broken off and the girl returned, it is rare that they do not accept the *fait accompli* and start negotiating the payment of bride-price. In practice the stubbornness of the couple or of one or both of the family heads can win the day.

---

46. Holleman 1952a, pp. 113f.

Another variation of traditional Shona marriage is found in child marriages which still occasionally take place in spite of legal prohibitions. In the past it was possible for a man to favour a friend or an associate with the promise of a small daughter in marriage. Now such promises are made rarely and only in times of dire need. Particularly after a bad harvest, a family without enough to live on may try to relieve the situation by marrying off a small girl and using the bride-price to buy food for the family. In such a case, the girl stays with her parents until she reaches a marriageable age, and even then the parties accept that should she refuse her husband they cannot force her to go ahead with the marriage — even should they wish to. In spite of the uncertain future of the marriage, there is an incentive to the husband in that it involves a smaller bride-price than is normal without stigmatizing the marriage as cheap, and in any case bride-price is returnable should the union not take place. In practice the girl may well accept her destined husband, proud to have been of service to her family in time of need.

There was a fourth type of traditional marriage for a poor man who had no way of raising necessary marriage payments. Such a man could arrange to work for his father-in-law instead of paying bride-price. He was likely to become something of a slave to his father-in-law's family for the rest of his life, although he could be freed of his obligations and allowed to set up an independent homestead after many years of marriage. I have mentioned that in some areas where cattle were scarce this used to be the normal marriage arrangement with the exception that the son-in-law's independence at the marriage of a daughter was a matter of right.[47] Now that all men can earn cash in wage employment, marriages based on long term service as opposed to bride-price payments have practically died out.

While the service marriage has died, other institutions have been added. One is the registration of marriages in accordance with the *African Marriages Act* which requires that traditional marriages are 'solemnized' by a marriage officer of the district of the bride: for such solemnization the marriage officer normally requires the agreement of both parties, the consent of the head of the girl's family or his representative, and the presence of a witness who is normally the girl's chief or headman. In practice not all marriages are 'solemnized' and registered; and when they are, registration is regarded as incidental to the traditional procedures: the modern version of the act recognises unregistered marriages as valid for the purpose of

---

47. Lancaster (1974) suggests that this can lead to a shift from patrilineal to matrilineal kinship.

status, guardianship, custody and rights of succession of the children,[48] which are the most evident practical implications of traditional marriages. One man explained his reasons for registering his marriage by pointing out that registration made it more difficult for his wife to divorce him: a registered marriage could be dissolved only by the district commissioner's court[49] whereas an unregistered marriage could be dissolved by a chief or headman — besides, he had to pay only five shillings to have a case heard at the district commissioner's court compared with the fee of fifteen shillings at the chief's court. When a marriage needs to be registered to obtain, for example, housing in an urban black township, it is an established practice for the couple to ask any acquaintance to pose as a girl's guardian — the deception cannot easily be established in a busy urban court. All this suggests that the 'solemnization' of marriage is to most Shona a technical legal triviality.

Christians may also go through a Church marriage with as much as the families can afford of the pomp and festivities borrowed from European marriage customs suitably adapted. Thus the bride may wear a European style of wedding dress and be accompanied by bridesmaids; though usually she will observe the traditional custom of expressing sorrow at leaving her own family — joy on the part of the bride is usually thought most inappropriate. Receptions are held at both family homes, and at each guests vie to outdo the other family in giving presents to help the couple establish their own home. The traditional insults and rivalry between the two families are rarely suppressed, and may cause disruptions or delays to the wedding proceedings. A Church marriage does not necessarily change the Shona perception of the union, and it is usually considered an incidental addition to a regular Shona marriage, often taking place after the birth of a child:[50] since divorce and remarriage is difficult or impossible in Christian communities, a husband wants to be sure that his wife is not barren before he enters the contract. A Church or state marriage without the customary payment of bride-price is considered a 'cheap' marriage and the resulting union akin to concubinage.

Although a large bride-price gives status to the wife and to the marriage, in the more developed areas bride-price payments have inflated to a degree that disturbs many — especially young men who, however, are like-

---

48. *African Marriages Act.* No. 23 of 1950, section 3(3). Originally passed as the *Native Marriage Ordinance.* Section 2 of the Ordinance No. 15 of 1917.
49. This no longer applies since some chiefs may now dissolve solemnized marriages.
50. See Weinrich 1963, p. 75.

ly to support the inflation as they grow up, and have marriageable daughters. The replacement of cattle by cash and consumer goods have diminished some of the group aspects of Shona marriage: the groom is now usually expected to earn his marriage payments himself, and his father is likely to regard cash received from bride-price as personal property for his own use rather than family property for the marriages of his sons. Partly on account of the growing cost of bringing up children, standard requirements have escalated: to marry a girl with a couple of years secondary education, a man may have to produce a full outfit of clothes for the father and for the mother of the girl costing him perhaps $150, bride-price payments in cash of about $500, and he may have to spend another $200 on wedding-day clothes for his bride. If the girl is earning a reasonable salary, the parents may increase their demands to delay the marriage and to compensate themselves for the prospective loss of income, and the girl may surreptitiously help her suitor to make the payments: should this become known, it would be very damaging to the characters of both parties since the man has not shown his worth or his love and the foolish girl did not expect him to prove either.

An attempt to limit bride-price by legislation[51] failed in its purpose of helping the younger men. The girl's parents could still demand the going price before consenting to their daughter's marriage, but on subsequent divorce the husband could enforce the repayment only of the legal limit. Since the father-in-law could not claim any court payments above the legal limit, he was likely to withhold his consent to have the marriage registered until all his demands were met, resulting in long delays in the legal recognition of the marriage. This type of delay by the father-in-law is still common in the urban areas where he may have difficulty in enforcing payments from a complete stranger without the sanction of refusing to agree to the solemnization of the marriage.

To the traditional Shona, the main purpose of a marriage contract was the continuation and growth of the family group, and for the modern Shona man it remains important to have sons to support him in old age and to carry his name to posterity. The importance of children to Shona marriage is illustrated by the custom that the wife got her own cooking stones, which, as we shall see, are symbolic of the marriage, only after the birth of her first child: prior to this she shared the kitchen and food supplies of her mother-in-law. Another illustration is that barrenness on the

---

51. Section 11(1) of Act No. 23 of 1950 limited official bride-price to £20. The limit was repealed by section 2 of Act No. 11 of 1962.

part of the wife, or her early death before she has given birth to many children, is regarded as failure by her family to fulfil their side of the contract. In such a case, either they must provide another daughter or the marriage will be dissolved with the return of bride-price (or a portion of it if the deceased wife had born some children before she died).

Sterility on the part of the husband, although not in itself a sufficient cause for the dissolution of the marriage, is shameful: if this is suspected, the husband may make secret arrangements with a close kinsman to impregnate his wife in his name. If, however, the husband cannot satisfy his wife sexually, relations between them may become intolerable and result in the dissolution of the contract. A boy may before marriage undergo a traditional test for fertility in which he is made to masturbate and his semen is dropped into water: if the semen sinks it is thought to be 'strong' and fertile, but if it floats it is considered 'weak' and infertile and the boy may be given traditional medicines to improve his fertility.[52]

The significance of parenthood also appears in the religious and ritual fields. The final funerary ceremony of bringing home the spirit of a dead person and installing it among the spirit elders of the community, only takes place if the deceased begot or bore children: other spirits have lesser status. Also significant is the purificatory killing of a beast at a girl's first pregnancy: although this is intended to protect her parents from supposed danger to themselves, even when the parents are dead, substitutes are found and the ritual is performed in full.[53]

So parenthood is necessary to establish status among the Shona. A man establishes his right to have children primarily in the marriage contract by which children born of the woman (even those begotten by another man) are his. A man can also obtain the right to his children by an unmarried girl on the payment of compensation, traditionally in the form of a number of head of cattle,[54] indicating further the link between recognition of parenthood and the transference of cattle. Otherwise children of an unmarried woman are retained by her own family and regarded as members of her lineage and clan. Thus central to Shona marriage and the payment of bride-price is the transference of rights over the offspring of a woman.

Shona marriage also confers on the husband exclusive sexual rights

52. Gelfand 1956a, p. 238.
53. Holleman 1952a, pp. 87f, 179.
54. This sometimes, but not always, applies to the adulterine child of a married woman (cf. Bullock 1950, pp. 265f; Stead 1946, p. 17; Holleman 1958a, p. 36).

over his wife[55] closely associated with the initial marriage payment of *rutsambo*. Although it is now generally accepted that young people have sexual intercouse before marriage, the seducer might find himself faced with legal action if the girl is betrothed to someone else, if he breaks off the informal relationship without reasonable cause, or if he impregnates the girl. Generally anything is permitted provided that the relationship is leading towards a satisfactory marriage, suggesting that implicit permission is conveyed by the anticipation of marriage. Adultery with a married woman is always unlawful, and if the husband finds out, he may beat his wife and sue the man for compensation which is higher than compensation for a betrothed girl. It is not unknown for a couple in need of money to arrange for the wife to seduce a more wealthy man at a prearranged spot where he can be caught in the act and will have to pay compensation to the husband.

A man who interferes with the wife of another is believed to have a dangerous influence over him, and should the latter fall ill, the adulterer must keep away, since his presence might cause death.[56] Especially sinister is adultery with the wife of a close kinsman: as one informant explained, 'If you sleep with the wife of your brother or father . . . it is as if you wanted to kill him so that you could marry the wife. It is something like witchcraft.'[57] In such a case, compensation may or may not be claimed depending on the proximity of the relationship, but the mystical threat to the husband must be averted by a symbolic gesture and solemn promise to leave the woman alone, followed by a public act of reconciliation such as eating, drinking or taking snuff together.

Marital fidelity on the part of the husband is not essential to Shona marriage, but the husband is supposed to keep his wife informed of his extra-marital relations, and a failure to do this may be regarded as endangering his children. Also a husband must satisfy the sexual needs of his wife, provide the necessaries of life for herself and her children, and respect her personal dignity. The wife will be jealous of extra-marital relations on the part of the husband, or even of his relations with co-wives, if she finds herself neglected as a result of them. Such neglect may be accepted as reasonable grounds for divorce.

---

55. This does not apply to those daughters of chiefs for whom no bride-price is (or was) paid, a fact which supports the relationship between sexual rights and the transfer of bride-price.
56. Howman 1948, p. 10.
57. Holleman 1952a, p. 230.

Rural homestead in Chibi Communal Lands Wall decorations are not so common.

Rural homestead in Chikwaka Communal Lands, near Harare

MOTHER'S BROTHER — SISTER'S SON RELATIONSHIP

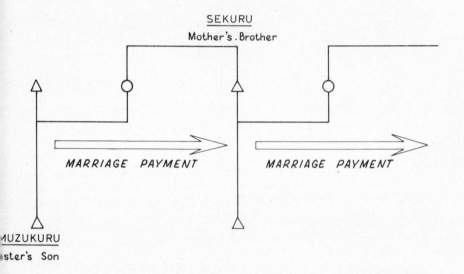

Typical homestead in the north amid dense bush.

Although sexual rights and rights over children are central to Shona marriage, there are other important aspects of the relations between man and wife. One important function of a wife is to provide food for her husband and her children. An inability to cook on the part of a wife is a serious shortcoming which may lead to the break-up of the marriage: many Shona men say that a husband may forgive a wife if she sleeps with another man, but if she cannot cook she is useless to him. In a traditional rural household, a woman's cooking stones are symbolic of the marriage: if a husband throws out the cooking stones or hands them in a basket to his wife, this is a clear token of rejection and the break-up of the marriage.[58] In rural areas, a wife must also be able to manage gardens and fields to produce food, especially now when husbands and wives must spend much of their time living apart. In the towns a wife must be able to stretch a meagre household budget to purchase essential supplies. Apart from his responsibility for the heavier agricultural tasks on the family fields, a modern husband must supply his family with a cash income. And mutual companionship is becoming ever more important to married couples as their ties with their extended families become weaker, and especially in the towns where a husband and wife may be living away from all their kin.

In a traditional Shona family a man could have as many wives as he could afford provided that he did not neglect any of them so much as to make them dissatisfied and ready to sue for divorce. The more wives a man had, the more children he was likely to have, and a large group of descendants meant a large labour force to work the fields of the family head, which in turn resulted in wealth and high status. In fact, few men are able to afford more than one wife until they are relatively old and influential members of the community, and not a few traditionalists remain with a single wife throughout their lives, whether by choice or for lack of means. So in practice, polygamous marriages have always been unusual except among the more senior members of a community. Now, a shortage of land in the rural areas, and the expense of keeping extra heads in the towns, make polygamy an economic burden rather than an asset. The influence of Christianity and European culture has reduced further the incidence of polygamous marriages. In upper class circles in the towns, people look down on a man who takes more than one wife.

---

58. Holleman 1952a, pp. 203f, 274, 282; Shropshire 1938, p. 269.

The position of women[59]

It is a common misconception that women had little or no status in traditional African societies. There are many reasons given for his view: women are said to be bought and sold in marriage like chattels; at the death of a husband, his widows are inherited with his estate; since women could not represent themselves in traditional courts but had to be represented by a senior male relative, it is said that legally they were minors all their lives; wives are said to be completely subject to their husbands who have the right to beat them within limits; women do most of the work in the fields and in the home while the men spend much of their time sitting in idle chatter. So some conclude that the traditional position of Shona women is little better than the position of a slave.

Taking the first point, we have already seen that a woman acquires status rather than loses it through the payment of bride-price. The payment of a high bride-price expresses and enhances the value the husband places on the marriage. Within her own family group, a woman's marriage brings wealth to her family and makes possible other marriages which can produce offspring to her lineage. This gives a woman high status within her own lineage, especially among the children of her brothers since their birth is ideally purchased with the bride-price received from her marriage. Owing to the institution of polygamy, any woman can find a husband as soon as she reaches a marriageable age and so any adult woman can acquire the consequent status in her own family.

Notice that the status acquired by marriage is not so much the status of wife but rather the status of provider to her own family. Few marriages in fact bring significant status within the husband's family. In a traditional marriage, the new wife lives as a young newcomer to her husband's extended family, and is under the control and direction of her husband's mother and sisters, who demand that she does the unpleasant chores around the home. Men and women usually eat, work and recreate separately, so during the day the new wife is confined for the most part to the company of the women of the family, among whom she is the junior. On the birth of children to the lineage, she acquires standing within it, which grows when her children marry and produce grandchildren for her. In the extended family system, the husband and wife relationship is not as important as it is when the nuclear family is emphasized. A Shona woman's status as wife is relatively unimportant; her social standing depends on her being an

---

59. The traditional position of women is briefly summarized in Gelfand 1973b. The contemporary position (legally and socially) is summarized in May 1983. A useful bibliography on the position of women in Zimbabwe is given in United Nations 1984.

influential person within her own lineage and the ancestor of a growing group of descendants.

As the immersion of the Shona into the monetary economy gives more emphasis to personal ownership, the group aspects of marriage payments are diminishing. This in turn diminishes the status of a woman within her own lineage, a change that is reinforced when a married couple live for a time away from the wife's kin and particularly from the children of her brothers. But the isolation of the towns and work centres applies also to her husband's family, and when the couple lives far from the husband's mother and sisters his wife is in charge of her own household. The sense of independence given to young wives when they are with their husbands away from their rural homes is one reason for the break-up of extended families in the rural areas. And apart from geographical isolation, the economic independence of a husband detracts from the authority of his sister over his wife and her children: when bride-price payments come from the husband's earnings rather than from his sister's marriage, the husband's sister can no longer claim responsibility for his marriage and for his children. The independence of the wife can further increase if she has a private source of income from some form of trade or employment. Thus in the changing Shona family structure, the woman's traditional status in her own kinship group is diminishing, a loss which has some compensation from her rising status as a housewife in control of her own home.[60]

It is true that at the death of the husband his widows are normally inherited by one of his kinsmen. But a widow may refuse to be inherited, and in any case she is usually asked to state her preference for a kinsman of her late husband. The inheritance of a widow provides her with a man to be responsible for her upkeep and for her children. Even an aged widow is inherited and can thus continue to find support in the home to which she has become accustomed and where she can continue to cultivate the fields originally allotted to her by her husband. Although widows are inherited when the late husband's estate is inherited, this does not mean that they are simply regarded as part of his estate. It is now not uncommon for a widow to choose to be inherited by her eldest son, in order to ensure that her late husband's estate remains within her sphere and influence, and largely under her control.

Although a woman could always acquire a position of standing with some authority, the traditional position of women had deficiencies relative to that of men, deficiencies which found clear expression on formal legal and ritual occasions.

---

60. See Holleman 1958c.

Women are supposed to be incapable of conducting a court case properly, and when bringing a dispute to a traditional court, a woman should have a male relative to represent her and to speak for her. He should advise her on how to present her evidence and on acceptable terms for the solution of the dispute. Also a woman traditionally has limited responsibility for offences, particularly obvious in cases of adultery which are treated by tribal courts as the sole responsibility of men. In practice, however, a husband may punish an unfaithful wife in private, and adultery with a woman known to be morally loose is not taken seriously; the woman's part is clearly recognised. And although a court may occasionally deride a woman for trying to conduct her own case, even in the 1970s women did sometimes take complete responsibility for the cases they brought before chiefs' courts, to the effect that practice did not strictly accord with the idea that women were always legally minors.[61]

In ritual too we find an inconsistency. Thus in some areas the final funerary ritual[62] to bring home the spirit of a dead person and install it among the spirit guardians of the family is not performed for a deceased woman. This ceremony is normally performed in conjunction with the inheritance ceremony for a man who has obtained full adult status by becoming the father of a family, and the fact that it is often omitted when the deceased is a woman suggests that women do not always acquire in life the full adult status necessary to be influential as spirit elders after death. Yet we have remarked that the spirits of a person's mother and mother's mother are considered to be strongly influential and sometimes dangerous.

Traditions concerning the spirits are considered to be in the male domain, and the men of a community normally conduct ceremonies in honour of the spirits. Yet women do interfere when they are not satisfied with the way the men are performing their duties, and occasionally a senior woman may preside over a ceremony when the men appropriately related to the spirit are absent or reluctant to perform the necessary rituals. Women can also play important roles as hosts to spirits in various possession cults.

In the traditional Shona family, the father is normally in charge. In particular, all family property belongs to him and his wife can claim little in the case of divorce or of the death of the husband: sometimes even the

---

61. Cf. Child 1958, pp 69f. District commissioners' courts were in fact lagging behind the changing practice in chiefs' courts which increasingly are accepting the emancipation of women.

62. This ritual is discussed in detail in chapter 8 below.

clothes a husband has given to his wife are successfully claimed by the husband when the marriage has broken up. Nevertheless, a woman could always acquire some property of her own by trading skills such as pottery or basket work, and many professional diviners and healers are women who can earn a healthy income from their art. A woman can build up a small herd from the cow of motherhood she receives at the marriage of a daughter, or from any other cattle she may acquire. And a woman's property is inherited on her death by her children or her patrilineal kin, not by her husband.[63] In the case of a wealthy woman, some kind of formal inheritance ceremony is essential for peace among her descendants. Nowadays, the opportunities for a woman to become financially independent through various kinds of trade have multiplied (though a woman in formal employment usually has to give her salary to her husband if she is married and to her guardian if she is not).

It is interesting to notice that women have more influence in the homestead than they dare, or their menfolk care, to admit. It has been found, for example, that the attitudes of wives are more influential in bringing about changes in medical practices, hygiene and even in agriculture than those of their husbands.[64] Although the husband officially controls his fields and the homestead, the fact that the wives do most of the work means that in practice their ideas receive little opposition. The influence of women in the rural areas has probably increased through the frequent absence of their husbands, who periodically leave home to seek wage employment, but it is probable that women always had more say in Shona society than was formally admitted. A man who publicly asserts the prerogative of men to make decisions and to control the economy, may in private regularly consult his wife on matters of importance and frequently defer to her judgement.

In many ancient traditions about the founding of chiefdoms and chiefly dynasties, women played a role in defeating the enemy by seduction or by magical knowledge. Thus in a number of Korekore chiefdoms, the chiefly dynasties are said to have been founded by a brother and a sister together. In each chiefdom, the brother and the sister became 'lion' spirits and through their mediums shared an uneasy balance of authority over the chiefship, the authority of each supported by contradictory traditions. In one chiefdom, there were two accounts of the founding of the dynasty: in one the sister was first in the country and killed the previous ruler after

63. See Holleman 1952a, pp. 350 – 368; Howman 1961.
64. See Theisen 1976, p. 96; also Mitchell 1952a.

seducing him, and in the other the brother arrived first and defeated the previous ruler in battle under the guidance of his sister; one old man, an acknowledged authority on tribal traditions, told both stories on different occasions, and when challenged on his inconsistency he explained that the brother ruled the chiefdom but his sister was the stronger. Her power was in fact associated with a mystical knowledge of 'medicines'; generally women are more readily associated with this kind of knowledge, in that accusations of witchcraft are most commonly made against women. This is partly due to the fact that women are often outsiders or strangers to the suspicious communities in which they live as wives, or due to the uncertainties of child bearing and the care of infants which are officially a woman's main function. But the clandestine power attributed to women appears also to be a recognition of their subtle influence in spite of the male-oriented structure of authority.

This kind of subtle influence and authority may have worked well enough in a relatively stable traditional society, but it is liable to be eroded as society changes. Because women's status was without overt recognition, people in authority do not see any reason to replace its supports. When a woman loses her role as supporter of the family through agriculture, and instead becomes totally dependent on her husband's salary, it is not immediately apparant that traditional norms concerning the relationship between husbands and wives will no longer apply. As land becomes short, and its usage changes, secondary rights in a husband's land no longer provide the security that they once did when land was plentiful. When people move into systems where land-holding is more formalised, such as irrigation schemes or onto commercial farms, the secondary rights of women to their husbands' lands are forgotten and lost — or are maintained only in contradiction to the formal legal situation.[65] Besides, in the past agricultural extension work was geared primarily towards men, on the erroneous assumption that women were more concerned with learning homecraft skills.[66] The result is that in both rural and urban areas, women have become increasingly worried by their lack of formal right to family property in the case of divorce or widowhood.

There have always been a few women with less subtle authority. Thus daughters of a Manyika paramount chief were sometimes appointed as headwomen over subject territories: these women were exceptional in that

65. See Cheater 1982.
66. See Muchena 1979, 1980b.

54

no bride-price was paid for them in marriage and they were not expected to remain faithful to their 'husbands'.[67] Elsewhere one finds occasional instances of famous headwomen and there is even a traditional Shona chieftainness. More commonly a woman could, and still can, hold significant sway in the government of a chiefdom by becoming a medium to a senior spirit, and female mediums to lesser spirits have, while possessed, authority over smaller groups of neighbours or kin. It has always been possible, albeit unusual, for a woman to hold a position of authority in Shona communities.

In modern times, and particularly in the towns, women are sometimes able to free themselves from subordination to their menfolk through economic independence. Women suffer considerable disadvantages in seeking employment, but employment is sometimes available in domestic service or in industry, and a living can be made through various types of trading.[69]

One sure way of achieving economic independence is through prostitution. Although there have always been a few morally loose women in Shona society, it was the introduction of money, together with labour migration, that made it possible for girls in significant numbers to earn a living through prostitution. In the work centres the large number of unmarried men, and of married men living away from their wives, provide a ready market for prostitutes, who in turn are out of the control that kinsmen can exert in the rural areas. Some professional prostitutes are rurally based and return home periodically, especially in the agricultural off-season when farming wives go to join their husbands in the work centres and the prostitutes become less wanted. A prostitute might also return to her rural home when she becomes pregnant: her children receive the clan names of their mother and become part of her patrilineal family. Although they are not respected by the community as a whole, prostitutes are often tolerated and well-treated within their own families on account of the substantial income they can acquire.

In the towns any woman who mixes with men in public places is assumed to be a prostitute, and faithful wives are discouraged or prohibited from passing their time with their husbands, who tend to recreate together in the traditional way. Yet at their homes the wives are normally cut off from

---

67. Bezeley 1940.
68. Murphree 1969, p. 16.
69. See May 1979, Muchena 1980a.

the women of the extended family with whom they would normally find company and who would provide mutual help for the running of the household. One young town wife remarked that she never dreamed that she would miss her mother-in-law; in town there is nobody to look after her children when she has work to do and she has to drag her three toddlers with her even when she goes to the market to buy groceries.[70]

Partly as a result of this kind of social isolation in the towns, women's clubs and church associations for women have developed and are growing rapidly to provide social gatherings for town wives. They also provide a ready means for the dissemination of ideas and new standards, domestic skills such as sewing and cooking, family budgeting, knowledge of hygiene and child care, and even a means for co-operative saving: these functions are equally effective in the rural areas where women's clubs have become a channel for adult education. In the towns, women's clubs have begun to be influential in local government: in the 1970s they controlled sufficient votes to be able to demand that representatives on advisory boards account for their position, and even to elect some of their own members on to these boards[71].

In modern Zimbabwe, many women have in practice acquired parity with men. Women can become owners and managers of businesses and farms. The status of women was helped by the official recognition of their part in the war of liberation, resulting in a woman in the cabinet of the first government of Zimbabwe. The legal Age of Majority Act (No. 15 of 1982) officially gave all people, including women, full adult status on reaching the age of eighteen. In practice, legal rights are of little use if social and economic pressures can be used to prevent women from asserting their rights (as often happens). And it is not clear how much independence the Act intended to give to women in such matters as contracting marriages without reference to the demands of bride-price by senior male kin. Nevertheless, the overt support that socialist ideology gives to women who are striving for equality, is likely to diminish some of the disadvantages under which women have been suffering.

So the subtle traditional influence of women is changing into an open force for progress and change. Although women are losing something of their traditional standing which relates to their position in the extended family rather than in a nuclear family of husband, wife and children, they

---

70. It is interesting to notice that women in the towns rely more on their kin than do men (see Stopforth 1972, p. 65).

71. May 1973b.

often acquire social and economic independence which improves their position in relation to their husbands. Some women are able to improve their position through the changes that are taking place, but many find themselves losing their traditional position without being able to find a new one.

The village

Among rural Shona, a number of extended families live together in a village community. The English word 'village' does not accurately convey the Shona *musha* (village, home) centred around the family of the headman and associated with him rather than with any locality or buildings: thus should a Shona headman move to new fields, his village is likely to maintain its identity (its name and much of its original population) at the headman's new home. Nevertheless a village usually does have territorial connotations, perhaps vaguely a cluster of homesteads and the surrounding fields, or often more precisely a ridge between two streams which mark it off from the territory of neighbouring villages. Now land is often short and, in accordance with government legislation, has been allocated to individuals, giving a more permanent and precise definition to village territory.

In the past, any man was a potential village headman should he acquire a sufficient following of dependants. The nucleus of a village is the founder and his patrilineal descendants. To these are added a few men who have married daughters of the family and have come to live in their wives' home, possibly bringing other members of their extended families with them. In subsequent generations, the children of sons-in-law who lived in the village form the nuclei of further patrilineal families cognatically related to the principal lineage of the village. And large villages usually have some unrelated families attached through ties of friendship.

Shona villages vary considerably in size. In some areas in central Shona country, the policy was to build up large villages, possibly fortified by a fence of stakes, which could form a defensive unit. In other areas, among the Valley Korekore for example, people preferred to live in small scattered hamlets from which they could disperse and hide in case of attack. The different policies were no doubt partly influenced by ecological conditions: the dry, infertile nature of much of Korekore country necessitated small mobile units to operate their shifting cultivation. Whatever the reason, village sizes did vary with a consequent variation in structure: small hamlets form a closer approximation to an extended family than do large villages which acquire numerous accretions to the principal lineage.

As a village grows to its optimum size, there is a tendency for it to split. The optimum size depends on the area, on available land and on the motivation keeping the group together. Among Valley Korekore, for example, a hamlet of a commoner head rarely survives the death of the founder who holds the group together, whereas a Zezuru village may grow to a population of couple of hundred when land is scarce.[72] Whatever the precise point, at some stage the tensions which arise in a growing community prove stronger than the bonds uniting the community and the village splits. The tensions are often expressed in suspicions and accusations of witchcraft, but these are usually related to personality conflict and demographic difficulties. Clearly the ability of the land to hold a growing population affects the tensions that can arise: when the land is less fertile, the split is likely to take place sooner. Another factor is conflict over authority and leadership: the split often occurs when two branches of the founder's family, each with a significant body of supporters, vie for the headmanship, in which case the village is likely to divide into two roughly equal units. The split may also take the form of a small branch of the community hiving off to start a new settlement without great disruption to the original community. Occasionally, when the headman is not able to inspire sufficient confidence and concord, individual families may leave the village which diminishes rapidly in numbers without any open split taking place.[73]

When a village does split, relations between the families concerned are likely to be forgotten and to die away.[74] Partly due to tensions prior to the split, and partly because the relationship becomes meaningless without contact and co-operation, the genealogy that is remembered and passed on to younger generations is likely to omit absent branches of the lineage.

The colonial administration has affected village structure in a number of ways. The administration preferred to keep large units together for the efficient collection of taxes or rates and so discouraged and hindered village fission. The role of the village headman as tax-collector has been institutionalized to the extent that his title has changed from *samusha*

72. Garbett 1963a, ch. 3; Chavunduka 1970a, p. 15.
73. Examples of this and of the process of village fission can be found in the series of studies on the Musami villages, Mrewa District (Bernadi 1950, Garbett 1960, Chavunduka 1970a).
74. Garbett 1960, p. 9.

(owner of the village or home) to *sabhuku* (owner of the book — the tax-register). Also in much Shona country the residential areas have been fixed along lines with fields for cultivation on either side surveyed and allotted to residents, all of which affects mobility.[75] And the shortage of land available to the growing population also deters mobility and village fission, with the result that generally villages have become larger. In many areas the villages now take the form of long scattered rows of brick houses, perhaps a kilometre or more in length, with access roads and sometimes an avenue of trees, all very different from the clusters of pole and mud huts of the past.

Yet in spite of the changes in appearance and in spite of the growth in size, Shona village structure has many of the features that it always had. In a series of studies over twenty years of five villages (which have become six, and unofficially seven) not far from Harare, we find that although the number of households and the population more than doubled, there was little change in the proportions of householders that belonged to the lineages of the headmen (31 per cent in 1948; 36 per cent in 1968), of householders who were spouses of members of the headmen's lineages (11 per cent in 1948; 14 per cent in 1968), of householders related to their headmen through female links (34 per cent in 1948; 23 per cent in 1968) and of unrelated householders (24 per cent in 1948; 27 per cent in 1968).[76]

Although changes have taken place in individual villages as they grew and split, the overall picture remains much the same. And within the village lines extended families and close relatives tend to occupy adjacent houses to the effect that the villages continue to be divided residentially into small family clusters.

In some areas, the growth in size of villages is an administrative fiction operative for little more than collecting rates. People continue to live in scattered hamlets, and residential locality may bear no relation to official village affliation as recorded in the tax registers.

The duties of a village headman are broadly similar to those of a family head, adapted for the larger community with which he has to deal. He must see to the sustenance of all members of the village, and it is his responsibility to distribute available land so that all can maintain

---

75. This was in connection with the *African Land Husbandry Act* (1951) which was intended to encourage improved farming and soil conservation. It comes under discussion in the next chapter.

76. Chavunduka 1970a, p. 16: these proportions are comparable with those of the Karanga villages studied by Daneel (1971, p. 33).

themselves. The headman may also be responsible for the performance of rituals to ensure rain and good crops. The headman should arbitrate any petty disputes that may arise within his village and for this he may have one or two senior kinsmen to help him. When a case is too complicated for his court, or when it involves someone outside his jurisdiction, the headman should make a preliminary enquiry into it before taking it to the court of the ward headman or chief, where he is expected to represent his villagers and account for them even when they are unrelated to him. His prestige largely depends on his advice in settling tensions within the community and his ability to support his villagers against outsiders. The headman is *baba* (father) to all the village and they are *vana* (children) to him.[77]

Yet the authority of a headman outside his own family group is limited. Thus he can expect help for the cultivation of his fields only from his close kinsmen who are normally juniors in his own family, and from his sons-in-law, but he may not demand help from any other person in his village. The only sanction he can exercise against these is to drive them away which would result in a loss in his own following.

There are various reasons why people may choose to live in a village whose headman belongs to a different lineage from their own. Often the cause is bad relations between the newcomer to a village and his own kin. The reason may be economic as when a husband works for his father-in-law in lieu of bride-price payments or when there is a shortage of land at the newcomer's village of origin. The most frequent reason, however, appears to be that people like to live close to those with whom they have a mutual understanding and friendship: it can be argued that personal relationships are more important in determining residential choice among the Shona than are kinship relations.[78] Whatever the reason for his choice of residence, once a man has obtained the right to cultivate land, he becomes a permanent member of the community, and his rights could not be unilaterally expropriated. Once he has settled in a village, he is likely to form ties with his neighbours which are more effective in daily life than kinship ties with those who live elsewhere.[79]

There is little co-operation between members of the same lineage if, as is often the case, they live far apart. But most people have some relatives

77. Holleman 1952a, pp. 9f
78. Bernardi 1950, p. 11.
79. See, for example, the story cited by Posselt (1920a, pp. 118f) in which the duiker is searching for the meaning of misfortune: the description of misfortune always involves two persons doing the same thing, the failure of one contrasting with success of the other.

living in their neighbourhood from whom they can expect close co-operation. Besides, the spread of kinship ties through marriage facilitates movement from one village to another, to the effect that even in a new village a man is likely to move into the neighbourhood of distant relatives. So kinship and neighbourhood tend to go together, and in daily life it is the latter that ultimately counts: neighbours who are not related are usually friends who have loyalties and obligations towards each other similar to those between kin.

In some situations the closeness of a kinship tie is measured by residential proximity. Thus Professor Holleman describes a clan which about six generations ago split into two segments living in different areas: although they still have the same clan names, and although in some cases the relationships between individuals could be traced, the relationship between the two groups is not recognised and they are allowed to intermarry freely on the grounds that they have been living apart for a long time. [80] Contrariwise, if two groups live close together an otherwise permissible marriage between distant kin may be regarded as incestuous. Also the distance that near kinsmen lived from a dead man can affect their share in his estate.[81] Thus genealogical distance, social distance and spatial distance are all associated in the Shona view.

Unrelated neighbours may adopt a bond of formal friendship expressed in the mutual *usahwira* relationship which is common in the north-east of Shona country.[82] A *sahwira* is strictly an unrelated person who has certain ritual functions, the most important of which is handling the corpse at a funeral. In practice the relationship of *usahwira* between two families usually has a long tradition and, at any death in one, the senior available member of the other performs the appropriate rites. In the absence of a traditional *sahwira*, any unrelated friend of the deceased or of his family may be appointed to the role, in which case a new *sahwira* relationship is created between the two families and inherited by their patrilineal descendants. In some areas the relationship may be created or confirmed by the exchange of tokens of friendship in the form of some small gift: friends bound in this way guarantee each other unlimited hospitality and help in times of need. Even when the ralationship is established through burial

---

80. Holleman 1949, pp. 29f.

8 1 Seed 1933, p. 52. Fr Seed also a case in which a Native Commissioner could not persuade the people that bulls from a distant district could be of the same stock as their own cattle.

8 2 See Holleman 1953, p. vii; 1958a, pp. 246f.; Cheater 1978.

rites, acts of friendship necessarily follow. At the meal after the funeral the *sahwira* receives special honour and, even when the family cannot afford meat for all the guests, a fowl must be killed for him. If a *sahwira* visits the home of his counterpart at any time, he can expect privileged treatment and he should not be refused any gift he may request (the mutual and friendly nature of the relationship is the sanction against asking too much). Generally, unrelated persons can call each other *sahwira* to indicate friendship.

Regarding relations between neighbours, Shona society is ideally egalitarian in the expectation that wealth should be evenly distributed throughout the community. The Shona idea of misfortune is defined in contrast to the good fortune of others, [83] and great success on the part of one man or family is believed to involve the detriment of others. Since 'medicines' are frequently used to obtain good luck, conspicuous good fortune naturally engenders the suspicion of witchcraft, using 'medicines' to the detriment of others. The norm of morality is the good of the group, and to work exclusively for one's own success, even by the use of 'good medicines' or simply by working hard on one's lands, meets with disapproval. A man who makes excessive efforts to obtain the help of the spirit elders can also be regarded as a witch. The rich bring unpopularity and suspicion on themselves[84] which can only be overcome by liberally using wealth for the benefit of kin and of the community as a whole[85] restoring the equality that is the norm.

In traditional Shona society, good relations with the neighbourhood require generosity and liberal hospitality: it is noticeable in folk tales that to refuse to offer food to a visitor who arrives when the host is eating is un-

---

83. See, for example, the story cited by Posselt (1920a, pp. 118f) in which the duiker is searching for the meaning of misfortune: the description of misfortune always involves two persons doing the same thing, the failure of one contrasting with the success of the other.

8 4 Essex-Capell (1946, p. 68) claims that no Korekore would wish his daughter to marry a rich man because such a man is proud and selfish and thinks only of his worldly goods; he illustrates this attitude by recounting a Shona tale against the rich in general. Such a principled antipathy to a financially favourable marriage is not dominant now.

8 5 The same applies, of course, to a person who is favourably placed in employment, and who is expected to bestow favours on kinsmen and neighbours who desire his help. It is extremely difficult, and contradicts much of traditional ideology, for a conscientious administrator to resist such demands of patronage as would appear nepotic to an outsider.

thought of, even when the host knows that the visitor is abusing his hospitality.[86] Negatively, a refusal to help a man in need is equated with wanting to see him and his children starve, clearly an indication of malevolence and witchcraft. To ridicule another member of the community may also be regarded as an offence, and it is particularly wrong to despise or ridicule a poor man in any way.

Nevertheless, even in pre-colonial times, there were in practice clear differences between rich and poor. With the labour of poor dependants, and through trade of surplus crops and of iron work, salt, tobacco or other valuables, wealthy individuals were able to acquire cloth for clothing instead of goatskins, to wear beads and other ornaments, to have large huts always in a good state of repair, to have others perform their unpleasant labour, and to have many wives and dependants. A man with many cattle lived noticeably better than the sons-in-law whose services he acquired.

With the introduction of monetary wealth on the one hand, and the shortage of available land on the other, the differences have widened somewhat, and many areas are fraught with 'competition' — keeping one up on the neighbours. Nevertheless, many remain secretive about their earnings and carefully avoid any exhibition of wealth which might provoke suspicion or jealousy, or simply demands for help.

---

86. E.g., Posselt 1929a, pp. 100f.

3

From Subsistence
to Cash Economy

The land

Before we discuss how rural Shona live off the soil, it will be helpful to consider their traditional relationship with the land. In doing this, we should bear in mind that the relationship has radically changed in most areas. In particular, as elsewhere in Africa,[1] when land becomes scarce, its economic value and the significance of rights of individuals in land become prominent, even when the old ideas about land are not completely forgotten. Even in the tribal trust lands, means have been found according to which land can be bought and sold: initially, the original user could demand compensation for the work of clearing and preparing farm land; but as land becomes more scarce, value for the land itself is added to the compensation fee, and chiefs and headmen can charge settlers a fee for the allocation of land. Now, in crowded areas, people expect to pay even for the allocation of a residential plot — as much as $70 near Harare.[2] In the early 1930s, the Southern Rhodesian government created "Purchase Lands" in which blacks could acquire freehold rights to land: land has become for the Shona living in these areas primarily an economic asset, and a source of security. The contemporary situation has of its nature brought about changes in practice, although traditional ideals linger on in the minds of many. According to these ideals, Shona people see more in their land than simply usable property.

The land is intimately associated with the history of a chiefdom, with the ruling chief and with ancestral spirits who lived on it. The significance of the land is illustrated in a Shona tale in which Mwari (the high god) distributes goods to men: to one man he gave people and cattle and to another only a handful of soil; the latter was able to claim as his own all that grew in or fell on the soil, including all the people and cattle born on the land. Through possession of the land he became a great chief while the man who received followers and cattle became a headman under the owner of the soil.[3]

Loyalty to the chief and respect due to to him are connected with his sovereignty over the land. If a man was rebuked for passing his chief with little or no formal salutation, he might reply, "Where is the land?", implying that since the white people had dominion over the land the chief had

---

1. Cf., e.g., Feldman 1974 on Ismani, Tanzania; Jones 1949 on the Igbo of Nigeria; Colson 1963 on the Valley Tonga of Zambia.
2. *The Herald*, 28 Nov. 1980, p. 1.
3. Posselt 1929a, p. 57.

lost his status.[4] On the other hand, the allegiance of townsmen to their tribal authorities depended on the fact that the tribal authorities controlled the use of land, which provides security in old age to townsmen and countrymen alike. The association of the chief with the land is symbolized in the instalment ceremonies of chiefs all over Shona country. Thus in the description of the instalment of Karanga Chief Ziki, we are told that the new chief opened his hands which were filled with two handfuls of earth while he was addressed: 'You are now Ziki. We hand you the country to hold. Look after us well.'[5] Similarly we find in the history of the vaShawasha people that when their chief had occupied the country and killed the old Rozvi chief, he called his people together; when they gathered, one of his followers dug a handful of soil, mixed it with water and gave it to him saying, 'Take this soil, Chinamora.' When he took it all the people clapped their hands in recognition of his chiefship.[6] Among the Korekore, the spirit medium appoints a chief by giving to the appointee a handful of medicated soil; although the full status of chiefship is acquired only during subsequent ceremonies, once a man has formally been given the soil, no one else can become chief until his death.

The chief's dominion over the land found practical expression in that only he could give permission for a group of foreigners to settle in the chiefdom and cultivate its soil. In the past various hunting tributes were payable to the chief in recognition of his dominion over the land in which the kill was made:[7] the chief received the elephant tusk nearest to the ground when the elephant fell, the skin or heart of any lion killed in his territory, a portion of certain kinds of big game, and he could claim any scaly ant-eater (believed to have strong medicinal properties) killed in his territory. In the old days, when a chief travelled through his country he received tribute from the crops of his subjects in recognition of the fact that they grew on the chief's land.[8] Subsequently the chief's dominion was confined principally to his control of immigration into his territory.

So the chief is in some sense owner of the land, but this 'ownership' is restricted to very limited rights over the land and certain duties towards it. Once the chief has granted cultivation rights to an immigrant, these rights are inalienable; the grantee has indisputable rights to the produce of his

4. Bullock 1928, p. 70.
5. Bullock 1928, p. 290.
6. Chidziwa 1964, p. 18.
7. Cf. Jackson 1950.
8. Marr 1962, p. 83.

land, to his herds and their offspring and he has the right to keep away trespassers. But he cannot sell his land rights and should he leave the territory these revert to the chief. Even when the chief was paid tribute, he was not entirely free as to its use but was bound by customary rules and especially by his obligation to help subjects in need. In return for his dominion, the chief has the duty to ensure good rains and good crops by performing the appropriate rituals to the spirit guardians of the chiefdom, and in the past he had also to protect his people from invaders and raiders. 'Ownership' or 'proprietorship' do not exactly convey the Shona idea of the relationship between the chief and the land.[9]

People often say that the real 'owners' of the land are the spirit guardians of the chiefdom, the spirits of founders or early rulers of the chiefdom and their immediate kin. In most chiefdoms, the ancestral spirit guardians of the chiefly dynasty have joint dominion over the chiefdom, and sometimes the spirits of a previous, ousted dynasty are believed to exercise some control over the country. Valley Korekore country is divided into clearly defined areas of varying sizes, each the domain of a particular guardian spirit; here the chiefdom and the chief have little significance outside the spirit domain in which the chief lives.[10] The spirit guardians of these domains, or elsewhere of the chiefdom as a whole, are said to own the territory and are believed to control rainfall and fertility in it. Newcomers to a chiefdom or spirit domain should offer a gift to the spirit owner through the medium on first arrival in the country, and should honour the spirit owners of the land with millet beer after building a homestead. Any projects of significance, such as the building of a dam or a school, should have the approval of the spirits of the area. These spirits are usually the ancestors of the chief who is their living representative: in such a case, they are approached through the chief, and the spirit mediums usually work in co-operation with the chief who is their appointee. The chief is closely associated with the land precisely because as the senior descendant of the original owners of the land he is the man who should intercede with their spirits. Occasionally, however, the most influential spirits are those of a defeated dynasty whose living descendants must co-operate with the chief when in times of distress the help of the spirits is needed for the good of the chiefdom.

Ultimate dominion over all the country is in the hands of the high god. It is the high god who provides and owns the wild fruits.[11]

---

9. Cf. Mitchell 1961a, pp. 30f.
10. Garbett 1966a, pp. 141ff.
11. Holleman 1958a, p. 145.

Particularly in the area of the oracle to the high Mwari, it is Mwari who is approached to provide rain and good crops. A universal drought that spreads beyond the boundaries of the domains of all lesser spirits is said to be caused by the high god. Nevertheless, the high god is for most Shona too remote from the concerns of men to be closely associated with something so intimate to the people as their land.

'Ownership' of the land by the spirits is bound up with the relationship between the spirits and the living community. The land forms a close and enduring bond between the living and the dead: through their control of the fertility of the land they once cultivated, the spirits are believed to continue to care for their descendants and the descendants are forced to remember and honour their ancestors. Chief Sileya says, 'The owners of the soil are the whole tribe, more especially the deceased members.'[12] If 'ownership' is to be understood in terms of rights and obligations, then all members of the chiefdom have some degree of ownership in the land, but it is the spirit ancestors who have the gravest obligations and the ultimate rights.

The association between the spirits and the land is expressed in the tradition of *chisi*, days sacred to the spirits, on which people should not work the soil in any way. It appears that usually these were originally connected with phases of the moon, and later became associated with a particular day of the week (the day varying from area to area). Even among commercial farmers, these days are often still observed, families using *chisi* to perform weekly tasks which do not involve work on the fields. In some areas, the only days sacred to the spirits are the rare days on which rituals are performed in their honour, and even then people sometimes have urgent ploughing done by children, explaining that since children do not know the customs of the people it does not matter if they break them. On the other hand, under the influence of economic demands or of Christianity or of both these, many Shona now ignore *chisi*, more or less openly, observing only Sunday as a rest day. But respect for the spirits' control over land in the observance of *chisi* remains a widespread practice in Shona country, often enforced by chiefly authority.

The territory of a chiefdom contains all its members, living and dead, and even those who may be away from home have rights in the land pending their return. The land thus becomes a tangible expression of the tribe as a whole. As neighbourhood is associated with kinship, so the chiefdom is associated with tribal affiliation.

---

12. Marr 1962, p. 83.

The land as a productive resource remains of crucial importance to the Shona even today, whether it be for subsistence during life or simply for security in old age. But it is far more than simply a productive resource. Since the Shona believe that the productivity of the land is in the power of its deceased owners, the land emphasizes their need of contact with their deceased ancestors. The land is thus important for the continuity of a people with its traditions. The land links past and present, the dead and the living, the chief and his people, and it binds the people together. It was thus no small thing for a people to be moved off their land by the white people: such a move can result in the disintegration of a tribe.[13]

Subsistence farming[14]

Apart from those who practised traditional skills professionally, the Shona have always traded to a limited degree, including trade in agricultural surpluses. In the south of Shona country, there is evidence of trade in precolonial times in surplus grain from the highveld for livestock from the lowveld. When whites first settled in the country, black farmers were ready to exploit the new market for their products: in 1903, African (and predominantly Shona) sales of grain and stock amounted to £350 000.[15] Subsequent pressure from white farmers brought about a deterioration in black agriculture, first by taking over large stretches of land, and later by pushing legislation which protected white farming against black competition.[16] So when we speak of traditional Shona agriculture as 'subsistence' farming, we must beware of belittling its economic viability.

Nevertheless, in the past, the Shona had not the technology for storing agricultural produce for long periods, or for protecting grain from such pests as borers and weevils; so there was little incentive to produce large surpluses. People grew only as much as they could use in a year or two. Indeed, the prevalence of game and wild fruits in the sparsely populated country of pre-colonial Zimbabwe provided a significant supplementary food supply and meant that people could survive even on an agriculture that was below the subsistence level.

13. Cf. Hove 1943, p. 45.
14. The best work on African Agriculture in Zimbabwe is Yudelman 1964.
15. Cf. Palmer 1977b, pp. 224f., 229.
16. The clearest illustration of this is the *Maize Control Amendment Act* of 1934. Cf. Palmer 1977b, pp. 239 – 243. Later, when white farming became more scientific, Shona farmers were often able to benefit from the expertise of white neighbours.

Now, most Shona still rely for their sustenance on their traditional sub-sistence farming, suitably adapted to the modern situation and with various types of supplementary income that the modern economy provides. Since the basic food of the Shona[17] is stiff porridge made from ground maize or millet, their main crop is maize or millet grown on fields of a few acres. The Shona may also grow vegetables to provide relish to eat with the porridge or to provide additions to the main diet. Sour milk and meat from domestic animals are also eaten as relish. The diet may be supplemented by various wild fruits and seeds, game and edible insects. In the dry low-lying areas, poor harvests of a drought year are supplemented by the plentiful fruit of the baobab tree which is traditionally protected for this purpose and which has acquired some religious significance. Other wild fruit trees[18] are also traditionally protected for the food they provide even when they are situated in the middle of field of grain. Nowadays the main supplement to subsistence farming is acquired through cash wages, but few Shona are able completely to replace their fields of grain with other forms of income.

In the traditional system of land tenure, a man was given his fields by his father with the consent of the village headman. A newcomer to the area was normally apportioned fields by the ward or village headman with the cognisance of the chief. He then cleared an area by cutting down and burning the trees and shrubs and hoeing the ground with a hand hoe. He grew his grain on the land, perhaps increasing the size of his field each year, until the land was exhausted, at which stage he could find and clear a new field. In some of the less developed and sparsely populated areas of Shona country, this system is still in operation with the exception that the ox-drawn plough has largely replaced the hand hoe. In these areas, a family might work the same fields for up to fifteen or even twenty years before moving to new ones: even then, aged couples with a dwindling number of dependants and without the vigour necessary for clearing new fields, may continue on their old unproductive land, sometimes eroded to little more than gravel. In granelitic sandy soils, fields become useless after four to five years. This system of agriculture is possible as long as land is available and it requires a minimum of capital expenditure, but it is wasteful of land resources.

In most areas the Shona population has grown and all the land avail-

17. Shona diet is discussed in Gelfand 1971a.
18. These include *muchakata* or *muucha* (*parinari curatellifolia*), *mubaba* (*piliostigma thonningii*) and *muzhumwi* (*strychnos cocculoides*).

able to them has been allocated, so that shifting cultivation is no longer possible. Arable land may be limited to as little as five acres a family, which must be used in perpetuity. The limitation of available land necessitates the use of fertilizers, crop rotation and contour ridging to keep the soil productive; it also means that sons of land holders are not always able to acquire their own plots as they grow up and marry.

Nevertheless, land rights and land usage in the Tribal Trust Lands are determined as far as possible by the traditional system. Thus rights to cultivate a plot of land are usually bestowed by the family head or village headman, though now the plot is likely to be clearly demarcated and to allow no room for expansion as the family grows. Although now a man officially loses his rights to land if he fails to pay the local council rates, in practice most headmen are slow and reluctant to evict any of the subjects for whom they are responsible. In practice, individual land rights are now vigorously defended. Traditionally land came from the chief or headman, to whose jurisdiction it returned when the person to whom it had been allocated ceased to use it for any reason; now land is effectively permanent private property, and can give rise to bitter inheritance disputes at the death of the person who held cultivation rights over it.

A household usually works its fields as a unit, but wives each have their own small gardens on which to grow relish or cash crops for their own personal use. The household head officially controls the use of the main fields but, especially if he is away at work, wives are influential in what is grown and how. In some areas, a man with more than one wife gives each wife a field and reserves one for himself. In such an arrangement, each wife is responsible for providing herself and her children with food from her field; the husband must provide for his guests from his field and he may also help out a wife who is short. Each wife may work her own field, or the co-wives may work together; in any case, all must help with the husband's field. Wives largely have their own discretion on what crops they plant, what type of grain and what subsidiary crops they may grow with or beside it (groundnuts, melons, cucumbers and various types of bean are common).

The heavy work on the fields must be done by men. This includes the initial clearing of a field, cutting out small trees and thorn bushes at the beginning of a season and often manipulating an ox-drawn plough. Other work, planting, hoeing, weeding, reaping and threshing can be done by women though the men usually help with planting, hoeing and reaping when they are available. The women are responsible for grinding the grain though the men sometimes take over this responsibility when motor driven mills are available. Women tend to perform the tasks which take up most time although they are not usually the most strenuous.

An important factor affecting this division of labour, and indeed the effectiveness of rural agriculture, is labour migration. When men are away at work, women and children take over some of their traditional tasks, such as ploughing. It is quite possible for two thirds of able-bodied males to be away in wage employment, leaving the majority of wives without husbands to do their heavy work.[19] When the absentee rate reaches these proportions, many families will not be able to rely on kinship networks for labour; and the hiring of labour for cash wages has become common even in the Tribal Trust Lands.

Larger groups of kin may co-operate for larger tasks such as ploughing or reaping. A householder may obtain help by hiring a plough and oxen from neighbours or by hiring labour. A more traditional means of obtaining help, which is still the practice in some areas, is to hold a work party: the land-holder brews a quantity of millet beer and invites friends and neighbours to help with his work (which apart from agricultural work may involve such tasks as building or roofing a house) for which they can enjoy the beer, which lasts considerably longer than the work. Such work parties involve reciprocal obligations: a man is expected to attend the work parties of all who attended his own.

Apart from their fields, many women also cultivate small gardens in their homesteads or near a water supply such as a dam or on a river bank. These may be used to produce a second subsidiary crop of maize after the first has been reaped, or more commonly to grow various vegetables to be used as relish. Such gardens are usually fertilized with cattle manure even in areas in which no fertilizers are used on the fields.

Over the last fifty years, governments have made a continuous effort to improve the agriculture of the indigenous peoples of Zimbabwe and to conserve the natural resources of their land. From the mid 1920s agricultural demonstrators and teachers have worked extensively in the rural areas and have been supported by the establishment of agricultural training schools in an attempt to teach and to show subsistence farmers how they can improve the productivity of their land.[20] Although some

---

19. Cf. Chavunduka 1970, pp. 14, 21.
20. The early attempts to improve agriculture in Zimbabwe are described concisely in Floyd 1963, vol. I, pp. 92 – 133. Some of the problems and some suggestions for overcoming them are outlined in Phillips *et al.* 1962, pp. 205 – 247. For a recent overview of development, cf. Hughes 1974.

progress was made, it was disappointingly slow, partly due to the fact that subsistence farmers had little permanent stake in the land they cultivated. When their fields were exhausted, they could easily find land elsewhere, reducing the incentive to improve and maintain the fertility of their fields, and in any case they had no security of tenure: headmen acting beyond their traditional powers occasionally moved farmers off fertile fields to make way for others, and the sense of insecurity was increased when the government moved people from scattered homesteads into larger villages in the 1940s. Another factor working against the most efficient use of land was that subsistence farmers who wanted or needed to increase their crop yields preferred simply to increase the size of their fields rather than change their farming methods, and many had fields too large to receive due care from the plot holders' families with their limited equipment. A crucial step was taken in 1951 when the *African Land Husbandry Act* was passed to control the utilization and allocation of land in favour of its efficient use for agriculture, and to require subsistence farmers to perform the labour necessary for good husbandry and for conserving the land against erosion. In the enforcement of the Act, villages were fixed in lines and permanent fields were allocated to householders to provide an incentive to spend money and effort on improving the land. In practice, people saw the legislation as limiting their land rights: a man could no longer expand his fields at will nor could he easily move elsewhere. Legislation on dipping cattle against ticks and on culling livestock to prevent overgrazing and the destruction of grazing land were also thought by Shona farmers to be unnecessarily restrictive. The legislation became a source of and focus for political agitation, and the policy had to be dropped.[21]

It is not that the Shona are against change, nor are they opposed to improving their agriculture. But many families living on or below the subsistence level do not have resources necessary for improving their lot: they have no cattle for ploughing or to provide manure, no surplus cash for fertilizer and no means of stopping their land and their crops from deteriorating further. Even when they have limited resources, the insecurity of subsistence agriculturalists make them reluctant to risk what little they have on something new.[22] Besides, people did not on the whole trust the

---

21. See Garbett 1963b; Floyd 1963. In practice the *African Land Husbandry Act* stabilized the old men, often at the cost of displacing the young: it may not have been a matter of chance that the act was passed when the labour supply was short and dropped when the supply of labour was plentiful.

22. The relevance of security to change is discussed in Theisen 1976.

white government and its employees, and they prefered to test any new ideas for themselves before committing much labour and capital to them. The use of animal and mineral fertilizers, which have been seen to work, has become commonplace, and dangerous insecticides are in all too frequent use. But it is difficult to convince people of the urgency of soil conservation when they see trees growing on rocky hill tops, and dropping their leaves, which turn into a rich nurture for plants. And many people claim that the crops on plots of extension workers are no better, and indeed sometimes worse, than their own. One extension officer admitted that the 'prejudice' of the local population against his use of fertilizers turned out to be correct when his crops, planted on spent land, failed completely after fertilization had induced initial rapid growth. Local farmers insisted that the application of ant-heap was of more use than artificial fertilizers and subsequent research showed that ant-heap was rich in trace elements which the soil lacked, making artificial fertilizers useless.[23] The people's intimate knowledge of local conditions turned out to be sounder than the prejudice of the extension worker's scientific training.

Many tribal areas are situated in rocky and hilly country with shallow sandy soils covering the sparsely arable land. In some places, people were originally moved off better land to make way for white farmers and resettled in the less arable country of neighbouring chiefdoms. In certain other areas, people are aware that they were left in peace because their land was too poor for white use. In those areas where more fertile heavy loams were originally avoided, because they were less suited to millet and sorghum, people are now confined for their modern crops to the less fertile soft sands. Besides, the low rainfall of many parts of the country prohibits commercial farming on small holdings.[24] The situation has been exacerbated by the failure to apply adequate and timely conservation measures in tribal areas with the result that it is often extremely difficult, if not impossible, to make an adequate living on the land available to any one family. The low productivity of tribal areas is not simply the result of apathy or entrenched conservatism.

A feature of the subsistence agriculture of the Shona is their attention to their domestic cattle: roughly fifty per cent of Shona farmers own cattle and many others have a stake in family herds controlled by their seniors.

23. Conversation with Mr R.J. Theisen.
24. Recent experiments at the Henderson Research Station into the possibilities of economic small-scale farming in tribal trust lands were valid only for areas with an annual rainfall of at least 700 mm (See Rodel and Hopley 1973) which excludes almost ninety per cent of tribal trust land (and nearly eighty per cent of Zimbabwe).

Operating an ox-drawn plough.

Poor subsistence farming with no crop-rotation.

Progressive farmer
going in for rabbit-
breeding as a profit-
able sideline.

Work on an irrigated
plot in Chirumhanzu
Communal Lands

We have already seen the significance to the Shona of cattle in marriage negotiations when they provide for the continuity of a lineage group. In the past, when there was no easy way of making durable profit from a good harvest, cattle provided the principal form of durable wealth, and the size of a man's herd of cattle remains a significant prestige rating. The Shona are quick to point out that the rate of increase of their cattle herds provides a greater dividend than the interest rate of banks or savings accounts. Now much of the money going into the tribal trust lands is realized from cattle sales, and even in ritual sacrifices the economic value of cattle comes to the surface when a poorer beast is selected because it would not fetch a good price on the market.[25] As we have seen, the association of cattle with bride-price payments gives to cattle a religious and social significance beyond the mere measurement of wealth. Indeed it is only in recent years, with the creation of rural cattle markets, that the full economic potential of cattle has been appreciated and now many people sell specially fattened cattle at the markets which have been established all over the Tribal Trust Lands. Others sell from their herds only when a particular need arises and without any preparation for selling: in a drought year in a more remote area people may walk their cattle as much as forty kilometres to the nearest market in order to obtain money for food, only to have their cattle rejected by the buyers as being too lean and poor in quality.

In many areas the herds, partly aided by the control of such plagues as rinderpest and trypanosomiasis which killed so many cattle in the past, have increased beyond the carrying capacity of the land, resulting in denuded grazing land and extensive soil erosion. Since it is the size rather than the quality of a man's herd which gives prestige, few people are prepared voluntarily to limit their herds in order to keep them within the carrying capacity of available grazing grounds, and in order to save natural resources the government has enforced in some areas large scale destocking, often reducing herds by thirty or forty per cent. Although a number of butchers and farmers were invited to attend the auctions of excess cattle in order to obtain for them the best possible price, in one area, where sixty per cent destocking was required, it was impossible to obtain a good price for the large surplus of lean cattle, many of which were sold cheaply to neighbouring white ranchers who controlled sufficient unused land to fatten them on.[26] Needless to say, the proud Shona owners of large herds regarded with displeasure and suspicion the move whereby over half of their cattle were handed over to white

---

25. Mitchell 1960a, pp. 132f.
26. Weinrich 1964, p. 19.

farmers at a nominal price. Yet herds must still be controlled in areas that are overstocked.

The Shona keep other livestock. Poultry have been a freature of Shona homesteads for centuries; fowls provide a ready relish for a meal and occasional ritual victims. Goats, swine and now sheep may provide meat to eat, though they can also damage crops and gardens; goats and sheep sometimes replace cattle for ritual purposes when they are consecrated to a family spirit and subsequently sacrificed. But this lesser livestock is kept primarily for utilitarian purposes and it does not have the association with family kin (including their spirits) that cattle have: it is interesting to notice that when a goat or sheep is dedicated to a sprit elder it is called for ritual purposes *mombe* (a head of cattle). There is a common belief that should a man drink water from a receptacle used by animals he would be in danger of incurring sickness and even death, but there is no danger of sharing a container of water with cattle because 'they are like people'.

The majority of Shona use their land for subsistence agriculture. They obtain from their land and the livestock kept on it the food necessary for life, and they rely for a cash income on hiring out their labour. This does not exclude limited local sales of livestock and of the produce of the land. But the harsh nature of much of the country, the difficulty in transporting produce from more distant areas, the capital necessary for agricultural equipment, fertilizers, water supplies, *et cetera*, all go to make small scale cash farming not feasible for the majority of the Shona.[27] Added to these difficulties, the dissipation of profits through the extended kinship ties and the fear of arousing the envy of witches reduce the incentive to great agricultural profit. Especially when a farmer's security is shaken by drought or pests, traditional religious leaders can be influential in hindering change.[28] Then there is apathy, possibly due to the absence of freehold tenure which gives a man a stake in his land and a sense of security, but also sometimes arising from a preference for idleness and beer drinking to the hard work that is necessary for progress. Nevertheless, many Shona have been able to overcome the numerous and varied obstacles to agricultural progress and have risen above the subsistence level, making an adequate living from their farms or plots of land.

Many farmers in the Communal Lands do earn considerable sums from cash cropping, using the best available agricultural techniques to make maximum use of the limited land available to them. The possibility of

---

27. The problems of agricultural development are discussed in Kay 1970, pp. 83-97, and Dunlop 1972. The problems of marketing are discussed in Dunlop 1970.

28. Chavunduka 1970b.

making a living in this way is, however, very limited for most rural residents, and especially for those in the more densely populated areas of central Shona country. In 1984, roughly two thirds of the communal lands were experiencing at least some pressure on land, and in some areas the situation was desperate. If all available arable communal land were to be divided equally between rural families, each would have less than half of what was conceived to be the minimum viable unit when the *Land Husbandry Act* was introduced in 1951. In a ward in Zvishavane in the Midlands, the average household holding of land was less than two hectares, and on recommended grazing practices, each household would have less than one and a half livestock units (say one adult cow or ox, and an adult goat) — not enough for draft power; let alone commercial breeding: most families therefore need some income from sources outside agriculture*. These findings seem typical of much of the country. The problems of young people in the crowded communal lands are compounded by the fact that older men usually have larger fields, allocated at the time when pressures on land were not so great; and such older men, with limited available labour, often do not fully utilise their land. Although reasonable incomes are still possible in some less densely populated communal lands, these calculations indicate the problems arising from a rapidly growing population. There are already too many people for the available land, and prospects for the future are bleak. Over half the rural population is aged fifteen and under, indicating a huge increase in demand for land holdings in the years to come; no development or resettlement scheme has yet been devised that might keep up with the growing population; and economic growth in the industrial sector is too slow to absorb the surplus rural population. Population growth must therefore be seen as a major problem facing rural Zimbabwe, and the Shona in particular.

Commercial Farming

Prior to independence, there were three systems by which Shona in Zimbabwe could acquire significant incomes from cash farming: they could improve their agriculture in the communal lands (which were then called Tribal Trust Lands), using their allotted fields and common grazing land; they could acquire small farms in designated African Purchases Land; or they could join irrigation schemes. Since independence, it has been possible for some to join a variety of types of co-operatives resettlement, and a very few have been able privately to purchase large scales commercial

---

*This information comes from as yet unpublished research by Michael Bratton, of the University of East Angola.

farms. Those making use of the last possibility are numerically insignificant. The co-operative resettlement schemes are recent, instituted since the independence of Zimbabwe in 1980, and it is too early to say precisely what changes to Shona life they bring about. We shall look briefly at each of the earlier possibilities in turn.

As has been pointed out, a rising population and a shortage of land has made commercial farming increasingly difficult in the communal lands. Nevertheless, in the past, and today in less densely populated areas, there are a number of successful communal land farmers. In the past, most of these were persons who had undergone a course of training in farming, and had been awarded their 'Master Farmer' certificates, based both on their knowledge and on their application of it to their holdings of land. Their knowledge has been disseminated through the communal lands, reinforced by agricultural extension services. Training in the economic use of artificial and natural fertilizers, in crop rotation and in animal husbandry, enables farmers to produce significantly higher crop yields than the traditionl methods allow and higher profits from their livestock, especially from fattened cattle. They may also increase their income by introducing cash crops such as cotton, which is resistent to drought and is more easily stored and transported than most food crops. Although the means and methods of master farmers spread slowly through the community, and although untrained farmers often show initiative in introducing new crops and new farming methods, those who have received the traaining are generally more successful than untrained farmers. Many master farmers are able to live, albeit poorly, on their land without the supplement of available wages for labour.[30]

The spread of progress from training selected individuals was initially slow. Persons who were most ready to change their farming methods were often poor persons of low prestige in the community who had nothing to lose by change. The subsequent success of such persons is regarded by

29. The black population of the Tribal Trust Lands in 1969 was 2 921 840 compared with 135 610 on Purchase Land (of whom about eleven thousand were squatters) There were 5 160 plot-holders on irrigation schemes compared with just over 9 000 Purchase Land farms. This means that for every 100 plot-holders in the Tribal Trust Lands, there are four owners of Purchase Land farms and between one and two plot-holders on irrigation schemes.
   Sources: 1969 Population Census (Interim Report 1971), vol. II, *The African population,* Central Statistical Office, Salisbury; *Agricultural Production in African Purchase Areas, 1969,* Central Statistical Office, Salisbury.
30. This comes from unpublished material which has since been incorporated into Weinrich 1975.

others with suspicion, since in traditional belief outstanding skills and success are associated with help from spirits and 'medicines' which often involve harm to others.[31] When the lead for change is set by more wealthy members of the community, their poorer neighbours may not be able to follow their example: they may not be able to buy fertilizer, they may have insufficient cattle to provide manure or to pull a plough, they may not be able to buy agricultural instruments, and their fields are often on less fertile soil. A further hindrance to the spread of the techniques of master farmers to other members of the community lies in the desire of successful master farmers to use their training and initial success as a stepping stone to moving out of the Tribal Trust Land and buying farms in the old 'Purchase Areas', where they can have larger areas under cultivation and they have control even of the grazing areas.

Nevertheless, improved methods of farming and cash cropping are spreading throughout Shona country. In 1975, agriculturalists from the Tribal Trust Lands marketed some $20 million worth of produce.[32] The bulk of this comes from the more well off households (about twenty per cent of the total), which have an average annual income in the order of $1 600. The study of one central Shona area shows that success in farming depends on a number of factors which tend to go together: cultivation rights in the more fertile vlei land, ownership of cattle to provide draft and natural fertilizer, ownership of agricultural implements, and background education (especially for plot-holders' wives) which creates a greater readiness to change.[33] These factors depend on initial wealth rather than on technical skills: wealthy families can farm economically, while poor families become poorer.

Attempts have been made, with considerable success in many parts of central Shona country, to overcome the economic disabilities of Tribal Trust Land farmers through the institution of co-operatives. These have been able to provide or obtain credit for individual farmers, and also to buy agricultural requirements and to sell produce more economically. The new government of Zimbabwe has further encouraged the supply of credit to black farmers.

I have mentioned that many Master Farmers have moved when possible onto their own farms in what used to be designated as African Purchase Lands.[34] Sixty-six separate Purchase Lands were created in different parts

31. Chavunduka 1970b.
32. Annual Report of the Registrar of Co-operatives.
33. Theisen 1976.
34. A good recent study of Purchase Land farming was made by Dr A.P. Cheater (cf. 1974a; 1974b; 1975). I am indebted to Dr Cheater for drafting for me much of what follows on this topic.

of the country by the *Land Apportionment Act*. Originally covering some seven million acres, these freehold areas were intended to compensate black farmers for their loss of right to purchase land in the areas designated by the Act as 'European'. In 1960, the total Purchase Area was reduced to about half, but not even this has ever been fully allocated: less than 10 000 of the estimated 14 000 potentially available farms have been surveyed and sold. The *Land Tenure Amendment Act* of 1977 formally abolished "Purchase Land" as a separate category, but each purchase area continues to retain its own name and identity.

Settlement in the Purchase Lands began in 1931, and for more than twenty years involved mainly the more educated members of the black population — teachers, evangelists, policemen, minor civil servants — who sought an alternative life style to that of tribesmen. Only in 1953 did an agricultural qualification (the Master Farmer Certificate) become a pre-requisite for obtaining a freehold farm. Yet some of the early settlers, without a farming background, have been amongst the most successful commercial producers in the Purchase Lands.

Although a Purchase Land farm, without mystical links with chiefly ancestors, is primarily an economic asset, it is also more than this. It represents long-term security to a family uncertain of its acceptance among more traditionally minded tribesmen. It is also a place where the dead are buried, thus fixing a spiritual link between the owners and the land. The importance of freehold land is reflected in the bitter inheritance disputes that follow the death of a titleholder, during which witchcraft as well as litigation may be used in the attempt to establish proprietorship over the valuable asset. The disposition of inherited land may follow the provisions of a will, but if no will exists, inheritance of freehold land follows customary law even though land was never traditionally in-heritable. By no means all Purchase Land farmers are satisfied with these legal arrangements, enacted on their behalf by previous white govern-ments: they feel that since customary law never defined immovable pro-perty in the past, it is an inappropriate guide for the disposition of such property in a modern, commercial economy.

There is a considerable range of success among Purchase Land farmers. Some farmers achieve no more than an expanded subsistence type of agriculture. A common pattern among purchase area farmers has been to show initial enthusiasm in developing their farms (development was often a condition of tenure), and subsequently to allow farm produc-tion to sink to something just above the subsistence level. One of the reasons for this is the adoption of a policy of increasing family size, particularly by marriage to a number of wives in order to provide labour for the farm. Subsequently, the large family can prove a burden on the resources of the farm, discouraging further development.[35]

Nevertheless, there is no doubt that serious commercial production is the norm in the Purchase Lands, and some farms have annual incomes of five figures. In the mid-1970s, farmers in the Purchase Lands were marketing around $10 million worth of produce annually,[36] about half what was produced from the Tribal Trust Lands which contain ten times the area of the Purchase Lands and twenty times the population. Given the shortage of financial credit, seasonal shortages of labour, fully-depreciated machinery, partial mechanization, distance from marketing centres, and many other disadvantages inherent in the small size of Purchase Land farms (the national average is two hundred acres, as opposed to an average of over 5 000 acres for previously white owned commercial farms), this contribution to the gross domestic product is significant.

The Purchase Lands have proportionately better soils and better rainfall than the Tribal Trust Lands, but the major reason why the Purchase Lands are more productive lies in the extent of capital investment in freehold land. Boundary fencing, paddocking, dams and boreholes, substantial housing and outbuildings, the mechanization of land preparation, planting and tillage (though not of reaping), all increase output. In tsetse areas, each farmer may own a tractor; whereas in those areas in which cattle can be used for draft power, owners of tractors may be as few as one in five farmers and three quarters of the land may be prepared by means of ox-drawn ploughs. Even where mechanization is least developed on purchase lands, it represents a substantial improvement on that of the tribal areas, reflecting greater wealth, larger investment, and better agricultural methods.

Purchase Land farms are, however, only partially mechanized, and to a large extent they are labour intensive. Ploughing by tractor allows for larger areas to produce increasing yields; it also increases the demand for labour for weeding, cultivating, the application of fertilizers and pesticides, and finally for harvesting. In the early 1970s in one long-

---

35. For a study of the kind of problems that farmers face in this respect see Long 1968 on the Lala of Zambia. Yudelman (1974, p. 142) pointed out that purchase area farmers produced about half the average yield per acre that Master Farmers in the Tribal Trust Lands produced.

36. Annual Reports of the Registrar of Co-operatives.

established freehold area in Central Mashonaland, where farms had an average of thirty-six acres each under crops, one third of the farmers employed resident labourers, and eighty-five per cent of the farmers hired casual labourers at times when labour was most needed.

One of the ways by which Purchase Land farmers have attempted to find labour for their farms is by marrying additional wives and procreating more children. The rate of polygamy is high in these areas in comparison with the Tribal Trust Lands, and the family size is larger: the average family size on Purchase Lands is approximately fourteen, as opposed to an average of less than eight in tribal homesteads.[37] This high figure represents many wives and many children, not the aggregation of members of an extended family on a single farm. Farmers have become most reluctant to recruit their relatives as labour, explaining that the obligations of kinship outweigh the additional labour such relatives might contribute, and in the long run the farmers would lose financially. Consequently, resident workers are either members of the immediate family, or unrelated strangers, in many cases foreigners from Mozambique, Malawi and Zambia. Hired resident workers live and work under conditions very similar to those on the larger commercial farms belonging to whites. Hired workers are not absorbed as 'part of the family'.

Although large families can hamper a farmer's attempts to develop their farms, a policy of increasing family size is not necessarily self-defeating in the long term. Until 1976, a Purchase Land farm could not legally be sub-divided among heirs. After the death of a titleholder, his family inevitably divided. Even when an heir permitted his siblings to remain temporarily on the farm, family quarrels would eventually drive away the siblings, leaving in the end only the heir's immediate family living on the farm. The rest would find homes in tribal areas, in towns, or, in the past, they would emigrate: a number of black commercial farmers in Zambia came from Purchase Land families in Zimbabwe. Thus in the past, the Purchase Lands have not had to cope with the long-term difficulties of recruiting labour by marrying and reproducing, difficulties which Purchase Land farmers have been able to shift onto other sections of the population. It is worthwhile noting that the use of polygamy to recruit labour for commercial agriculture distorts traditional relationships betwen the spouses involved, destroying much of the respect and equality in

---

37. Hughes 1974, pp. 229, 20. Weinrich (1975, p. 162) notes that in one Purchase Land in the mid 1960s, 43 per cent of farmers had two or more wives.

production that, in the past, linked the sexes in mutually beneficial trust: wives can become commercial assets to be exploited.

Although there are major economic and social differences between tribal trust lands and freehold areas, the two types of land are frequently contiguous, and there are important social links between the communities of each, especially in those parts of the country where particular Purchase Lands were settled *en masse* by people from a neighbouring tribal area. In such circumstances, those in the Purchase Lands may simply be an extension of tribal society, even to the extent of acknowledging the social jurisdiction of the local chief although he has no official administrative authority in the freehold area. Such Purchase Lands appear much closer to custom and tradition than do others that attracted settlers from widely dispersed origins and different ethnic groups. These have generated a totally new form of society, very open to modern institutions, including bureaucratic forms of administration. Such polyethnic, modernizing Purchase Lands are governed by independent local councils, which are responsible for education, health, roads, public water supplies, dipping services, and other community matters; and the residents reject any formal association with the impoverished tribal areas, which they regard as culturally backward and lacking any spirit of progress. Yet it is mainly from the Tribal Trust Lands that Purchase Land farmers obtain their casual labour and many of their wives, and to which they export their surplus kinsfolk when farms are inherited and families fragmented. It is from peasants that commercial farmers, both black and white, buy inferior cattle at rock-bottom prices, to fatten and resell at a large profit. It is to those on the margin of subsistence that Purchase Land farmers may sell grain, especially in the season in which food is scarce, at somewhat inflated prices. While rejecting institutional ties with tribal neighbours, commercial producers rely on these neighbours in many ways for their own relative prosperity.

Even though the Purchase Lands are numerically insignificant in terms of both population and of land area, their importance is considerable. Over their fifty years of existence, they have carved out a reputation in social, economic and political matters, that reflects an alternative to tribal society. This alternative stresses individualism and privacy, in contrast with the more open community of a tribal village. Land is privately owned; family relationships are removed from public scrutiny and traditional norms of behaviour are dropped; wealth is usually a matter for proud display. Education and professional employment are emphasized; but agriculture is not rejected or derided (provided it is based on the role of 'gentleman farmer'), since commercial farming is a respected modern occupation, guaranteeing productive independence as well as a decent living. Periodic migration to sell unskilled labour from the purchase lands is minimal. Local government emphasizes elected representation and administrative competence, rather than traditional authority. The model for purchase land society is the white, urban lifestyle. Even the residues of traditional behaviour that remain are often distorted: I have mentioned the loss of status to wives of polygamous marriages; the conditions under which *chisi*, the traditional rest day, is observed are redefined to exclude any real threat to agricultural production; the ancestors are approached about lack of employment among the younger generation; bride-price revalues women as workers in inflated payments; councils of family elders who own freehold farms usurp the powers of traditional courts to decide matters of dispute within and between families. Where tradition can serve increased productivity, it is retained and modified; other customs are subject to widespread evasion or outright rejection. Farmers openly debate the possibility of abolishing hampering customs, such as the customary law of inheritance. Thus the major hindrances to further increases of productivity in the Purchase Lands lie not in the constraints of custom, but rather in the availability of credit and machinery, in the facilities for marketing, and in the supply of labour.

A few Shona have been able to move into irrigation schemes designed for small scale, very intensive farming. Considerable government capital is required to initiate such a scheme in which all the plots have a constant supply of water to enable the intensive cultivation of such cash crops as wheat and various vegetables.[38] In order to guarantee returns for this expenditure, government maintains strict control on the policies and methods of plot-holders, insisting that irrigated plots are used to the maximum of their potential. Plot-holders in such a scheme are allowed to keep only a few cattle for draft purposes and to grow limited subsistence crops: they must use most of their land and energy growing specified cash crops. Enterprising farmers, who believe that they know best how to use their resources to make money from their plots, resent these controls on their farming, and are often hostile to the agriculturual advisers who have to enforce them. A number of successful farmers use the schemes simply to make sufficient capital to establish themselves on purchase area farms where they can be their own masters.[39] For all the disadvantages of settling

---

38. For an analysis of one such scheme, see Roder 1965.
39. Cf. Weinrich 1975, p. 284.

in a scheme, plot-holders are safeguarded against poor rains and in any case are able to earn more than traditional dry land farmers.

Unlike purchase area farms, plots on irrigation projects are not privately owned; neither are rights conveyed through headmen in the traditional way, and plot-holders sometimes feel insecure about the permanence of their position. The settlers in the Sabi Valley project, for example, remembered that their people were moved off the more fertile highlands to make way for white settler farmers, and commonly believed that the irrigation project was simply an experiment: should it prove successful, many plot-holders presumed it would be made over to the whites.

The Shona are traditionally a farming people who have had, with a minimum of capital expenditure, to eke out their subsistence in the country they know. They are the experts on their own local conditions, and they are the most experienced at this type of cheap farming. While most are keen to find ways of improving their situation, they, like any other people, resent being told by outsiders that they do not know how to do their work, and they resent being compelled to make changes that they neither understand nor trust.

Migrant labour

We have seen one way in which the Shona have moved from subsistence farming into the cash economy, namely through commercial farming at various levels of competence and sophistication. But to move into commercial farming even at the lowest level, a man must have capital to acquire ploughs and other farm equipment, draft oxen, seed and fertilizer, capital which is normally acquired through wage employment. So time spent in wage employment is usually necessary to provide the means for passage from subsistence to commercial farming. The growing population on limited available land[40] means that many are unable to farm commercially even if they have the necessary capital and technical knowledge. Besides, the low rainfall and poor soils in many areas, together with the heavy transport costs to and from outlying regions, make it impossible for

---

40. By limited I mean locally limited. The bulk (about 73 per cent) of the population increase in Zimbabwe over the last twenty years has been absorbed by the Tribal Trust Lands. The proportion of black people living in the urban areas, on mines and in white-owned farm land has dropped from 46 per cent in 1954 to 38 per cent in 1971 (from estimates given in Dunlop, 1974, p. 3).

most men to earn on their small holdings sufficient income for all the modern needs of rural Shona.

A few are able to earn an income in their rural areas through the practice of specialist crafts. Such are the ever-present diviner-healers (*n'anga*) who charge their patients and clients fees which may be very substantial in the case of a diviner and healer of some repute. The hired services of musicians of various instruments are in demand if the musicians are sufficiently skilled: an expert on the *mbira*, who requires both technical skill and considerable musical sense to pluck the metal reeds of this instrument to good effect, may earn all he needs by playing on ritual occasions. The ancient craft of a blacksmith, adapted to include repairs and renovations of remarkable ingenuity on ploughs and other steel goods, can provide a small cash income. Basket-makers and potters can also earn a little cash. Newer crafts such as carpentry, which is especially common in the south-east around the long-standing school at Mount Selinda, can provide larger incomes. It can be lucrative (provided sufficient initial capital) to keep a small country store. The men at home can plough for a fee the fields of those who are away, and surplus grain can be sold within a rural community. Nevertheless, although individuals may be able to live on their rural activities, the economy of the rural community as a whole demands that cash comes in from outside, and even those who do earn a cash income in the rural areas usually have to spend some time away in wage employment before they acquire a regular clientele at home. For the majority of Shona, the only way of acquiring a cash income is by leaving their rural homes for a time and hiring out their labour.

Men have regularly left their homes to seek employment since the turn of the century when the new white administration started to impose taxes on the black population precisely in order to induce men to hire their labour to farms and mines. It is true that the taxes were considered by many a reasonable contribution towards the costs of administering the country, and it is also true that some tribesmen needed no incentive to earn money to buy the newly imported goods that only money could buy. Nevertheless, for the majority the initial incentive to leave home and seek wage employment was the necessity of paying taxes. Since those early days, labour migration has become part of the way of life of rural Shona.[41]

Now there are a number of needs that demand a cash income. The old personal taxes have in most areas been replaced by council personal taxes

---

41. The causes of labour migration are discussed in Mitchell 1959b and 1969.

to support the local government schemes. These are payable by every adult man who wishes to maintain his right to a home in the council district; a man who leaves home with his wife and family must continue to pay his taxes if he intends to return to his rural home later in his life.

Modern marriage payments normally include a substantial cash payment by the prospective groom who may also be obliged to buy his bride's parents gifts of expensive clothing before the marriage is formalized. Since young single men have no fields of their own, time spent away from home in wage employment is a necessary prelude to marriage. The glamour of travel and stories of town experiences may also be an aid to successful courting.

Money is also needed to pay for education. In some areas in Zimbabwe nearly all children receive at least primary education and in all areas every family attempts to have at least some of its children able to read and write, though some disillusionment is setting in as employment becomes more difficult to find for the semi-educated and the expenses incurred bring no visible returns. Nevertheless, some education is seen to be essential and parents must earn the school expenses at least for their oldest children. As the older children go into employment, especially if through their education they obtain better paid jobs, they are expected to contribute towards the education of their younger brothers and sisters.

A family must have cash to buy clothes, a considerable recurrent expense relative to the meagre incomes most are able to acquire. Oxen, ploughs and other agricultural implements are bought for cash. And cash is needed to buy grain to supplement a poor harvest: the traditional support from wild game and fruits is rarely adequate to meet the growing population. Apart from these essentials to life, in many Shona communities money is needed to pay for brick houses, bicycles or cars, radios, household furniture, supplementary food and drink, and other items considered luxuries in the past, but now essential in the 'competition' to keep one's standard of living up to the level of the neighbourhood. Life in the Tribal Trust Lands involves a battle to keep within a very limited budget obtainable by most only in wage employment.

So labour migration has become an economic necessity and must go on even if it is extremely difficult to find work at the employment centres, and however bad the conditions of living and working may be.

A man may have reasons other than economic for leaving his rural home and seeking wage employment. Not infrequently, a man in conflict with his neighbours or kin sets off to seek work in the hope that the problems will have sorted themselves out by the time he returns some years later with his savings. More generally, young men wish to see more of the world than their rural villages, and a young man returning from a spell at work with new possessions, smart clothes, tales of his experiences in the towns and cities, new words and new ideas met in the towns, will readily flaunt all these in the presence of young ladies: travel has become a means of prestige, almost a customary initiation into adulthood.

Nevertheless, the glamour of the cities for the rural Shona should not be exaggerated. It is true that they do present attractions to young men about to embark on their first journey from home. It is also true that many in the more undeveloped areas consider life in the cities better than life at home: a number of Korekore men remark that people age much more quickly in their rural homeland where the weather is hot and dry, the water supply is limited and often dirty, and food is often scarce. Yet people are aware of the economic insecurity in the towns and of the difficulty of living family life in them. Many migrants are unable to afford the time and money to enjoy the entertainments that the towns may offer. The glamour may quickly die and temporary city dwellers soon hanker for the leisurely existence of life amid their kinsfolk in their rural homes.

At least in old age, most labour migrants express a desire to return to their rural homes where they have to work for no one but themselves, where they have the secure companionship of close kin around them, and where they do not have to pay cash for their food. The low salaries most unskilled workers receive are insufficient to pay for the upkeep of their families in the towns.[42] Still less are unskilled migrant workers able to set aside sufficient for their keep in old age and only a few can rely on pensions after retirement.[43] So they look to their rural homes and a return to subsistence farming for their retirement; this means that they must retain throughout their working lives their place in the rural community and their rights to a home and to land.

Even while they are still working, many migrants have to utilize their rural property rights. Housing shortages in the towns and cities and, until recently, residential rules for the families of black domestic servants in white-owned suburbs, have made it impossible for most workers to have their wives and families with them while they were away from home: these had to remain in their rural homesteads. Besides, the incomes most men

---

42. The situation has improved for those substantially affected by minimum wage legislation in 1980. There are, however, now more people unable to find formal employment.
43. Old age presents problems even in the Tribal Trust Lands where aged and absent landholders inhibit the most efficient use of the land (cf. Hunt 1963).

received required supplementary sources of food for their wives and growing children, and they obtained this supplementary food by the cultivation of rural holdings, which also provide security against unemployment through redundancy or bad health. In the current economic structure of Zimbabwe, wages usually provide only for the workers in employment: in effect, the industrial and commercial sectors demand from the under-developed rural areas a subsidy for the subsistence of their workers while growing up and in old age, for the subsistence of the families of the workers, and to maintain the surplus of workers necessary to meet varying demands on labour. In practice this subsidy is arranged by the workers who maintain rural homesteads for their wives and families. Such an arrangement encourages husbands to spend only short periods in employment and to return frequently to spend time with their families in the rural areas.[44]

The career of a typical labour migrant starts when at the age of eighteen he is expected to go off to work to fulfil his obligations towards the rearing and education of younger brothers and sisters and to start saving to marry. After a few years he returns home to visit his family with gifts from his earnings, and to marry and set up his own homestead. In the past, this usually involved a substantial break in the migrant's working career, but now the pattern is increasingly for the migrant to stay at the work centres throughout his working life.[45] This working life is extended by the need to meet costs of further bride-price payments, of clothes for the growing family, and later the cost of educating children. Further visits home, which nowadays do not necessarily involve breaks in employment, result from the need to repair the homestead and to perform necessary heavy work in the fields. As the migrant reaches middle age, he commits himself more to his rural home where he is acquiring the status of seniority. To this end he buys cattle and agricultural equipment or tries to set himself up in some other rural enterprise such as a small store or a grinding mill; this demands capital gained from further wage labour. Finally, as he grows old and finds it more difficult to find work, his sons are beginning to earn cash wages, and at the same time he retires to the status of a respected elder in the rural community.[46]

There are of course, considerable variations in labour careers. Some

44. See Bourdillon 1977; also for discussions of the economics of urban living see Mswaka 1974, Clarke 1974 and Harris 1974.
45. Moller (1978, p. 391) points out that it is the norm for all urban workers to settle in town for the period of their working lives.
46. See Mitchell 1969, p. 179.

men are soon able to establish an income in their rural homes to overcome the necessity of leaving in search of work; others stay away continuously for most of their lives, to return home only in old age. Some men spend little time away from home, preferring to remain poor and relying on kinsmen for their bare monetary necessities. Members with some status in the rural communities, headmen, for example, and members of the chiefly lineages, are less likely to leave home.[47] Men with no traditional status are likely to gain prestige through economic success or the introduction of new ideas and techniques, and these men are likely to spend more time away from home. In areas where cash farming is feasible, more men are likely to stay at home. In times of drought, more men are likely to leave. Then there are incidental factors such as conflicts with neighbours or kin driving people away from home, or conflicts with employers driving people back. A labour career may be shortened by bad health in a worker, or sickness in his family, or by the influence of relatives and friends persuading a man to return. Clearly many careers do not correspond with the paradigm I have described; it nevertheless indicates some of the forces which bear on a man who is deciding whether to leave home in search of wage employment, or whether to leave his employment to return home.

We have seen that labour migrants earning cash wages have to maintain a stake in the rural community and economy. As a result, their tribal associations are emphasized rather than undermined by their temporary incursion into modern society:[48] a man must continue to respect his headman and chief, who have authority over the land to which he intends to retire; he must maintain the appropriate relationships with his various kin to be sure of their support in times of need; he must equip himself with an understanding of community affairs, in order to acquire a position of due prestige when he joins the elders of the community. Involvement in the modern economy does not necessarily disrupt traditional life; rather it results in a new set of norms and techniques which are applied only on appropriate occasions, and which exist along with more traditional ways.[49]

Tribal associations are in fact brought even into the places of work. A young man on his first trip away from home often travels with his father or another senior kinsman, and he usually makes his initial lodging with relatives who introduce him to the ways of the wider world. On subsequent journeys, a man may have other contacts and may have arranged a

---

47. This is discussed in Garbett 1967, pp. 310ff.
48. This theme is well elucidated in Watson 1958 on the Mambwe of Zambia.
49. Cf. Mitchell 1960, pp. 19f.

position for himself prior to leaving home, but the majority continue to rely on the support of relatives if there is any delay in finding employment. Many migrants choose their place of work because of the presence of relatives or friends from their home community, on whom they can rely for help in times of emergency, and with whom they can chat about home: news of importance, such as the rain and crop situation in the rural area or the death of a chief, spreads rapidly in a large centre like Harare where there is likely to be an expansive network of relatives and friends from any given rural area. Apart from the social support of relatives, labour migrants often use the network to obtain employment: especially in domestic service, where relations between employers and employees are personal, and where the employment turnover is high because few employees are able to live with their families, it is a common practice for a worker returning home to find a kinsman to replace him, and so to keep the job within the family. Advice from contacts at the work centres may also be useful in warning a work-seeker against employment in particularly hard conditions or under a particularly unpleasant task-master.

The presence of a home social network is likely to be particularly prevalent among those working for the low wages in agriculture: close contact with members of the home community may partially offset the economic disadvantage of low wages. Certainly working on farms has disadvantages: occasionally a man might remark that he wants to return home but that on his salary he cannot save enough even for the bus fare. Farm workers are rarely able to save enough for more than a set of cheap clothing. Nevertheless, employment has been easy to find on the commercial farms and a minority of Shona migrants trickle into this field. Farm work does have the advantage that there are normally facilities for wives and families to live with their working husbands, with the result that the few who go into farm work tend to stay much longer in their posts than do, for example, domestic servants. The life style on the farms differs little from life in the more backward rural areas and, in spite of their low wages, farm workers have less incentive to return home.[50]

A common practice on farms and elsewhere if wages are low, is for two or more workers to pool some or all of their wages and take it in turn to receive the collected sum. Since saving is difficult in the face of continual petty expenses which rapidly eat away the low salaries unskilled workers

---

50. For comments on farm workers, see Clarke 1977a; Chavunduka 1972a. The situation has been changed by minimum wage legislation in 1980, which substantially increased the earnings of most farm workers, but which made employment in this field harder to find.

receive, this institution helps the workers to buy more expensive items when their turn comes around to receive the pool. It is interesting to notice that although these groups comprise friends and perhaps distant relatives who can be trusted, they rarely include close kin: the traditional demands of respect and authority make it difficult for a man to claim, when his turn for the pool comes round, the contribution of a senior kinsman.

Some Shona men go into domestic service which is better paid than farm labour, but salaries are rarely adequate to support a family in town and domestic servants usually live with little privacy in cramped servants' quarters in the city suburbs. Domestic servants readily complain about their low incomes, also about the long hours they have to work which include much or most of the weekends. Another cause for complaint is the absence of wives, most of whom are allowed to visit their husbands only for a few weeks in the year. One man described the visit of his wife whom he had not seen for two years: his employer forbade her permission to stay on his property, so she had to sneak in after dark and leave before dawn during the course of her stay in town, spending the days on her own in the open with nowhere to go and nothing to do. It is not surprising that men are not prepared to put up with these conditions for extended periods, and the labour turnover in domestic service is understandably high.

Commerce and industry pay higher salaries, but for unskilled workers even these usually fall below the cost of raising a family in town.[51] The higher cash incomes in this sector are diminished by the absence of payments in kind common to agriculture and domestic service: all food must be bought for cash and accommodation must be rented — with the current housing shortages in black townships, accommodation may be a room illegally let and shared with one or more others, not necessarily of the lodger's choice. Although some still rely on kinsmen, people working in the industrial sector tend to be more independent of their kin, usually acquiring their more highly paid jobs through their own efforts and in competition with others.

Some earn their living in towns in more informal employment.[52] This

---

51. In 1974, a family of five needed about $60 a month to cover essential costs while living in a black township in Salisbury (cf. Cubitt & Riddell 1974, table 26). For the first quarter of 1974, the average monthly earnings of black employees excluding domestic service, agriculture and forestry, was about $47 (calculated from *Monthly Digest of Statistics*, Central Statistical Office Salisbury, June 1974, tables 14 & 16). The estimated needs had increased to $90 by the end of 1978 (Cubitt 1979, p. 24). The minimum wage of $70 for industrial workers, introduced in 1980, still falls short of family needs.

52. For a discussion of the economic importance of the informal sector, cf. Davis 1974. Also Cheater 1979.

ranges from small trading, often illegal, which may provide for subsistence while regular wage employment is sought, to larger trading enterprises and the exercise of various skills such as carpentry, decorating or traditional herbalism, which may earn from black or white clienteles an income far in excess of available wages. People working on an informal basis are often able to save on living expenses by lodging with relatives in the suburbs from where they can operate during the day. Thus one man learnt to paint with a firm of decorators and doubled his income immediately after leaving it by hiring himself out to do casual painting jobs in a number of suburbs around Harare, in each of which he had a brother or cousin with whom to stay.

There are few men and women who maintain a footing in the rural areas and yet are continuously away in semi-skilled, skilled or professional employment, earning salaries well above the poverty level. Such people tend to weaken their ties with their kin and their rural homes (without breaking them entirely) and may settle permanently in the urban areas. These are the wealthy few who have been able to break out of the tight circle of economically enforced travel between town and country, and are not strictly migrant labourers.

Although certain aspects of tribal life are reinforced by the brief incursions of migrant labourers into modern industrialized society, the constant flow of workers between town and country does effect some changes in the rural communities. There are obvious changes in the style of life: standards of clothing have changed over the past seventy years in all Shona country; enamelled metal cooking pots, dishes and cups, together with some chinaware and glassware, have largely replaced the older baked clay pots, gourd drinking vessels and wooden plates; the diet has broadened to include bread, tea, tinned foods, bottled drinks and a variety of new vegetables and fruits; house furnishings from wooden stools and simple bedsteads to elaborate lounge and diningroom suites are widely purchased; brick houses predominate in many parts of Shona country; roads penetrate all areas providing bus routes and allowing the use of private cars; and there are many other novelties. People coming into contact with white society aspire to the greater comforts its way of life provides.

Less obvious, but perhaps more significant, are the changes wrought on the kinship structure. We have already seen that the introduction of money into Shona marriage payments has reduced the group aspect of marriage and made young men more independent of their families. This growing independence shows itself in other ways. A young wife who has been mistress of her own household away from her husband's kin does not readily submit to becoming subservient to her husband's mother and sisters when she returns to live with his extended family, and wives exert considerable pressure on their husbands to break out of the extended family as a residential unit. Besides, the men adopt a freer kinship structure away from home: although the bonds of kinship are emphasized in places of work, migrant labourers are free to choose the kinsmen with whom to associate and they are not constricted to maintain close contact with the immediate extended family. Kinship as such is strengthened, but the internal structure of the kinship group is weakened, a fact that is reflected by a greater residential freedom of returning migrants. The weakening of close kinship ties is exacerbated by growing wealth differentials: a man who has worked hard and saved hard may on his return home find his wealth rapidly dissipated by the demands of less thrifty kinsfolk, and some ambitious young men openly admit that they prefer to live away from their kin. Nevertheless, the break must not be too complete since kin provide ultimate security in times of calamity and need: one wealthy householder in a Harare suburb decided to strengthen his kinship ties after a motor accident had made him aware of the precarious nature of his position. He commented of his family, 'If I become totally broke, they would look after me.'[53]

The demographic changes produced by labour migration also have an effect on the rural areas.[54] The fact that the rural community loses many of its young men in their prime can have a detrimental effect on agriculture and other necessary work, though this depends on the numbers involved and varies from district to district. The absence of young husbands from the rural community certainly has a detrimental effect on marriage stability since in the circumstances not all wives remain faithful and not all who remain at home are dutiful in looking after the wives of absent kinsmen. The corresponding preponderance of males in the work centres results in prostitution and numerous loose and temporary unions,[55] but these do not necessarily break up the rural homes.

In this section I have been speaking primarily of migrants who circulate between the work centres and their rural homes, keeping a firm foothold in the latter. There are people who leave their rural homes, possibly with an original intention of returning, and eventually settle permanently elsewhere. A few settle in other rural areas, whether because of social contacts

---

53. Kileff 1975, p. 94.
54. See Chavunduka 1976.
55. See May 1973b.

made while they were working or because they wish to invest their savings in establishing a farm for cash agriculture. More frequently, migrants become reluctant after years in the urban areas to revert to the inconveniences of their undeveloped rural homes. As one old man who had retired on a pension explained, his wife and family had got used to town life and the high standard of hygiene that running water allows; they would find it hard to live at home; even if they wanted to return, he would not be able to transport all the furniture he had acquired. Another man, who was living on a small, irregular and largely illegal income after living in a city for over fifty years, remarked that his relatives condemned him for not returning home (such 'deserters' do not generally meet with approval) but he would never go back.

There are others who are torn between a desire to return home and life at their places of work. One such who has been working for over thirty years in domestic service in a city has no desire to return home to live, but realises that in old age he will have no viable alternative: he would need a cash income in the towns which he is not likely to have when he is old and he would need more capital than he is likely to acquire in order to settle in a more developed rural area. Another example of a marginal case is an old man aged about seventy who had built up a small herd of cattle in his rural home and wished to return there, but was constrained by family tensions (a number of grandchildren had died and the deaths were believed to be due to an angry spirit which it was his duty to appease): the family was breaking up at home and he stayed away from all his relatives on a farm saying that he would stay there until he was too old to work.

In conclusion, there are a number of forces which drive people to and from employment centres and to and from their rural homes. Some of these are ambitions to be fulfilled, and the journeys do provide some excitement and variety to life. More commonly and more fundamentally, men travel driven by the dull and pervading necessity of making ends meet.

The use of wealth

The majority of Shona have to live on an income little above the subsistence level and obtained by tapping both the land at home and the labour market elsewhere. Some, however, manage to break out of the low income group and a few, usually through judicious use of capital, become very wealthy.

Wealth in the monetary economy often makes little difference to the lives of older men, apart from the addition of a motor vehicle and a few luxuries at home. Thus one very wealthy man I met lives much like the neighbours: he wears shabby old clothes and his homestead is arranged like others in his line, a small two-roomed brick house for himself facing four rondavels for his four wives, and the usual scattering of chickens, small gardens and paw-paw trees. The only external signs of his wealth were an old lorry parked outside his house and a television aerial on the roof of his house (he had a power plant to operate his television set).

There were, however, other wealthy men in the area, who were somewhat younger and who lived quite differently. These lived in bungalows, wore smart new suits and drove flashy cars. They quite clearly had access to wealth far beyond the reach of the majority of their neighbours. Younger men who emulate the life style of the more affluent white society often display their wealth in this way, and find themselves engaged in burdensome 'competition' to keep up with and outdo their neighbours. In the battle for the comforts and the prestige bestowed by wealth, clear differences between rich and poor arise. Although even in pre-colonial times a wealthy man could acquire status and a following of dependants (sons-in-law, for example, who were unable to pay full bride-price), now wealth provides new ways of eating and living, creating differences that were impossible in the old subsistence economy and benefitting a few individuals rather than a whole kinship group.

The wealth differentials in turn break society up into classes. Those who have achieved a high standard of living tend to keep their distance from poorer acquaintances and relatives who would like to see the wealth spread more evenly around the community. Besides, the second generation of a wealthy family acquires tastes and habits beyond the means of others in the community which create barriers against free mixing.

These barriers are not impassable: especially in the rural areas a wealthy capitalist might be seen sitting on a stone among his poorer relatives at some important family gathering, and even the most wealthy need to maintain family ties as a security against financial ruin. In many business enterprises, poorer relatives and affines are employed especially where trust is necessary in the care of cash and goods, though these employees are rarely so closely related to the owner of the business that they could claim from him in the traditional structure hospitality and gifts without payment. The old social structure is not cast away; it is used and adapted to meet the new economic structure.

Although some men have acquired wealth through a shrewd financial sense without the help of formal education, the acquisition of wealth is usually associated with education. In the rural areas the most common way of reaching a higher standard of living has been through the profession of school teaching, and this requires formal education. Education also provides a way into better paid, white-collar employment and some education is now becoming necessary for any employment. A few Shona have been able to enter other more lucrative professions such as medicine or law, through a more lengthy and more expensive education. The clear association between affluence and education gives rise to a growing demand for education.

This growing demand in turn gives rise to disillusionment and frustration when it is not satisfied. One difficulty is the gross shortage of school places higher up in the educational system. Of the 1959 intake at the first year of primary school, just over a third (thirty-seven per cent) went on after five years of schooling in 1964. Fewer than one in four of those who completed eight years of primary education in 1966 were able to find places in secondary schools in 1967. Numbers were again cut by over a half after two years of secondary education and they were cut again after four years. Only one in five hundred of the 1959 intake were in the sixth form in 1969.[56] Many pupils with first division passes in the Ordinary Level public examinations are not able to find places in sixth forms. So there is a constant struggle to find places for school children and to keep them in school as they advance: even when places are found, many children have to drop out for lack of finance. The chances of receiving technical training have not been much better. It was even more rare for a black man to become a registered apprentice in Rhodesia than to be admitted into a university;[57] there are limited possibilities of obtaining skills in other ways, in technical training schools for example, but employment opportunities afterwards are hampered by industrial agreements which favour the apprenticeship system.

Even when a child had managed to work his way through secondary school and his parents had scraped up the necessary fees, there was no guarantee of satisfactory employment. One family from an economically backward area managed to get a son through two years of secondary

56. *News Sheet of the Rhodesia Catholic Bishops' Conference*, 25th June 1973, Mambo Press. The figures were obtained from the annual reports of the Ministry of African Education from 1962 to 1972.
57. In the eight-year period of 1961 to 1969 only 114 African apprentices were registered (See Harris 1972).

education with the relatively high expense of boarding school fees, a feat achieved by not more than half a dozen in the chiefdom: but the young man would be glad even of employment in domestic service with a salary no higher than his uneducated father receives. This kind of situation was common and applied at all levels of employment: there were black university graduates who would have been glad of the·employment opportunities that relatively uneducated whites have enjoyed in the past. This kind of frustration leads not only to disillusionment in education, but also to a mistrust of white people who appeared to have been collecting the meagre earnings of black parents in school fees only to deny them equality of opportunity when they had been through the European education system. The frustrations were exacerbated in the case of those who continued their education at the secondary level by the fact that their expectations were very high. Those who reached secondary school were only a small percentage of the black population, a small educational elite of children who stood out markedly from their peers. They aspired to the best, but in the past have found their position threatened because so many of the better occupations were reserved (at least in practice) largely for the whites.[58]

Now, in independent Zimbabwe, as many blacks are pushed through to high posts in all branches of society, often with far less experience and knowledge of the job than the whites who have become their subordinates, they regard it as a rightful redress of the injustices of the past. Since the educational system has been expanding rapidly since indepence in contrast with the stagnant or diminishing employment opportunities as a result of economic depression in the early 1980s, we are likely to see again the kind of disillusionment of people who have struggled for years to receive a higher degree of education for no reward.

Relative wealth has been necessary for high education, so that on the whole successful members of the younger generation have been children of wealthy parents, reinforcing the division of Shona society into economic classes. In the past, since high academic performance was necessary for a child to remain in the educational system, relative wealth was no guarantee of success for the children of a family, and success did not exclusively depend on wealth. Now that education is more widely available, the crucial issue is entry into employment, for which the contacts and the home background of a wealthy family are likely to prove more useful than academic achievement.

---

58. This is discussed in B.J. Murphree 1974.

4

Chiefship

The chiefdom

A chiefdom is a tract of land under the jurisdiction of a traditional ruler. Chiefdoms vary greatly in size, population and significance: the smallest may have no more than a couple of thousand inhabitants whose ruler may be subordinate to a neighbouring paramount chief, whereas the largest accommodate tens of thousands of subjects.

The boundaries of a chiefdom are usually clearly defined by natural features such as hills and rivers well known to its inhabitants, but precise agreement over these boundaries are not always shared with inhabitants of neighbouring chiefdoms. The country within the boundaries of a long established chiefdom usually has a traditional name apart from the dynastic title of the chief who rules over it, and the people distinguish themselves from their neighbours by using the name of their chiefdom: thus the people from the Korekore chiefdom of Diwa (under Chief Makuni) call themselves Shona as opposed to Malawians on the farms, Korekore as opposed to other Shona groups, but at home they call themselves vaDiwa distinguishing themselves from their Korekore neighbours.

Each chiefdom has its traditions about the founding of the chiefly dynasty and about its history to the present day. Sometimes the first chief and his followers moved into empty country: in other chiefdoms there were older inhabitants to be conquered, whose descendants may form part of the present day community. Some peoples have detailed histories of migration before settling in their present land: for others history starts with the founding of their present chiefdom. In many cases the history contains an association with a more powerful or more famous neighbouring dynasty as for example small and recent chiefly families among the Korekore claim to have been granted land by Mutota, the legendary founder of the Korekore nation. In all cases the history claims to justify the right of the present chiefly dynasty to rule over the country as an independent chiefdom, and any particular history is likely to emphasize points against current doubts or disputes to this claim.

In legends about the origins of chiefdoms, some special spiritual power is usually ascribed to the founder chief. Thus the founders of the vaMari (Southern Karanga) are said to have had medicines which enabled them to change the colours of stolen livestock so that it could never be reclaimed, and the owners of the horn could become exceedingly wealthy.[1] The vaShawasha (central Zezuru) are said to have obtained their independence from the traditionally powerful Rozvi when an ancient chief demonstrated

1. Tagwireya 1950, p. 63.

his magical power to protect his people from being wounded by spears.[2] One eastern chiefly dynasty is supposed to have established itself by stealing a powerful rain charm from the ruling Rozvi.[3] Often a chiefly dynasty is said to have been established simply through success in battle as when the leader of the vaShawasha is said to have become a chief after defeating resistance to his people's occupation of the country,[4] or even by guile as was the case when the Rozvi Chief Sileya (north-western Shona) defeated the last Shangwe chief by using his sister who seduced and murdered the latter;[5] but the use of 'medicines' usually comes in as an additional help. The early chiefs are associated with extraordinary power, whether it came from natural leadership, cunning, a knowledge of 'medicines' or, as is most usual, a combination of these.

The legendary power of early members of the chiefly families is further expressed in the belief that their spirits remain the powerful guardians of the chiefdom. They are believed to continue their rule through the chiefs, their successors, whom they protect and support.

The descendants of the founding ancestors form a dominant group in any chiefdom. Although there is normally no territorial definition of clans[6] and any chiefdom is likely to contain a spectrum of clan names, the clan of the chief usually forms the largest group in any chiefdom and the country is to some extent associated with the chief's clan. Thus even those who are in no way related to the chiefly family speak of the spirit guardians of the chiefdom as their ancestors who have a duty towards their descendants of providing rain and caring for their crops. In some areas, when a headman of a commoner clan holds a festival in honour of the spirit guardians, a member of the chiefly clan must be present to establish contact with the spirit guardians of the land;[7] and again in some areas, members of the chiefly clan may make offerings at local rain ceremonies, although all inhabitants of the neighbourhood should be present or represented. The chiefly clan is especially associated with the chiefdom and has special status in obtaining the help of the guardian spirits or spirit owners of the land.

Nevertheless, apart from the immediate family of the ruling chief, members of the chiefly clan receive little if any special honour in daily life. The majority of the subjects of a chief belong to other clans, some of which

2. Chidziwa 1964, pp. 23f.
3. Meredith 1925, pp.77f.
4. Chidziwa 1964, p. 18.
5. Coley 1927.
6. Cf. Bernardi 1950, p. 58.
7. Holleman 1952a, p. 17n.

are associated with the founding of the chiefdom and have their part to play at important ceremonies. The clan of an older defeated dynasty may be specially important when the original owner of the land is believed to maintain some of his power over it: defeated autochthons often become the centre of the most important rain-making cults. Prominent elders in a chiefdom need not be members of the chiefly clan, and not infrequently the appointed advisers to the chief are not related to him.

Most chiefdoms are subdivided into wards, each under a ward headman. A traditional ward, like a chiefdom, has clearly defined boundaries which give it a permanence that villages do not have, yet it contains a smaller and more closely knit community than the chiefdom as a whole. The permanence of the ward which holds the graves of ancestors often makes it more important to the Shona than a village; the ward is 'home' to them, where they can always return and obtain cultivation rights and where they hope eventually to be buried.[8]

Sometimes the chiefdom is divided into wards each of which is ruled by a branch of the chiefly family, in which case the chiefship is likely to alternate between the wards. Wards may also be assigned to branches of the chiefly family excluded from succession to the chiefship, perhaps the senior house excluded from succession because the living members are a generation below members of other houses and therefore junior to them. Wards may also be governed by some other family, either because it was prominent in the early days of the chiefdom or because its ancestors led an immigrant group into the chiefdom and obtained land for a promise of allegiance. Many modern wards were traditionally independent chiefdoms which have been grouped together under one chief for adminstrative convenience; in some cases they comprise the people of a chiefdom whose land was expropriated for settler farmers and who were given instead land within the boundaries of some other traditional chiefdom. Such chiefs, who have lost their autonomous status, complain bitterly about being made subject to some 'paramount', a complaint which is exacerbated when they have also lost their fertile land and have been given instead inferior status in uninhabited rocky hill country.

The hereditary role of a ward headman is similar to that of a chief. It includes both religious and secular functions, the precise definition of which depends on the status of the ward and its particular traditions.

---

8. Holleman 1958a, p. 205. Professor Holleman remarks that traditionally a village was not 'home' on account of its mobility; nor was the tribal territory 'home' since it was too wide and vague.

The appointment and instalment of a new chief[9]

We have already mentioned the Shona inheritance system which is both unilineal and collateral; in simpler terms, a position is inherited only through males and circulates in one generation before passing on to the next. In succession to the chiefship, the collateral aspect is institutionalized in a number of houses of the chiefly family between which the chiefship alternates, arising from the succession in turn of each of the founder chief's sons before any of his grandsons became chief.

In the extended Shona family, a man cannot be head of the family while he has a 'father' (that is, a brother or agnatic cousin of his father) alive and living with him. Similarly, in the traditional system, a man cannot be chief while he has a 'father' alive over whom he has to rule. This system ensures that the chief is always an elderly and senior man, but it results in a certain amount of confusion over a chief's successor. It can happen for example that a man's oldest son is older than his father's youngest brother or half-brother; the junior line is thus a generation more senior than the senior line. In the illustrative diagram (following p. 108), the first chief (A1) had three wives (A2, A3 and A4). On the death of the chief, ideally the chiefship should be inherited by the house of each wife in order of seniority; thus the second chief should be B1, the third B4 and the fourth B7. On the death of B7, there may be younger brothers in his house (B8 and B9) still alive while all of that generation in the other houses are dead, in which case a dispute may arise over whether the chiefship should remain with the senior generation or move back to one of the senior houses. When the chiefship is due to return to the first house, it is possible that all the sons of B1 are already dead; in such a case, people may dispute over whether men of a junior branch of the house (C3, 4 or 5) should succeed or whether they are disqualifed on the grunds that their father was not a chief. If the junior wife of the first chief was very much younger than the senior wife, it is quite possible that all of generation C have died in the senior house before the last of generation B in the junior house; in such a case, the senior house is likely to be excluded from the chiefship since members of generation D in the senior house should not rule over their 'fathers' of the senior generation C in the junior houses.

---

9. I do not discuss the more exotic ideas about the ancient Rozvi Mambos or the ancient Mutasas of the Manyika, including ritual or approved regicide (cf. Posselt 1935, pp. 91f., 150f.; Franklin 1927, p. 59f.). These are exaggerations of what actually happened, and in any case do not apply to the Shona people as a whole.

After a number of generations the question of seniority can become exceedingly confused. It is not uncommon among the Shona for the chiefship to be taken over by junior lineages, the senior houses sometimes acquiring ritual office in compensation.[10] Sometimes strict adherence to the generation principle is over-ruled when the senior house successfully presses its claims to the chiefship. Even when the generation levels are not involved, there can be disputes about seniority: in one Korekore succession dispute, one man refused to give way to his elder cousin because the latter's father was younger than his own, while the elder cousin insisted that the ages of their respective fathers were irrelevant.

Difficulties can arise from other considerations. Certain branches of the chiefly family may be excluded on account of some offence on the part of an ancestor: the offence may have been real or it may have been no more than a malicious rumour, and in any case members of the family concerned are likely to dispute their exclusion. Debates can arise over points in the genealogies of the various families, whether one man had two names or two men had the same name, or whether a particular branch of the family was descended from a slave, and so on. And people may occasionally dispute whether a particular candidate is unfit to rule on account of extreme old age or some other deficiency.

Accordingly, at the death of a chief there are usually a number of claimants to succeed him. In a dispute I witnessed, there were as many as ten claimants from five branches of the chiefly family each of whom could produce a case in his favour; although there are usually fewer claimants, this case is not unique and succession to the chiefship rarely takes place without debate, perhaps several years of debate.

It appears that succession to the chiefship has always given rise to some debate, and many chiefdoms have traditions of feuds between branches of the chiefly family with rivals (even brothers) murdering each other. The competition for the prized salary paid by government intensified the debate, and with a growing emphasis on personal rather than family wealth, members of a branch of the chiefly family are less ready to unite in support of one of their number. In recent times some administrators have attempted to forestall disputes by writing out the chiefly genealogies for future record, but debates still take place, occasionally with professional legal help; the records show that successive administrators have found it necessary to alter and correct the genealogies

---

10. Weinrich 1971, pp. 108f.

recorded by their predecessors, which suggests that oral genealogies are being adapted to suit new circumstances.

Most Shona say that the senior spirits of the chiefdom, speaking through their mediums, should decide which of the candidates should succeed to the chiefship, and the mediums are usually consulted at various stages during the succession dispute. Although in theory the possessed medium of the senior spirit of the chiefdom is supposed to have the last word, in practice his decision may be disputed. Thus if a medium appears to be favouring a candidate with whom he is personally friendly or with whom he has some connection, he is liable to suspicion: people might say that he only pretends to be possessed and speaks with his own voice rather than that of the spirit. Dissatisfied candidates may spread rumours that the spirits have been bribed, or they can consult another medium and incorporate a power struggle between two mediums into the succession dispute. Disputants may press the District Commissioner to oppose a decision of the spirit mediums. So although the possessed mediums are said to have the final say on who is to be chief, and although the mediums can insist on their own candidates, in practice people do argue with the mediums, who do under pressure sometimes change their choice. The prestige and status of the mediums to some extent depends on their ability to choose a good man as chief, and often they delay their decision until public opinion has crystalized on the man they should appoint.[11]

Although theoretically the Shona system involves clear rules to be followed and enforced by the spirit mediums, in practice succession to the chiefship is very flexible. The complexity of the rules provides for an element of choice. The arbitrators are members of the community and depend upon the community for their position and their livelihood, to the effect that the needs of the changing community can influence their decisions. In practice, a suitable and popular candidate can usually be appointed with popular consent on the grounds of qualities of character associated with the chiefship. This practical democracy is not, however, generally recognised by the Shona themselves: for them the chiefs are not elected by anybody, but are born chiefs, with the blood of their fathers and the power of their ancestors to help them.

Even when pressure is put on spirit mediums to appoint a popular candidate, their final acceptance of the chief elect is necessary. The good of the chiefdom and of all its inhabitants is believed to rest with the spirit guardians, who will not be willing to bestow their favours on a man they do

---

11. See Garbett 1966a, p. 155; Howman 1959, p. 42; Bourdillon 1974b, pp. 35ff.

not want. Besides, a chief is believed to require the support of the senior spirits of the chiefdom to protect him from the malice and witchcraft of jealous rivals, and the political power of the chiefly family is associated with the magical power of the founding ancestors which must be behind a successful chief. Thus Processor Gelfand describes a case in which a senior man in the chiefdom was influential enough to argue against the medium's choice of a chiefly successor, but his own candidate could not be proposed to the District Commissioner until he had come to an agreement with the medium.[12] In another case, a succession dispute lasted seven years because the medium of the senior spirit of the chiefdom had died away from home and the spirit had not yet 'come out' again in a new medium: when appropriate rituals had been performed and the new medium was recognised, the dispute was solved immediately.[13] In yet another case, after a number of incumbents of a government created chiefship had died in rapid succession, the senior spirit mediums of the area explained that this was because they had previously had no say in the elections.[14] Most chiefs need some recognition from a senior spirit medium, and in the minds of their subjects they are appointed by the spirits who control the resources of the land.

In some areas, the connection between chiefs and their spirit ancestors is expressed in other ways. Karanga chiefs are often nominated by descendants of senior branches of the chiefly family which have been eliminated from the chiefly succession. These branches acquire ritual status to compensate for the loss of political status, and are important in rituals to the ancestral spirits of the dynasty. Thus their nomination of a successor to the chiefship represents the choice of the ancestral spirits: nevertheless, it may have to be ratified by a spirit medium or by the oracle of the Mwari cult, which we will be discussing later. Among the Ndau-Shangaans of the Chipinga district, the most important chiefship is decided when one of the candidates can show that he is possessed as the medium of Musikavanhu, the most famous and important rain spirit in the area: the spirit makes its appointment by speaking through the man of its choice. So even where the chief is not appointed by spirit mediums, the traditional Shona chiefship is associated with the spiritual powers which are believed to control the chiefdom.

Often a chief must undergo some trial before his succession. The chief

12. Gelfand 1966, p. 40.
13. Howman 1966, p. 11.
14. Garbett 1966a, p. 160.

elect of the Korekore chiefdom of Chesa has to keep a handful of meal dry while he is carried into a pool and held submerged by the senior medium's acolyte for about half a minute.[15] Other reported ordeals include carrying the corpse of the predecessor over a slippery rock to lower it gently into a pool, standing all night in some sacred and dangerous place, smearing sacrificial blood over the grave of a predecessor, and climbing blind-folded a steep bare rock.[16] Successful completion of the ordeal, which is normally believed to involve grave ritual dangers, is taken as a further sign that the ancestors and spirits of the land approve of the appointment. In practice, the ordeal shows the courage and good faith of the chief elect, who is prepared to submit himself to the dangers of the ordeal, confident of the support of the senior spirits of the chiefdom.

At the ceremonial accession of a new chief, all sections of the chiefdom must be represented. The chief elect sits in a prominent position in front of all his people. He takes up or is given any emblems of office associated with the chiefship: in the past these included a handful of soil to indicate owner-ship of the land (still commonly given to the appointee by some senior ritual figure), a ritual head-dress and a spear or staff of office; now the government emblems of office (a cloak, a pith helmet, a stick and a large brass pendant) receive prominence and they are presented to the new chief by a representative of government.[17] Modern accession has two elements: a representative of government must formally install the new chief and a senior man of the dynasty must formally bestow on him the dynastic title of the chiefship. All ward headmen, village headmen and important members of the chief's family must give the new chief a formal gift, whether a substantial present or a mere token, as a sign of recognition, and neighbouring chiefs may send gifts in order not to appear hostile. The ac-cession is a festive occasion accompanied by music and dancing and feasting on millet beer and meat supplied by the new chief.

The succession ceremonies of many non-Rozvi chiefships in central Shona country show traces of past Rozvi dominance in that a represen-tative of the Rozvi clan must ratify the instalment.[18] Sometimes a chief claims to be paramount over neighbouring chiefdoms whose chiefs must

---

15. Gelfand 1962, p. 13.
16. Bullock 1928, p. 289; Howman 1959, p. 41; I also draw on my Korekore material.
17. I refer here to the situation under the Rhodesian Front government. It is not yet clear how the war and the new independent government of Zimbabwe will affect the pro-cedures.
18. Holleman 1952a, p. 22.

consequently have his formal approval before their instalment.[19] In present times, however, chiefdoms are for practical purposes independent units and are regarded as such by most Shona.

The degree to which the period of white domination influenced the accession ceremonies varied. In some cases the new chief received the government emblems of office at the administrative headquarters of the district and received a traditional welcome on his return home. Elsewhere an administrator or government official formally installed the chief in the presence of his people. Dr Weinrich describes one installation ceremony at which white guests, some of whom had helped the chief elect in his campaign with advice and legal aid, received prominence and were entertained with expensive European drinks, while the chief's subjects complained of a shortage of meat and beer at their more traditional feast: this chief from his election campaign onwards clearly associated himself with the white administration and became unpopular among his subjects.[20] In contrast to him are the many chiefs who associated themselves more with their people, and who pay more attention to the customary care of their people at their instalment ceremonies.

Now the installation of a chief is frequently attended by representatives of the government, who use such ceremonies to emphasize the role of the chief as a religious and cultural leader, embodying the history and traditions of his people. Such presence lends status and dignity to the installation proceedings. To what extent it enables the chiefship to maintain any long term influence remains to be seen.

The role of the chief
The chief is traditionally guardian of the fundamental values of *rupenyu* (life) and *simba* (strength, vitality, well being). Life comes from the land of which the chief is the 'owner', and strength or power comes from the chief's status and his accession rituals. Both life and strength are necessary for the prosperity of the people. The chief is responsible for the prosperity of his people and particularly for the land and its produce. Thus drought may be blamed on the general incompetence of the chief or on the fact that the wrong person was appointed. It is perhaps a common human trait that political figures receive the burnt of any dissatisfaction felt by their subjects.

---

19. E.g., Marr 1962, p. 83.
20. Weinrich 1971, pp. — 5: comments on Chief 'Shoko' occur *passim*.

Until 1981 when these functions were placed in elected presiding officers, the most significant task of the chief was to preside over his court: indeed, in many cases the chief still unofficially presides over the hearing of disputes among his people. The word for this, *'kutonga'*, is also used in the more general sense of 'to rule': 'to rule' and to judge' are thus virtually synonymous. We shall be considering the aims and procedures of Shona courts later and at this stage need only to notice that ideally the chief was not so much a judge as chairman or president of his court. When a case was being tried any man present who felt he had anything to say on the matter had a right to express his opinions, and according to government regulations two elders of the community were appointed to help and advise the chief in judging any cases that are brought to him. Although some chiefs were authoritarian and took complete control of the proceedings, a shrewd chief would usually wait until his advisers had spoken before making his own assessment of the case. In any case the ideal of the Shona courts is reconciliation rather than the imposition of a judgement, so that the successful conclusion of a case depends more on the disputing parties and the pressure put on them by their acquaintances than on a decision of the chief officer, whose role is primarily to guide and assess the proceedings.

It is in court that the authority of the chief was most often seen in practice, and the limitations on his power to judge reflect the limited political power of a traditional chief. Many old men say that in the remote past no chief could impose his own will on unwilling subjects: if he tried, they would simply move elsewhere and the chief would be left without a following. Also a chief needed supporters to protect him against jealous rivals. It is true that the chief could exercise control over individuals provided he had the support of the community: an individual could not move off of his own into the hostile environment or into some foreign community as easily as could a large group of dissatisfied subjects. Also in the larger chiefdoms with some bureaucratic organization (as in the case of the larger Shona states of the past) the chiefs could exercise more control. But generally the chief could not rule with tyrannical coercion; rather he reigned as the centre and figurehead of the community.

In colonial times the authority of the chiefs was supported by government policy with all the forces behind it. Dissatisfed subjects could not so easily hive off and found a new colony since land was all carefully allocated and available land was in short supply. It is true that some of the powers of chiefs were removed by the early white administration, particularly the power to try what Roman-Dutch law defines as criminal cases and to mete out traditional punishments to witches and other malefactors. It is also true that chiefs came under government jurisdiction in such things as the use of land. Nevertheless, the official powers of chiefs were being increased in the years immediately prior to independence — they were given, for example, in 1967 jurisdiction over the distribution of their land and the right to try minor criminal offences[21] — and the government gave them all the protection they needed from their rivals. In the eyes of many of their subjects the chiefs were able to exercise more control than ever they could before the arrival of the white people.

On the other hand, their clear subjection to a national government deprived the chiefs of some of their traditional status: we have already commented on the relevance to dominion over the land to this status. In colonial times, the political power of a chief came from the government rather than from his ritual association with the spirit guardians of his chiefdom. Consequently, chiefs were believed to have less ritual power than the chiefs of the remote past. One old man, when explaining the ritual incest performed by the most powerful chiefs of the legendary past, commented that no contemporary chief could perform the rite: since they were ruled by white people, chiefs did not have the strength to overcome the dangers incurred by performing the rite.

In independent Zimbabwe, the political power of the chiefs has been further diminished. In most of Shona country, the ZANU (PF) party network has been established; and this often takes over the consultative role of the chief and communication with administrators. District councils too have acquired more autonomy than they had in the past. The community courts have officially been taken over by elected officers. Religious symbols of power normally derive their significance from economic and political power, and it is rare in human history that the two have successfully been divorced from each other. It is perhaps significant that many rural people blamed the successive droughts from 1981 to 1984 on the fact that government was taking away the authority of the chiefs, and so insulting the spirit ancestors who owned the land. Although government ministers have made statements that chiefs are the custodians of the cultural heritage of the people, it seems unlikely that the religious symbols which support them will maintain their force without something material to back them up. Nevertheless, at least for the present, the chiefship is much desired and often hotly contested, which suggests that at least in the eyes of the claimants it confers status and influence in the community.

---

21. See *Tribal Trust Land Act*, no. 9 of 1967; *African Law and Tribal Courts Act*, no. 24 of 1969, §.12, 13.

The traditional role of the chief is an extension of the ideal patriarchal system. The chief is the senior member of the dominant clan of the chiefdom. He is called *baba* (father) or *baba mukuru* (great father) and he refers to his people as his children.[22] The succession rules ensure that the chief is an elderly man who can be respected as the father of the chiefdom and who can exercise the authority of a father over all his subjects. In the past he could demand help in his fields from all his subjects and was under no obligation to compensate them for their work (although he usually did so by killing a beast and providing a feast) and hungry subjects could, as his children, claim support from his fields. In return the chief is expected to look after his people, providing them with land for their subsistence, propitiating the spirit guardians of the land, settling conflicts within the community and so on. Although these responsibilities tend to be more formalized at the level of the chiefship, they are associated with the responsibilities of the father of a family. It is clear that the chief was traditionally a father figure for the chiefdom.

Towards the end of the colonial era, there was a tendency to prefer as chief a younger man who could travel on behalf of his subjects and who could cope with the institutions of local government; a man who could speak to the administration and obtain for his subjects schools, clinics, dams, roads and other amenities. This was an adaptation of, rather than a complete break from, the traditional fatherly chief: the chief was still expected to represent his people with respect to the government and to care for all the needs of his people.

Now the chief cannot enforce or expect substantial tribute from his subjects. Before the independence of Zimbabwe, he depended on his government salary to supplement an income from agriculture. The salary provided a substantial income[23] which he could use exclusively for his personal benefit; and was supplemented by the payment of court fees, a substantial

---

22. This is illustrated in the speeches by chiefs at the Domboshawa conference immediately before the Rhodesian Government's declaration of independence: they asserted their authority and right to speak for their people, referring to nationalist politicians as children and minors (Government publication, *The Demand for Independence in Rhodesia: Consultation with African Tribesmen through their Chiefs and Headmen. The* DOMBOSHAWA INDABA. *1965).*

23. The salaries and allowances of individual chiefs were not available to the public while the Rhodesian Front was in power. Each chief received a salary which, though small, was in excess of the average earnings of black workers in the country, and many received considerable allowances depending partly on their co-operation with the government (see Palley 1966, pp. 478f).

part of which he kept for himself (some payment must be made to advisers present and messengers involved in the case), and from charges for making grants of land and bestowing other favours. The traditional income coming from the people and used for the benefit of the people had been replaced by a government salary and smaller subsidiary payments during the time of white domination, all for the chief's personal gain. As a result, many Shona presumed that the loyalty of their chiefs was directed away from their people towards their source of income. The system of government salaries for chiefs has been maintained*, which could strengthen cooperation between these leaders of local communities and government.

Apart from the position of the chief and the attitude of his people *vis-a-vis* the government (which we shall consider shortly), the status of a reigning chief depends on a number of factors. One is the influence of religious figures in his area. The position of a chief can be overshadowed by a famous spirit medium in his country. Thus Chief Sileya said that he could not disobey the senior spirit of his chiefdom speaking through its medium, since if he did, the whole country would dry up;[24] among the Korekore of the Zambezi Valley, the spirit cult receives such prominence that the chief has little influence outside the territorial spirit domain in which he lives,[25] and one spirit cult in Budya country in the north-east is a political centre with a court of its own, and it controls the election of a neighbouring chief.[26]

A weak personality would not be highly respected as a chief, nor would a financially poor man. Persons have occasionally been turned out of a chiefship because they could not meet the expenses demanded of them for rituals, hospitality and generosity associated with the chiefship.[27] On the other hand, a domineering chief is also disliked and quickly loses respect and influence, as would a wealthy yet close chief. A chief should be authoritative and firm, but he should speak with the voice of his people and act for the good of his people.

The chief's status can also be affected by his family. Professor Holleman cites the case of a chief who had five sons and only one daughter. This weakened his position in two ways: firstly, the fact that he had to pay so

---

24. Marr 1962, p. 82.
25. Dr Garbett (1966a, p. 139) remarks that Korekore chiefdoms are loosely structured and that their chiefship is not a highly developed institution: Dr Garbett's studies generally and my own visits to the areas give the impression that the chiefship among the Valley Korekore is less influential than it is among other Shona groups.
26. See Holleman 1959a, pp. 266f.; Murphree 1969, p 16.
27. Howman 1959, p. 40.

much for the marriages of his sons and received so little in return was a strain on his estate. But more significant was the fact that he had few sons-in-law who would honour and serve him as their father-in-law: of his own clansmen he confided, 'They say I am their "father", but they cannot forget that I am only their "brother".'[28] Some of the greater chiefs of the past used this effect of the kinship system by bestowing their daughters and girls captured from other tribes on their entourage without accepting bride-price payments in return; in this way they were able to rely on a loyal body of servants and fighting men.[29] In the wider political sphere, the leader of a group of immigrants may arrange a marriage with a daughter of the powerful paramount chief who allowed the immigrant group to settle: in this way the relationship between the two chiefly families is established and guaranteed as one between father-in-law and son-in-law.[30]

A fundamental aspect of the traditional chiefship is its association with religious and magical powers. We have seen that the founding ancestors of many chiefly dynasties are said to have obtained their positions through knowledge of 'medicines'; that the founding ancestors of chiefly dynasties are usually the spirits believed to control the productivity of the chiefdom; that the ruling chiefs are successors to these founding ancestors and must have their approval and protection; that the chief's political power arises from the religious power of his ancestors. From all this arises the role of the chief to mediate between his people and the spirit guardians of the chiefdom. Thus in times of drought or when pests threaten crops in a chiefdom, it is the responsibility of the chief to arrange for a consultation with the medium of the senior spirit guardian and to organize appropriate rituals. Some people say that no one should approach a senior medium on a public matter without first consulting the chief; in any séance the chief has a place of honour beside the possessed mediums and the senior spirit mediums generally take an interest in the private affairs of the chief's family. In many chiefdoms the chief is responsible for holding on behalf of all his people a thanksgiving festival after harvesting, or at least after a particularly good harvest;[31] all villages are represented at these ceremonies and a large crowd gathers to dance in honour of the spirits and to drink the millet beer brewed in their honour.

---

28. Holleman 1958a, p. 114.
29. Cf. Bullock 1913, p. 21; Edwards 1929, p. 32.
30. Cf. Weinrich 1971, pp. 44f.
31. In some areas consultation with spirit mediums and festivals in honour of the territorial spirit guardians operate at a local level and do not involve the chiefdom as a whole.

Among the Karanga where the centralized cult of the high god, Mwari, is strong, the chief is responsible for sending delegations to the oracle of Mwari when consultation is deemed necessary, and for sending contributions to important festivals at the cult centre. The traditional chief is thus a religious as well as a political ruler.

Although there is always some association between a traditional chief and the spirit guardians of the land, the precise nature of this relationship varies and depends partly on the traditional history of the particular chiefdom. In most long established chiefdoms the chief is the senior descendant of the most important spirits of the land, and the chief shares with the spirits their relationships to other long established families in the chiefdom. Occasionally the spirit of a conquered chief is considered primarily responsible for the fertility of the land, in which case the clan of the conquered chief becomes ritually important and the hereditary head of this clan is required to propitiate the original owners of the land from whom he is descended: in such a situation, the chief is likely to be the senior acolyte to the spirits rather than the mediating priest.[32] Among the Valley Korekore the land is divided into spirit domains independent of political boundaries, and here the ritual status of the chief is reduced to that of headman of his neighbourhood.[33]

The relationship of a chief to spiritual powers is further expressed in the burial of a chief, which is always more elaborate than that of a deceased commoner. The senior spirit mediums are usually prominent in the burial ceremonies for a deceased chief. A chief is usually buried at a sacred ground with his famous chiefly ancestors; the site is believed to be particularly dangerous to anyone approaching it without the sanction and protection of the senior spirits. When the chief is buried, special ritual arrangements are made to facilitate the emergence of his spirit should it become active as a 'lion' spirit of the chiefdom.

While they are by no means completely eclipsed, the religious aspects of the chiefship gave way to the political and economic aspects. In the election of a new chief importance of recognition by the spirits has given way to the greater importance of government recognition and its accompanying salary: thus unsuccessful candidates for the chiefship may attempt to persuade government administrators to override the spirit mediums. In one chiefdom, the spirit medium's candidate in the 1930s performed all the

---

32.   See, e.g. Mitchell 1961a, pp. 31ff; Bourdillon 1970, p. 105.
33.   Garbett 1966a, p. 144.

religious duties of a chief and was generally recognised as the real chief for seven years until his death, although another man held the government emblems of office and received the government salary: in a more recent dispute in the same chiefdom none of the candidates was prepared even to consider performing any of the duties of a chief without receipt of the salary. Prior to independence, the administrative duties of a chief and his role *vis-a-vis* the government with respect to the development of the chiefdom and the implementation of government policy, received as much attention as his traditional religious functions, which have been weakened by changes in the religious beliefs and practices of the people.

The present government of Zimbabwe has formally separated the chiefship from administration, although in practice as has been mentioned, chiefs are sometimes elected to leading administrative roles. The *de facto* authority of chiefs is, therefore, more dependent than it was in the past on the ability of each chief to inspire the confidence of his people and of government administrators. It remains to be seen whether stated support for the chiefs as religious and cultural leaders has the effect of restoring the importance of traditional religious functions.

Chiefship and government administration

The main problems facing modern Shona chiefs (and chiefs elsewhere in Africa) arise from the intermediate position of chiefs between their people and the centralized government of the state. The position became acutely problematic under the Rhodesian Front government and remains difficult in independent Africa.[34]

On the one hand, the chief is the traditional 'father' of his people and represents them and speaks for them both to the spiritual powers believed to control the land and to other powers his people may have to deal with, particularly the power of the national government. The chief is the senior descendant of the founders of the chiefdom, the link with the traditional past, and he is supposed to represent his people, speaking their mind. The traditional status of the chief depends on his ability to attract and to inspire confidence in his followers.

---

34. The marginal status of chiefs is discussed in Garbett 1966b and Weinrich 1973 *passim*. Cf. also Howman 1956; Otite 1973 (on Nigeria); Deng 1972, pp. 141-152 (on the Sudan).

On the other hand, the chief was a government employee. Although colonial administrators normally tried to follow traditional election procedures, the Shona knew that government could veto any candidate for the chiefship or favour a co-operative candidate. In fact, a number of chiefly dynasties have been affected by government interference, whether installing chiefs who were not strictly eligible or raising or lowering the status of a chiefship. The chief received a relatively large salary from government which could be supplemented by allowances in the case of co-operative chiefs. The government could depose an unco-operative chief: although this is rare, occasionally a popular chief was deposed by the government for reasons which his subjects find unconvincing.[35] Many chiefs saw their status as depending on government support, especially when they saw the weakening position of traditional rulers elsewhere in the world. Apart from personal gain, many chiefs saw that their ability to acquire for their people support for development projects depended on their co-operation with government. As one chief commented on his return from the conference organized by government to discuss the proposed 1969 constitution, 'It is a very bad constitution, but what can we do? If we say "no" we can't get money for roads and schools. So we said "yes".' Although the chiefs were supposed to be the leaders and representatives of their people, they often appeared to their people simply as government employees, under the control of the white administration. This position of dependence on government remains after indepence, and while conflicts of interest between government and rural communities are not expected on the same scale as in the past, when such conflicts do arise the pressures on the chief to conform to government demands remain.

A further complication arises when the more educated of their subjects regard the chiefship as an outmoded institution, or an institution with limited value in the modern world. In the changing Shona society, traditional leaders are usually accepted for traditional roles (most agree, for example, that chiefs should continue to control the allocation of rural land), but new situations require a new type of leadership. In a 1971 survey of an African township near Harare, informants were asked if the chiefs should be represented in parliament; many agreed that they should be represented, but by younger educated men.[36] Even without the problem of government control, the position of a chief as the political (rather than religious or symbolic) head of his people was being questioned.

35. A case in point is that of Chief Mangwende described briefly below.
36. Stopforth 1972, pp. 114f.

The difficult position of chiefs in the colonial era was well exemplified in their role in the developing rural councils. From the late 1930s various Rhodesian governments encouraged the formation of African rural councils to initiate the population into responsibility for administration and development. The early councils were composed of equal numbers of traditional leaders and of elected members who could represent the growing educated class. The councils were never widely popular, partly because of the lack of effective power of the councils (they were advisory bodies only and their advice was often ignored), partly because of the political force of African nationalism working against them as government creations, and partly because of the opposition of most chiefs who saw in the elected members to the councils a threat to their traditional leadership.[37]

Councils became more widespread in the early 1960s under government policy of community development. Community development is the name given to a type of programme in which the communities to be developed are made responsible for initiating change. In the ideal form of community development, outside agencies (such as government) provide financial and technical assistance and guidance to make the people aware of their real needs and of ways of meeting them: community development thus essentially includes practical adult education. As they grow, community development schemes should ideally give rise to rural local government to consolidate the efforts of smaller communities, and to effect larger enterprises such as building and running a secondary school. The Rhodesian Government officially adopted the policy of community development in 1962.[38]

The chiefs were given an ever increasing role in community development in an attempt to use the full influence of traditional leadership. Chiefs had virtual control of many of the newly created councils, and the right to veto any proposition made by the councils. The consequent support of the chiefs was influential in what success the scheme has had.

There are however, inherent difficulties in the progress of such a scheme. Inevitably, a community occasionally wants something which the responsible administrators deem not to be in their interests, whether it be expensive corrugated iron school roofs to replace the cheaper and cooler (and hence more practical) thatched roofs, or something more serious such

---

37. Cf. Weinrich 1971, pp. 14f.
38. The history of community development in Rhodesia is given in Passmore 1972.

as a secondary school, the running of which would involve an intolerable burden on the community's resources. Besides, the local community is not always the most efficient body to run development schemes. Impatient district commissioners, many of whom never fully understood the ideals of community development, began to impose their own plans for development on the councils. Often they even coerced communities to form councils which the people neither understood nor wanted. Some community projects, particularly the small village primary schools ubiquitous in the Tribal Trust Lands, were taken out of the hands of the local communities which started them, and put in the control of a council which the local community regarded as remote and foreign.[39] The result was far from the ideal of community development: instead of local communities initiating action through accepted leaders, we find a form of local government, the primary function of which was to provide a local mechanism for implementing policies determined by agencies of central government.[40] In community development, chiefs in the councils should be leaders of their communities in determining their development: instead they often found themselves to be mere instruments for enforcing on the council and the people decisions made by white administrators.

The conflict between local councils and administrators preceded the official implementation of community development. A clear example of such a conflict, based on misunderstanding rather than ill will, is the case of the Mangwende council in the 1950s.[41] The Chief Mangwende concerned was a progressive man, keen on the development of his chiefdom, and initially favoured by the district administration. Although he met with opposition from rivals in the early years of his rule, he was popular with his people who respected him highly even after he was deposed by the government. The Mangwende Council was founded in 1946 under his leadership. Within the council the chief found himself struggling for status *vis-a-vis* the district commissioner, who was *ex officio* the chairman of the council. The chief, with the support of the council and his people, staked his status on building a school independent of missionary educators in the area, an idea which went through various mutations as it was opposed by successive district commissioners. The school issue interfered with various

---

39. An example of such an inversion of the principles of community development is described in Murphree 1970.
40. The difference between the theory of community development and government practice in Rhodesia of promoting local government is discussed in detail in Passmore 1971.
41. See Holleman 1969.

other council activities and resulted in a personal animosity between chief and district commissioner, an animosity which was reflected by general unrest in the chiefdom at the time of the political troubles of the late 1950s. Finally in 1960 the chief was deposed on the grounds of perjury committed two years previously: the deposition was interpreted by the people as government retaliation against a chief who was prepared to stand up for the wishes of his people.

As the policy of community development changed to directed development through local government, more and more chiefs found themselves in the same kind of predicament. The community through its leaders decided on one programme and the chief found that he was to implement the administration's decision in favour of another. The deposed Chief Mangwende identified himself with his people in his antipathy towards district commissioners. Other chiefs identified themselves with the government and a few managed to integrate the demands of government with the wishes of their people. Some associated themselves with the white people in a way which alienated them from their own people. One example is the chief mentioned earlier, who catered more for his white guests than for his people at his installation ceremony: during his rule he showed himself clearly on the side of unpopular government policies and regularly frequented the district commissioner's office; as he became more divorced from his people, he spent much of his time drinking and gambling in townships and hotels outside his chiefdom.[42]

Some chiefs managed to show their opposition to unpopular government policies and yet brought their people to see the advantages of reluctant cooperation. One such chief, known by his people to be against the government, established a successful council to promote community development, which the people saw to be to their advantage in spite of their initial hostility to the government sponsored scheme. He received some opposition from illiterate elders in his court and some from the district commissioner, but with popular support he was able to make use of government aid without compromising his opposition in the eyes of his people.[43]

The position of any particular chief depends on a number of factors. His support within the traditional system was important as were his personal qualities of leadership. The political feeling in his chiefdom was also

42. Weinrich 1971, pp. 88-91.
43. Weinrich 1971, pp. 100-103, 210-215.

relevant to his standing: where African nationalism engendered strong opposition to the white administration, the chief's position as a government employee was more blantantly opposed to his role as leader of his people and it was consequently more difficult for him to steer an intermediate course. Another factor which could affect the position of a chief was the attitude of the government administrators in his area: an autocratic district commissioner was likely to engender hostility and to exacerbate the difficulties facing the chiefs under him, whereas an understanding and capable district commissioner was likely to receive some co-operation from people and to ease the position of the chief (and thus to promote successful community development).

The difficult position of chiefs was due to their intermediate status between undeveloped rural communities and a bureaucratic central government. This difficulty was exacerbated when central government was in the hands of unpopular white rulers, especially during the war in the 1970s, when a number of chiefs were killed and many more lost effective power over their peoples.

In other African countries, traditional rulers have maintained positions of leadership in local communities, even occasionally in spite of official government policy abolishing their status.[44] In independent Zimbabwe, the religious status of the chiefs has been emphasized, and some of their powers lost to guerrillas during the war have been officially returned to them. In practice, it appears that chiefs who lost popularity on account of suspected co-operation with the white government, or because of such abuses as the misallocation of land, are being largely ignored by their peoples (where they were not eliminated during the war). Others are playing a prominent role in local government, and are likely to remain influential leaders in the development of their communities.

---

44. Cf., e.g., Kuper and Gillett 1970, showing how chiefs in independent Botswana retained a position virtually identical to the one they had held under colonial rule; Bond 1975, which gives an example of a Zambian traditional ruler who had lost his position under nationalist pressure prior to independence, and who regained his powers after independence; and Miller 1968, showing how traditional headmen and some chiefs maintained their influence after the abolition of chiefship in Tanzania in 1963.

5

Courts

Aims and procedures of traditional Shona courts

When disputes arise within a Shona community, there are various levels at which people can attempt to solve them, corresponding with a hierarchy of courts and courts of appeal. In the past, the hierarchy ranged from a family meeting, to meetings presided over by village or ward headman and finally the chief. In the colonial era, various administrative courts were added at the top of the hierarchy. In independent Zimbabwe, primary courts with elected presiding officers have replaced the chiefs' courts, though chiefs and headmen may still sometimes preside over unofficial or informal meetings concerning disputes within their communities; and 'community courts', attached to district administrative offices and of which presiding officers receive formal government training for their work, function as central courts of appeal from primary courts.[1]

Family disputes should never come before a public court; they should be solved within the family. I once came across a case in which the chief referred disputing patrilineal cousins to their family head with the comment that the quarrel should never have reached the chief's court. When there is a serious quarrel within a family, an attempt should be made to solve it at an informal gathering of the senior men of the family with the family head or a senior *muzukuru* ('sister's son') presiding. Nevertheless it does sometimes happen that a rift within a family is irreconcilable and the case may be taken to a higher court.[2]

Any village headman may hold an informal court (or *dare*) to try to solve conflict within the community for which he is responsible. In practice only minor cases, or cases in which the rights and wrongs are very clear, are solved at this level, and if a case has a clear and ready solution it may be solved by a headman's court, even when people outside the village community are involved. In the past, if a village headman could not solve a case, or often in the first instance, any dispute could be taken to the higher court of a ward headman or minor chief. The highest court in the traditional system was the chief's court, and this was the only one that received official recognition from the white administration of Rhodesia. The chief's court operated in practice as a court of appeal from the more informal

---

1. The *Customary Law and Primary Courts Act* (Act No. 6 of 1981, and ammended in 1982) replaced the older *African Law and Tribal Courts Act* (No. 24 of 1969).
2. One example is the case between a father and son described by Professor Holleman (1952b) to which we shall refer later.

lower courts, and many difficult cases were taken straight to the chief's court. Under the white administration, disputing parties could agree to go to the court of a neighbouring chief when one or both believed that they would not get a fair hearing from their own chief, and if the case was serious either party could take it to the district commissioner's court which could override the decision of a traditional court.[3]

Within the traditional system, the most important court was the chief's court. Lesser courts operated according to the same principles but with less formality. The current 'primary courts', presided over by elected presiding officers, are normally modelled on the traditional operation of a chief's court: indeed the presiding officer is sometimes given the title *mambo* (chief) in recognition of his chiefly role. In their aims and procedures, primary courts are assumed to be 'traditional'. This chapter focuses on the traditional operation of chiefs' courts, and the term 'president' is used to cover both traditional chief and contemporary presiding officer.

Most chiefs set aside one or two days a week on which they presided over their courts, but in smaller chiefdoms the courts do not always have business to deal with on the appointed days, and in any case officials at the court may demand that they be informed in advance of any case they may have to try. One or both parties may consult the chief privately in advance of the public hearing in order to obtain his advice and good-will, and possibly also to obtain the chief's help and authority in bringing a reluctant adversary to court.

When the court meets, the chief presides and usually sits in a conspicuous position apart from the gathering of attendants. These include the chief's appointed advisers, his messengers, his secretary to write down a brief summary of cases heard and their conclusions, the disputing parties with their supporters and any men who have an interest in the case or who simply wish to be present. The supporters of each of the disputants usually sit together; in some chiefdoms they arrange themselves on either side of judge or president, expressing visibly that direct contact between the parties is impeded by the conflict and can only be achieved through his jurisdiction.[4]

The plaintiff opens the proceedings by placing before the court a token with which he expresses his submission to the court's jurisdiction and

---

3. *The African Law and Tribal Courts Act* (No. 24 of 1969, s. 21 instituted a court of appeal consisting of three chiefs, to hear appeals from chiefs' courts. This institution was widely established when war broke out.

4. This and other procedures are described in detail in Holleman 1952b.

whereby he obtains a hearing. When the defendant has heard the complaint, he too must submit a token by which he accepts the jurisdiction of the court. These tokens are often the court fees (in the order of $1,50 for the plaintiff and 50c for the defendant) which are placed for all to see during the case; after the case they are divided between the chief (who takes the greatest share), his messengers and the appointed advisers. Some courts, however, demand small tokens of submission distinct from the court fees which may be paid at some other time.

Material tokens are frequently demanded in court procedures: thus the proceedings are opened by a token of submission by each party in turn; a token is required as an admission of guilt and it must be physically given to the other party as such an admission; a material sign of reconciliation between the disputants may be required. A verbal statement alone is of little importance to the Shona; since one of the purposes of conversation is to be polite and pleasing, a Shona person often says what he thinks his audience wishes to hear rather than the strict truth, especially when speakng to someone he regards with deference. This is illustrated by the complete incomprehension of a witness who was sentenced to six months imprisonment for perjury, while the man who admitted to the charge of homicide was discharged: he was called to witness against a friend who had killed a man in the sight of all at a beer party, and did not wish to say all that he had seen; instead he simply agreed with the suggestions put to him by the lawyer, who seemed pleased when he did agree.[5] In traditional Shona courts, the aim is to reconcile disputing parties and this would not be helped by witnesses with no interest in the original dispute saying things that might offend: people even on occasion try to suppress particularly sinister facts relevant to dispute in an attempt to solve the quarrel without unpleasantness.[6] Important statements of a case must be supported by visible action involving the transference of some token which can later be exhibited as proof of what has been said.

The use of material tokens occurs elsewhere among Shona institutions. The exchange of tokens in a friendship pact can bind the friends even to risk their lives for one another. The love token given by a girl is also thought to be powerful: should the relationship subsequently be broken, it is believed that the token could be used to harm the girl, especially to make her barren; in such an event, the girl's family demand the return of the

5. 'Mapanabomvu' 1924.
6. An example of this is given in Holleman 1958a, p. 256.

token and can impose a severe fine if the man claims to have lost it — especially if the girl subsequently fails to bear children.[7] A token is given by the party of the suitor to open marriage negotiations and the subsequent proceedings involve a number of token gifts. In most religious rituals, token offerings are made to the spirit or spirits concerned, especially to emphasize a formal address or entreaty to a spirit. A man settling in a new area gives a token to the medium of the territorial spirit guardian and to the local headman or chief in order to introduce himself. Tokens are exchanged to bind the parties to an agreed but suspended sale. And there are many other examples.

These tokens materialize words or actions of particular significance into some tangible object which is more permanent and accessible than the passing sound of words. Professor Hollenman explains:

> The use these tokens is based on teh obvious urge to express — or stress — important but abstract thoughts or communications (a proposal, promise, notification, admission, etc.) by means of something more tangible than words: a concrete *thing*. Such a thing (a string of beads, a hoe, a calabash with snuff or oil, a fowl, button, anklet, hairpin, pocket-knife, coin or amount of cash) is not so much a "symbol" or "reflection" of the idea which is thereby communicated, as the idea itself couched in a tangible form. It can be handled, stored and produced at will by the party who has acquired it, and it can be used as irrebuttable "evidence" that such a proposal, notification, etc., has been communicated by the donor to the recipient, because the token is, in fact, the communication itself.[8]

Perhaps the best European parallel to this kind of activity is signing a document which may require a stamp of some monetary value to endorse its validity. Although the terms of the agreement and the contents of the document must be known and understood before the signature is added, signing the document is not simply a 'reflection' or 'symbol' of an agreement, but the agreement itself. By signing his name a man commits himself to a particular course of action. Similarly when a Shona man endorses a statement by giving a visible token, it is his personal and irrevocable commitment to what has been said in words. The token shows that a man is serious in the matter.

So each party to a court case must present a token to show that they are

---

7. Cf. Holleman 1952a, pp. 76f. The power of this token depends on the nature of the object used: a strip cut from the girl's skirt or a bit of pubic hair is believed to be especially potent.

8. Holleman 1952a, pp. 135f.

serious in submitting themselves to the court's attempt to solve the conflict.

Each of the disputing parties is normally supported by close kinsmen. a woman or a young man rarely comes to court without a senior relative to present her or his case, and a senior man may hae adult sons with him, with whom he can discuss tactics and policy as the case proceeds. In many courts, village headman of each party must be present to introduce the case, especially if the case has received a preliminary hearing in his village court. The supporters to some extent accept group responsibility for the actions of the disputant: thus the senior representative of the defendant may speak of the charges as directed against himself, and I have seen a son taking personal responsibility for accusations against his elder brother who was a minor chief and could not himself take up the role of defendant. Nevertheless, support for their party is not blind: one of the functions of supporting kinsmen is to argue with the disputants when they are being unreasonable, and to help effect a compromise solution to the dispute.

After each party has made a formal statement of their case, the discussion is thrown open to the public. In his account of court proceedings in the north-east of Zimbabwe, Professor Holleman described how any member of the public could take up the cause of one of the parties, impersonating him even to the extent of mimicking him: in this way all possible aspects of the case could be fully discussed without the proceedings being disturbed by the emotive bitterness of the disputants themselves. At no stage in the proceedings may the disputants argue directly with one another: whatever they have to say may be addressed only to the court, and even then often through the mediation of a senior representative. [9]

At this stage in the traditional proceedings, all pretence to formality falls down, although order may be restored from time to time to see if any progress has been made. The reason for the informal and unrestricted nature of the discussion is that the subject matter extends far beyond the particular incident that sparked off the dispute. When the disputants are members of a close knit community, the aim of the proceedings is to get at the heart of the conflict and to reconccile the parties. To this end, every aspect of their relationship can be, and is, brought into the discussion. The

---

9. Holleman 1958a, pp. 251f. This has obvious parallels with courts in the Roman-Dutch legal system in which disputants operate through advocates.

court may on occasion refuse to dismiss a case until the disputants publicly show friendship by, for example, taking snuff or drinking beer together.

In a case described by Professor Holleman to illustrate the aims and procedures of Shona courts, once a public reconciliation had been achieved, a second charge against the defendant was dropped. Apart from damaging the plaintiff's private property, the defendant had also chopped down some wild fruit trees and trees that normally contained wild honey: the village headman concerned charged him with damaging property which belonged to the community as a whole. But when it was seen that this action was due to the defendant's anger towards the plaintiff, with whom he was now reconciled, public opinion regarded the matter as settled and the headman let the subject drop.[10]

Normally before settlement is reached, one of the parties must give a token to show that he admits his guilt and asks what compensation is required (in some areas this involves two separate tokens). The token (usually a small coin, but it can be any personal object such as a coat button) is handed to the other party. In the case just mentioned, the accused wanted to give as his admission of guilt the change owing to him from the halfcrown he had given as a token of submission to the court, but the court insisted that the change be found and given publicly as a separate visible token.[11] At formal court sessions, court assessors or members of the public often insist, 'We have heard you saying that you were wrong (guilty), but we must *see* it too.'[12]

Not all cases, however, are solved to the satisfaction of all parties, and the president may have to insist on one party being punished even without an admission of guilt. Punishment may include compensation to the other party in the dispute, a small fine to the chief, and the guilty party may have to pay the full costs of the case, refunding his adversary the courts fees paid at the beginning. The party who wins the case may be asked to give the president a portion of the compensation he receives as a token of his gratitude for a fair hearing.

It has been said that the primary aim of traditional courts is to reconcile disputants rather than to decide on the legal aspects of a case in terms of

---

10. Holleman 1952b, pp. 36f.
11. Holleman 1952b, p. 33f. In this case the token of guilt was refused by the Plaintiff, who was the son of the defendant and did not want compensation from his father; he simply wanted to be left in peace.
12. Holleman 1952a, p. 136.

law.[13] Certainly this is one aim, but we find a divergence from it in the conduct of many divorce cases.[14]

Divorce cases

The most common type of case to come before traditional courts are marriage cases, whether between the quarrelling husband and wife or, less frequently, between father-in-law and son-in-law over marriage payments. Divorce has always been possible in Shona society, but the dissolution of a marriage contract normally involves the return of a proportion of the bride-price.[15] The exact amount that is to be returned depends on how long the couple have lived together, on how many children the wife has born to her husband, and, marginally, on who is to blame for the dissolution of the marriage. If the marriage was of long standing, the court may decide that nothing is to be returned even if no children were born, whereas if the marriage was of brief duration and unfruitful, and especially if the wife appears responsible for its failure, the court may decide that everything should be returned to the husband, including gifts he had made to his wife. The birth of children always results in some of the *roora* being retained by the wife's family, and *rutsambo* payments are rarely returnable once the couple have begun to live together. If the husband is deemed responsible for the failure of the marriage, the terms of the return of the agreed portion of the bride-price may be unfavourable to him: he may, for example, have to wait until his wife is remarried before receiving his due.

Since the marriage contract is between families rather than between the spouses, proceedings for the dissolution of the contract may be necessary on the death of one of the spouses. If the wife dies soon after the marriage (and the same applies if she proves to be barren), it is the duty of her family to provide her husband with a younger sister as a second wife with no further payments, and it is the duty of the groom's family to accept the girl that is offered to them. Should the husband die, it is the duty of his family to see that the wife is cared for by his successor or by some other man in the family (and care here includes all the obligations due to a wife),

---

13. Holleman 1955, pp. 42f.
14. I discuss this contrast in detail in Bourdillon 1974a.
15. Until 1969, chiefs' courts were not competent to dissolve a marriage which had been 'solemnized' according to the law. In practice, they disolved unregistered marriages, and often decided on the terms of dissolution of solemnized marriages before these were brought to a competent court.

and it is the duty of the wife to accept a successor (often the man of her choice) as her husband. Should either party fail in their duties, the other family may demand the dissoution of the marriage contract.

Initially, the purpose of the court is to save the marriage if at all possible, and the kinsmen of the two parties together with the elders of the court try to arrange a compromise solution. The wife's family especially have a vested interest in preserving the marriage since otherwise they have to return some of the bride-price they have received, which may already have been dissipated on other marriages in the family or on expensive consumer goods. The husband's family have a smaller financial interest in effecting a compromise, but a blatantly unreasonable man, as an unreasonable woman, is bad for the reputation of the family and the husband's kinsmen normally put pressure on him to accept a reasonable compromise. Some presidents may refuse to allow the dissolution of a marriage when the case first comes before the court, demanding instead that a compromise be attempted for some months to see if the marriage can be salvaged. In such a case, it is important for the court to delve deeply into the grievances of each side and to try to expose the root cause of the quarrel.

But often the break-up of the home is established before the case comes before the court and, especially if the case has been before the court previously, only the terms of the dissolution of the contract need to be decided. In such a case the debate and the tactics centre on which is the 'guilty' party and which party 'refuses' to continue the marriage: to lay 'guilt' and 'refusal' or either one of these as far as possible on the other party increases the chances of a favourable decision on the return of brideprice.[16] In this context, 'guilt' implies any action or omission which gives the other party a potential cause to seek the dissolution of marriage. It includes on the part of the wife barrenness, desertion, serious failure as a housewife, repeated unfaithfulness, the practice of witchcraft, and so on; on the part of the husband, 'guilt' can mean, for example, maltreatment of the wife (for which she should show bruises in evidence) or failure to pay the agreed bride-price. 'Refusal' may simply be obstinate 'guilt' when one spouse persists in a repudiation or desertion of the other without just cause; but it may also be the refusal of the innocent party to continue marriage relations when the guilty party makes an apparent effort to save the marriage — an attitude which tends to impair the innocent party's ability to obtain a favourable ruling from the court. For this reason, a categorical rejection is avoided as far as possible by each party to the case.

16.   Holleman 1952a, pp. 280ff.

Neither 'guilt' nor 'refusal' necessarily imply moral culpability. In fact a certain amount of provocation, such as veiled threats or accusations of witchcraft by the husband or slipshod work by the wife, may take place in order to make the other party responsible for the apparent 'guilt' or ultimate 'refusal'. These provocations are often naively ignored by traditional courts which tend to judge a divorce case by apparent and evident facts rather than by motives which require explanation.

Quite clearly in such cases the courts become legalistic in their approach, concerning themselves with applying recognised laws or customs rather than finding out the root of the trouble. In cases involving the dissolution of a marriage contract, the disputing parties are not kinsmen and not usually close neighbours, and hence they are not likely to be involved together in communal activities. When there is a chance of saving a marriage and keeping the families together, discussions in the courts may take several hours to cover all aspects of the relations between husband and wife in an attempt to expose the root cause of the conflict. When the families involved in a divorce case are close neighbours the courts attempt to get the disputing families to reach an agreement even though the marriage is terminated. But in most marriage cases, the failure of the marriage is an established fact, and the disputing families neither need nor intend to have any further relations with each other. Yet the marriage is not finally dissolved until an agreement is reached on the return of the bride-price or a portion of it to the husband's family, and until this happens reconciliation is theoretically possible — hence the tactics of trying to put the other party in the wrong. In practice, the dispute brought before the court is not so much a conflict within the local community that needs to be resolved as a wrangle between distant families about the portion of bride-price to be returned and the terms of its return.

A parallel situation arises when one party to a case before the court is foreign to the chiefdom and not an integral part of the community. The court is likely to deal with such a case in a brisk and legalistic manner, without a full discussion of the background to the case.

Reconciliation and the administration of law

We have seen that one of the aims of traditional Shona courts is to reconcile disputing parties within a community and to restore social harmony: to this end the courts delve into the root cause of disputes that come before them. Occasionally courts even go against accepted custom in order to appease the disputants; the Shona do not generally make the law more important than the people it is supposed to serve. We have seen one illustration of this in the case of the headman dropping his charges of damaging community property, once the conflict in the community which gave rise to the offence had been eliminated. Professor Holleman gives another illustration in the case of a woman who said that she would return to her husband only if her illegitimate child were given to its physical father, and not to her husband as custom decrees; when she explained that her husband would hate this child, the court overruled accepted custom and let her have her way.[17] Apart from court decisions against accepted custom, customs are frequently bent to suit particular occasions, as when rules of inheritance and succession are altered in consideration of the characters of, and the actual relations between, the persons concerned. Shona customary law is flexible, and the traditional courts make use of this flexibility.

It is true that in certain types of case, particularly in divorce cases, Shona courts sometimes adopt a legalistic approach which does not take into account the background to a dispute. Occasionally the law overrules what is clearly just. I once heard a chief sympathizing with a man who had just lost his case in the chief's court: although the chief supported the decision of the court, he commented that the plaintiff had lost his case only because he had made mistakes in procedure, and that he would have done well to seek prior advice on the matter. Nevertheless, traditional Shona courts attempt to persuade disputants to come to a reasonable agreement in a spirit of give and take. In this process, customary law provides no more than a broad and flexible basis for discussion. It can be argued that the purpose of Shona courts is to solve conflicts rather than rationally and impartially to apply abstract rules of law.[18]

The emphasis on the solution of conflict over the enforcement of law is reflected in the absence of a developed concept of crime among the Shona, corresponding perhaps with an absence of a developed concept of state. The vast majority cases brought to traditional courts are civil cases between two disputants,[19] not involving the 'state' or chiefdom. Even such offences as theft, which the national law regards as crime punishable by the state, are among the Shona civil offences: a case of theft is a case between two parties and concerns the return of the stolen property together with

17. Holleman 1958, p. 36.
18. See Holleman 1955, p. 43.
19. Until recently, chiefs' courts were officially allowed to try only civil cases, but common practice did not correspond exactly with government legislation.

compensation to be paid to the rightful owner.[20] In a small, closely knit community, the owner is as likely as anybody else to find out who the thief is, and once this is established the court need only to consider how the breach in community relations can be repaired in a way which will discourage future breaches: there is no need for retributive punishment over and above this.

Nevertheless, offences against the community as a whole, rather than against particular individuals in it, do occasionally come before the courts, and such cases may be regarded as criminal in an elementary way. Thus a man who cuts down wild fruit trees near a village can be punished at the instance of the village headman on behalf of his people. The fruit can be taken by anyone and is seen as belonging to the community. Should a man wantonly destroy such a source of food for all, it is the responsibility of the village headman to bring the culprit to justice. Yet we have seen that in a case of this kind the headman dropped his charges when the quarrel behind the misdemeanour had been settled. So the Shona do have a traditional means for coping with 'crimes' against the community, but this is subordinated to their desire for social harmony.

Perhaps closer to the European concept of 'crime' are certain offences against the spirit guardians of the chiefdom. To work in the fields on a holy day of rest or to defile the shrine of an important spirit is believed to endanger the whole community: the spirit, if angry, may with hold rain from the chiefdom, and an offending party must appease them even if he has good relatives with all his neighbours. Another crime of this kind is incest. If a man has sexual intercourse with a girl forbidden to him by the incest taboo (apart from close kin, members of the same clan and certain affinal relatives come under the taboo), the case must be judged in the presence of the possessed mediums of the spirit guardians of the chiefdom. A man found guilty of incest must pay not only the common damages for adultery to the family of the girl, but also a fine to the spirits[21] on account of the criminal nature of the offence.

Another type of offence which may be regarded as criminal is witch-

---

20. In some African societies, such as the Lozi with their complex bureaucratic state, offences such as theft have always been regarded as crimes punishable, for example, by amputation of fingers or limbs. Possibly the Shona had a clearer concept of crime under the greater states of the past.

21. The fine may be one or two head of cattle or it may be a cash fine. It is kept by the senior medium who may use it for his own purposes or to help needy persons living under the care of the spirit, depending on local custom and no doubt on the integrity of the medium.

craft. This is considered thoroughly evil, and in the past was sometimes punished by ostracism or even death. Another crime which used to be punished by death was the seduction of a woman consecrated to an important spirit: such a crime was believed to result in severe drought which could be relieved only by burning the offender to death. Clearly this kind of punishment precluded an attempt at reconciliation within the community.

So the traditional Shona idea of justice does not exclude the punishment of crime, nor does it exclude the application of an accepted code of law. But the customary code of law has not been written down by the Shona, and the precedents from customary courts are not accurately recorded. This allows a flexibility in the traditional system. Traditional Shona courts apply a kind of situation ethic which aims to solve problems before them in accordance with general social values rather than predetermined laws. They are thus able to adjust their decisions in accordance with the changing values and standards of a community. Such a flexible legal system readily adapts itself when this is necessary to maintain some social unity, and unity was a condition for survival in small closely knit communities of the Shona past.

The modern situation shows a number of changes: the people are involved in a broader plural society with a variety of codes of behaviour; they are economically more independent of one another, diminishing the importance of social harmony; the facility of modern travel also detracts from the emphasis on community concord; the court presidents are subordinate to an administration concerned with conformity to a written law. Although many of the features of traditional procedure remain in practice in modern Shona courts, these form only part of a more complex system.

Shona courts in contemporary society

Although African customary law was always recognised in the white administration of Rhodesia, orginally customary law was officially enforced only by the magistrates' courts, the High Court, and later by the district commissioners' courts.[22] In 1937, traditional courts, consisting of a chief or headman and at least two councillors, received official recognition when they were allowed to try civil cases pertaining to customary law.[23] In practice, the chiefs' courts continued to operate in the intervening period, as

---

22. *Southern Rhodesia Order in Council*, 1898, articles 50 & 51; *Southern Rhodesia Native Regulations Proclamation*, 1910, §14.
23. *Native Law and Courts Act*. No. 33 of 1937.

today many village and ward headmen, and even some chiefs, continue to hear cases in their courts which have no official recognition: the function of the traditional system does not depend on government recognition. In 1969, more powers were given to certain chiefs' courts, to allow them to try small crimes such as petty theft or offences against a number of statutes controlling the Tribal Trust Lands[24] (chiefs were thus expected to enforce government statutory law). Again, offences of petty theft within a community have always been dealt with by the traditional courts, but as civil cases and without official recognition; under the 1969 legislation, certain chiefs could try such cases as crimes, and could impose fines on guilty parties over and above traditional compensation.

Yet in many ways, traditional courts are unreliable and unsatisfactory when compared with the Roman-Dutch legal system imported into the country. They appear unsatisfactory not only to some magistrates who come into contact with them, but also to many of the people who may come under the jurisdiction of such a court.

The first deficiency is in the sifting of evidence. In the small, close-knit communities for which traditional courts are ideally suited, the facts of most cases are known to everybody, as are the characters of the persons involved: sophisticated rules for weighing evidence are not so important in this kind of situation. But as the communities have grown and broadened their contacts with outsiders, the situation has changed, and convincing evidence plays a greater part in deciding a case. Although many presidents are discerning about evidence and demand independent and preferably disinterested witnesses, traditional courts follow no clear rules in the matter. Public rumours and gossip about a person are often presumed to be true.

And certain traditional types of evidence, unacceptable to the Law of Zimbabwe, are presumed by traditional courts to be reliable. It is often presumed, for example, that a girl would never lie over the name of a lover. Although I have come across a case in which the court accepted that the defendant had proved his innocence and that the woman had been forced to mention a name by her suspicious husband, this is rare and people commonly assert that if a girl or woman mentions the name of a lover the man must be guilty. This belief in a woman's word applies even when the name has been forced out of her by means of torture when a difficult childbirth is believed to be the result of adultery: if after mentioning a

---

24. *African Law and Tribal Courts Act.* No. 24 of 1969, §§ 9 & 12.

name the woman gives birth to a healthy child, the named man has little chance of asserting his innocence.[25]

Divination by prophets or traditional diviners is often accepted as convincing evidence in cases of witchcraft or adultery, and very occasionally traditionally ordeals may still be applied. It is true that these may be supported by more modern procedures, such as a blood test to determine the paternity of a child, and it is also true that resort to divination normally requires the prior consent of both parties. Nevertheless, refusal to consult a diviner of repute is readily interpreted as tantamount to an admission of guilt, and a party who has agreed to divination is rarely able to dispute its result. Even though a prophet I came across once in a divination on an adultery case accused a man who had been away in town at the time of the offence, the prophet's evidence was still accepted as sufficient to apportion guilt in other cases. The acceptance of this kind of evidence by traditional courts poses problems for the growing number of people under their jurisdiction who do not believe in it: if such a person refuses to submit to divination, a traditional court may interpret his refusal as an admission of guilt.

Finally on the matter of evidence, the question of relevance is loosely interpreted. Although a president or members of his court may occasionally criticize a witness for wandering off the point, generally evidence not strictly relevant to the case in question is accepted in order to help determine the root cause of conflict within the community. This type of procedure is inefficient and time-consuming, becoming more difficult as the courts have to deal with expanding and diversifying communities, and some presidents deal with cases before them rather more briskly than traditional procedures would allow. But the acceptance of evidence not immediately relevant to the case in question may introduce prejudice against one of the parties. This can penalize a man who is trying to break out of the traditional system (thereby showing a lack of respect for traditional values) in order to improve his standard of living.

Another problem facing the acceptance of traditional courts is the part public opinion plays in their proceedings. The traditionally run courts are

---

25. The common belief is that difficulty in labour is due to unconfessed adultery. Thus in order to save the life of both mother and child it is believed necessary to force the mother to confess the name of her lover. A safe delivery is believed to evidence that a true confession has been made.

open to all and all may speak; cases are ideally decided on a consensus of public opinion. Although this helps to preserve harmony in a small community, it often results in injustice to an unpopular person or in rash judgements in emotional situations. For these reasons the European legal system has been moving away from judgement by peers with a personal knowledge of the background to the case, towards judgement by disinterested persons, and there is a movement away from untrained juries, to place judgement in the hands of persons trained to assess evidence and to make a sound judgement based on it.[26]

The deficiency of public opinion is especially evident when there is a conflict of values or of legal norms. Traditional courts worked well enough in traditional small communities which had a common way of life and common customs and values. There was no provision in traditional procedures for conflict between two systems of laws since such a conflict rarely or never arose: a stranger generally had to fit into the local way of life, and norms. Now communities are becoming more heterogeneous. Wide contacts with different peoples in different situations have introduced a diversity in values and norms. When one of the disputing parties has adopted values different from those of the majority of the community (if a man emphasizes, for example, his obligations to his wife and children to the neglect of his extended family), public opinion is likely to work against him. And when the community has a diverse collection of norms, 'public opinion' becomes almost meaningless.

We should notice that courts of a traditional type have proved capable of coping with conflicting norms from different African societies. Urban courts have been able to draw on widely accepted African (or at least Bantu) values to arrive at a reasonable way of coping with conflicting tribal customs.[27] The problem arises when traditional courts try to deal with people who are breaking away from any traditionally African mode of behaviour.

This leads us to the question of the applicability of customary law in the modern context. Something more formal than the flexible situational approach is required when people with different backgrounds and dif-

---

26. In the Middle Ages, English juries consisted of persons with personal knowledge of cases to be decided and were expected to be able to answer the questions put to them without need of witnesses. Now few civil cases are tried by jury and more and more criminal cases are tried summarily by magistrates in England. Trial by jury has been abolished in South Africa and there was a move to do likewise in Zimbabwe (cf. *Report of the Courts Inquiry Commissioner* , 1971. Government Printer, Salisbury,§137).

27. Cf. Chavunduka 1979; Epstein 1958.

ferent values wish to know exactly where they stand in the eyes of the law. Yet simply to formulate the principles and rules of customary law is hardly satisfactory, since these are applicable to small-scale rural communities based on kinship, rather than to the modern urban situation with which customary courts are usually only marginally familiar. Urban patterns of residence, new economic systems encouraging self-sufficiency and independence, new values encountered in formal education, have all affected the ideals and norms of living for many. It is hard to see why people who have adopted a way of life suitable to their position in the urban economic environment, should continue to be bound by traditional rules of kinship obligations and inheritance, which are suited to a traditional rural society based on the residential family. It is hard to see why, for example, when a man has been living with his wife away from his kin, his estate should be inherited on his death by his brothers according to 'customary law' (in traditional society he would be sharing a homestead with them) rather than by his wife.[28]

Another difficulty in the traditional system is that the role of the president of the court, particularly the role of the chief in the chief's court, was not clearly defined. According to traditional ideals, a chief could never force his people to do what they did not want to do: he was a leader rather than a ruler, relying for his position on influence rather than force. This ideal comes into the traditional courts where ideally the chief was a chairman rather than a judge. Some chiefs conducted their courts according to this ideal, overseeing the conduct of the case, helping parties who appear unable to put their case to its best advantage, and allowing his elders and people to speak their minds before giving his own summing up, which depended largely on expressed public opinion. Other chiefs took complete charge of the cases that came before them and decided the cases on their own autocratic decisions. Such an attitude need not make the chief unpopular if he was a competent judge: I knew of one court in which the chief boasted that he had no need of advisers and it was generally acknowledged that the aged official advisers to the chief would be afraid to dispute any of his findings; yet this chief was respected as a good and popular ruler. Nevertheless, the ability of chiefs, supported by governments, to take power completely into their own hands was open to abuse and led to some corruption.

---

28. See Bourdillon 1975a. For a full recent discussion of the application of customary law in the changing society in Zimbabwe, see Chizengeni, 1979.

Thus a traditional chief's court very much depended on the person of the chief, who was often selected with little consideration of his ability in this field. Apart from his attitude to the opinions of his advisers and of members of the public, there are many other variables in a chief's conduct of his court. Some chiefs and headmen had reputations for taking bribes or for allowing consideration of relatives and friends to influence their judgements; although there were channels of appeal over a chief's court, few people had the knowledge or the nerve to use them. Some chiefs were ignorant or even stupid, and occasionally a chief was overimpressed by the education and life style of more wealthy subjects who consequently had undue influence over his decisions. Other chiefs were intelligent, perhaps openminded and educated, scrupulously fair and very good rulers, but the significance of these characteristics received little explicit consideration when a cheif was appointed to office.

Now, of course, there are parallel legal systems which operate among the Zimbabwean Shona. Crimes and more serious civil cases come before the magistrates' courts and the High Court. These courts have an advantage in that they are believed to be generally free from corruption and also from the ignorance and primitive prejudices of many of the traditional courts. But for the majority of rural Shona they also have considerable disadvantages.

One is that they do not go to the root of a dispute and apparently deal instead with legal superficialities. Many Shona consequently distrust the results of courts conducted by the legal elite as being unpredictable and to a certain extent arbitrary. The difficulty these courts face in coming to a correct decision is exacerbated when witnesses omit to mention facts relevant to the conclusion of the case because they are so well known within the local community that they are presumed to be known to all the world and are not deemed worth mentioning in court.[29]

Another disadvantage of the magistrates' courts and the High Court is that they do not always take full account of the traditional legal system. Sometimes a person sentenced to a fine or a term of imprisonment by a magistrate's court is also summoned before a traditonal court and further punished by, for example, being ordered to pay compensation to the owner of stolen or damaged property. Occasionally a man has been.

---

29. See, for example, Holleman 1958a, pp. 264f.

sentenced to death for murder by the High Court, and his family have had to pay heavy compensation besides to the victim's family who raised the case anew in their chief's court.

Magistrates' courts act according to laws not readily intelligible to the majority of Shona. Thus the heavy penalties connected with the illegal distillation of liquor or with growing and smoking cannabis (both ancient and accepted practices in Shona society) appeared as an arbitrary attempt by the white government to stifle cheap forms of entertainment for the black people. Similarly the requirement of a licence in order to trade appeared to many simply as a protection of white commerce against the initiative of poorer blacks trying to earn a living through petty trade.

District commissioner's courts were an improvement on magistrates' courts in that they primarily administered customary law. They were sometimes used by litigants as a court of appeal from the chiefs' courts. District commissioners were reputed to be incorrupt and without bias, but they delt with cases more briskly than a traditional court would do and were not usually fully cognisant of the background to the cases that came before them. Also district commissioners' courts were more rigid than traditional courts: since a district commissioner was not fully in touch with the changing norms of the communities for whom he had to arbitrate, he had to rely for his judgement on written accounts of customary law often based on research performed many local chiefs in raising payments for damages in accordance with rising standards and costs of living, and it was noticeable that many district commissioners went on insisting that according to customary law women were legally minors long after tribal courts had been accepting their emancipation.

So the impartiality of migistrates' courts, (and to a lesser extent of district commissioners courts) brings with it a mutual lack of understanding. Poorly educated rural Shona on the whole prefer their traditional courts, or perhaps in the past the court of their district commissioner who was fair and familiar with African custom and who could enforce his decisions. More educated and wealthy Shona are likely to prefer the impartiality and competence of a magistrate.[30]

The declared policy of past governments was freedom to choose between

---

30. This is indicated by my Korekore material taken in conjuction with comparative surveys in the elite 'Chitepo Road' and the rest of Highfield African Township, Salisbury (Stopforth 1973a, Table XLIV).

courts and legal systems. In practice, there have always been restrictions on the choice of legal system, criminal cases and substantial civil cases being beyond the jurisdiction of traditional courts, and most matters concerning African marriage and family being confined to the customary system.[31] District commissioners often referred petitioners to chiefs' courts, refusing to consider cases which they believed to be in the chiefs' domain of competence. The cost of using the formal legal system, and the knowledge required, put it beyond the means of most Shona, who consequently are constrained to have recourse to traditional courts for the settlement of any dispute.

During the war, a new type of court had emerged, theoretically based on traditional community courts, but in practice often conducted by youthful guerrillas, who automatically imposed their decisions on the communities concerned, by force of arms if necessary. Those who administered these courts handed back their power to traditional authorities only slowly and reluctantly, resulting in occasional conflicts between 'kangaroo' courts and the official forces of law and order. In some areas, traditional authorities never regained their status.

The government of Zimbabwe quickly passed a bill[32] which provided for greater freedom of choice between courts and legal systems, and which provided for a greater diversity of informal courts under elected presiding officers. Sometimes, chiefs or members of the chiefly families have been elected to preside over community courts: I came across one case in which the presiding officer and his two successors came from the three main houses of the chiefly family.

In practice, the legislation is unlikely to make the more complex systems readily available to rural Shona, but it does leave the traditional courts in the hands of democratically elected persons, offering some protection to the rural people from some of the abuses which occasionally occurred in chiefs' courts during the colonial era.

---

31. Cf May 1980, especially pp. 73-79.
32. *Customary Law and Primary Courts Act,* 1981.

Mr Lazarus Muketiwa Zonde Gwanzura, a widely respected *n'anga* from Mufakose. According to him there is no discrepancy between Christianity and his way of healing. He himself is a Christian.

(Photo: MAMBO MAGAZINE)

Two sets of *hakata* (divining "bones") with different designs.

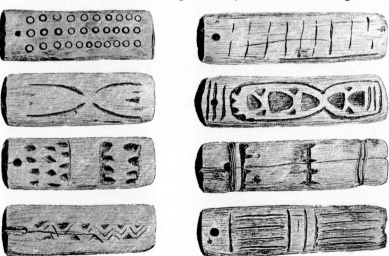

Some instruments used by the n'anga

The n'anga's knife for cutting _nyora_ (tattoo marks)

The _murimiko_ used for cupping

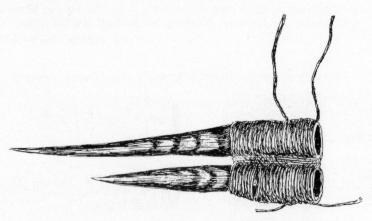

Small horns for storing powdered medicinal roots

A hollow reed used for storing powdered medicine

6

Sickness and Personal Misfortune

Consulting the medicine man

There are illnesses (particularly of children), such as coughs, colds, influenza and slight fevers, which are seen to be quite 'natural' or normal and do not perturb the Shona since they are of a fleeting nature and resolve themselves completely. There are also some more serious ailments, such as venereal disease, of which the Shona are not particularly afraid since they know how these diseases arise. But should an ailment linger, or should it become serious and threaten life, it requires an explanation beyond the natural causes. Thus if a man has a pain in the stomach or diarrhoea, everyone knows that this may be due to something he has eaten; but if the trouble lasts for a week or more, it is not so readily explained in terms of something that passes rapidly through his system. Similarly, if a man gets caught in the rain and catches a chill, he might end up with a slight cough; but if it lasts ten days, the chill seems too remote to explain it adequately. A prolonged or serious illness is presumed to have some invisible cause and a diviner should be consulted to determine it and to state the necessary remedy.

On the one hand, the Shona are often terrified by serious illness; on the other hand, they often appear indifferent to the outcome of treatment received from doctors of western medicine and to have no incentive to fight an illness.[1] The reason behind these two attitudes lies in the belief that serious or abnormal illness, like anything out of the ordinary, is caused by spirits, perhaps angered spirits, or by witchcraft or sorcery. Until the ultimate cause of the trouble is discovered and appeased or overcome, there remains the frightening possibility of further trouble, and it is hopeless to expect complete relief from the present affliction. According to Shona belief, western medicinal treatment can only alleviate symptoms of abnormal illness, or at best it can cure the present illness, but it remains useless against the original cause of an illness which can always strike again. Thus even when he is treated by western medicine, a Shona patient is likely to consult as well a *n'anga* (traditional diviner-healer) whose main function is to communicate with the spirit world.[2]

Nowadays, the Shona use extensively hospitals and clinics which

---

1. Contrast, for example, the statement that serious illness terrifies the Shona (Gelfand 1956, p. 167) with the remark that they have little interest in the outcome of an illness (Gelfand 1944, pp. 3f).
2. Shona reactions to sickness are analysed in detail in Chavunduka 1978; also in Gelfand 1964b.

dispense western medicine; so they do understand the kind of complaint which comes under the western category of physical disease. This type of disease is also traditionally treated by *n'anga*, about which western medicine is thought to know nothing. As one Shona diviner stated, 'They (the white doctors) are good. They can operate. But they don't know about poison (witchcraft), and about protecting people; they can't mix thunder.'[3] So whenever a person has reason to believe that he is being troubled by spirits or other malign influences with which he cannot cope himself, he consults a *n'anga*. And he might alternate between western medicine and traditional treatment if each in turn fails to bring about a satisfactory cure.

A *n'anga* may be consulted to cure any form of misfortune or bad luck, and he treats it in much the same way as he treats any physical illness. Thus an unsatisfactory wife may blame her indolence on bewitchment, and her husband might blame her obstinacy on his bad 'luck' which can only be overcome by new and more powerful medicines. Bad luck in marriage may be attributed to an alien spirit which must be exorcised. Some forms of misfortune, if a man will not marry, for example, or if he wastes his wealth or is inherently lazy, are thought to be due to a substance or spirit (it is not clear which) called *chitsina* which must be sucked out or exorcised by a *n'anga* and prevented from re-entering the patient.[4] A man might even consult a diviner because his sons never or rarely return home from work.

Bad luck always has a cause. It may be simply that loose living and witchcraft among the people in one's vicinity spoil one's protective medicines. But a more common explanation is that bad luck is sent deliberately by spirits or by fellow men.

A person's fate or fortune is associated with the general relationship supposed to exist between a man and the spirits who control this world, and who to some extent take responsibility for his life out of his own hands. When some particular misfortune befalls him, it must be examined in the general context of this relationship in order to find out exactly what is required to maintain or to restore harmony with the unseen forces that control his life. So a *n'anga*'s first task is to find out the general relationship between his clients and their spirit guardians, and on this his recommendations and treatment depend.

Tension in a community is often associated with the invisible powers

3. Sachs 1937, p. 146.
4. See Davis 1931; Gelfand 1957.

that bring trouble. Indeed some claim that quarrelling and bickering can themselves be the cause of sickness. Any tension between persons, whether due to suspicion or simply to incompatibility, is likely soon to come into the open, and a diviner is approached to find an immediate answer and a solution to secret fears. Thus if a man suspects his wife of adultery, rather than wait for the outcome of slow legal procedures, he might try to discover the truth of his suspicion at once by divination or ordeal. This is especially the case when there is some tension in the relations of a man towards his spirit elders: resort to a diviner is the first step towards resolving any such tension or anxiety.

But it is not only trouble which brings about an appeal to a *n'anga*. A man may consult a diviner before making a long journey, both on the safety of the journey and on the success of its outcome. A man might also consult a diviner to find out the result of a coming court case, or of some forthcoming examination or trial. A *n'anga* provides 'medicines' for success in various enterprises: in love-making, for example, also for good crops, for success in finding employment, for good relations with employers, for success in gambling, and so on. 'Medicines' against witchcraft, theft or other misfortunes are also obtainable from *n'anga*, and some claim to be able to recover lost or stolen property.[5]

Generally, *n'anga* deal with any problem of an individual and his family. Occasionally he may be asked to resolve the problems of a village community, especially if witchcraft is involved. But problems which affect a neighbourhood community as a whole, such as famine caused by locusts or drought, are normally the concern of the mediums of the local spirit guardians (whom we will be discussing later).

To summarize, the Shona believe that their well-being depends on their relationships with spirit guardians who control their lives. Any persistent trouble or anxiety is likely to be interpreted in terms of this relationship and in terms of tensions and ill-will within the local community. Sickness is the most common such trouble, but by no means the only one. Whenever there is unease concerning the spirits, a diviner in touch with the spiritual powers is consulted in order to resolve it.

Divining

Any person whose troubles and anxieties are not serious may approach a

---

5. Ways of achieving this are described in Gelfand 1964a, pp. 54f.

neighbour or relative with an elementary knowledge of divining: this is especially likely if he has a strong opinion on what the outcome of the divination will be and merely wants confirmation. But for more serious matters a diviner of some repute is required with a powerful healing spirit to support him. Although for serious matters, and especially when death is feared or has occurred, people prefer to consult a diviner living some distance away, who is less likely to bring personal prejudices to bear on his divination and who can show his contact with the spiritual powers by displaying knowledge about his clients which a stranger would not normally know, more commonly the diviner is a member of the local community, thoroughly acquainted with the history and current relations of his clients.

In a matter of some moment the consultation becomes a family affair usually arranged and financed by the family head. If someone in the family is seriously ill, he will not be able to travel himself to a distant diviner. So a delegation including, or at least representing, the family head is made responsible for the consultation.

It is said that a good diviner should know of his prospective clients before their arrival and go out to meet them before they reach his homestead, though in practice this rarely happens. In any case, the diviner is supposed to be able to tell the clients what their trouble is before they say anything. The diviner makes his first statements vague, and keeps talking, becoming more and more precise while the clients remain silent or react positively depending on how close to the mark the diviner's statement is. In practice, the diviner is able to tell the delegation the reason for their errand through an astute assessment, possibly unconscious and aided by a heightened awareness induced by the possession trance,[6] of their reactions as he feels his way with his statements. In cases where the diviner provides hospitality to the clients before making his divination, the diviner and his assistants are probably helped by a certain amount of eavesdropping. The degree of the diviner's foreknowledge, which he is supposed to have received in a dream while his clients were on their way to consult him, affects his prestige. A good diviner is supposed even to know how much the delegation has brought to pay him, and if he demands too much they may lose confidence in him and go elsewhere.[7] When he has shown his clients that he is able to discover the cause of their errand without having to be told, they can consult his oracles with confidence.

Different diviners use various methods to diagnose the causes of the

6. Cf Fry 1976, pp. 35f.
7. Gelfand 1966a, p. 83.

misfortunes or illnesses over which they are consulted, or to answer questions about the future. The Revd Shropshire described a diviner who used a calabash on a string one end of which was fastened to the roof of his house and the other held by the diviner: he threw the calabash up as he asked the question put to him and the answer depended on whether the calabash stayed up or came straight down again[8] — in practice it could be controlled by the diviner since it depended on how taut he held the string. Another method involves two clay 'horns', one 'male' and the other 'female': after the diviner has rubbed them in his hands and on the client's head, he puts them in a calabash which he holds apparently rigidly in his hands. In fact, the diviner's wrists are kept loose and vibrating so that the movement of the horns which is supposed to give the result of the divination are controlled (perhaps unconsciously) by the operator, and the interpretations given to the movement depends on the information gleaned from the client and his reactions to the diviner's suggestions.[9] Other methods of divination include staring into a special calabash or horn containing 'medicines' and the use of 'talking images', but the most common and important methods involve either spirit possession or throwing divining dice (*hakata*) or both of these together.

The usual procedure adopted when a diviner uses divining dice is for the client (or, in the case of serious sickness, a near relative with one or two witnesses if the cause of the illness is thought to be serious, such as witchcraft) to visit the diviner at his home. The diviner dresses himself in his ritual regalia which consist of skins or a cloth around the waist, a cloth around the shoulders, an ornamental head-dress, strings of beads around the neck and various charms and ornaments on various parts of the body. He also carries a ceremonial axe or a whisk made from an animal tail. The diviner sits facing his client and receives an initial fee to put him in touch with the client: this is said to depend on the requirements of his dice, and may be as little as a token pinch of snuff or a considerable sum in cash for a diviner of some repute. The diviner usually gives his dice to his client to make the first throw and to make contact with the dice. The diviner then begins to throw the dice himself and to interpret the answers to his questions.

There are three types of divining dice used by the Shona, and occasionally a diviner may use a combination of two or three kinds of dice. In the north of Shona country, diviners usually use sets of six half shells of a

---

8. Shropshire 1928, pp. 29f.
9. Sachs 1937, pp. 108, 156f.

certain fruit seed that are collected from elephant turds and ritually prepared. Some diviners prepare their own sets, but many obtain their sets from more famous practitioners: in any case the shells require an elaborate 'medication' in order to enable them to 'see', and many diviners treat their dice regularly, perhaps after each full moon. A diviner usually has three or more sets of six shells which he throws more or less in turn: a satisfactory divination should be confirmed by all three sets, and if two sets agree, the diviner may throw the third two or three times in an attempt to make it agree. In any case, the diviner throws all the sets a number of times, starting with general and vague questions before reaching the precise cause of the trouble. The answer to any particular question depends on how many of the shells land with the concave side up and how many with the convex side up: each of the seven combinations has a name and a vague range of meanings depending on the context of the question asked.[10] The meanings of the different throws are sufficiently well known for a client to be able to check the diviner's interpretation of them, but the diviner exercises some specialized skill in interpreting the throws to suit the particular context of a divination, and especially in explaining ambiguous combinations of throws. In the Shona view, his skill lies principally in his ability to throw the dice to make them 'see': indeed, diviners do in practice appear to exercise some skill in obtaining the throws they require.

In the eastern districts, the dice are frequently made from bone, often taken from animals killed for the purpose. The number of bones in a set and the types of bones used vary considerably. Generally they are small flat bones with recognisable convex and concave sides and are used in much the same manner as the seed shells.[11]

The most widespread form of divining dice are sets of four carved from wood, or occasionally from ivory or bone. These dice are about ten centimetres long and two or three centimentres wide and each dice has a pattern carved on one side which in spite of local variations is sufficiently fixed for anyone to be able to distinguish the four dice of a set (see illustration). Of the four, one *chirume* (manhood), is identified with the male sex and one, *nhokwara* (one which scratches), has female associations. A third, *chitokwadzima* (something becoming blind, dead), is associated with, and sometimes called, *ngwena* (crocodile) which its carved pattern sometimes resembles: the tail of the crocodile in the carving is sometimes intended and recognised as a phallic symbol and the crocodile carries in folklore a reputation for cunning,

10. Gelfand 1964a, pp. 77f.
11. Gelfand 1956a, pp. 116f.

sometimes with phallic overtones.[12] When the crocodile alone turns up in divination, it may mean success in answer to questions about hunting, guilty in an examination on witchcraft, and bad news about a sick relative, but it is not dominant when other dice turn up as well.[13] The fourth dice of any set, *kwami* (togetherness), has strong sexual associations and sometimes represents womanhood but its meaning varies from one diviner to another.[14] Depending on which of the dice fall with the carved side uppermost, there are sixteen possible throws, for each of which the diviner has a name and a range of meanings.

Although some throws have meanings which are well and widely known, the meanings of many are vague and vary from one diviner to another.[15] People generally are not able to interpret the throws for a given context, and diviners are reluctant to talk about their art. Where these sets of four are used, divining is a more specialized art and the interpretation of throws is more under the control of the diviner. In practice, diviners often use two, four or eight sets of dice thrown together, making possible combinations and interpretations yet more complicated. During divination, a diviner repeatedly gathers up and throws his dice as he asks questions of them, sometimes too rapidly for any but the practised diviner to recognise all the throws. Even when the clients are able carefully to consider all the throws, it is extremely rare that the combination of the different sets used in a divination provides an unequivocal answer to the questions asked of the dice. The diviner must work out a plausible message on the subject of the divination based not only on the throws that appear but also on significant combinations that fail to come up. His explanations utilize his prior knowledge of the background to the case in question if he has any, and whatever a skilled diviner may infer from an asute assessment of the reactions of his clients during the course of the divination. The diviner's standing in the community, his ritual attire and the eloquence of his explanation may all help to convey a conviction that cannot come solely from his

12. Tracey 1934a, p. 24. Cf. the stories cited in Posselt 1929a, pp. 29f, 92ff.

13. The names and interpretations of different throws in various districts are given in Hunt 1950, 1954 and 1962. Von Sicard (1959) speculates on the origins of the names of the four dice.

14. Gelfand 1964a, p. 75.

15. Mr H. Tracey (1963) claims that in spite of local variations there are general meanings for the throws based on a polarity ranging from *chirume* at the masculine and negative pole through *chitokwadzima* and *nhokwara* to *kwami* at the feminine and positive pole. He claims that the ranges of meaning obtained from this polarity are generally consistent with Hunt's tabulations of interpretations given to the various throws in different contexts by diviners from four different regions (Hunt 1950, 1954 & 1962). In fact, a detailed comparison of these shows little correspondence with Tracey's scheme and previously

(continued on p. 156)

dice.[16] In the eyes of his clients, however, the diviner obtains information from his dice, which have been ritually treated to enable him to 'see' into the troubles of his clients.

Many people who do not claim to be *n'anga* (traditional diviner-healers) do claim to be able to divine with dice for matters of lesser importance. This applies particularly to Korekore country in the north where the seed shells are used, but elsewhere a family head may have his own set of dice which he can consult on minor matters.[17] But the dice in the hands of a family head are not regarded as being very reliable, and in a serious situation a professional diviner is always consulted.

The Shona admit that even a professional diviner can make a mistake in divination, and a dissatisfied client always has the right to consult a second opinion. But when someone expresses such scepticism over divination, it is not that he doubts the efficacy of the process of divination, but rather he suspects the particular diviner of being incompetent or a charlatan. Even the most sceptical of Shona can usually cite at least one diviner, often someone living some distance away, whom they believe to be genuinely able to divine.

A professional diviner is consulted partly because of his skills in manipulating the dice, in reading the more complicated throws and in interpreting them for any given situation. He is also believed to be more skilful in making the dice 'see', since he knows the best medicines and procedures for this. But these skills and the prestige of the diviner are believed to depend on his contact with the spirit world through the assistance given to him by a healing spirit. As in the case of many skills among the Shona, the skill of a professional diviner is attributed to some spirit which has singled out its human host to be the medium through which it can exercise its powers. The spirit may be a deceased ancestor or close relative who was a diviner when alive, or it may be a wandering *shave* spirit,[18] often inherited from a deceased ancestor who was helped by it during life. It is considered essential for a successful *n'anga* to be the host to some healing or divining spirit: a man who learns all the techniques of a diviner from his

---

(1934b, p. 46) Tracey expressed the opinion that the diviner uses his dice to give his client confidence while the result of the divination depends on information gleaned from the client.

16. Werbner 1973 provides a detailed analysis of the relevance of rhetoric to domestic diviners among the Kalanga.

17. Gelfand 1962, p. 106; see also Werbner 1973.

18. A *shave* is the spirit of some stranger. This type of spirit and its relevance to the practice of skills is discussed below in chapter 9.

father may feel unable to practice until he inherits or acquires the necessary healing spirit.[19]

Some diviners rely entirely on the powers of their spirits in ritual possession, and do not use dice at all. For this type of divination the procedure is different in that the diviner needs an assistant (often a spouse or an appropriate relative), who receives the fee and who must perform some ritual to induce the spirit to enter the diviner. This may be as simple as the assistant clapping his hands and asking the spirit to come out in the medium, or passing the medium medicated snuff. Some spirits require the medium first to don the ritual dress of the spirit, and the medium may require music and dancing to induce possession. Generally, an experienced diviner is possessed more quickly and easily than one who has only just started to practise. Once the spirit has possessed the host, the client can address it often using the assistant as an intermediary. The spirit may speak to the client about spiritual and ritual affairs and answer questions the client or other onlookers may have to ask.

The diviner might remain in the state of possession for some hours during which the spirit speaks through him at convenient intervals; the intervening time may be spent in casual conversation and possibly some dancing. During this period the diviner is supposed to be taken over completely by the spirit, and he acts and speaks in a manner appropriate to the spirit. Finally the diviner is dispossessed, often indicated by yawning and stretching as if coming out of a deep sleep, after which he is supposed to remember nothing of what happened while he was in a state of possession. We shall discuss the phenomenon of spirit possession later; here it is sufficient to see that the validity of divination depends on the belief that a spirit takes possession of a human host in order to tell people about their relations with the spirit world.

We can turn now to the possible results of divination which can tell us more of the Shona understanding of personal misfortune.

Ideally, before making a diagnosis, a diviner shares with his client every detail of the client's private life: his family relations, his fears, his enemies, his past history. The diviner establishes intimate contact with the client from which he is able to discover his general relationships with his spirit guardians which is the determining factor in treatment. (Relating treatment to hidden anxieties and fears has obvious parallels with modern psycho-therapy.)

In this process, any qualms of conscience are likely to be brought into

---

19. Cf. Howman 1948, p. 13.

the open and might suggest possible causes of the troubles of the client. Any serious immoral or anti-social act is likely to suggest itself as the cause of misfortune, in which case confession and the consequent release of tension is usually a step towards overcoming the problem. Confession is particularly important in cases of adultery, which is supposed to endanger a woman's young children or to cause protracted labour — in such a case, a woman may be tortured to force a confession out of her and so save herself and her child. Crimes such as theft against which protective 'medicine' is used are also especially likely to be diagnosed as the causes of illness, and confession to the owner of the property may be necessary since he alone is believed to know the antidote to the protective 'medicines' he has used.

More frequently, the diviner finds some ritual which has been neglected for some time, or some other reason why one or several of the family spirits should be upset. Although this may be due to neglect, it may be that the spirits have a special request to make and are not displeased at all; a spirit may, for example, wish to possess the sick person as its host. The diviner divines what spirit is involved and what ritual is required to appease it, the most common being to brew beer in honour of the spirit. The family ancestral spirits, particularly the spirit of the paternal grandfather, are most commonly involved, since even when there is some other immediate cause of the trouble they are believed to have withdrawn their protective power. Other spirits may also be diagnosed as causing illness in a request to be honoured with beer.

In some parts of Shona country, people test when they can a diviner's diagnosis before they perform a ceremony in honour of a spirit.[20] Usually the subject of divination is the cause of sickness and the prescribed ritual involves the use of grain for beer (or possibly a meal). In such a case, towards evening the family head takes a little grain in a gourd cup and formally addresses the spirit divined to be the cause of the trouble in words as: 'Grandfather N., here is your grain. We are brewing the beer you have asked for. Make your grandchild well and stop causing trouble in the home.' Provided that the patient shows some sign of improvement by morning, the grain is mixed with sufficient grain for the ceremony and preparations proceed.

If it is decided that the trouble is simply due to a spirit guardian asking to be honoured with millet beer, the matter is treated lightly, provided the

---

20. This comes from my Korekore material, but cf. also Gelfand 1966a, p. 61, where the Karanga are described as expecting signs of improvement in the patient before they offer beer to a deceased ancestor.

patient begins to improve when the beer is brewed: such spirits have a right to be honoured in this way and they have no way of making their wishes known except through mild illness in the community. The illness is not necessarily a sign that the spirit is unfriendly. But occasionally trouble is diagnosed as being caused by an angry avenging spirit (*ngozi*) of a relative or acquaintance who died with a grudge over a grave injustice suffered during his life, or the spirit may have been stirred to take revenge for the bad treatment of its living descendants. An attack by such a spirit is a serious and frightening affair, often involving a number of deaths in quick succession. Appeasement is difficult and may involve heavy compensation to the spirit's descendants.

Another common cause of serious illness is believed to be witchcraft, possibly in conjunction with dissatisfaction on the part of spirit guardians. This is often described as 'poisoning' by some jealous or otherwise malicious person, who may be named by the diviner. In such a case, the most satisfactory action is to obtain from the witch an antidote to the poison, or to remove her harmful influence by breaking all contact with her. But some diviners claim to be able to provide antidotes to witchcraft, in which case no personal accusation is necessary.

There are some vague associations between certain symptoms and particular types of causes, but diviners do not stick rigidly to these associations. Diseases of the genitals or of a child at breast are generally attributed to sexual offences, though other diseases may be attributed to this kind of cause as well. The sudden, acute and painful onset of rheumatic disorders is generally associated with witchcraft, but in circumstances which make witchcraft unlikely this may be attributed to common spiritual causes; and in practice any kind of disease or trouble may be diagnosed as the result of witchcraft. In most cases, the final diagnosis comes from the client's general circumstances rather than from the physical symptoms which would be the concern of a western doctor. The social environment and the politics of the local community provide strong influences on the explanation of misfortune.[21]

Besides divining the ultimate causes of illness or misfortune, a professional diviner should prescribe herbal remedies for the immediate symptoms of the disease. Some diviners do not deal with herbs in which case they may recommend a herbalist, and a diviner may even recommend western medicinal treatment for the removal of symptoms. Or a possessing spirit may tell the client to ask the human host for medicines when he is no

21. Cf. Fry 1976, p. 98. Also Gelfand 1967a, pp. 86 – 100, where a list of cases and ascribed causes is given.

longer possessed. In any case, the appeasement of the spiritual cause of the disease is normally complemented by the medicinal treatment of the physical symptoms.

Treatment

Especially in the towns, where the dense population allows for a higher degree of specialization than in the more sparsely populated rural areas, it is a common procedure to go in the case of serious illness first to a *n'anga* who specializes in divining to find out the cause, and then to consult a *n'anga* specializing in herbalism to treat the symptoms. Sometimes, however, medicines are obtained first for immediate relief, possibly from a healer with a reputation for being able to cure a particular type of illness. Or if the patient is well enough to consult the *n'anga* himself, it is often the same man who divines the cause and prescribes the necessary herbal remedies. Although a *n'anga* tends to acquire a reputation in a particular field (such as the knowledge of medical herbs for certain illnesses, divining the cause of death, dealing with the recovery of lost property, love potions or some other such field), most *n'anga* practice both divination and herbalism and claim to be able to treat any complaint.

Even when only one diviner-healer is consulted, there are two distinct aspects of the Shona reaction to personal misfortune. The first is to determine the ultimate spiritual cause and to appease it in order to prevent any further misfortune. The second is the 'natural' rectification of the disorder caused by the initial misfortune, and in the case of disease this involves the treatment of the symptoms usually with some form of medicine.

This is why there is no contradiction in the fact that some *n'anga* advise the use of western medicinal or surgical treatment for certain disorders, nor in the fact that many Shona who make use of western medicine also consult a *n'anga* to discover the ultimate cause of their troubles. Although in the past there may have been some opposition to a science that not only ignored the spirits, but even defied their authority,[22] now there is little hostility to western practice which, in spite of its shortcomings in some fields, is recognised to be for the most part superior. Traditional diviner healers are prepared occasionally to recommend western practice where they themselves have failed, in much the same way they might very occasionally recommended another *n'anga* with a particular reputation.

Some of the traditional medical practice of traditional healers does

22. Cf. Burbridge 1923, p. 95; also Gelfand 1944, p. 4.

have a sound empirical basis. Thus many herbalists have a knowledge of purgatives and emetics, and certain diseases (such as smallpox and syphilis) are recognised to be contagious and to require isolation. Although it may be true that this isolation is based at least partly on a fear of coming into contact with the unseen evil powers causing the illness,[23] the theory is empirically sound in that it recognises the danger of the ultimate cause of disease being passed on through contact.[24] But the Shona themselves regard all their medicines as working in much the same way, and do not necessarily distinguish those which western medicine recognises as having a sound basis from others which western medicine would regard as magico-religious.

Since the ultimate cause of serious or abnormal disease is seen in terms of spiritual forces, most remedies of traditional healers are directed simply at apparent symptoms without any reference to anatomical causes. Thus aches and pains may be treated by making incisions in the skin over the sore places and rubbing some medicinal powder into them. Another treatment for pain is 'sucking out' the sickness either by placing a horn over the sore place and sucking through it or by sucking directly with the mouth: usually by sleight of hand the healer produces the 'sickness' from the horn or from his mouth in the form of a small worm or similar small object which he subsequently ritually disposes of. Ailments involving breathing, asthma for example, are treated by inhalation of smoke or steam produced either by burning medicinal leaves or boiling them in water. The most common forms of medicine are taken by the mouth, either in the form of powders mixed with food, or in the liquid form of water in which appropriate medicines have been soaked or boiled.

Traditional healers do not normally exchange information on the preparation of medicines, which requires great care and a certain amount of secret ritual. The reason for this is mainly economic: a diviner can attract more clients if he has medicines that no one else knows about. But power is always associated with secret knowledge, usually concerning the spirits or imparted by them, and this should not be bandied about too lightly for fear of showing disrespect and making the spirits angry. The result is that traditional healers are not able to rely on a solid stock of traditional knowledge and tend to have an individualistic approach to the preparation of their medicines. The criteria on which the ingredients of

23. Cf. Gelfand 1944, p. 7.
24. Professor Gelfand (1967a, p. 51) draws a parallel between the Shona attitude to witchcraft and the European attitude to germs.

medicines are chosen appear to be based primarily on the conceptual associations of the healer who makes them. Some of these, such as the use of the heart of a lion to give strength,[25] are obvious even to the western mind. Others carry clear Shona symbolism in the use of the colour red (which conveys danger or insidious power) or in associations with water (spirits are often associated with pools or rivers). Other medicines still involve a specialized conceptual system, the logic of which may be evident only to the diviner who makes them, and perhaps his reasoning is at the subconscious level.[26] The same applies to the numerous protective charms, love potions, and other concoctions that herbalists supply to their clienteles.

Professor Gelfand emphasizes the effectiveness of suggestive therapy in some of the cases treated by traditional healers. The clients of a traditional healer believe that he has the help of a healing spirit whom he regularly honours. They know that he has much secret knowledge of medicines and that he has to observe ritual taboos on which the efficacy of his practice depends. His distinctive dress, his incantations, his collections of roots and herbs in decorated horns and calabashes all displayed in full view of the patient, his supposed knowledge about the preparation of medicines, the confidence with which he deals with his patients, all these help to impress the patient and give him confidence in the powers of the healer.[27] This effect provides some success especially in psychological cases. It also makes the client ready to see physical improvement where there is none.

The change in attitude to sickness after the performance of appropriate rituals is an important factor in the apparent success of traditional *n'anga*. This is illustrated by the case of an old man suffering from chronic lumbago. After he had rejected one divination since there was no improvement when he started to appease the designated spirit, he spent some weeks under treatment at a mission hospital. On his return, he went to a second diviner on whose advice he proceeded to honour the spirit of his father's father with millet beer. Some months later the old man explained that he had been well ever since he had honoured his grandfather: he ad-

---

25. Gelfand 1964a, p. 70.
26. This will become clearer in the light of the remarks on the training of a traditional healer in the next section.
27. Cf. Gelfand 1967a, p. 139. It is doubtful to what extent *n'anga* deliberately deceive their clients in order to impress them. Sometimes, as when the 'sickness' is produced by sleight of hand after it has been 'sucked out', the deception is clearly deliberate, but the degree to which this kind of dramatic effect is carried depends on the personal traits of the particular *n'anga*. Cf. also Gelfand 1964c on Shona treatment of psychiatric disorders.

mitted that he still sometimes had pains in his back, but remarked that this was to be expected in an old man. Before consulting the diviner, he was suffering from a complaint which made him anxious: after taking the diviner's advice, the anxiety ceased and the complaint was no longer considered abnormal or serious. The improvement may have been psychological, but the old man certainly felt it as real.

In the eyes of the patient the power of a traditional healer lies with his healing spirit, which teaches him how to prepare and apply medicines which can produce required physical effects. This belief is confirmed by the evident improvements often seen in the state of patients who consult *n'anga*.

Once the medicines have been prepared and correctly prescribed, the Shona have great faith in their efficacy, independently of any spiritual powers. In Shona myths and legends, there are frequent references to political power being obtained through possession of efficacious medicines and charms; such power is often lost through the medicine being stolen or its secret betrayed, indicating further the belief in the power of traditional medicines and the importance of exclusive medicinal knowledge.

The Shona believe that traditional medicines can cause physical harm. Medicines against theft, for example, are supposed to cause serious sickness in a thief, and even death unless he confesses to the owner of the medicine and obtains a cure. So the power of a traditional healer could be used for evil purposes as well as good. It is generally believed that there are *n'anga* who employ their powers for evil ends, and cases of extortion or even murder by *n'anga* have occasionally come to light.[28] In fact, the *n'anga* occupies a very ambiguous position in Shona society and is treated with both respect and caution.

Becoming a n'anga[29]

There are two types of *n'anga* in Shona society. Some are believed to operate under the direction of healing spirits and with the aid of their power. Others simply use the skills they have learnt from their tuition by experts.

It is possible to acquire the title of *n'anga* simply by learning the art of

---

28. Cf. Gelfand 1967a, pp. 43ff.
29. Much of the material in this section comes from Gelfand 1964a, pp. 56 – 64; 1967, pp. 114 – 133.

herbalism during a period of apprenticeship with a senior herbalist, in the course of which the apprentice must pay his teacher formal fees for imparting the secrets of his art. Or a man may learn herbalism or the art of divining with dice from his father or a senior relative. Although such a *n'anga* may acquire a regular clientele, he can never acquire the reputation and income of someone reputed to be able to cope with more serious spiritual troubles. To deal professionally with the spirit world requires the help of a specialist healing spirit.

The most important qualification by which a person, whether man or woman,[30] may be recognised as a *n'anga* is evidence that he or she has the help of a healing spirit. Often this is the spirit of a deceased close relative (usually a parent or grandparent) who was a *n'anga* during life and wishes to continue his (or her) work through a living descendant. Frequently, the healing spirit is a wandering *shave* spirit which may pick on any person, but once it has been accepted it generally remains within the family, so that after some generations of *n'anga* people may ignore the distinction between the *shave* which helped a deceased parent or grandparent and the personal spirit of the deceased. A *n'anga* who practises through the help of a family spirit elder is likely to be regarded as more powerful than the host of a wandering *shave* spirit, and if the profession has been in a family for some generations, the healing powers of the family spirit elders are emphasized.

An indication that someone is wanted to be the host of a healing spirit is for that person to dream about practising as a diviner or healer. This is usually accompanied by illness, often some kind of mental disorder, which is diagnosed to be a request by the healing spirit to enter the sick person and to continue its work through him. Neither the dreams nor the illness are absolutely essential, but it is rare for a person to be accepted as a professional *n'anga* without at least one of these signs, and the majority of successful *n'anga* experience both before they begin to practise.

Often the call by the healing spirit comes when the prospective *n'anga* is too young to practise, in which case the spirit is placated immediately but the recipient of the spirit waits until he receives some further sign or simply until he is older. When there is a traditional and inherited healing spirit in a family, the future *n'anga* receives informal training from his boyhood onwards at the hands of his predecessor. Alternatively, after receiving the call from the spirit, a prospective *n'anga* may undergo a year or more of

---

30. Although *n'anga* are more usually male than female, there are many female *n'anga* who are in no way deemed inferior to their male counterparts.

apprenticeship under some *n'anga* of renown. Some, however, practice without having received any formal instruction and learn their art from their spirits, usually through dreams. And those who have received instruction from a senior *n'anga* invariably supplement their knowledge with what they claim to learn directly from their healing spirits. The normal way in which this takes place is for the *n'anga* to dream of herbal concoctions at night and the places in which the ingredients are to be found, and to go out and find the herbs in the morning. Spirits are believed also to impart other information through dreams and signs, about problems of clients, perhaps, or glimpses into the future. Sometimes a *n'anga* simply feels his spirit talking within him, dictating to him his own half-formulated ideas.[31] Thus many herbal medicines are based on subconscious or semi-conscious symbolic associations.

There is little or no communication of medical knowledge between *n'anga*. To reveal to an outsider what the spirit has taught in secret (except to an apprentice who has paid a ritual fee) would be regarded as a betrayal of trust, and is anyway financially inadvisable. Thus the only chance there is of building up a tradition of empirical knowledge arises when a healing spirit is inherited for a number of generations from father to son, and it may not be entirely fortuitous that *n'anga* with such a family tradition are regarded particularly highly. But in the Shona view, the knowledge gained from such a tradition is indistinguishable from the additions made by any particular member of it: all is believed to come from the healing spirits, whether learnt from a late father during his life or in dreams after his death.

There are legends about *n'anga* who qualify by learning their art from ancestral spirits while living with them for a few days at the bottom of a pool or river bed.[32] The person concerned disappears for a few days and then comes back into the community with the full regalia of a deceased *n'anga* and a story of how he acquired it under the water. In one account, the man was said to have risen out of a pool in front of his brother and a number of people.[33] Although *n'anga* who claim to have received their powers in this way are extremely rare,[34] the belief that some do illustrates the importance of an intimate relationship between a *n'anga* and his spirits.

---

31. Sachs 1937, pp. 21f, 27.
32. Burbridge 1923, pp. 98ff; Edwards 1928, pp. 26f; cf. also Daneel 1971, p. 129.
33. Burbridge 1923, pp. 98ff.
34. Professor Gelfand remarks (1964a, p. 63) that he has never met a *n'anga* who claims to have qualified in this way. Neither have I.

This is further emphasized in the initiation ceremony with which most *n'anga* begin their practice. The ceremony is similar to that of any person who is to be consecrated as the host or medium of a spirit (a topic we will be discussing later). The ceremony is performed under the directions of a senior *n'anga*. Beer is brewed in honour of the healing spirit and a libation may be poured for the spirit. The new *n'anga* usually becomes possessed by his healing spirit during the singing and dancing which lasts through the night. In the morning, the new *n'anga* is consecrated by having his hair ritually cut, the instructor's fees are agreed as are the arrangements for paying them, and after this the new *n'anga* may practise on his own.

Most *n'anga* hold, or claim to hold, an annual ceremony in honour of their healing spirits. At such a ceremony beer is offered to the healing spirit and the *n'anga* usually becomes possessed. At the first of these, the instructor of the new *n'anga* is especially honoured, but at subsequent ceremonies he is treated as an equal together with other local colleagues who are always invited. The purpose of this annual ceremony is to thank the healing spirit for its help and so guarantee its continued assistance, without which the *n'anga* would be powerless.

Once he has been initiated, a *n'anga* needs to acquire a good reputation in order to gain a regular clientele. His position is helped if his family already has a reputation for divining and healing, and he may enhance his position by impressive paraphernalia and dramatic ritual when divining. Stories of wonders performed with the help of the spirit may also help. But generally the reputation of a *n'anga* is based on the observed recovery of his clients. When asked why they consult a particular *n'anga*, Shona people often cite past cases of sick persons who recovered after consulting him. Faith in a traditional diviner-healer depends at least partly on empirical observations.

The treatment of sickness today

Nowadays more and more Shona are relying on the proven success of western medicine especially for curing specific and clearly physical complaints. Nevertheless, traditional healers are numerous even in the towns and cities where their numbers are increasing. And there is no shortage of clients, both rich and poor, illiterate and educated, Christian and pagan, who are ready to pay good money for the advice of *n'anga*:[35] a *n'anga* in

---

35. Cf Chavunduka 1973, where the relevance of stress to traditional therapy is discussed.

Harare may regularly earn thirty to fifty dollars a week.[36] The tensions and uncertainties of modern life readily provoke suspicions of invisible forces, especially of witchcraft, and few Shona can resist going to a diviner when things are going badly. For traditionalists, *n'anga* provide a variety of cures, prophylactics and charms to ensure good fortune. And *n'anga* provide for all a last resort to whom one can appeal when western medicine has dismissed a case as hopeless, or has simply failed to cure it, or when a person is unable to survive financially, when a man cannot find work, or in any of the intolerable situations that so readily arise in the towns. Even a person who is sceptical about the powers of *n'anga* or who positively disbelieves in the efficacy of divination and traditional treatment is likely to consult a *n'anga* in time of crisis. (As many a European agnostic or atheist prays in time of crisis.)

Traditional healers are more successful than western medicine in treating many psychiatric cases or in calming patients with terminal diseases, and some western doctors occasionally send patients suffering from such disorders to traditional *n'anga*.[37] Their greater success with these cases is partly due to the fact that they are able to give more personal attention to their patients than is possible in a large and busy western-type hospital. But more relevant is the fact that traditional healers are intimately concerned with the anxieties and hidden fears of the people they are dealing with. Since psychological troubles are not likely to decline with industrialization and modernization, neither is the traditional art of the *n'anga*.

There have been some superficial changes in the practices of *n'anga*. In many rural areas, a professional herbalist is now supposed to have the permission of his chief to practise, perhaps in the form of a written permit. And a written permit from a chief, or better from a government official, offers some prestige to a *n'anga* which may be important when he is operating in a town or city in competition with others. A progressive *n'anga* in a town might wear a white clinical coat instead of his traditional ritual regalia and keep records of all his patients in a card index,[38] but his concern is still to discover and appease the spiritual cause of troubles and he still deals in traditional herbal remedies.

In the cities, a number of associations of traditional healers arose,

36. Private communication from Professor G.L. Chavunduka.
37. Cf. Gelfand 1964c for an appreciative account of traditional ways of coping with psychiatric disorders.
38. Mitchell 1960b, pp. 16f.

which used to vie with one another for the allegiance of practitioners: a large membership gives prestige to an association and to its leaders, and a distinguished association gives status to its members. In July 1980, at the suggestion of the Minister of Health, the more significant of these associations dissolved themselves in order to form a single national union, *The Zimbabwe African Traditional Healers Association.* The aim of the Association is to protect the interests of its members, and also to protect the public from abuses by traditional healers. It is already involved in undertaking and controlling research into traditional methods of healing. The Association also receives complaints against particular traditional healers, but at the moment the only sanction it can apply against malpractice is expulsion from the Association. In practice, the Association has not been able to satisfy everyone that it has control of its members.[39]

Nevertheless, for the treatment of most physical ailments, western medicine has surpassed traditional practice. Patent remedies are sold and bought throughout the country for petty ailments like headaches or a passing cold. And throughout the country there are hospitals and clinics which are rarely able to meet the demands on their facilities: the queues at the main hospitals became so long that the Ministry of Health has been compelled to filter patients through outlying clinics run by nurses, and a number of doctors have been able to set up lucrative private practices in the high density suburbs. Even from the most backward rural areas, people may travel hundreds of kilometres to obtain for themselves or their children hospital treatment which is not available locally.

The adaptation to western medicine has not, however, been complete. Doctors of western medicine still face the problem of patients who expect the medical expert to find out for himself what is wrong with them and who feel no obligation to impart information about their symptoms. Also a slow cure may be disrupted when the sick person becomes impatient and decides it is time for further divination and ritual to appease the troubling spirits.

A third way of coping with disease today, a way that opposes both traditional and modern medical practices and which is growing in popularity throughout Shona country, is faith healing. Many of the new independent Christian churches (which we shall be discussing later) claim

---

39. When the Prime Minister commented that perhaps one in a hundred *n'anga* are genuine, Professor Chavunduka, supported the statement (The Herald, 24 Sept., 1984)

to follow the example of the Biblical Christ and his Apostles by healing all kinds of diseases through faith; they preach that the use of medicines of any kind displays a failing in faith and is wrong. The prophets and healers of these churches to some extent replace traditional diviners and healers: they practice divination, accept traditional explanations of the spiritual causes of misfortune and they deal with witches and witchcraft, all practices outside the domain of western medicine. Yet their treatment is clearly new, relying largely on symbolic ritual from Biblical and Christian sources: thus the healer usually wears long white robes and heals by laying his hands on the patient and sprinkling the patient with consecrated water. Where witchcraft or evil spirits (and in these churches all spirits causing illness are considered evil) are believed to be involved, exorcism takes the form of a command (as Christ commanded evil spirits to leave their victims) rather than the traditional magico-religious rite of transferring the spirit into a fowl or goat which must be driven away. Still less do these churches condone traditional rituals to appease the spirit.

In practice, Shona people may try all three types of healing in turn when they do not receive satisfaction at first. Although some may stick to their commitment to a doctrine or sect or way of life, come what may, more commonly theoretical beliefs are not as strong as the practical necessity of finding some solution to a present crisis.

7

Witchcraft

The belief in witchcraft

The Shona very often explain disease and misfortune in terms of witchcraft. Witchcraft can explain all types of misfortune, from minor ailments to conflict with an employer or losing one's job, and many Shona believe that death is always due to witchcraft. The art of witchcraft is believed to be as wide in its scope as the art of a traditional herbalist, and the belief in witchcraft persists strongly in all strata of Shona society.

Belief in witchcraft does not necessarily contradict belief in natural causes. We have seen that invisible causes are sought to explain sickness only when natural causes appear to be inadequate. Often when witchcraft is believed to be operative, it acts in conjunction with evident natural causes. Thus should a man be killed in a drunken brawl, the natural cause of death is obvious and nobody denies it: but the Shona would want to know what made the aggressor kill his victim on this occasion — they argue that he has drunk beer on other occasions and may even have been in fights before, so the tragedy on this occasion must be due to witchcraft. A man was washed away and drowned in the Mazoe River: again the natural cause of death was obvious, but his relatives still wanted to know what had blinded him to the danger and why he tried to cross the swollen river against the advice of his companions. If a man loses his employment after a quarrel with his employer, he can still ask what jealous witch created the misunderstanding and the rift between himself and his employer. And even when a very old man dies, some claim that the only explanation of why he died precisely at the time he did is that a witch killed him (though others accept that he may have died simply because he was 'tired').

Natural causes can answer the question of *how* something happens. But there is the further question of *why*, why to this particular person and why at this time and place. Europeans are likely to speak of chance or perhaps of divine providence, but the Shona find a more ready answer in terms of witchcraft.[1] So the Shona belief in witchcraft deals with a realm beyond the more natural series of events; it neither conflicts with empirical evidence nor is it essentially irrational. Indeed there is evidence which in the Shona view confirms their beliefs.

We have already seen that a traditional herbalist or diviner often acquires a reputation from his apparent results, and it is presumed that if he can do good through his medicines he can also do harm which would be

---

1. The best exposition of this kind of reasoning in an African society is Evans-Pritchard 1937, especially pp. 63 – 83.

witchcraft: the belief in the power of a traditional medicine man to bewitch is based on his observed success in healing. There is further evidence in support of a belief in witchcraft when persons occasionally admit to performing the horrible actions associated with it,[2] and occasionally convincing physical evidence is unearthed of the atrocious rituals of witches.[3] Then there is often circumstantial evidence suggesting that certain persons are witches, sometimes involving misfortune following a quarrel or a veiled threat: thus when a young man died suddenly of meningitis after a suggestion by a jealous woman that a death might occur in the family, nothing could persuade his relatives that she had not bewitched him. Occasionally deaths have occurred for which western medicine could find no other explanation than that the patient believed himself to be bewitched. All this supports the Shona belief in witchcraft, but for the people themselves the most telling evidence is that troubles and misfortune, presumed to be the result of witchcraft, are always present and have for the Shona no more satisfactory explanation.

The belief in witchcraft is practically universal among the Shona, as indeed among many peoples throughout the world. But the details of the belief and the emphasis placed on different aspects of it vary. To show too much knowledge of witchcraft is tantamount to admitting to being a witch, so people do not readily speak about the subject in public and private views and variations are rife. Nevertheless, there appears a body of belief held by most, if not all, the Shona people.[4]

The paradigm of witchcraft

The paradigm of a witch, and indeed the worst kind of witch, is a person who wanders about at night performing weird and horrible deeds. Such witches are almost always thought to be women. Although it is believed that a witch of this kind can acquire her powers of witchcraft through medicines provided by another witch, usually, and certainly in the case of a more powerful and senior witch, she is believed to inherit her witchcraft from her mother or some maternal ancestor whose spirit assists her in her evil activities. The children of a reputed witch are always suspected of being witches themselves. These witches are supposed to meet late at night

---

2. See Crawford 1967, pp. 44 – 59.

3. Professor Gelfand (1967a, pp. 32f) describes a case in which the corpse of a child killed by a self-confessed witch was found to have a fractured skull and skin removed from the left cheek and the genitals.

4. The beliefs are given in some detail in Gelfand 1967 and Crawford 1967.

when they go about naked to perform their nefarious deeds, acting together in cultic collusion. They are believed to have various poisons or charms with which they can kill anyone at will. Although they are particularly likely to bewitch somebody against whom one of the coven bears a grudge, they do not necessarily have any other reason for killing than the pleasure of doing evil, and husbands, children and close relatives of the witches can be their victims: many believe that a witch must kill her own first-born child. Witches are supposed secretly to keep familiar beasts of the night or of stealth, such as hyenas, owls, antbears and snakes,[5] which they can ride or send on their evil errands: these beasts can be used to bewitch a victim (their presence in a homestead is considered evidence of an attack by witches), or they may simply be used by witches at play. Witches are thought to be able to fly great distances at night. They are supposed to be able to arouse and influence an avenging *ngozi* spirit[6] to help achieve their ends, and also to have some control over the forces of nature: in particular, they can send lightning as easily as any animal.[7]

The most atrocious aspect of these witches is that they are supposed to be very fond of eating human flesh, especially the flesh of children, and they are believed often to desecrate graves in order to obtain it. For this reason a barren woman, or a woman who aborts or whose children die young, is likely to be suspected of deliberately killing her children for the purposes of her witchcraft. Human flesh is believed to be the most powerful of a witch's 'medicines'. These 'medicines' may be used to cause harm or they may be used for socially acceptable purposes, for luck in gambling, for example, or success in business,[8] or to obtain good crops; nevertheless, by their nature they are evil, and their use is held to convey an unfair advantage over others in the community. Power is always associated with power to

---

5. Snakes normally are strongly associated with witchcraft, but they do signify different things in different contexts. Thus life is believed to begin as a snake or worm in the mother's womb. Snake skins can be used for auspicious medicines (see Gelfand 1964a, p. 173). Pythons are often associated with guardian spirits of a chiefdom. Snakes may have phallic associations (see Tracey 1934a, p. 24) and they may be associated with private tutelary spirits (see Sachs 1937, p. 11).

6. This is a very frightening and dangerous type of spirit that we shall discuss later.

7. Lightning is said to be a bird which lays eggs in the ground where it strikes. An object or place struck by lightning is feard or taboo (except possibly for making 'medicines') at least until it is purified by a traditional diviner-healer, who usually produces eggs or egg-like objects from the ground near where the lightning struck. These he removes or destroys. Cf. Mbizo 1924; Dicke 1931.

8. See The State v. Chitongo (Harare, 1985), concerning a dead child which had had organs from its neck removed, allegedly to obtain 'medicines' to improve the accused's business.

harm: thus a death in a chiefly family followed shortly by a badly deformed birth was attributed to a renowned witch attacking his relatives to strengthen his own medicines in his campaign to acquire the chiefship.

Some of the activities attributed to witches appear to be purely imaginary, especially when by their very nature they are empirically unverifiable: thus some witches are said to be so powerful with their medicines that they are able to tamper with a corpse without leaving any sign of injury to the body. Similarly many claim that a witch can leave her body asleep in her house while she flies around on her nefarious nocturnal activities. On the other hand, there is occasional empirical evidence of witches performing horrible rites together, as when fifteen persons were convicted in Fort Victoria (now Masvingo) after they had exhumed the body of a dead baby and eaten it between them.[9] But whether or not the activities of a witch are in what we might call the psychic sphere is irrelevant to the Shona view of them, according to which all the activities associated with witchcraft are equally real and all are thoroughly evil. The evidence indicates to the traditional Shona that there are persons who have extraordinary powers and who delight in horrific deeds. It is undeniable that some witches willingly and openly confess to these deeds and admit to having caused serious harm to others by their secret powers. This itself puts a person into the category of evil and horrible, and the other less probable phenomena associated with witchcraft fit readily into this category. When a witch leaves no visible sign of her activities, this is explained by her power to conceal them from all except a diviner, and the nature of what the diviner reveals is as horrifying as any physical evidence that may be produced.

The most powerful witches are believed to be hosts to evil ancestral spirits or to *mashave* (alien spirits) just as the best diviners and healers are believed to be aided by healing spirits. A witch may become possessed by her evil spirit, or the evil spirit may simply hover around the living witch as any spirit elder looks after his living descendants. Although either may be emphasized in any particular situation, the physical powers of the witch and the powers of attendant spirits are closely associated.

The spirit is believed to be the driving force behind the witch and may occasionally speak through her when she is in a state of ritual possession. It is believed that the spirit may sometimes act without the knowledge or consent of the human host, but even then people hold the witch responsible for the activities of the spirit. Thus revenge may be taken against a man when

---

9. Reported in *The Times*, London, 19th January, 1968.

death results from sickness divined to be caused by his father's spirit.[10] In one case, the death of a child was divined to have been caused by a spirit of its mother's family and, in the ensuing divorce suit of two three-hour sessions at the chief's court, the court never distinguished between the working of the spirit and the supposed witchcraft on the part of the mother. In fact there is no clear distinction between witchcraft and harm supposedly caused by spirits, as is further illustrated by a family spirit who told the people through its medium that they were all bewitched, and explained this by saying that there was sickness in the family because they had not brewed beer for their spirits.[11] The witch and her spirit are both agents in the practice of witchcraft, and the resulting ambiguity corresponds with the more general Shona attitude according to which responsibility is shared between a living person and his tutelary spirits. As in the case of other tutelary spirits, it is believed that the witch's spirit demands to be propitiated with occasional ceremonies in its honour: in the case of a witch's spirit, however, the ceremony is presumed to involve evil rites associated with witchcraft, possibly including the sacrifice of a baby.[12]

The parallel between a witch and a professional diviner-healer is particularly close. Apart from the similarity in the concept of the living person being host to a spirit which gives him his power, there is the similarity in the use of secret 'medicines' taught either by another practitioner or more usually by a spirit. Like those of a traditional healer, the 'medicines' of a witch (usually 'poisons') comprise both genuine physical poisons, such as arsenic from cattle dips, and symbolic mixtures which work only by suggestion, if they work at all.[13] Just as a professional healer uses suggestive therapy, so a witch can sometimes produce her effect when a patient dies through a conviction that he has been bewitched.[14] Medicines, particularly secret medicines, are closely associated with witchcraft, and when they are found about a suspected witch's dwelling or possessions, they may be taken as convincing evidence that she is in fact a witch, although they may have been originally intended for perfectly acceptable purposes. The knowledge of witchcraft is believed often to come through dreams, which is reminiscent of a traditional

---

10. Crawford 1967, pp. 261ff.
11. Gelfand 1966a, p. 51.
12. Crawford cites some evidence in support of such a ritual having taken place (1967, p. 79), but elsewhere he remarks that the evidence is, if anything, against such rituals being performed in practice (1967, p. 64).
13. Crawford 1967, pp. 79; 56 where the author cites a 'poisonous' herb used by a witch but found to be quite harmless.
14. This appears to have been operative in the case cited in Crawford 1967, p. 98.

healer learning his art in dreams. Finally, the way in which a person becomes a witch reflects the ideal manner of the vocation of a traditional healer.

Some Shona claim that a person first knows she is wanted by the spirit of a witch when she starts to dream about the deceased witch (often her mother's mother), who teaches her how to practice the craft. Some misfortune, especially barrenness or sickness in a woman's very young children, may also be divined to be a sign that a person is wanted as host to the spirit of a witch. The prospective witch may try with the help of a traditional healer to refuse to become host to the evil spirit by having it transferred into a fowl or goat which is driven away into the wild, or with the help of a modern faith-healer to have the witchcraft spirit exorcised. But since a spirit can rarely be thwarted from achieving its purpose, these attempts may fail, and the person concerned may in the end accept the spirit and become a witch, this being in her view a lesser evil than the trouble caused by the spirit. Sometimes a witch is persuaded to practice by other witches, and is trained in the secrets of the craft by them, and occasionally the influence of other witches is emphasized to the neglect of the spiritual realm. But normally it is assumed that the witches who teach the new witch her craft also provide her with a helping spirit.

Thus the rationale behind the belief in witchcraft is the same as that behind the powers of a traditional healer. The difference is that the healer normally uses his powers for good, whereas a witch uses her powers for evil. This difference is not always clear with respect to any particular practitioner: as one man explained, just as a European doctor knows a lot about poisons, so a traditional healer knows how to cause harm. Some traditional healers are believed to use their powers for harmful ends, in which case they are regarded as witches: some people go so far as to say that all professional healers are witches, and certainly all are feared and treated with respect. Nevertheless, there is a difference between traditional healers and witches in that the latter are believed normally to work in groups and to entice other persons to join them, whereas professional healers normally work alone and do not encourage rivals.

Once a witch has accepted a bewitching spirit and is confirmed in her evil ways, she is considered to be virtually incurable. A hereditary witch is supposed to get satisfaction and enjoyment out of doing evil, just as a normal person feels satisfaction from doing good, and consequently a witch would not normally want a cure. This is particularly the case when a woman is thought deliberately to acquire 'medicines' to make her a witch. It is not, however, absolutely impossible to cure a witch: a rite by which the source of witchcraft is transferred into a domestic animal is believed sometimes to be effective, as is a rite in which a witch takes medicines to make her vomit out her witchcraft. Nowadays many Christian faith-healers and prophets and other religious leaders claim to be able to exorcise witchcraft, and have a regular clientele (sometimes partly of their own making, when they divine out the witches to be exorcised). But even when a witch is believed cured, this does not prevent a relapse, and should further harm happen within her community, she is likely again to fall under suspicion.

A final point about witches who are hosts to witchcraft spirits is that the Shona accept that a person may be a witch, possessed by a bewitching spirit, without knowing it. Normally it is assumed that a witch is fully conscious of her activities and enjoys them, but sometimes a person accepts the result of a divination that she is a witch even when it comes as a complete surprise. In one case, a woman demanded to undergo a traditional ordeal because she had lost so many children that she wanted to know if she was a witch and was bewitching them.[15] Such a witch is likely to be treated less harshly than one who enjoys her witchcraft, but is nevertheless associated with the greatest of evils.

Sorcerers

As there are *n'anga* who operate without the help of a spirit, so the Shona believe in a second kind of witch who, though called by the same name (*muroyi*), is less bizarre and evil than are full hereditary witches. Such a lesser witch is usually a man and, far from partaking in the bizarre rites of witches' covens, he usually has a deliberate purpose for his witchcraft, whether it is to harm someone he dislikes or to acquire some benefit for himself to the detriment of another. This kind of witch does not necessarily have a helping spirit, though he does have some secret knowledge of the powerful 'medicines' that he uses. In anthropological literature this kind of person is called a sorcerer, distinct from a witch which normally means someone like the Shona hereditary witch.

The Shona believe that sorcerers usually buy their powers from a corrupt herbalist who is prepared to sell harmful 'medicines'. The most common procedure is to obtain a charm that can be placed at the entrance to the victim's house or by a path along which the victim is liable to pass. This is usually a thorn or bone with a sharp point which will enter the victim's

---

15. Crawford 1967, p. 216. A possible motive was to prove her innocence to others.

foot when he stands on it. But physical contact with the charm is not necessary, and in any case the 'poison' is supposed usually to be able to select the appropriate victim and leave others unharmed. The poison may be of the type that is put into the victim's food or drink, or even his tobacco, and it may be a physical poison such as arsenic obtained from cattle dips: in Shona view, all evil 'medicines' are classed as witchcraft. A sorcerer is also supposed to be able to attack his victim by performing an appropriate rite using the victim's excreta, nail pairings, underclothing or anything else that has once been in close contact with the victim.

The use of powerful 'medicines' that can only be obtained by harming others is also regarded as sorcery, although the purpose of the medicine maybe to fulfil a perfectly acceptable desire. Examples of this are the use of parts of a murdered infant for success in business or for abundant crops. Similarly a man who tries to obtain good crops through committing incest (which is liable to bring the wrath of the territorial spirit guardians down on all, and in any case is a horrifying crime in itself) may be regarded as a sorcerer. Medicines used or prescribed to procure an abortion or to induce sterility are also regarded as sorcery since these destroy or prevent life.[16]

When the victim comes into contact with the sorcerer's 'poison', it is believed that he is likely to suffer pains, with or without swelling, in the elbows or knees or in the limb itself so severe that the victim cannot use the limb (common rheumatic disorders are often attributed to witchcraft). This may spread to other parts of the body and may even cause death. The sorcerer's poisons can also cause stomach and intestinal troubles, and there is one that is supposed to befuddle the victim so that he gets killed, for example, in a road accident.

The herbalist who provides 'poisons' may himself perform the sorcery, or he may simply prescribe the poisons and indicate the appropriate use of them to his client. In either case, both the client and the herbalist are called sorcerers. Although some say that no proper healer would abuse his healing spirit by prescribing poisons in this way, and that poisons can be obtained only from a man possessed by the spirit of a witch, the more common view is that any traditional doctor can become a witch by misusing his spiritual powers for his own ends. Even a right-minded herbalist may have 'medicines' which can cause personal harm in legitimate circumstances; he may have and sell, for example, charms against theft, which are supposed to cause the thief's abdomen to swell, and 'medicines' against adultery,

---

16. Gelfand 1967a, pp. 44f, 146f; 1964a, p. 46.

with which a man can make a wife's lover severely ill.[17] Such a herbalist has the requirements for the practice of sorcery, and a creditable herbalist may become a sorcerer because of his desire to become rich, either from the sale of his poisons or by using his powers to extort money from people — perhaps even his legitimate fees.

On the one hand, an evil herbalist is said to be aided in his evil ways by his tutelary spirits and to obtain his evil powers from them which suggests that he is a real witch. On the other hand, he normally works by day in the manner of a sorcerer, administering his poison to achieve some specific end. We have noted that hereditary witches may resort to sorcery by using poisons to achieve some end. Conversely, if people find any medicines in the possession of a suspect, they are likely to conclude that she is in fact a witch. The distinction between witches and sorcerers is not, therefore, very rigid in the Shona view, as is suggested by the use of the same word, *varoyi*, for both.

Nevertheless the Shona do distinguish witchcraft from sorcery, and they react differently to the two types of activity. An allegation of sorcery is not considered as serious as an allegation of witchcraft, since the sorcerer is not inherently evil as is the witch. Although a particular deed ascribed to a sorcerer may be serious enough, he does not represent an insidious and permanent danger to the community as does a witch, who is consequently more feared. Whereas the witch performs her evil actions according to caprice, the sorcerer always has some reason for his action (usually anger or the desire for revenge), and it is possible to avoid situations in which sorcery is likely to be used. Although the same word is used for both sorcerer and witch, when an accusation of witchcraft is made, it is often supported by mention of attributes, such as eating human flesh or the possession of animals associated with witchcraft, in order to distinguish the accusation from one of sorcery.[18]

The word *muroyi* (witch or sorcerer) can be used in other contexts.[19] 'Muroyi' is a common swear word used when a person is incensed at the behaviour of another; an ill-mannered child who, for example, refuses to share his food may be called a little witch. An emotional person who too readily gives vent to feelings of jealousy, greed, hatred, frustration, or any

---

17. Gelfand 1967a, pp. 144, 150. Elsewhere Professor Gelfand says that the 'medicine' that makes a thief's abdomen swell is regarded as evil and that the herbalist who prescribes it is therefore considered a witch (1964, p. 47). Both views are held by the Shona, depending partly on which party they may happen to be related to.

18. See Crawford 1967, pp. 76f.

19 See Howman 1948.

very unpopular person may be called a witch. These characteristics are associated with witches, and lightly to call a person of this nature a witch may carry a hint of an accusation of witchcraft: certainly a domineering person who often uses threatening or abusive language, is likely to acquire the reputation of being a witch and therefore afraid of nobody.

People who break serious taboos are also liable to be called witches. Thus a family in which members 'burn the grave' of a deceased man by allowing sexual intercourse with his widow before the spirit has been settled, may be called witches. Intimacies between a grown-up son and one of his father's younger wives while the father is still alive would horrify the Shona and are regarded as witchcraft, since the son, by placing himself in his father's position, would 'like to see his father dead.'[20] Although these actions are strictly neither witchcraft nor sorcery, they are associated with witchcraft and sorcery in that they are horrifying violations of socially accepted behaviour; the association is reinforced by the belief that these crimes, like witchcraft, sometimes result in personal harm.

Witchcraft does not necessarily involve the use of some preternatural force: to lie in wait for and assault someone who passes along a path is labelled *uroyi* (witchcraft),[21] also to poison someone with cattle dip, the effects of which are well known to all. Although witches are believed to have special powers to do their evil, these need to be no more unnatural to the Shona than, for example, the power of a scientist with a knowledge of germ warfare would be to us. It is not so much the means used that classifies an action as witchcraft or sorcery; it is rather the evil intentions of the witch, together with the secret and furtive way he puts them into practice.

It might appear that witchcraft does not always involve a deliberate intention to do harm.[22] Thus if a person's crops have an extraordinarily good yield, he may well be regarded as a witch or sorcerer. Yet it is an acceptable and common practice to use 'medicines' which, without causing anyone any harm, are believed to produce a more bountiful harvest. If, however, anybody's crops are singularly better than those of others in the community, it is presumed that an unfair advantage has been gained through, for example, the use of evil 'medicines' involving incest or murder; when a man sees that his own crops are significantly poorer than his neighbour's, he may readily assume that the neighbour's success has been gained to his

---

20. Holleman 1949, p. 36.
21. Cited by Fr. M. Hannan, SJ, in Gelfand 1967a, p. x.
22. Fr M. Hannan, SJ, expresses this view in his foreword to Gelfand 1967a, (p. x).

disadvantage. Another example of witchcraft without apparent harm is found in the belief that witches are able to enter a house in which people are sleeping, to remove the head of a sleeper, play ball with it and return it to its proper place, leaving no trace of their activity and in no way affecting the sleeper, who does not even know what has happened. In fact, the belief clearly arises from the concept of a witch who is thoroughly evil and who cares neither for the dignity nor the rights of her victims: it is at least distasteful to have one's head used as a football. Witchcraft is thoroughly evil and anything that a witch may do in the practice of her craft is evil, precisely because it is witchcraft.

Witchcraft is the paradigm of all evil and anti-social behaviour, but not all such behaviour is witchcraft. Thus to injure or even to kill a person in an open fight is not normally witchcraft, though a witch may be involved as a third party. Simple theft in which the thief is simply out to further his own ends is not normally witchcraft, though theft intended as a personal attack is likely to arouse suspicions of witchcraft, and the use of 'medicines' by the thief to avoid detection is certainly witchcraft.

In this respect, what appears to be witchcraft, to one party may seem perfectly justifiable to another. Thus if a man believes he is suffering from the 'medicines' another used to protect his home or his crops from intrusion or theft, he may regard the use of these 'medicines' as witchcraft, while the owner of the property would maintain that he had acted well within his rights. Similarly an adulterer suffering from the 'medicines' used by a jealous husband, may accuse the husband of witchcraft, while the latter denies the charge claiming that his action was perfectly justifiable. The spirit of a person who was owed a beast before he died, may inflict disease on the family of the debtor, which would appear quite natural and even laudable to the spirit's family who stand to gain; the debtors, however, may accuse the spirit's family of practising witchcraft or sorcery.[23]

So witchcraft can refer to any threat, involving an element of furtiveness, to personal security by the violation of the human person or of human life, or by the violation of any deeply held value. A witch or sorcerer (*muroyi*) is a person in any way responsible for such a violation.

Suspicions of witchcraft

Although practically any misfortune can be attributed to witchcraft or

---

23. Howman 1948, pp. 9f.

sorcery, there are certain types of events particularly associated with these practices. Any death is likely to be attributed to witchcraft. Sickness of a pregnant mother, or of the mother or child soon after birth, are also likely to be attributed to witchcraft, and an abortion or the death of a small child is often interpreted as witchcraft on the part of the mother. The sudden and sharp pains of rheumatic disorders are associated with witchcraft, as are diseases of an uncanny nature such as 'mamhepo', a contagious psychological affliction making children delirious. The appearance or repeated appearance of will-o'-the-wisp, or of the snakes, owls or other animals associated with witchcraft, is likely to arouse suspicions that there is a witch in the community, especially if thoughts are directed to the possibility of witchcraft by friction or other troubles within the community.

Open accusations of witchcraft are almost always preceded by tension and conflict within the community.[24] These may be the result of conflict over succession and leadership or they may come from disagreements over the distribution of family wealth or some other conflict within the family group: since such conflicts are supposed to be solved at the family level and should not be brought to a public court, the tensions created readily find expression in accusations of witchcraft, which provide an excuse for breaking up the group. But the tension may be psychological: when a person in his mature years has been thwarted in any way, and the smooth running of his life has been interrupted by illness, death or some other disappointment, he is likely to look for a possible witch or sorcerer. In tension arising from conflict or frustration, people are likely to nurture suspicions of unseen powers working against them.

From the Shona point of view there are normally two requirements for an accusation of witchcraft: a suspicious person, and proof that the suspect is using her evil powers in a suspicious event. In the case of a very serious event, even a previously unsuspected person may be convicted and punished as a result of divination; and in the case of a very suspicious (anti-social) person the slighest mishap may be sufficient to punish her. If both conditions are present, an accusation of witchcraft is almost certain to arise.

Strictly a witch is only proved to be such by divination, at which the accused person or at least a token of hers should be present, or in the past by ordeal. In the most well known form of ordeal, the suspect drinks a little 'medicine' provided by a traditional herbalist: vomiting is believed to show

---

24. This is supported by both Gelfand 1967a, p. 50, and Crawford 1967, p. 72, but it should be noticed that their material only covers the relatively rare cases of witchcraft accusations which have come before the courts.

innocence while diarrhoea or sickness indicates guilt. An accusation of witchcraft or sorcery should never be made without first consulting a diviner, and the accused can always claim the right to be tried by divination or ordeal: should the accusation prove to be false, the accused may demand heavy damages for defamation of character. Some cases, however, occur in which the accused is confronted without prior divination[25] either because the circumstantial evidence is considered sufficient to convict the suspect, or because the victim and his family are so incensed that they become imprudent. Even should the victim restrain himself in such a situation, he is likely to let the diviner know his thoughts.

We have already mentioned that extreme success is likely to result in suspicions of witchcraft, and an emotional or aggressive or unpopular person is likely to be suspected. Further characteristics associated with witchcraft are a sullen disposition, an unhappy demeanour and appearance, a quiet and reserved character, jealousy, selfishness and miserliness. A boastful and corpulent person, who openly displays his riches and his success, is also likely to be associated with witchcraft. A person who is not afraid of arousing envy or resentment is presumed to place his confidence in his own powers of witchcraft. Any kind of power may be associated with witchcraft (since power includes power to harm), and some express the view that no one would dare to put in a disputed claim for the chiefship without some witch in the family to support him. Activity during the night is another sure sign that a person is a witch.

Although barrenness or the death of infants are not always blamed on the woman concerned if some other scapegoat can be found, a childless woman is suspect when witchcraft is considered, partly because a witch is supposed to be fond of destroying her children, and also because a childless woman is expected to be jealous of those who have children. Barrenness is considered shameful and a traditional healer's fee for curing a woman of it is relatively high.[26] Repeated still births or repeated deaths of children in their infancy are very likely to arouse suspicions that the mother is a witch. A woman whose child dies as a result of an obstructed labour is almost certain to be called a witch since the Shona believe that obstructed labour is caused by adultery and can be relieved by confession: a woman who refuses

---

25. Crawford says these are 'comparatively few' (1967a, p. 161). But in Gelfand's study of 90 accusations coming before the courts between 1959 and 1963, only 27 were openly preceded by divination (1967, p. 77): some may have consulted a diviner and refused to mention it for fear of getting the diviner into trouble and incurring his anger and possible revenge.

26. See Gelfand 1964a, p. 105f.

to save her child by a timely confession must clearly be a witch. When a woman is married, she is brought at some expense as a stranger into her husband's family to produce children to his lineage: the tensions created when such a woman fails in her obligations to the family among whom she is living, create an atmosphere in which witchcraft accusations are likely to occur.[27]

Witchcraft accusations normally arise in a community that is already divided, whether by quarrels, unpaid debts or conflicts of character. It follows from this that accusations of witchcraft normally arise between persons living in the same community. Many accusations occur between close kin who cannot readily bring their differences to a public court. The wives of a lineage group are also likely to be accused of witchcraft: apart from the difficulties of child-bearing, these women are outsiders to the lineage in which they live and, until they have established themselves by bearing a number of children, they are likely to fall under suspicion if anything goes wrong without a ready explanation.

Complete strangers are not above suspicions of witchcraft.[28] A stranger is not normally allowed to come into contact with the food supply or with drying crops in case he should poison them, and a traditional Shona would not normally shake hands with a stranger lest the hand clasp of a witch should bring trouble to himself or to his family. People may be afraid to receive a total stranger, even an orphaned child, into a village for fear that he may be a witch. Nevertheless it is rare that contact with a stranger produces the type of tension likely to result in an accusation of witchcraft. Thus the study of a central Shona ward revealed that there were no suggestions of attacks by witches on Malawians living in the villages: although the Shona attributed this to powerful anti-witchcraft medicines in the possession of the Malawians, in fact the reason appears to be that Shona witchcraft accusations centre around the kinship group.[29] In towns and cities, the Shona believe that witchcraft is rife (an impression conveyed by the competition and insecurity of urban life), but explicit accusations are rare since these normally require more personal encounters than urban contact with neighbours and competitors usually provides.

So serious accusations of witchcraft normally follow tensions within a community accompanied by some misfortune. Nevertheless, in the Shona

---

27. See Crawford 1967, p. 156.
28. White people, however, are normally believed to be free from both the effects and the practice of witchcraft.
29. Garbett 1960, p. 4.

view an accusation is made because the accused is believed to be a witch, often confirmed to be a witch by divination, not simply because there was some social conflict. The fact that divination usually confirms prior suspicions only strengthens the Shona beliefs on the sort of person a witch is likely to be. Sometimes a diviner fails to confirm prior suspicions and occasionally makes a surprising accusation. If such a divination is accepted, the accused may be treated as any other witch, but some scepticism in the divination is likely to mitigate the treatment of the witch.

Reactions to witchcraft

If a person falls ill and witchcraft is thought to be the cause, it may happen that the case is not sufficiently serious to name and accuse the witch, or that the diviner does not wish to expose himself to the penalties that the law imposes on such an accusation. When the witch is not named, treatment is sought from a traditional herbalist or a faith-healer (western medicine can only be a subsidiary aid when witchcraft is the ultimate cause). Treatment may involve simple herbal medication, 'sucking out' the witchcraft, or exorcism either by traditional ritual or by faith-healers. The treatment of the results or symptoms of witchcraft may be the only action taken, or it may coincide with action to remove the influence of the witch behind it. In any case, should the attempts at a cure fail, the patient's family are likely to take further action to find out who the witch is.

A witch or sorcerer is believed to know the antidotes to his or her poisons. If the disease believed to have been caused by witchcraft becomes serious, the patient's family may try to discover the witch by divination in order to obtain the required remedy by persuasion or threat. The remedy is usually a herbal concoction mixed with thin porridge which the witch sips herself before administering to her victim.[30] Occasionally, before the witch is publicly exposed, all the women of the community may be told to administer a little thin porridge to a witchcraft victim: this gives the witch an opportunity to cure her victim and thus to save herself from detection and punishment.[31] But such action is extremely rare in practice and in any case if no cure takes place, the victim's family is likely to introduce proceedings to reveal the person of the witch.

When a diviner indicates a witch from a number of people, he does not

---

30. Cf. Crawford 1967, pp. 267ff; Gelfand 1966a, p. 75.
31. Howman 1948, p. 11.

usually openly state who the witch is, but identifies her by some sign: he may for example pluck a little hair from her head or, if she is not present but gave instead a token to the consulting party, he may simply return the token. Also, when a witch is named in her absence, she may be informed by someone placing ash or possibly a symbol for a stretcher in her doorway at night. The use of these signs as opposed to verbal accusations may be partly due to fear of the law against accusations of witchcraft, but another reason for them is that people are reluctant and afraid to confront a known witch openly.

Although in theory a witch is able to harm people at a distance, the Shona recognise that allegations of witchcraft generally occur within the local group, and the power of a witch is assumed to some extent to be limited to her locality. Thus a person who believes himself to be bewitched may try to free himself of the evil influence by moving to a new home some distance away, beyond the social sphere of the suspected witch. A similar effect may be obtained when the witch is driven out of the locality, as when a suspected wife is sent home.[32] Thus witchcraft allegations are often a prelude to the break up of a community, with one section hiving off, either in defence of an alleged witch whom others want expelled, or in order to escape from a witch in the settled community. Nevertheless, further trouble may readily be blamed on the continued influence of a powerful witch from whom spatial distance is not a reliable safeguard.

More important than locality and spatial distance is social contact. The supposed action of a witch normally affects those who have social contact with her, and she may be accused of harming any of her social contacts wherever they may be. Thus when a witch is expelled from a community, or when a family moves homestead after a death is believed to have been caused by witchcraft, or when a village community splits after accusations of witchcraft, the important consideration is to break all contact with the witch: to place the witch at a distance is only a means to this end. Often a person believes himself to be the victim of a witch living miles away — possibly past conflict was the reason for witch or victim moving home; but rarely does a person believe himself to be bewitched by someone with whom he has had no contact at all, though the contact may be no more than, for example, the witch and the victim applying for the same job.

---

32. A suspected wife may be rejected even by her own family, but more often she is taken back and her family may refuse to accept that she is in fact a witch (cf. Holleman 1952a, p. 279). I discuss the connection between social relations and believed causality in Bourdillon 1974c.

Although government legislation against the accusation and punishment of witches has reduced the incidence of physical attacks on suspected witches, so great is the anger that is sometimes roused against the witch that in spite of the penalties of the law, physical violence to a convicted person and her property remains a real possibility. In cases where people are particularly incensed, either because of the nature of the affliction believed to have been caused by witchcraft or because of the attitude of the accused person, the convicted witch is liable to be assaulted or even beaten to death.[33] The assault is to some extent a ritualized way of expressing indignation, and a person arrested for murder or rape is also liable to be assaulted. Apart from a physical beating, the witch may also be driven away by, for example, having all her property burnt — preferably anonymously so that the witch does not know who the aggressor is.

The whole community may take part in the punishment of a witch, or at least provide passive co-operation, since to be a witch is a public crime against the community. In the past, serious accusations of witchcraft were supposed to be referred to the chief or headman who was responsible for the trial (normally by divination or ordeal) and punishment of a witch, and even today chiefs and headmen occasionally risk their office by taking an active part in the divination of witchcraft. But now these authorities rarely, if ever, have anything to do with the execution of a witch (presumably for fear of losing their posts), and this sometimes becomes a matter for private revenge. Shona people often say that in the past witches were always put to death or driven away by the chief, and they blame the government law against witchcraft accusations for present troubles and misfortunes, which result, it is supposed, from the freedom now given to witches. Certainly some people make use of this freedom by acquiring a reputation for witchcraft and then holding considerable sway over the community in which they live through the judicious use of thinly veiled threats.

The tradition of rites to cure a witch suggests, however, that even in precolonial times death or exile did not always follow a conviction of witchcraft, and now only a small minority of cases results in physical violence.[34]

---

33. Cf. e.g., Crawford 1967, pp. 253ff.
34. Out of 35 cases of witchcraft accusations appearing before the courts between 1899 and 1930, the accused was not apparently affected in 27 cases; in 108 cases between 1959 and 1963, 73 resulted in neither attack nor injury to the accused (Gelfand 1967, p. 60).
   In Crawford's study of cases appearing before the courts from 1956 to 1962, of 28 witches convicted by divination, 4 were violently treated, 14 were ostracized, divorced or otherwise adversely affected without violence, and 10 suffered no recorded consequences; of 19 persons accused of witchcraft without prior divination, 8 were violently treated, 5

After the first emotional reaction to a conviction of witchcraft has subsided, it is unlikely that any violence will take place since the fear of the witch overcomes the desire to punish her. Also a witch's family may prefer to keep it secret if they are told privately that one of their number is a witch, whether because they think it advantageous to have a witch in the family, or to prevent scandal and suspicion falling on the whole family; whatever the reason, secrecy precludes the possibility of physical violence.

It is possible to have a known witch living in a community provided she does not use her powers for harm. People are careful to treat her with respect in order not to aggravate her into using her witchcraft: a woman may be seen chatting apparently amicably with a person who is believed to have killed her own son, rather than provoke the witch into further acts of violence against her family. A witch may even be permitted to wander around the homestead at night when she wishes to. If a witch continues to live a normal life after she has been accused, the diviner's findings may be forgotten and the witch may be reinstated in the community, possibly on the presumption that she has been cured. A friend of a convicted witch may ignore the divination on the grounds that diviners sometimes make mistakes, and a popular person is less likely to be badly treated on being divined to be a witch, if indeed the result of the divination is ever accepted. But no one knows when a witch may strike, and a convicted witch is generally avoided at least until the affair blows over. Should an event indicative of witchcraft take place within the community at some future time, forgotten divinations are likely to be remembered and reinstated witches are likely to become suspect again.

When a witch recieves no observable punishment, the victim or his family may resort to vengeance magic against her, usually in the form of some 'poison' obtained from a traditional herbalist. In the case of death by witchcraft, the family of the deceased may perform rites to turn the deceased's spirit into an avenging *ngozi*,[35] a powerful and dangerous spirit capable of causing havoc in an enemy's family, in which case the witch may expect a number of deaths in her family unless she pays a substantial fine to the family of the avenging spirit. 'Medicines' (sorcery in the eyes of some) are also used to take revenge for crimes other than witchcraft, and the fear of such retaliation is a deterrent against crime and an encouragement to reconciliation between families in conflict.

---

were punished without violence and 6 suffered no recorded consequences (cf. Crawford 1967, p. 250). It should be noticed that these are all cases which appeared before the courts and are not representative of all incidents of witchcraft accusations.

35. *Ngozi* will be considered in chapter 9.

The reaction of a person accused of witchcraft varies considerably. There are some who readily admit to being witches and confess to all kinds of nefarious nocturnal activities associated with traditional hereditary witches. A woman who stubbornly refuses to confess her witchcraft is likely to be treated more harshly than one who shows some co-operation by admitting her crimes, and this may be the motive for some confessions. A person might also confess to witchcraft because she accepts the validity of divination although she was not aware of being a witch, and confession is the first step towards reconciliation with the community and a cure for her disposition. On the other hand, there are some witches who eagerly recount a diary of horrific deeds which they claim to have performed and are ready to show evidence of their nocturnal wanderings.[36] This may be due to the psychotic state of the person concerned, but also relevant is the status a woman may receive in the community arising from the fear and respect shown towards a known witch; this is a particularly likely motive in the case of a childless woman or a widow or divorcee who has not been remarried, all of whom in normal circumstances would have low status within the community. But even if people recognise that the motive for the confession is its consequent influence over the community, they reason that anyone who openly confesses the crimes of witchcraft has so little respect for values that she must in fact be a witch, and a person who boasts about being a witch confirms the Shona belief in the perversion of witchcraft.

Other persons may show anger at being accused of witchcraft and hotly deny the charge. An accused woman may be bewildered by the divination or indignant at it, and an influential person may be able to get the decision reversed. But normally nothing can be done against the result of a divination, and the accused must either escape from the community or simply wait until the affair blows over. The latter course would be made easier were the accused to confess her guilt and undergo a ritual cure by a herbalist or faith-healer. Very occasionally a conviction of witchcraft may lead to suicide,[37] which indicates how seriously such a conviction can be taken by the accused, and how intolerable the reputation may be.

During the war of liberation, a number of persons were executed by guerrillas on the grounds that they practised witchcraft. In one chiefdom I have been in contact with, there was one such execution, that of a woman who had long had a reputation of witchcraft and who was held responsible at divinations following a recent death. The guerrillas obtained the

---

36. Cf. e.g. Crawford 1967, pp. 49 – 56.
37. Crawford 1967, p. 245.

approval of the senior spirit medium of the chiefdom before carrying out the execution. Generally, it appears that the execution of witches had the approval of local communities, and indicates the strength of feeling against the white government's protection of people who were believed to be witches.

Witchcraft in daily life

Although a serious accusation is a comparatively rare phenomenon among contemporary Shona, the belief in witchcraft is very real and very strong. Many hamlets in the rural areas and not a few urban homes are protected against witchcraft by ritual and charms. Persons often wear charms and take medicines to protect themselves from witchcraft. It can be argued that the Shona believe there is a continual threat from persons endowed with evil just as every European today accepts that we are continually exposed to germs.

The belief in witchcraft has an influence on attention to good manners and etiquette. No one would want to show the unlikable characteristics associated with a witch. Certain customs, such as sharing food or eating and drinking from the same pot or plate, reflect a fear of witchcraft or of being suspected of witchcraft or sorcery: thus a traditional host should take a taste of any food or drink offered to a guest 'to take away witchcraft' (to show that there is none). I have already mentioned a cautious attitude to strangers arising from a fear of witchcraft. Also the fear that discarded property or anything coming from the body could be used to bewitch a person results in a high standard of cleanliness and hygiene.

Witchcraft beliefs act as a deterrent to crime. A man may be afraid of picking up objects found lying around in case they have been bewitched; this applies particularly to wandering domestic animals which may have been involved in an exorcism bringing evil and calamity to anyone who took possession of them. The fear of being bewitched encourages good relations within a community, and the fear of revenge or protective medicines makes crime against members of the community seem dangerous even when detection is escaped. Also a reluctance to wander late at night for fear of being suspected of witchcraft or, worse, for fear of meeting a witch on her nocturnal escapades, minimizes the possibility of petty theft and like crimes.

It has been argued that witchcraft beliefs comprise a barrier to material progress.[38] A man who has significantly altered his life style in accordance with technological and economic advancement is endangered in two ways: he may readily be suspected of using witchcraft to obtain the wealth necessary for his change of life and, secondly, he is likely to arouse envy and so become the victim of witchcraft or sorcery. A man who through hard work is slightly better off than the common run is usually respected, but in a traditional community there is little incentive to outstanding success, and if it is achieved it should not be openly displayed and flaunted. In communities which have had more contact with European ways, however, people are not so afraid to stand out from the rest: indeed this has become the ideal for most, but they must still take precautions against jealous witchcraft. In practice most communities have members who are conspicuous for the material progress they have made, so belief in witchcraft is not so much a barrier as a slight deterrent to material progress.

The Shona belief in witchcraft is also relevant to their general reaction against the white people. Some of the older people blame *chirungu* (meaning anything associated with the whites) for the troubles of present times ranging from bad crops and poverty to various social tensions. They base this vague and not always justifiable opinion on the law preventing the conviction and punishment of witches who are consequently believed to be more numerous and more free in their activities than they were in the past — and certainly some people who foster the reputation they have as witches, flaunt this freedom.

Witchcraft beliefs provide a rationalization of suspicion and tension. Although to the modern western mind these beliefs may appear as irrational superstitions which can divide a community or bring unjust opprobrium on persons who have fallen victim to vague suspicion, to the Shona mind the beliefs are based on a real experience of the world about them. Evil, troubles, sickness are undeniable and demand explanation; social tension and conflict frequently arise, a clear sign that some people are careless of the good of their neighbours; bad people are to be found and appear at times to have their way; some of these claim to be witches; people do sometimes suffer after quarrels or threats; some people do have knowledge not available to other members of the community; suspicions of witchcraft are often confirmed by subsequent events, especially by divination. These empirical observations may not prove the reality of witchcraft to the satisfaction of western science, but they do give some credence to Shona beliefs.

---

38. Gelfand 1967a, pp. 168f.

Witchcraft eradication

There have been various attempts from outside Shona society to eradicate the belief in witchcraft and the practices associated with it. Prominent among these was the early attempt by the colonial administration to eliminate accusations of witchcraft.[39] The government was convinced that belief in witchcraft is basically false and that the process of discovering and trying witches through divination and ordeal is thoroughly unreliable, often resulting in the conviction and punishment of innocent persons: accordingly an ordinance was introduced to convict any person who tries to injure another or his property by means of witchcraft, and also any person who imputes to another the use of non-natural means to cause disease or injury to person or property. The law was normally applied only against those who made accusations of witchcraft: witches have escaped conviction, even on some occasions when clear and concrete evidence of witchcraft practice was produced against them. Although people undoubtedly need to be protected from false accusations of witchcraft, there is some justification for the Shona view that the law provides protection for witches.[40] Certainly the law has failed in its aim of diminishing witchcraft beliefs.

Besides government administrators, many European missionaries have denied or ignored the Shona belief in witchcraft and have forbidden their converts to take part in associated practices. None of these measures have been significantly successful in destroying the belief in witchcraft, and the forbidden practices have on the whole merely become clandestine.

Within traditional African society there have been periodic attempts to eradicate witchcraft, but these attempts have been concerned with curing witches of their evil ways and in no way question the validity of the common beliefs. One such attempt was made through the famous Mchape movement in the 1930s, which originated in Malawi and spread throughout central Africa.[41] The agents of this movement were young men, dressed in European clothes, who claimed to be followers of the founder of the movement. They would arrive in a village, assemble all the inhabitants, give them a sermon on the evils of witchcraft and then line them up for the witchcraft ritual. In this, witches were allegedly detected with the aid of small mirrors and were ordered to give up their hoards of harmful

---

39. The current *Witchcraft Suppression Act (Statute Law of Rhodesia*, Cap. 50) is contained in substance in the *Witchcraft Suppression Ordinance* (No. 14 of 1899).
40. Cf. Chavunduka 1980.
41. See Richards 1935; Marwick 1950, pp. 100f, 111f.

'medicines'. If they refused, the witchfinders were reputed to find with unfailing perspicacity where these medicines were hidden. After detecting the witches, the witchfinders proceeded to cure them by giving each a sip of the famous *mchape* medicine which, it was claimed, would cause any witch who returned to her evil ways to die. It was believed that any witch who escaped detection by refusing to pass in front of the magic mirror would be caught and exposed at a second coming of the founder of the movement. In addition, the witchfinders sold protective charms against witchcraft. Although from the point of view of the officials this movement may have been primarily a money-making racket, for the people who welcomed it (including many Shona communities) it was an opportunity to rid the community of the troubles and tensions associated with witchcraft. They were ready to pay well for such an utopian situation.

There have also been a number of lesser movements acting in different ways but to achieve the same end. One of these is the Mai Chaza Church, a *quasi* religious movement named after its foundress who was said to have come back from the dead to cleanse the country of witchcraft. The movement started in the early 1950s; it was very popular in central Shona country for ten years until the death of the foundress, and it still has some adherents today. The officials wear a uniform for ritual occasions at which they heal the sick and cure witches. Witches are invited to confess their witchcraft and to throw away all their charms and medicines into a pit; an official of the movement (in the old days usually the foundress herself) cures witches by touching each and sprinkling her with consecrated water. Many people travelled spontaneously to a cult centre to be cured of their witchcraft, and many communities got temporary relief from suspicions of witchcraft through the activities of this movement.[42]

Now prophets of the new independent Christian churches are often asked to cleanse a community of witchcraft. A prophet might be invited into a homestead, where he finds hidden medicines and charms in and around the houses and 'sees' any witch in the community. He destroys the charms and exorcises the witches, usually by commanding the evil spirit to leave its host in the tradition of the Christian gospels.

Rites against witchcraft feature in the practices of most independent African churches.[43] The principal religious celebrations of the year are

---

42. This information comes from conversations with my colleague, Professor G.L. Chavunduka. Cf. also Martin 1971, which emphasizes the healing practices of this church.
43. These will be considered later in chapter 11. It is interesting to notice that the Mchape movement stopped short of Karanga (Southern Shona) country where independent churches were strong.

often preceded by penitentiary rites, during which all members of the congregation confess their offences (including witchcraft) and are forgiven. In some churches members of the congregation must pass between two prophets who may add to a person's confessed offences faults which they claim to see through their prophetic vision, and the offence of witchcraft is a common addition. Witches are then cleansed or exorcised through prayer and a symbolic cleansing with consecrated water. The attitude of the independent churches towards witchcraft is one of the reasons for their popularity *vis-à-vis* the mission churches: as the Shona people explain, you can belong to a mission church and still be a witch, but you cannot be at once a member of an independent church and a practising witch. Witchcraft is considered to be the worst evil in Shona society, involving deliberate harm to members of a community, and yet it is ignored in the moral teachings of most mission churches, which claim to emphasize love of one's neighbour as a cardinal value.

So, even in a changing situation, the Shona remain convinced of the real evils of witchcraft, and they wish to be free of these evils. Especially in times of tension and stress in a community when suspicions of malevolence readily arise, members of the community may take active steps in the wishful hope that they can rid themselves of witchcraft and the evils associated with it. But the state of supposed freedom from witchcraft cannot last long. Even in the congregation of a church which emphasizes eradication of witchcraft, members of the congregation are believed to lapse occasionally into the practice of witchcraft and have to be cleansed. No utopian ideal can eliminate the evils of disease and death, or social conflict and frustration in a community. From the Shona point of view, these evils are evidence of the practice of witchcraft, so no eradication of witchcraft can endure.

8

Death and After

Death and burial

In all Shona institutions we have so far described, we find frequent references to the spirits and spiritual powers. In fact, the spirits of the dead are so much part of Shona life that they can aptly be called spirit elders, the senior members of the community who now act as spirits. To understand Shona attitudes towards them, it is useful to look at the rituals surrounding death, by which a person undergoes the change of status from being one of the living community to being a family spirit.

As is the case with most Shona rituals, the details of the rites surrounding death and burial vary from area to area, and they vary even for different clans within a given locality. Yet we can find a general structure of the rituals which is common to all or most Shona peoples.

When a person is seen to be dying he may be moved out of his homestead, but this appears to be mainly for his own comfort (away from the noise of children and others in the home) since the corpse is taken back to the room of the deceased immediately after death.[1] The dying man is expected to reveal the whereabouts of any hidden resources, arrange for the settlement of the outstanding debts, and to confess any outstanding offences against members of the community in order to avoid recriminations on surviving members of his family. He may be given traditional medicines to make his passing easier.[2]

At death, all relations and friends are informed, either by some ritual act such as beating a drum or blowing a horn audible in the neighbourhood of the deceased's home, or by word of mouth. The body is washed and prepared for burial by close kin among the Zezuru and Karanga,[3] but by an unrelated ritual friend possibly helped by non-agnatic kin in the north of Shona country. In the past the legs were usually flexed against the body, though now it is becoming customary to bury a corpse stretched out straight. The corpse is wrapped in a new cloth or blanket and laid on a reed sleeping mat (though now a coffin may be used). Sometimes a beast is ritually killed and its meat roasted and given to attendants; in any case, food is prepared for all attendants, who continue to arrive as the news of the death spreads.

When the corpse is ready for burial, all kinsmen and friends pay their last respects to the deceased, bringing a farewell present usually in the

1. Edwards 1929, pp. 34f.
2. Gelfand 1966a, p. 80; 1962, p. 132.
3. Gelfand 1959, p. 184; 1966a, p. 80.

form of a small coin. The donor places the gift near the head of the corpse and formally addresses the deceased: 'So-and-so, it is I your child (brother, sister, friend, etc.). You have left us today. Look after us well.' Some may make a slightly longer speech. Before leaving the corpse, each person respectfully claps his hands to the deceased.

It is generally believed that every person has two 'shadows', the black reflection of physical stature and also a white shadow which is *munhu*, the person, and which becomes the *mudzimu* (spirit) after death. The white shadow should disappear as soon as the person dies, but it may linger as a sign of the deceased's displeasure on the wall or floor of the room while the corpse is lying in state.[4] In such a situation, no one may enter the room or touch the corpse until the shadow disappears. A diviner may be consulted on the reason for the appearance of the shadow, which may be that some ritual has been omitted, that a witch is present, or that some relative or friend has failed to pay his respects to the deceased. In the last case, the person concerned may be summoned, or if he is not present a proxy may present a farewell token on his behalf.

I have not been able to discover the exact form this 'shadow' takes: it appears that no observer outside the family of mourners has seen one. But the readiness of relatives to see the shadow illustrates their fear of displeasing the deceased, and it also indicates the importance of each relative and friend paying his respects to the deceased and obtaining his goodwill. One reason for desiring the immediate disappearance of the shadow is that should it remain visible some witch may be able to rouse it to anger, which could be disastrous for the family of the deceased. We shall see that later in the funerary ceremonies care is taken to rest the spirit and to keep it 'cool'.

In many areas, people sing and dance in honour of the deceased outside the room in which the corpse is lying: the songs express the merits of the deceased and the grief of the community. This may go on thoughout the night if burial is to be deferred to the morning, in which case attendants are usually fed.

In central Shona country, tension is often relieved by the antics of one or more ritual friends *(sahwira)* who are honoured guests at the funeral, and who have a permanent joking relationship with the deceased and his or her family. A *sahwira* may freely make fun of the immediate relatives of the

---

4. Kumbirai 1966/7 V (July 1966). A number of accounts mention this shadow, though not all specify that it is white and some imply that it is dark: cf. Edwards 1929, p. 35; Shropshire 1931, p. 270; Holleman 1953, p. 28; Crawford 1967, pp. 211f.

deceased, and so break the intensity of mourning by introducing a certain amount of laughter into the proceedings.[5]

Normally the corpse is buried within twenty-four hours of death. In the case of a chief or headman, however, it lies in state for a longer period in order that representatives of the deceased's children can pay their last respects. The corpse may be kept for up to a week or a little more, and in one description of the burial rites of a chief the corpse was kept on a plaform in his hut for some months: the walls were kept free from cracks to prevent the spirit from escaping, pots were placed under the corpse to collect the body fluids, and any maggots falling from the body were carefully collected to be buried with the corpse since they may contain the spirit of the dead chief.[6] The death of a chief or headman does not usually involve such a long delay, but it may involve other elaborations, such as screening off the corpse from the eyes of commoners or shrouding it in the skin of a black ox.

Soon after death, an appropriate relative (the relationship varying with local custom) is appointed to choose and mark the site for the grave. A small cave or cleft in a rocky outcrop may be chosen, or the soft damp soil by a river bed or in an ant heap. The site is normally within a couple of kilometres of the homestead of the deceased, though Professor Holleman describes one case in which the grave, at the request of the deceased, was ten kilometres from his homestead, in the land from which his family originally came,[7] and graves of chiefs are often sited together in a remote spot far from any habitation and taboo to all except on ritual occassions. When the site has been chosen, relatives and friends of the deceased prepare the grave: a grave dug in soil is normally dug to a deapth of six feet and then an inlet is dug out to take the corpse.

Although now it is becoming more and more common for the family of the deceased to obtain a coffin, the corpse is still often carried to the grave simply wrapped in a clean white cloth and tied to a bier especially made for the occasion. In some areas, the task of cutting poles and bark to make the bier is the task of sons-in-law to the family of the deceased, since it is associated with the chores they are supposed to perform for the family in everyday life. The body is often carried around the homestead in a last

---

5. See 1978, p. 125. This appears to be a relatively new institution in Shona society, perhaps a Malawian influence.
6. Edwards 1929, p. 38.
7. Holleman 1953, p. 11.

farewell before the funeral procession sets off briskly towards the grave.

The funeral procession may be announced by a drum or horn and attendants may dance or sing funeral songs, though in some areas the funeral is conducted in silence. There may also be a certain amount of wild, aggressive behaviour such as throwing sticks or spears into the air, leaping about and pulling at branches of trees, and in the case of an important person discharging fire-arms in honour of the deceased.

All adults take part in the procession to the grave except possibly some young women married into the family of the deceased who are assigned the tasks of purifying the house in which the corpse lay (traditionally by smearing it with fresh cow dung) and preparing a meal for all attendants at the funeral. Young children are not allowed to take part: they used to be shut away in a hut or granary for fear that sight of the corpse would make them blind, but now people do not bother too much — they say that since the coming of the white people it does not matter.

Men married into the family and unrelated friends carry the bier out of the homestead and distant kin may help on the way to the grave. The body is at first carried with the head towards the homestead until some distance from the homestead it is lowered to the ground to give the spirit a rest. The attendants sit and salute the spirit, the men respectfully clapping their hands and the women shrilling. Before proceeding the corpse is turned around two or three times to make it difficult for the spirit to find its way back to the homestead should the spirit wish to return and scourge the community. This may happen two or three times, and after the last stop the corpse is carried with the head towards the grave. Soon after reaching the grave, singing and wailing stops and the burial takes place in silence.

Among the Manyika, the grave may be lined with wet clay to keep the spirit 'cool';[8] and to keep the spirit 'cool' is one motive for burying a corpse in damp soil.[9] In some areas, a person dying of leprosy, a disease which is believed to be caused by the high god, is customarily buried in swampy ground to 'cool' the body; elsewhere the custom is (or was) for a leper to be burnt and his bones and ashes thrown into a pool.[10] We shall see that the metaphor of 'cooling' occurs frequently in funerary rites and that the

8. Shropshire 1931, p. 270.
9. Broderick 1956, p. 61.
10. Holleman 1953, p. 38; Edwards 1929, p. 40.

metaphor occurs in situations which are associated with spirits and in which tension is felt. There is certainly tension at a funeral, which is evident in the complete silence in which the corpse is lowered into the grave.

There are various rules about which way the corpse should face, depending on local and family tradition: I attended one funeral at which the corpse was laid three times in different positions while two elders argued about the way the head should point. Normally the corpse is laid on its right side 'so that he cannot kill the people so easily with his left arm',[11] and facing the opening of the grave. The corpse is sealed off with half the sleeping mat on which it is lying and the grave is filled with earth and stones. In the case of a chief or senior spirit medium, a hollow reed may be placed against the ear of the corpse, leading out of the grave to facilitate the emergence of the spirit. The poles of the bier are broken and thrown into the grave before it is filled, together with anything else without value and associated with the funeral procession. In most areas, all present throw a handful of soil into the grave to cast away evil and misfortune, and this action may be performed on behalf of those who are absent.[12] The grave may be left at ground level, though nowadays it usually has a mound of stones over it, or a stone border with a large stone at the head. Traditionally a dish, a calabash or cup and a small pot are punctured (to ensure them against theft) and left over the grave: these are to ease the deceased's passage to a new environment, leaving him with the essential utensils for food, drink and washing to which he is accustomed.

Sometimes further elaborate rituals are carried out at the grave, such as the sacrifice of a goat which has been brought in the funeral procession.[13] There may, however, be no more than a sprinkling of the grave with water to cool the spirit and a short address to the family spirits asking that the deceased be received and cared for, before the attendants respectfully salute the spirit and return to the homestead. The area around the grave is carefully swept with the branch of a tree (which is afterwards left on the grave as a shade) so that any footprints indicating violation of the grave will be clearly visible on inspection the following morning. In some areas, representatives of the deceased's family secretly guard the grave overnight to make sure that no witches come to desecrate the corpse. Sometimes a thorny branch is left on the path away from the grave to discourage the

---

11. Shropshire 1931, p. 270.
12. Cf. Edwards 1929, p. 36; Gelfand 1966a, p. 81.
13. Gelfand 1959, pp. 186f.

spirit of the deceased from returning home to worry his family.

Before returning to the homestead, all who took part in the funeral must purify themselves by washing their hands and their faces or sprinkling themselves with medicated water. Some of those who had close contact with the corpse may have to wash themselves completely and take prophylactic medicines as well.

Back at the homestead, a meal of meat and stiff porridge is provided for all who have helped or taken part in the funeral: the considerable expense involved is shared out between the family of the deceased. The homestead must be purified of the ashes of fires that burnt while waiting for the burial, and of any valueless items associated with the deceased or with the funeral. There may be further rites involving the adoption of mourning symbols (commonly a widow wears a bark string around her neck and close relatives have some hair cut or shaved off), collecting the deceased's possessions to be sealed away in a granary until the succession ceremony, and staking claims to the deceased's estate. Nothing personal belonging to the deceased should be available for use until after the inheritance ceremony.

At this stage the spirit of the deceased is thought to be vaguely 'outside', wandering about the veld or floating somewhere in the air, or possibly in the ground, or finding a temporary residence in some large tree.[14] The white shadow is invisible but is believed to be somehow in or about the grave.

A grave always carries with it the danger associated with death, but it also has a sacred character. The salutation of the funeral party before they leave the grave is reminiscent of salutations at spirit shrines and is intended as an honour to the deceased. Graves are always avoided except for ritual purposes, and mingled with the fear of death is a fear of the occult powers which are believed to linger around any grave. Thus a case of madness in a small boy may be attributed to his stumbling across a grave while herding cattle in the veld, and other mishaps may be attributed to the proximity of graves.

At death, a new spirit with its appropriate superior powers enters the conceptual world of the community. Nobody knows quite how the spirit will react to its new environment nor what secret grudges the deceased may have harboured before his death, which explains the necessity of keeping the spirit 'cool' and of discouraging it from returning to the homestead. In

---

14. Holleman 1953, p. 2.

the Shona idiom, as in the English, the concept of 'coolness' carries over tones of calm, placid peacefulness; the opposite of 'cool' is 'hot', much as the concept is used in the English expression, 'hot-tempered'. In the social upheaval caused by death in the community, calm is a benefit, and calm is essential for the spirit of the deceased, which is believed to have passed from the life of the living community to a completely novel existene in the community of the spirits. The presumed readiness of the deceased to use his newly acquired spiritual powers, and his possible touchiness after the upheaval, is a powerful sanction for performing the rituals properly.

The power the spirit is believed to wield, and the consequent danger, depends to some extend on the status of the deceased. Graves of chiefs are treated with special respect and anyone approaching them frivolously is supposed to be in danger of his life. A person who has acquired full adult status requires more 'cooling' ritual than a person who died without progeny, indicating that the former is believed to be more dangerous. At the funeral of a very small child, the danger is considered to be so slight that some attendants do not bother to purify themselves after it. Most people, however, maintain that such an omission is wrong: as one old man put it, 'A dead child is a person of God (*munhu waMwari):* we clap to him (the spirit of the child, before leaving the grave).' Even the weakest of spirits is feared and must be treated with respect.

At this stage the spirit is regarded as unpredictable. Its name is not mentioned with the names of other spirit elders in prayer or ritual, and in many areas it may not be honoured in the homestead. It is said that should the spirit cause illness among the family it has left soon after the funeral and before subsequent funerary rites have been performed, the situation is serious and the sick person is likely to die. 'Who knows if he does not feel angry with us because of some old grievance?'[15]

After the funeral

Immediately after the burial (if this did not take place during the illness preceding death), near kinsmen of the deceased usually appoint a delegation to consult a diviner on the cause of death. Among the Korekore in the north of Shona country, they may decide that the death was quite natural

---

15. Holleman 1953, p. 22.

and that a diviner need not be consulted, especially if the deceased was very elderly: they might say that an old man died because he was 'tired' or that the death was caused by the high god alone. In the case of a younger person, however, death is always considered to be unnatural and in most areas every death is considered to demand divination. Even when the kinsmen think that a death was natural or that they know the cause of the death, they are still likely to arrange a consultation with a diviner in order to confirm their opinions.

The diviner chosen is usually a specialist in divining the causes of deaths, and a man living some distance away is preferred in order to avoid the possibility of prejudice. The delegation may be prepared to make a week's journey to consult a famous diviner.[16] The fee paid for divining the cause of death is usually considerably higher than the normal fees charged by a diviner, on account of the association with witchcraft and danger that death involves. As in other cases of divination, a skilful diviner usually manages to produce an answer that confirms his clients' prior suspicions, and if he comes up with something they consider to be grossly unlikely, they are free to consult a second opinion. The final outcome is generally that they believe their own suspicions to have been confirmed by an un-biased outsider with powers of divination.

Regarding the cause of death, we have remarked that some Shona accept the possibility of a purely natural death: even when a diviner has been consulted over the cause of death, he may diagnose that there was no witch or spirit involved.[17] But many Shona do not accept this as a possibility and believe that any death is caused by evil spirits or more probably by witchcraft.[18] Witchcraft is thought to be the most common cause of death even among those who believe that a purely natural death is possible.

When the diviner diagnoses the cause of death to be a spirit, he prescribes some ritual action to prevent further catastrophies. The Shona say that family spirit elders (*midzimu*) never directly cause death in their own families, but they may withdraw their protection if they are displeased, and allow some witch or evil spirit to do its work. If such is believed to be the case, the diviner usually finds some ritual in honour of the spirit elders which has been neglected for some time and he states what is re-quired of the family to make amends: often it involves the sacrifice of a

---

16. Gelfand 1962, p. 110.
17. Cf. Gelfand 1959, pp. 188f.
18. Cf. Gelfand 1966a, p. 47; Powell 1953, p. 17.

beast to the spirit elder and libations of millet beer. The principal cause may, however, be diagnosed as the avenging spirit (*ngozi*) of some close relative or acquaintance who suffered serious wrong at the hands of the deceased or his family. Such a spirit is believed to be very dangerous and must be appeased directly.

Most commonly death is believed to be caused by witchcraft or 'poisoning' by some malevolent person. People say that in the past, when a diviner identified a witch guilty of having caused the death, the delegation would go immediately to the hut of the person nominated and accuse him of witchcraft, a charge which could be refuted only by successfully vomiting up the ordeal poison. It is said that if the accused failed to prove his innocence through an ordeal, he and his family would have to flee or they would be driven out or killed. Alternatively, the family of the deceased may have been prepared to settle for compensation of a girl or the brideprice equivalent from the witch's family.[19] If, however, the accused were proved innocent by the ordeal, his accusers would have to pay him the equivalent compensation. Nowadays, the revenge on a person believed to be guilty of murder by means of witchcraft has to be more circumspect: it may consist in making life generally so unpleasant for the suspected witch that he is forced to move out of the community, or it may involve the use of vengeance magic against the witch.

The person accused of being a witch is usually some very unpopular member of the community or someone who is supposed to have had some reason for wishing to harm the deceased. This provides a further reason why everyone must be so careful to show their respect and goodwill towards the deceased during the funeral ceremonies. Apart from the possibility of angering the spirit, to fail to give a parting present to the spirit of the deceased is likely to arouse suspicions of malevolence and witchcraft — or rather such a failure is anti-social and would be unthinkable by any except a witch.

There is usually a further ceremony shortly after the funeral, which varies considerably according to local custom and to circumstances. It may involve an elaborate ceremony akin to the rite of settling the spirit with formal libations of millet beer at a temporary shrine in the bush or, more commonly, it may involve little more than a beer party for relatives and friends of the deceased. The delay between the funeral and this ceremony can be as little as ten days (the time required to brew millet beer) and it

---

19. Powell 1953, p. 17; Gelfand 1962, p. 129.

can be a number of months. In any case, grain contributed by guests at the funeral is brewed into millet beer and relatives and friends of the deceased are invited to attend.

The ceremony serves a number of functions, one of which is to gather all the deceased's kin including those who were too far from home to attend the funeral. It also provides an opportunity for the kin of the deceased to gather at his home when the deceased died and was buried elsewhere. At this gathering, the estate of the deceased can be collected and, if necessary, arrangements can be made for its safe keeping pending the inheritance ceremony. The dissolution of marriages or the care of the deceased's family may also be arranged at this time. The delegation which consulted the diviner on the cause of death can reveal the result of the divination to this gathering of kin who can then agree on what action, if any, they should take. Occasionally, the full inheritance ritual takes place at this ceremony shortly after death, but it is normally deferred until after the later ceremony of settling the spirit of the deceased.

A second function of the ceremony shortly after the funeral is to mark the end of official mourning. Any ritual signs of mourning, such as a bark string worn by a widow, are removed or ended at this ceremony. Also the weeping as the deceased is remembered early in the ceremony slowly gives way to gaier singing and dancing as the influence of millet beer takes its effect on the participants, and many Shona blatantly admit that they brew beer on these occasions to help them to drown their sorrows in a drunken stupor.

From the ritual point of view, the main purpose of the ceremony is said to be to 'cool' the spirit. Prior to the ceremony, the spirit of the deceased is greatly feared and people sometimes say that should it cause illness in the family it has left, death would certainly follow. After a few weeks have passed, the tensions arising from death in the community begin to relax. This relaxation is helped by the end of official mourning and the preliminary settlement of the affairs of the deceased at the second funerary ceremony. The settling of the community reduces the tense fear in which they hold the spirit. Thus the unpredictable spirit is said to be 'cooled' by the ceremony: most Shona say that from now on it can influence the lives of its descendants in a friendly way just as any other spirit elder can. Nevertheless, at this stage the spirit of the deceased may be honoured only outside the family homestead: the full status of family spirit guardian is acquired only at a later funerary rite, the rite of settling the spirit.

Settling the spirit of the deceased

In most areas, the most important funerary rites for a deceased man take place a year or more after burial[20] when the spirit of the deceased receives the full status of a family spirit guardian (the ceremony is not usually performed for women or unmarried boys). Again there are considerable local variations: in some areas the principal rites take place at the grave of the deceased, in others the grave is left untouched and the ceremony is performed at some tree in the bush. Usually a beast is sacrificed to the spirit, but this is not always necessary. Even the names of the ceremony vary: *kurova guva* (to beat the grave) or *kugadzira mudzimu* (to prepare the spirit) in central and south Shona country, and *kutamba n'ombe, kutamba mudzimu* (to dance to the sacrificial beast, spirit), *kutora mudzimu* (to bring the spirit home) or *bona* (just the name of the ceremony) in the north. Yet in spite of the differences in name, time and performance of the ceremony, in all areas it has a common pattern and function. A large number of relatives and friends of the deceased gather to sing and dance in honour of the spirit through most of one night; there follows in the morning a procession to the grave or some other spot outside the homestead where various rituals are performed including generous libations of millet beer, and the spirit is requested to come home; this is followed by further music and feasting in the homestead to welcome the spirit home.

The ritual of settling the spirit of the deceased ideally takes place about a year after burial. Since a large circle of kin and acquaintances gathers for the ceremony, it is usually held in the dry season when there is little work to be done in the fields and gardens, and when grain from the previous harvest is still plentiful. Since a large quantity of grain is required for the feasting and drinking, in times of scarcity the ceremony might be postponed a year or two unless the spirit demands an earlier performance by making someone in the family ill. There could be other reasons for delays: the family of the deceased might delay the ceremony for a number of years if nobody is prepared to take over responsibility for elderly widows of the deceased (a matter that should be decided immediately after the ceremony), or it may be delayed on account of poverty or sheer apathy until sickness in the family stirs the head into action. Difficulty in settling the estate of a wealthy man, which should immediately follow the

---

20. An exception is to be found among some Manyika people who perform the ceremony immediately after death (Daneel 1971, p. 334).

ceremony, is another cause of lengthy delays. On the other hand, the ceremony may be held as little as a couple of weeks after death if there is some reason for hurry: Professor Holleman cites a case in which these final rites were held ten days after the burial since the deceased had left a young widow and an unmarried youth, and relatives were worried that they would 'burn the grave' by undulging in sexual intercourse before the spirit was settled, an offence which would incur the anger of the spirit and invite trouble on the family.[21]

In most areas the ceremony is followed by, and associated with, the final dissolution of the deceased's estate and the re-marriage of his widows, which may give rise to some tension in the family. In any case, the ceremony recalls the recent death in the family and revives a degree of the sorrow and the tension that followed it. The fear of the spirit after death is not entirely abated until it has been settled with the spirit guardians of the family homestead: some consider the spirit dangerous and capable only of harm until it has been so settled.[22] The ceremony is often delayed until the spirit of the deceased is divined to request it by making someone ill, and in this unsettled atmosphere, if the ceremony is unduly delayed for any reason, any misfortune is readily interpreted as a demand by the spirit to be settled in the ranks of the family spirit guardians. So the ceremony is normally held amid a certain anxiety and tension, which persists during the rites.

The immediate kin of the deceased decide when the ceremony is to be performed and inform other kin, various affines and the deceased's associates. Much beer is brewed and food is prepared, to which all are expected to contribute, the size of the contribution depending on the relationship between the donor and the deceased. A large gathering of unrelated neighbours also attends the rituals, and all enjoy the singing and dancing and the beer. Many of these contribute to the feast, either as the result of guilty conscience towards the deceased or, more usually, as a spontaneous and tangible expression of goodwill.

The guests begin to gather on the evening before the ritual is to be performed. Some of the millet beer is consecrated to the spirit and the spirit is informed of the forthcoming ceremony in a formal address by the senior *muzukuru* (sister's son) of the family. Others present may also make a formal address to the spirit and pay their respects with token gifts. Late into the night, funerary songs are sung in mourning for the deceased and

---

21. Holleman 1953, p. 2.
22. Kumbirai 1966/7 VIII (Jan. 1967).

in honour of his spirit, and men and women dance in his honour. Then young boys and girls take over with a gay dance lasting into the following morning to welcome the spirit and make it happy.

Early the following morning a girl married into the family of the deceased cleans the consecrated pot of beer and carries it in procession usually to the grave, but in some areas to a temporary tree shrine outside the homestead. In most areas, a beast (a head of cattle or a black sheep or goat) is also taken to the grave to be sacrificed. The grave is 'opened' by removing one or two stones, generous libations of porridge and beer are smeared and poured over it, and the spirit is invited to come home. If a beast is to be sacrificed, it is ritually killed, skinned and roasted, and some of the meat is offered to the spirit. All present may be invited to make a formal address to the spirit while pouring a libation of beer or leaving an offering of roasted meat: each person announces himself and makes some plea for the guardianship of the spirit. Offerings are also made on behalf of absent relatives of the deceased. Then all return to the homestead, where there is much music and feasting to welcome the spirit home.

Sometimes the spirit is symbolically brought home. Thus on the evening before the main rituals, the Shangwe tie a black cloth around the neck of a goat which is then taken to represent the deceased. It is taken to a tree in the bush outside the homestead, and there the appropriate functionary addresses the spirit and informs it that they are bringing it home. The goat is then led back into the homestead and into the hut of one of the deceased's closest relatives. It is kept apart from other goats until it is sacrificed the following day.[23] In the north-east, a small branch is cut from the ceremonial tree, when the tension among the attendants indicates that this is one of the most important moments of the ritual. The severed end of the branch is immediately covered to prevent the spirit from escaping, and the branch is dragged into the homestead with frequent pauses to rest the spirit and to cool it by pouring millet beer over the branch. The branch is then fastened to the wall of the house of the family head.[24] Among the Valley Korekore, a pathway is made from the grave to the family homestead and the spirit is symbolically brought into the homestead.[25]

But even when this visible act does not form part of the ritual, at some stage in the ceremony the leading functionary addresses the spirit and

23. Powell 1953, pp. 17ff.
24. See Holleman 1953, pp. 7f.
25. Garbett 1963a, p. 79.

informs it that the people want it to return home.[26] The importance of this ceremony is to install the spirit of the deceased among the spirit elders of the family, expressed in terms of a physical journey from the bush outside the homestead (where the deceased was buried) into the homestead. This does not imply that the Shona believe that the spirit has to be physically moved: no further ceremony is required if the family head moves his homestead, and once the spirit has become a spirit guardian, it is believed to remain with its descendants wherever they are. Once established among the family spirit elders, the spirit may be honoured in the homestead with millet beer and the name of the spirit may be mentioned when other spirit elders are honoured. The ceremony of bringing the spirit home is essential to obtain the guardianship of the spirit, and some such rite should be performed for those who have died away from home or who have been killed by wild beasts and so could not receive an ordinary burial.[27] Thus if a person dies and is buried while at work in a town, his relatives may take home a handful of soil from his grave and perform a small ceremony to bring the spirit home and install it among the family spirit elders.[28]

Throughout the ceremony of bringing the spirit home, great care is taken to please the spirit of the deceased. The dancing and singing through the night before the ceremony include dances of mourning and lament to honour the spirit and gay dances with sexual overtones 'to make the spirit happy', and boys and girls dance right through early morning rituals for the same purpose. When the party first approaches the grave, they take care not to disturb the spirit with excessive noise. When the beast is sacrificed, people try to prevent it from bleating and disturbing the spirit. When a branch is cut from the ceremonial tree, the man who performs this rite must take care to cut the branch with one clean stroke of his

---

26. A possible exception is to be found in the Manyika *'tsvitsa'* ceremony (described in Shropshire 1931) where the emphasis is on the spirit joining the ranks of the family spirits, and no mention is made of bringing the spirit home: as we will see, these two ideas are closely associated which brings the Manyika ritual into line with the ritual performed elsewhere. Professor Gelfand's remark, 'There is no bringing back the spirit from the grave to the village,' (1962, pp. 134f.) when describing funeral rites in Chesa (Darwin District) presumably refers to the separate ceremony of bringing home the spirit which he describes earlier (pp. 125f.)

27. Edwards 1929, p. 39.

28. Cf. also Howman 1969, p. 11, in which he describes how a lion spirit guardian of the chiefdom would come out in a new medium only after the spirit of the late medium, who had died away from home, was brought home in a handful of soil from his grave.

axe lest the sleeping spirit be wakened and escape. Libations of millet beer to the spirit are always very generous: one pot may be emptied and a couple of calabashes poured from a second pot to give the impression of an unlimited supply, or the pots may be filled until they overflow before the beer is poured onto the grave.[29] The spirit of the deceased must be kept 'cool': thus the Shangwe build a rough thatch shelter over the grave at the beginning of the ceremony to provide shade for the spirit,[30] and elsewhere straw or a branch may be placed over the libations for the same reason. Sometimes water or a weaker beer is mixed with the beer that is poured in libation in order to keep the spirit 'cool', and water may be sprinkled over the grave for the same purpose. When the spirit is brought home in a branch, several stops are made on the way to rest the spirit and to 'cool' it with millet beer.[31] Thus the spirit must be honoured, entertained and thoroughly feasted; it should not be disturbed and it must be kept 'cool'.

The fear of annoying the spirit is further illustrated by the ceremony for a man whose widow had returned to her own people and was suspected of having broken the prohibition on sexual intercourse: the head of the deceased's family insisted that the libations be poured at the side of the grave instead of on it since he was not sure that the spirit would accept them.[32] Great care is taken over the performance of the rituals since anything going wrong is believed to be a sign that the spirit 'refuses' and will consequently remain unsettled in the forest. The ceremony is generally regarded as the most exacting of all Shona rituals.

Yet when things do go wrong in practice, they are as often as not regarded as unimportant. Although the belief in the serious consequences of a mishap is strong enough to make one man run away rather than perform his task of cutting the branch in which the spirit was to be brought home,[33] when in fact the person performing this rite fails to make a clean cut people may shrug the incident off with a joke. In one ceremony at a

---

29. Professor Holleman (1953, pp. 32f.) suggests that one reason for this generosity is to improve the position of the deceased in the eyes of the spirits whose ranks he is about to enter. This is certainly true in the case of the Manyika ceremony in which the deceased is expressly intended to entertain with millet beer those who have gone before him (Shropshire 1931, p. 272).
30. Powell 1953, p. 18.
31. Cf. Holleman 1953, pp. 37f.
32. Holleman 1953, p. 16.
33. Holleman 1953, p. 7.

grave some kilometres from the homestead, the party excused themselves from the usual abstention from beer during the preliminary dancing on the grounds that they needed strength for the long journey. As a result, they were all rather drunk for the ritual, many mistakes were made, and a certain amount of quarrellimg took place. When questioned on the ceremony a few days later, the attitude of the deceased's kin was that they had made an effort and had performed the essential parts of the ceremony, and that this should satisfy the spirit.[34]

The ceremony thus reveals an ambiguous attitude towards the spirit. In some respects the spirit is presumed to wish to be settled in the homestead and to be co-operating with the living community performing the rituals, but in other respects the spirit is believed to be very demanding and has to be cajoled into co-operation. As the Shona themselves explalin, it 'is difficult to know what the spirit wants'.[35] The unease after death lingers on into the ceremony. The ceremony is conducted specifically to overcome this unease by cooling the spirit and settling it in the ranks of the spirit elders who are more predictably beneficent, but even these the Shona hold in a mingling of fear and confidence.

Thus the final funerary ceremony attempts to resolve the tension caused by death in the community by installing the spirit of the deceased among the family spirit guardians who take care over the family homesteads. For the Shona, the living and the dead form part of the same community, and the ritual which installs the spirit of a recently deceased member of the living community into the community of the departed ancestors must be the ritual which brings the spirit home.

The inheritance ceremony

Once the spirit of the deceased has been finally settled in his family home, his estate and his widows can be distributed among his heirs. In many areas, the inheritance ceremony is part of the ritual of settling the spirit, but often there are two separate ceremonies and sometimes the inheritance ceremony takes place soon after death before the spirit of the deceased has been finally settled.

Inheritance is supervised by a close kinsman or kinswoman of the deceased who is not entitled to receive, the most usual being a sister or a

---

34. Holleman 1953, pp. 17ff.
35. Holleman 1953, pp. 32f.

sister's son of the deceased, or possibly both in consultation with each other. The general principle of inheritance is that a man's personal name and position can be inherited only by a son, but his position as head of a larger family group may be inherited by a younger brother. There are, however, borderline cases between these categories, and these and the precise distribution of the deceased's property is decided according to the previous relationships between the deceased and his various kinsmen and also according to local custom. Each of the deceased's widows is expected to accept the inheritor or some other close kinsman of her late husband, possibly a senior son by another wife, as her husband, who in turn accepts responsibility for the widow and her children. Her objections to any particular kinsman of her late husband are respected and she is usually asked to choose her new husband, or if she objects to all her late husband's agnates, the marrige is readily dissolved. Also widows often go through a rite which is supposed to prove that they have not committed adultery since their late husband's death.

Once the inheritor to the deceased has been decided and the senior widow has agreed verbally to accept him, he goes through the formal ceremony. The inheritor sits on a mat with the senior widow, who is given a cup of water or millet beer which she sips before passing on to the inheritor to show her acceptance of him. After the inheritor has sipped from the cup, it is passed to the widow's senior kinsman, who drinks from it to indicate his acceptance of his new 'son-in-law'. Then each person present in order of seniority places a token gift on the head of the inheritor and formally addresses him by the name or the kinship title of the deceased, exhorting him to perform properly the duties he has received with his new position. The inheritor becomes responsible for the estate of the deceased which, in consultation with the deceased's sister, he is expected to distribute equitably to appropriate kin. He is also responsible for the social relations of the deceased, including responsibility of service and payment towards the deceased's in-laws.

In the traditional inheritance systems, widows do not receive any of the deceased's property, though they do keep their own personal effects including any personal gifts the husband may have made over to them during his life. In the rural subsistence economy, a widow continues to work the fields her late husband allocated to her and she is cared for either by his relatives or by her own family if she refuses to accept an inheritor. In the urban situation, however, a widow may well be left destitute by her husband's kin who often claim all his property, including house furniture and items purchased with the husband's and wife's joint income, immediately on the death of their kinsman and without bothering to decide who is responsible for the maintenance of the widow. The traditional rules of inheritance applied outside the context of the extended family structure and without the traditional social restraints can have disastrous social consequences.

The formal inheritance ceremony is not in most areas customary for a woman or for a man without offspring. In the case of a wealthy person, however, inheritance needs to be formally settled, and some kind of ceremony modelled on the rites just described may be performed. More usually, a dead woman's personal property is given to the head of her own family (as opposed to her husband's), who in turn normally distributes it to her children (his grandchildren or sister's children), and possibly also to her siblings of her mother's house.

In most areas, but not in all, the dead man's name is inherited by his successor. Even where this is not the case, a man's spirit may demand that some descendant be named after him by making the descendant ill, and a woman's name may be taken by a grand-daughter if the dead grandmother is believed to demand it. The Shona regard the name given to a person as relevant to their relations with their ancestral spirits and a diviner may prescribe a change of name in case of sickness, especially in the case of an infant that continually cries.[36] The inheritance of a dead man's (or woman's) name by one of his descendants is one aspect of the full adult status acquired by having children.

---

36. Cf. Wieschoff 1937, p. 499.

Kinship and the rituals of death

Kinship relations feature prominently at all the rituals associated with death, as indeed they do on most ritual occasions. All close kin should be present at the funeral (or at least at the ceremony shortly after it) and again at the rite of the final settling of the spirit of the deceased. One sanction bringing kin together is the heavy cost of the funerary ceremonies in grain for food and for millet beer, a beast for sacrifice and meat to eat: if a member of an extended family is not present and fails to contribute towards the costs, he will be left to bear the full expense of any funeral for which he is responsible and his relatives are unlikely to be lavish at his own funeral. Another sanction is that absence is likely to arouse suspicions of ill-will and witchcraft: indeed strife between branches of a family is occasionally expressed in a refusal by members of one branch to attend the funeral of a member of another.

So the extended family must gather and co-operate in the performance of the funerary rituals. Other families related by blood and marriage must also attend, and their various relationships are dramatized in the course of the rituals. A *muzukuru* ('sister's son') always has a part to play: among the Korekore he acts as mediator between the living and the dead of the patrilineal family, leading any formal address to the spirit of the deceased, and he is in charge of all the rituals actions associated with the tasks of a son-in-law: they are often responsible for digging the grave, collecting firewood for brewing millet beer, clearing away the ashes from funerary fires and performing other heavy chores around the homestead; they may also have to provide the sacrificial beast which is associated with bride-price cattle, and they are always involved in slaughtering it. Likewise women married into the family perform chores proper to a daughter-in-law, such as cleaning and carrying pots used in the rituals and cooking for guests. In areas where friendship is formalized in ritual, friends perform tasks invollving contact with the corpse and take any gifts offered to the spirit. The community comes together and dramatizes the relationships around which it is structured so that, far from being disrupted by the death of one of its members, it is in fact drawn together and the kinship ties created through the deceased are reinforced.

It is noticeable that although the agnatic kin of the deceased are primarily responsible for the funerary rituals, in some areas the principal functionary roles in the rituals are performed by people who are not agnates.[37] Thus the agnates provide most of the food and drink and arrange when the rituals are to take place, and it is the agnates who would suffer from the spirits if the rituals were not properly performed. But a non-agnatic kinsman (the deceased's sister's son or his equivalent) is often master of ceremonies taking responsibility for the organization of the rituals and giving all instructions. Where the deceased has a ritual friend, he is responsible for handling the corpse[38] and sons-in-law help to carry it to the grave. Sons-in-law and daughters-in-law are in charge of sacrificial beasts and consecrated pots of beer.

The Shona see death as some as yet undetermined force striking at the family. The whole family group is vaguely threatened and the evil is particularly associated with the body of the deceased: contact with a human corpse always requires traditional prophylactic medicines. the danger diminishes as the blood relationship becomes more remote and those least threatened are persons unrelated to the deceased. On the other hand, the funerary rites involve serious responsibilities towards the deceased on the part of his kinsmen, which cannot be passed off lightly to anyone not closely associated with the family. Thus when a friend of the family is pledged by an exchange of tokens or by previous ritual ties, he may be given the more dangerous tasks to perform. Men and women married into the family are also people whose service is institutionalized and trusted. The close relationship between a sister's son and his mother's brother makes the sister's son an ideal person to conduct the funerary rituals and to plead for the spirit's care and protection.

For their services in the rituals, the various functionaries are specially honoured and rewarded by the family of the deceased in the feasts and drinking associated with the rituals.

In urban situations families are scattered. When death occurs in the towns, it may be difficult to gather the kinsmen appropriate to the various burial functions. Besides, expenses are increased by transport and cemetery costs, and there are few local kinsmen to provide financial support. To replace the functions of extended families in the rural areas, burial societies have grown up in the towns and for a small regular subscription they guarantee a good funeral, possibly even the finance necessary to transport the body home for burial. These societies sometimes centre around a

---

37. This applies particularly to the north-east of Shona country. The relevance of kinship to funerary rituals in this area is analysed in Holleman 1953, pp. 21 – 26.

38. This does not, however, apply in the south of Shona country where no one but a close agnate would be allowed to come into contact with the corpse.

band to play traditional funeral music. Or sometimes church groups provide mutual support for burials.

The spiritual aspect of man

We are now in a position to begin to understand Shona ideas about life and spirits of the dead.

According to Shona beliefs, life begins as a snake or worm in the mother's womb.[39] The spirit of a boy's deceased paternal grandfather (or his grandfather's paternal grandfather if the child's grandfather is still alive) is believed to enter the child while he is still in his mother's womb or, according to some, when the child utters his first cry.[40] In the case of a girl, some say that she receives the spirit of her paternal grandfather, but others say that a female agnate, perhaps the grandfather's sister, enters the child; a girl also has close ties with the spirit of her mother's mother from whom she is supposed to receive her procreative powers, but her mother's mother has nothing to do with the girl's personal spirit.[41]

The Shona do not have a systematic body of beliefs about the spirit world and when we try to elucidate their beliefs we come across ambiguities and contradictions. Shona beliefs do not form a rigid body of acceptable doctrine, but rather they provide a general way of looking at and understanding things, and they can be adapted to meet particular situations or particular points of view. Thus when we try to elucidate exactly how an ancestral spirit is believed to enter a child, we meet with vagueness and confusion: in some respects the ancestral spirit appears to dominate the living person and in other respects the ancestral spirit appears to beget a new and separate personal spirit.

A man's own spirit cannot reveal itself by 'coming out' during his lifetime. Any special powers a person may have, whether these be special skills in hunting or music or healing or whether they are the evil powers of a witch, are attributed to the spirits of the dead and often involve the spirit of a close ancestor. Bad health and any unusual behaviour or character traits may be attributed to the spirits of deceased ancestors. Thus ancestral spirits are believed to be dominant in controlling a person's life, and his

---

39. Relevant to this belief is the taboo against a pregnant woman killing a snake (Gelfand 1956a, pp. 218f.).
40. Holleman 1958a, p. 258.
41. See Holleman 1953, p. 27.

own personal spirit could be said to be embryonic, maturing as the person matures, until it is pushed out of the body at death.[42]

The maturity of the spirit is believed to depend on the maturity of the living person. In particular, parenthood is a prerequisite for a person to acquire the full status of a spirit elder after death. We have already seen how parenthood affects the status of Shona men and women during their lifetime. In some areas, an indication in ritual of the greater independence and full adult status achieved by parents at the birth of their first child is seen in the fact that both parents are then, and not before, allowed to pray directly to their family spirit elders on matters of personal concern.[43] But the main ritual effects of parenthood are seen after a person's death: the full series of funerary rituals are performed only for parents of children. People sometimes say that a man can only live through his son: thus a man's position and name are inherited by a son, his spirit enters his son's children, and, most of all, his spirit is remembered and honoured by his patrilineal descendants on ritual and other occasions. In theory, the spirit of any unmarried person is powerless and unimportant, although in practice rites may be deemed necessary to ward off the spirit of a bachelor of marriageable age from trying to enter a sister's son.[44] According to some, the worm containing the spirit of an unmarried person comes out of the grave and wanders about with nowhere to go since an unmarried person has no place in society, whereas the worm of a baby cannot even speak.[45] The spirit of a person who dies without children can never be fully mature. On the other hand, as a person becomes very aged, he is thought to grow closer to the spirits. Old people are believed to be very influential with spiritual powers and are regarded with a certain amount of fear and sometimes even suspicion: they are believed to become similar to spirits and occasionally to cause illness in their descendants. Thus there is a correlation between the maturity of a living person and the believed maturity of his spirit.

Notice that it is the social rather than the physical aspects of maturity

---

42. Holleman 1953, pp. 27ff. Professor Murphree (1969, p. 33, & n. 2) criticizes Professor Holleman's analysis on the grounds that the spirit is not believed to be incarnate in a person during his lifetime but is rather a 'shadow' existence beside him, that the term *kubuda* (come out) does not in this context have spatial overtones, and that the importance of physical maturation does not lie in quasi-corporal links between the spirit and the body. The differences of opinion have little, if any, practical implications, and the Shona's casual and practical approach to their beliefs make it difficult to settle such differences.

43. Murphree 1969, p. 34.

44. Holleman 1953, p. 28.

45. Kumbirai 1964, p. 8.

Dancing in honour of a territorial spirit at the shrine (partly obscured) at the foot of a baobab tree in Korekore country. One possessed lion spirit medium is lying on the reed mat and another (in the bead cap) is dancing.

The shrine to a territorial spirit guardian at the foot of a baobab tree in the Mount Darwin district.

Possessed hosts of family spirit elders in Korekore country await the next dance.

An offering of millet beer for a deceased family head in Korekore country. Since in this case the dead man had been a chief, two possessed lion spirit mediums take an active interest in the proceedings.

which count: parenthood rather than puberty or age gives status to the spirit, and the spirit of a chief is more significant than the spirit of a commoner. The spirit is regarded not so much as incarnate in the body maturing through some *quasi* corporal links, but more as a kind of separate or shadow existence beside the living body.

In any case, little emphasis is given to the spirit during life. The spirits of the deceased are believed to be the active agents in a community, and the responsibility of a person for his own behaviour is considerably diminished in the Shona view. The spirits of the dead can be blamed for any misadventure that takes place and they should be thanked for any good that happens. Thus the activity of the spirits through the living community is very much part of the Shona view of life. Consequently, various forms of spirit possession (which we will be discussing later) are not necessarily exotic or unnatural to the Shona,[46] but are often simply special cases of an everyday phenomenon.

This is not to say that the possession of every living person by his tutelary spirit is as absolute as the ritual possession of a powerful spirit medium. In the latter case, the spirit is believed completely to take over the living body so that the medium's words are taken to be the very words of the spirit. The same phenomenon occurs when the deceased head of an extended family comes out in his chosen medium. An ordinary individual however, has only his own authority and reputation for what he says and does, and he carries some of the responsibility for it. Although some blame can be attributed to tutelary spirits, a living person can be the subject of moral disapproval and an anti-social person can be said to have an evil *mweya* (wind, spirit), which refers to his personal vitality and life principle.

But in his description of *mweya* as 'that unique combination of characteristics that constitute a human personality', Professor Murphree points out that during a person's lifetime it (*mweya*) is under the tutelage of an ancestral spirit.[47] So even an evil disposition can be blamed partly on the spirits. The principal practical effect of this way of thinking is that reconciliation after any anti-social activity is facilitated since the responsibility of the parties concerned is diminished.

The *mudzimu* (spirit of a dead person) is said to 'come out' at death. Although this is sometimes understood in a physical sense as coming out of the grave in the form of an animal, the term *kubuda* (to 'come out') means

---

46. This is not to deny that greater mediums make use of exotica to boost their prestige.
47. Murphree 1969, pp. 31f.

more to reveal oneself: on the death of a man his spirit can 'come out' and reveal itself as an independent and active entity. Thus the spirit revealing itself by possessing a medium is also said to 'come out'.

The spirit is supposed to hover about the corpse as a shadow and then to vanish 'like air'. From then on, the spirit is released from the confines of a single spot in place and time. 'He (the spirit) is like air (*mhepo*), and he may be everywhere.' But, particularly in ritual, attention to the spirit is often focused on one object, such as the grave, a consecrated pot of millet beer, a tree shrine or a branch cut from it.[48] The Shona are vague as to the nature of the spirit's presence in any of these objects: when questioned, they say that the spirit might be in the object concerned, but that they do not really know since one cannot see the spirit and their fathers never explained it to them. They tend to get impatient with attempts to record a verbal explanation: for them it is sufficient to perform the rites as they have been instructed, and our understanding of their beliefs must be based on ritual expression and association rather than on verbal theory.

The spirit comes nearest to being identified with a material symbol in the belief that when the body decomposes the spirit comes out of the head in the form of a worm which is associated with the 'white shadow'.[49] Especially in the case of a chiefly spirit, this worm is believed to come out of the grave and to grow into a small animal which can be seen around the grave six months or so after burial, scurrying back into the grave when disturbed. The most powerful spirits are believed to take the form of lion cubs, but the spirit may be associated with one of a number of animals and birds. An animal associated with a spirit must be treated with respect and may not be hunted or chased away. It is supposed to be able to move about anywhere without normal spatial limitations and to be immortal. But the spirit remains a spirit and is not simply identified with the animal. Thus the spirit can possess its medium while the animal remains outside in the bush where it can sometimes be heard. The spirit can exist apart from the animal, but it is believed that the animal has no independent existence: it exists only as the manifestation of the spirit. The spirit identifies itself with the animal when it meets people in the bush or when it is ill-treated by people. The spirit is said to live in the animal, and the relationship between the two is similar to that between the shadow *mweya* and the living body of a man. Thus it is the animal and not the spirit that eats and drinks, and the spirit is vaguely in it or about it.[50] The spirit appears to be

---

48. Cf. Holleman 1953, pp. 28, 35.
49. Kumbirai 1966/7 V (July 1966).
50. See Kumbirai 1964, pp. 3 – 8.

quite independent of anything in the physical world, but requires some physical object as a focus of attention.

The Shona regard death as a frightening entry into the unknown, a complete break from the community of the living. But after the spirit is brought home, it is believed to be on friendly terms with the living and can readily be approached for the help whenever help is needed. The spirit is believed to be able to ask favours in return by causing illness in the family it has left. The past influence of the deceased remains observable among the descendants he has left, and the kinship relationships of these descendants are still traced through the deceased. The structure of the family remains dependent on the deceased, and the continued good of the community is presumed to depend on his spiritual power. Thus to the living community, family ancestors maintain as spirits the influence they had over their descendants when they were alive.

9

Traditional Religion in the Family

Family spirit elders

We have seen that the Shona believe in life as a spirit after death, during which a dead person can continue to bear influence on the community he has left. Immediately after death the spirit is feared as unpredictable and dangerous, and a fear of their superior power covers all dealings with the spirits. Nevertheless, sometime after death the deceased is settled back at home in the community, and from this time on is regarded as a friendly spirit guardian to the family that survives him. The presence of these spirit guardians and their power over the lives of their descendants are so real to the traditional Shona that in many respects they remain part of the community, spirit elders whose influence remains very much alive.

The most important spirit elder is the deceased head of an effective extended family, the father or grandfather of the senior living generation who brings the group together on ritual occasions and ensures that it continues as a group. The group he created during his life survives after his death. Whenever members of the group come together, they can see and feel the influence of their dead ancestor. The spirit is presumed to maintain responsibility for the group he founded during his life. Particularly in central Shona country, the spirit of the deceased family head usually has a medium through whom he can from time to time talk with his living descendants. Again in central Shona country, the presence of spirit elders is emphasized by a shrine in every homestead, at which their descendants regularly approach them for help and thank and honour them.

The spirit of the deceased head of the family should be honoured regularly (perhaps annually) with millet beer, which is ritually brewed for the occasion: sons-in-law to the family must bring firewood for cooking the beer (performing the chores appropriate to their relationship with the family and the spirit), daughters-in-law should grind the grain and prepare the pots, and other functionaries may have tasks to perform depending on local custom. I have known a man to offer to the spirit of his grandfather a commercially sold substitute for home-brewed beer, but few of his acquaintances approved of this departure from tradition, and many pointed to trouble in his family as a sign that the spirit was not pleased.

The ceremony usually starts the evening before the beer is ready for drinking, when the adult members of the family gather with their senior *muzukuru* (sister's son) to inform the spirit of the ceremony of the morrow and to consecrate to the spirit a pot or two, or perhaps a small gourd container, of fermenting beer.[1] After sunset the people gather around the shrine in the principal room of the homestead, or in some areas a temporary shrine in the courtyard outside, and salute the spirit by rhythmic clapping of hands. The *muzukuru* or the family head then pours an offering of beer while formally addressing the spirit, announcing that this is the beer brewed in his (the spirit's) honour, and saying that he should not ask for more beer but should look after his grandchildren and should refrain from causing trouble in the family. If the family considers that the spirit has been failing in his obligations towards them, the formal address may involve an harangue with shouts of support from attendants. When the libation has been poured and the address has been made, all clap in honour of the spirit and disperse.

During the night, people may dance in honour of the spirit, and young boys and girls may be asked to dance their gay dance through to the morning to keep the spirit happy. But this depends on local custom and the solemnity of the occasion.

Early next morning a larger group of attendants gathers, including more relatives and most neighbours, who come to share the millet beer. Again the rites depend on local custom and on how much of the ceremony has been performed the previous evening. Often the small offering of the previous evening is replaced by two large pots of beer, one on the right for the spirit of the family head and one on the left for his principal wife, the grandmother to the senior branch of the family. The spirit's pot is consecrated with a smearing of meal around the top and the living head of the family may place a token offering of snuff tobacco by the beer. Again, attendants gather around to honour the spirit, and a formal address is made to the spirit explaining the ceremony and reminding the spirit of his obligations towards the family. Then the people disperse to that part of the courtyard where men normally sit and chat.

Further pots of millet beer are brought out and distributed to all who are present. Sometime during the drinking, the senior son-in-law to the family takes the pot of the wife of the spirit (a son-in-law can always expect hospitality from the senior woman in his wife's family in return for the services they demand of him). When all the beer except the last consecrated pot is finished, the crowd usually disperses to gather again in the evening for the final ceremony.

---

1. I am relying largely on my own Korekore material in the description of this ceremony. For descriptions of the ceremonies elsewhere, see Gelfand 1959, pp. 79f; 1962, pp. 55f; 1966a, pp. 60f; 1977, pp. 107 – 111; Fry 1976, pp. 31f.

Again the people gather around the consecrated pot of beer and salute the spirit. A son-in-law removes the pot. Depending on local custom, this may be replaced by two small gourds or pots into which are poured a libation for the spirit and his wife, with yet another formal address to the spirit: at this stage of the proceedings the address is usually light-hearted in tone and often abusive. After a final salute to the spirit, the remainder of the beer is distributed.

The primary symbolism of this ceremony is in honouring the spirit with millet beer. Apart from religious occasions, millet beer may be brewed for a number of reasons: the most common is simply to raise money by selling the beer by the cup; if a man has a big job of work to do, such as building a house or clearing or ploughing a field, he may brew beer for a party at which the attendants are all expected to do their share of the work; beer may also be brewed simply for fun, to celebrate, for example, the completion of a homestead or to welcome home some member of the family. On all such occasions, as at religious ceremonies, friends, relatives and other neighbours are expected to show their goodwill by their presence. And whenever beer is to be drunk, an important guest may expect to be honoured with a pot of beer which he should distribute to those present, or at least with a large cupful of beer.[2] When the beer is presented to such a guest, the head of the homestead makes a short formal speech in which he explains that the beer is to express how glad he is at the presence of the guest. After this formality, he respectfully claps his hands.

In this way, the spirits too must occasionally be honoured with millet beer in order to keep them happy. When beer is brewed for a spirit elder, one pot is formally presented to the spirit concerned and one to his wife (or occasionally to her husband). The beer is distributed to all present, but a little is poured as the personal share of the spirits, which can be taken only by the appropriate functionary.

In central Shona country, the senior spirit guardian of the family often has a medium, who becomes ritually possessed when the spirit is to be honoured with millet beer. In such a case, the spirit is believed to be present in the medium and is honoured as any living dignitary would be honoured. The ritual possession, which usually lasts through the night and which is accompanied by *mbira* music, overshadows or replaces all other ritual.

The ceremony of brewing beer for the spirit elders of a family may be the spontaneous thanks for the spirits' care of the family, ensuring continued

---

2. A reigning chief can always expect a pot of beer if he is present at a beer drink, but other offerings to senior persons depend on the quantity of beer available and the purpose of the brew.

favour. But most frequently the spirit has to ask for the honour by causing illness in the family or some other relatively minor trouble that is divined to be such a request. The fact that the spirits normally have to make their presence felt by illness does not necessarily mean that their influence is regarded as evil. Although some people regard such requests by their spirits as a nuisance, people generally say that if the spirit is simply asking for beer or for some other ritual to which it has the right, it is a good spirit. The spirit is only regarded as evil if the trouble persists after the beer has been brewed, and should the illness become serious, especially should it result in death, the accompanying work of a witch is normally presumed. It is considered quite natural and right that certain spirits should ask to be honoured in various ways, and the only way they can make such a request is by inducing in one of their descendants a mild illness, which they remove as soon as the request is answered.

Nevertheless, the presence of the spirit elders is felt most strongly in times of anxiety and tension. The care of the spirit elders is noticed in its absence. Thus a family living close to or below the subsistence level, with the poor health which results from a scanty diet and the consequent continual problems and tensions, is likely to pay more attention to its spirit elders than a wealthy family for whom life runs smoothly.[3] There are affluent Shona who remain devout to their traditional religious practices, and there are many poor people who neglect their family spirits or at least resent them, but on the whole, more sophisticated and wealthy people tend to revert to their traditional religion only in time of crisis.

Communication with the spirit world provides a link with the traditional past. When asked why they perform particular rites in a religious ceremony, Shona usually reply that they were taught to do these things by their elders. Sometimes they can supply explanations of the symbolism and functions of particular rites, but this usually comes after the first response, and ultimately when they can explain no more they refer questions to their elders. In this context, even the oldest people alive are called *vadiki* (juniors) and the elders who could explain the rites are all said to be dead. Questions could be addressed to the possessed mediums of the senior spirits, but in practice people are satisfied that they are following the customs taught them by their ancestors and are not usually concerned with explanations of these customs.

---

3. Theisen 1976, p. 95. It is of course common to many cultures that the poor and the oppressed tend to be more strongly religious than the affluent. Later, Theisen (1979) pointed out that attendance at Christian services correlates with positive attidudes to extension workers and to agricultural innovation.

In the context of religious ceremonies, the persons who are honoured or appeased are precisely those ancestors who passed on the custom, and tradition is respected simply because it is the tradition of the ancestors. Deceased ancestors must be honoured in the way they wish, which is the way they taught their descendants. Spirit elders maintain their positions as heads of their family groups, and the regular change of older generations passing away to be replaced by their juniors is absorbed into a more permanent view of society in which the dead remain part of the community. Since religion is concerned with persons who lived in the past and their supposed control of present events, religion serves to bring the past and the present together, promoting in the living community a respect for tradition. In this way traditional Shona religion tends to encourage conservatism.

This conservative influence is emphasized by the fact that ritual and remembrance of the ancestors is usually the consequence of some anxiety. Trouble to be averted reinforces a respect for tradition. A poorer family is more frequently likely to be in the sort of trouble which demands attention to their spirit elders, and the family is likely to be more respectful of tradition.

In particular, religion draws together the extended family group. We have seen how various kinship and affinal roles are dramatized in funerary rituals and the same applies to other rituals in honour of the spirit elders.[4] The importance of drinking beer together has also been remarked. Notable absence from a ritual in honour of a spirit elder without good reason would be displeasing to the spirit, who might show his displeasure by causing further trouble in the community. If the ritual was initiated by sickness in the family, the spirit would presumably make it worse rather than cure the patient. Similarly quarrels in the family are presumed displeasing to the spirit elders. So when there is reason to perform a ritual in honour of a family spirit elder, all the family must come together and co-operate for the common good. Thus the Shona are right in seeing the continued influence of their deceased elders in maintaining the family group.[5]

The spirit head of a family may also be honoured by having a bull from

---

4. Cf. Werbner 1964, p. 212, where the author claims that certain Kalanga rituals serve to dramatize social ranking. The kinship group also expresses areas of tension and hostility at the rituals.
5. This is perhaps a further reason why the break up of extended families is more evident among the more wealthy who suffer less anxiety and have less reason to pay attention to their spirits.

the family herd dedicated to him.[6] Again this may be the result of sickness in the family interpreted as a request for the dedication of a bull, or it may come from the spontaneous piety of the living head of the family. Once consecrated, the bull continues with the herd, but represents the spirit elder after whom it is named. When cattle are added to or taken from the herd, the family head should approach the bull and, sprinkling meal or meal and water on its back, address the spirit to explain the transaction. The living head of the family may also address the spirit in this way at other times. The bull becomes symbolic of the power and dignity of the spirit, well illustrated by a schoolboy's account of Digma, his deceased grandfather's bull: 'The very name to me conveys more than anything else the character of a bull. Digma: might, solidity, demure dignity, diabolical majesty. . . . Indeed, one is led to believe that the spirit in him (or suppos-ed to be in him) gives him supernatural intelligence.' And he goes on to speak of how the bull shows the characteristics of gentleness to the weak but jealousy for its honour and dignity in the face of possible rivals.[7]

The spirit may ask for the sacrifice of the dedicated beast, which would be performed by sons-in-law and be accompanied by an offering of millet beer.[8] In such a case, or should the bull die naturally, it may be replaced by another beast.

Besides the spirit head of a family, other spirit elders may be honoured formally or informally. We have seen that the wife of the spirit head is honoured with him and her care over her descendants is also requested. Divination may point to trouble being caused by deceased grandparents on the mother's side, who may also be honoured occasionally with millet beer. A woman's mother's mother is believed to be very influential as a spirit, especially responsible for the woman's child-bearing capacity: the cow of motherhood that a woman receives at her daughter's marriage may be con-secrated to the spirit of her mother's mother. Many Shona respect the spirits of their deceased parents with filial piety and often ask for the aid of these spirits in the running of their lives, especially when they are about to undertake difficult or dangerous enterprises. But in public and on ritual occasions, relations between parents and children remain formal, and communications with the spirits are normally made through a grandchild or sister's child of the spirit. We have remarked on the belief that a spirit

6. In some areas a black goat is used instead of a bull.
7. Sadza 1954.
8. Sacrifices of dedicated beasts are described in Gelfand 1959, pp. 80 – 91; 1962, pp. 60f; 1966a, pp. 63 – 69.

elder never asks for beer by causing sickness in his own child: should sickness be divined to have been caused by the spirit of a parent, it is regarded as a dangerous sign of the spirit's anger.

Angry spirits[9]

An angry spirit is terrifying. Such a spirit attacks suddenly and very harshly. It usually attacks an individual through his family causing a succession of deaths, or death followed by serious illness in other members of the family. And an angry spirit is not easily appeased. Thus the angry spirit of a man murdered some eighty years ago is believed to have caused the deaths of the two brothers who plotted the murder, their father and six of their children, and still to claim the occasional victim among their descendants while the surviving relatives are still trying to raise the large fine in cattle necessary to appease the spirit. The Shona believe that an angry spirit can also cause serious quarrels within a family, loss of property and wealth, or any devastating misfortune. In practice, the tensions and fears following death believed to be caused by such a spirit, and the difficulty in appeasing it do on occasion lead to the break up of a family group.

The cause of the disaster is diagnosed by a diviner who sometimes names the angry spirit and indicates the necessary propitiation. Often, however, the spirit itself speaks out, choosing as its medium a member of its own family if it is unrelated to its victims, or preferably someone who has some connection with both groups by blood or marriage, or possibly even a member of the victim's family whom it has made ill: by possessing a medium, the spirit can make known who it is, why it is angry and what it requires in compensation before it will relent. Generally, the spirit is that of an acquaintance or relative who had been angered or wronged during life, such as an ill-treated parent, a neglected spouse, a creditor or a victim of murder (either by sorcery or by physical means: it is a common belief that many ex-guerrillas are suffering from madness and other disasters induced by the angry spirits of people they killed during the recent war). Sometimes the spirit is believed to become angry years after the death of

9. The name for such spirits is *ngozi*. Among the Korekore this name also applies to commoner family spirits which possess mediums. Accounts of *ngozi* are given in Gelfand 1959, pp. 153 – 161; 1962, pp. 69 – 83; 1966a, pp. 70 – 72; from all of which I have taken material.

the person owing to a failure on the part of the victims to fulfil obligations towards its descendants or towards itself. Sometimes too, it is said that an angry spirit has been stirred up, possibly by a witch, without serious provocation on the part of its victims, and occasionally people say that an attack can be due to the angry spirits of certain animals.[10]

The fear of avenging spirits can act as a sanction for ethical behaviour. During life a person must never do anything that might provoke someone to return as an avenging spirit, and this sanction is particularly relevant in the payment of debts and in the distribution of property after death. Occasionally a person may threaten to become an avenging spirit in order to obtain what he believes to be his due, and in extreme circumstances the person may even threaten to commit suicide in order to hasten this revenge.[11] The fear of making a spirit angry is also a sanction for performing funerary ceremonies carefully and correctly.

Methods of appeasing the action of an angry spirit vary according to the relationship between victims and the spirit, the crime that provoked the spirit, and the nature of the spirit's supposed activity. In the case of murder, the murderer might try to avoid the avenging action of his victim's spirit by eating flesh cut from certain parts of the victim's body.[12] But once the spirit has become active, the mediumship of a diviner specialized in dealing with avenging spirits is usually required (an unspecialized diviner would not dare to meddle in the affairs of an angry spirit for fear of bringing its anger upon himself), and some *n'anga* claim to be able to drive an angry spirit away without any propitiatory fine being paid, although such a course of action is believed to be dangerous to the diviner and liable to end in a recurrence of attacks by the spirit. Particularly for murder, a large fine in cattle must be paid to the family of the spirit: a large fine may also be necessary when the grievance concerns debts or bride-price payments. The sacrifice of two or three beasts might be necessary to appease the spirit of an ill-treated father and to obtain again the protection of the family spirit elders. The avenging spirit of an ill-treated mother may require the offending child to humiliate himself by dressing in rags and begging grain for a feast in her honour, at which a beast should be killed and from which the offending child must be absent. An offending husband may have to live in his dead wife's room, keeping it clean and performing her duties. If the angry spirit is the spirit of an unrelated person,

---

10. Crawford 1967, p. 89.
11. Cf. Holleman 1952a, pp. 257, 357f; 1958a, pp. 187f; Kumbirai 1964, p. 63.
12. Cf. Gelfand 1959, p. 157; Crawford 1967, p. 88.

besides appeasing the spirit it may be necessary to take measures against any further visitations by the spirit: these are performed by a *n'anga* and consist principally in planting protective charms in and around the homestead and treating all the inhabitants — similar to preventive measures taken against witchcraft. In all cases, the full appeasement of the angry spirit involves severe punishment, either in loss of wealth or in extreme humiliation, which further indicates how fearful such a spirit is to the Shona.

A family may try to avenge the death of one of its members or to enforce the payment of debts by raising or 'awakening' a spirit against the offending family, either with the help of a professional *n'anga* or by some commonly known rite over the grave of the person concerned.[13] It is also believed that a witch can raise an angry spirit to take unjustifiable action against its victims: a malevolent spirit is a ready-made weapon in the hands of a witch. And what is regarded as the justifiable action of an angry spirit by one family may be regarded as witchcraft by the family of the victims. Yet theoretically the action of an angry spirit is quite distinct from witchcraft in that the former is usually thought to be the righteous action of an offended spirit — a physical rather than the moral evil that witchcraft is.

If the avenging spirit is a family spirit, it may become a friendly spirit elder once it has been appeased. Thus during a quarrel within a family, somebody associated with the family may become the medium of an angry spirit elder. The medium is usually someone associated with both sides (perhaps a woman married into the family) or someone more closely associated with the branch that has offended the spirit: the possessed medium, supported by the threatening spirit, is thus in an ideal position to act as mediator in the quarrel.[14] Once the quarrel has been settled, the host remains the medium of the spirit through whom it can maintain friendly communication with its descendants.

Of all evil influences, an angry spirit (*ngozi*) is perhaps the most greatly feared by the Shona. It should be noticed that under this category come a variety of spirits. A *ngozi* may be some alien spirit aroused by a witch and the havoc it wreaks is akin to witchcraft. It may be the spirit of some unrelated acquaintance avenging mercilessly some wrong. Or the spirit may be a spirit elder angry at the bad behaviour of its living descendants. Thus the concept of *ngozi* refers not so much to a type of spirit as to its supposed action: death and destruction in the victim's family.

---

13. Cf.Crawford 1967, p. 260; Gelfand 1962, pp. 69f; 1966a, p. 70.
14. A case of this is described in Garbett 1969, pp. 123f.

Spirit possession

We have frequently had to refer to spirit mediumship and possession. Possessed spirit mediums elect a new chief. Many diviner-healers divine and heal by the power of a spirit which possesses them. Family spirit elders and angry spirits sometimes possess mediums in order to communicate with the living community. Spirit possession appears at all levels of Shona religion.

Some people become mediums or hosts to spirits, and periodically a medium becomes possessed when the spirit is believed to take complete control over his or her body. When this happens, the medium enters some kind of trance.[15] At the beginning of the trance, the medium usually starts to twitch and shake violently, sometimes uttering sharp cries and moans: he or she may require support and help from attendants before entering into the full trance or the state of full possession by the spirit. For this, the medium dons, possibly with the help of attendants, the full ritual dress of the spirit which varies from plain white or blue cloths for some lion spirits to colourful skirts, beads, rattles and head-dress for the gayer dancing spirits. The spirit also has a ritual staff, a ceremonial axe or an animal tail which the medium holds in his hand. While possessed by the spirit, the medium speaks in an unnatural voice associated with the spirit: a female medium of a male spirit speaks in a deep, gruff voice; some male mediums use a falsetto voice; very common is a lilting, sing-song manner of speaking associated with spirits. It is important that the voice of the spirit (when the medium is possessed) is recognizably different from the voice of the medium when not possessed, although the former may differ markedly from the voice of the person of the spirit while he was still alive or even from the spirit voice of the previous medium of the same spirit. Possessed mediums of very ancient spirits often speak in what is supposed to be an ancient dialect which is not readily intelligible to modern people and which includes words known only to the more elderly in the community. The possessed medium also adopts a typical expression, rigid and often tense, rarely showing any reaction to events and conversation around him (though a medium may relax a little during the course of a long séance). The medium adopts stances and postures associated with the possessing spirit, and certain mannerisms associated with the spirit which usually include frequent taking of snuff tobacco. Thus while possessed, the medium

---

15. Professor Gelfand (1962, pp. 167 – 170) discusses the trance state of the Shona with reference to psychiatric theory.

speaks and acts the part of the spirit and behaves in a way that is markedly in contrast to his normal behaviour. Often the character of the medium while possessed is so different from his normal personality that it becomes quite natural even for the unbeliever to treat the spirit (the medium possessed) and the medium (when not possessed) as two distinct persons.

Depending on the type of spirit and the experience of the medium, the medium may require music and dancing to go into the trance state, or possession may be induced relatively easily, requiring merely that attendants welcome the spirit by rhythmic clapping of hands or simply giving the medium a little snuff tobacco. Most mediums occasionally become possessed spontaneously when inspired to say something relevant to the situation in which they find themselves. The trance may be very brief, dealing merely with the business for which the medium has become possessed (possibly divination of the cause of sickness), or it may last several hours, perhaps all one night and the following morning on ritual occasions.

At the end of a séance, the medium goes outside the homestead or into a house, alone or with one assistant, and comes out of the trance, often with a sharp cry. After washing his face and usually rinsing out his mouth, he may then join those who attended the seance. He is supposed to remember nothing of what happened while he was possessed — it was the spirit and not himself who was supposedly present — so usually the attendants immediately inform him of what the spirit did and said.

Likewise, the spirit should not show knowledge of what is proper to the medium, though there is some ambiguity about the limits of the knowledge of the spirit. Thus the spirit is believed to look after his medium when not possessed (often called *homwe*, an empty bag or purse) and to punish anyone who tries to hurt or harm the medium. Also the spirit usually imposes a number of taboos on the medium (which we shall look at later) and is presumed to know at once should these be broken. Yet the spirit is not supposed to know what has been told privately to the medium and should be repeated formally to the spirit: thus when a man, suspicious of an adverse pronouncement by a possessed medium during a chiefly succession dispute, asked, 'How did they (the possessed mediums) know what they were told when they were not possessed?', everyone understood the implication that the mediums were only pretending to speak with the voices of the spirits and were not really possessed at all.

The Shona are vague as to how the spirits know some things in the lives of their mediums and not others. One explanation is that the spirits move about: sometimes a spirit is hovering around the homestead of its medium and at other times it wanders off into the bush. In practice, people expect the spirit to know most of what happens provided that the important distinction between the medium and the spirit is maintained:[16] thus conversations of one should never be confused with conversations of the other.

We must now consider how a person becomes accepted as the medium or host of a spirit. We have already seen that a diviner-healer's vocation often starts with dreams or sickness divined to be a request by a healing spirit for the person to be initiated as its host. Persistent illness is a common prelude to spirit possession, and mental disturbances are usually interpreted as a demand by a spirit to have the patient as its medium. A divination to this effect is especially likely if the patient has a late close relative who was a medium, or if the general circumstances are such that the emergence of a medium is likely: this may be because some current event or dispute is thought to be the concern of a spirit who needs to communicate with persons concerned, or simply that some spirit possession cult is growing in popularity and becoming fashionable. Occasionally a person simply becomes possessed without any prior disturbance and without prior divination: in such a case the new medium may have some difficulty in being accepted by other mediums of the cult.

Occasionally too a person may try to resist the demands of the spirit. Thus one reluctant Korekore medium had a long illness affecting his head and stomach which lasted for four years until he accepted the spirit divined to have caused it. It started when he was in his twenties away at work on a farm. His white employer had him examined by a doctor several times and he was given western medicines, but without effect. He consulted five diviners and they all agreed on the cause of his trouble, namely that he was going to be possessed by the great spirit that had previously possessed his deceased grandfather. Eventually the spirit came out, possessing him early one morning while he was still away at work in Bulawayo. He left for home shortly afterwards. But he did not want to be a spirit medium, so he joined the Church of the Apostles, a new independent Christian Church; he was baptized by church officials who tried and failed to exorcise the spirit. He then went to a traditional healer who gave him cannabis to smoke and powdered medicine to take, but this too failed to drive away the influence of the spirit. Finally he went home and accepted the spirit, becoming the

---

16. I have once come across an a-typical medium whose general arrogant behaviour was so similar to his possession ritual that people were never sure whether or not he was possessed. This medium was, however, acknowledged by all to be very unusual and his influence was short-lived.

senior medium of the chiefdom — but has twice since been in serious trouble for breaking the spirit's taboos. It is a common saying that a spirit will always have its way.

When the host decides to accept the spirit, he must be ceremonially initiated as a medium. The ceremony should be arranged by a senior kinsman of the new medium (a person normally becomes a medium while still in his late teens or early twenties), by the husband of a female medium or by someone associated with the spirit (such as the chief in the case of a chiefly spirit): the medium himself (or herself) should take no part in the preparations for a ceremony in honour of his spirit. Musicians competent in the music appropriate to the spirit must be hired. A senior medium of the type of spirit coming out must be invited to perform the initiation, and in most cases the senior medium charges a substantial fee for his services.

The ceremony usually starts late in the night before the initiation ritual when the senior medium, the initiand and often other hosts in the cult become possessed to the accompaniment of appropriate music. It occasionally happens that the initiand fails to enter the trance state. The senior medium may try to help by providing medicated snuff and medicinal vapours, but occasionally even these fail to induce possession. I once attended two lengthy night sessions organized to initiate a new host before the husband and kin of the initiand decided that the diviner who prescribed the initiation ceremony must have been wrong; an expensive mistake, since the husband had to prepare two feasts and to pay the drummers and the senior medium twice for their services plus an extra payment 'for wasting their time'.

But usually the initiand becomes possessed and the ceremony can proceed. First, with the help of the senior medium, the initiand dons the ritual dress of the spirit. Then the new spirit may be interrogated. It should be able to recognise the spirits of all other mediums present and know something about them. In the case of a family spirit or the spirit guardian of a chiefdom, the newly possessed medium may be tested on the history of the family or chiefdom concerned. The spirit should also reveal its own identity if this is not previously known, and say something of its own history. When the senior medium is satisfied, he introduces the new spirit to the assembled people, including members of the new medium's family. The mediums spend much of the night in consultation, discussion and instruction.

Early in the morning, the senior medium initiates the new medium with a hair-cutting ritual. The senior medium, or some functionary instructed by the possessed medium, cuts all the hair from the initiand's head, continually demanding token payments from spectators in order to continue. The hair is wrapped in a white cloth and deposited in the veld outside the homestead. A second hair-cutting ritual takes place soon after the first: the ceremony is similar to the first, but the medium has only his back and sides cut and millet beer is brewed in honour of the new spirit. It is said that the new hair belongs to the spirit and must never be cut off (though it can be trimmed occasionally without further ritual) and many mediums keep their hair noticeably long. The ceremony, however, appears to have little significance other than to set the medium in some way apart from other people and in some way belonging to the spirit.

Once initiated, the new medium may hold seances whenever he wishes. About a year later, he should normally hold a seance for which millet beer has been brewed in honour of his spirit and to which the senior medium who initiated him should be invited. Subsequently, a medium may hold an annual or occasional seance at which his spirit is honoured with music and beer, or he may hold such a séance only when the spirit requests it by making him ill. At any séance for spirits in the same category as his own, a medium may join other mediums in the trance state.

If the medium has a family spirit or a healing or divining spirit, he may become possessed from time to time for private deliberation or consultation, or the seance may be instigated by the medium when there is trouble in the family due to sickness or social conflict. Especially if he or she is possessed by a family spirit elder, a medium, supported by the believed power of the spirit, is in an ideal position to mediate between conflicting parties within a family group or to bring out into the open latent hostilities within it.[17]

A person who wishes to become a medium or who claims to be a medium is not always recognised as genuine. Thus a man who spontaneously goes into a trance at a spirit dance may be accepted by the other possessed hosts as a new member of their cult, or they may reject him, claiming that he is only pretending to be possessed, for which he is in danger of death from their spirits. Or a medium claiming to be possessed by a spirit of some moment in the community may fail the tests imposed upon him, in which case the senior mediums may inform the new medium that the possessing spirit is of some lesser variety. And even should a person be accepted as the medium of, say, a healing spirit, he must acquire respect and show by his results that he can divine and heal.

Theoretically the Shona say that a spirit can desert its human host. In

17. Cf. Garbett 1969; also Werbner 1972.

the gay dancing spirit cults, a man may cease to become possessed as he acquires the status of seniority: usually in such a case, he remains the nominal host of the spirit which will not come out in another host until the first dies. Occasionally, a lesser spirit may be replaced by a more senior spirit as when the host to a dancing alien spirit becomes the host to a family spirit elder, in which case the alien spirit must find some other host. It sometimes also happens that a more important spirit is believed to be dissatisfied with its medium and to leave him. In practice, this belief may arise when a medium breaks his taboos or behaves in a way not becoming to a medium, or when a rival claims the mediumship of the same spirit. People say that when the spirit leaves its medium, the medium will shortly die. In practice, should circumstances arise to make people suspect that a medium has been deserted by his spirit, there are usually confusing and contradictory opinions voiced, and the only certain sign that the spirit has left its medium is when the medium does in fact die.

Even when there is no doubt that a medium is the host of a particular spirit, the Shona believe that he could occasionally fake possession, leaving room for doubt at any particular séance. So although the Shona believe that a medium is chosen by his spirit, and that he is proved to be genuine by divination and the clairvoyance of other mediums, in practice the recognition and respect paid to a medium depend on his ability to convince peole when in the possession trance. He must act in accordance with what is expected of his spirit.[18]

The respect due to the host of a spirit in daily life depends on the status of his spirit. Hosts to the common dancing spirits receive no special attention between seances although they are supposed to be under the protection of their spirits and to receive certain skills from them. On the other hand, mediums of the senior spirit guardians of a chiefdom have high status in their communities: in some areas they wear ritual dress at all times, clearly distinguishing themselves from other members of the community, though elsewhere they confine themselves to a few beads and charms hidden under ordinary clothing.

Most mediums have some taboos imposed on them by their spirits, the precise nature of which depends on local custom and on the status of the spirits. A very common taboo is one against eating the produce of a new harvest before a first fruits ritual, in which the medium eats a little new grain cooked with a little old grain and some herbal 'medicines'. Some mediums must avoid certain types of meat or any strong smells. Some

---

18. This point is argued at greater length in Bourdillon 1979c and 1982.

mediums taboo things particularly associated with the white man's culture. The taboos do, however, tend to change with the times: thus when a young man who had travelled extensively became the medium of a spirit which traditionally forbade its medium the use of motorized transport, the spirit (that is, the possessed medium) followed popular opinion and dispensed the new medium from this rule. The medium of an important spirit should undertake no radical change to his life (such as a move of home or marriage) without first arranging for a relative or friend to consult the spirit (that is, the medium himself when possessed) on the matter. The degree to which mediumship affects the medium's daily life thus depends on the status of his spirit and to some extent on the whim of the medium.

Of the various kinds of spirit that can come out in a medium, one is a family spirit elder. A spirit elder who possesses a medium is likely to be consulted on any significant decision to be made in the family. The spirit is likely to come out in a séance to greet senior members of the family who have returned after some time away from home, or who are about to leave on a long wage-seeking journey. The institution of spirit mediumship thus allows for friendly communication between members of a family and the spirit elders who are believed to control their lives. This emphasizes the belief in the real influence and presence of the spirits of the dead. Unlike Christian missionaries whose God is silent, the Shona can hear their spirits speak.[19]

Alien spirits

A very common type of spirit occurring in Shona ritual and belief are those called *mashave*. When one asks Shona people what *mashave* are, a common explanation is that they are spirits of aliens who died away from home or of young unmarried persons. Such spirits would not have been settled with the final funerary ceremony and therefore wander around restlessly. Having no living descendants they seek to express themselves by taking possession of unrelated persons.[20] *Mashave* include the spirits of neighbouring peoples, of white people, of certain animals (especially baboons) and occasionally of other objects such as aeroplanes. But little is usually known about the person or animal during its life, and these spirits normally come out as complete strangers to the communities of their

19. Cf. Gelfand 1973a, p. 133.
20. Cf. Hugo 1935, p. 52; Gelfand 1959, p. 121; Kumbirai 1966/7 VII (Dec. 1966).

mediums. Sometimes a *shave* is said to possess a medium in order to help him or her perform a particular task (as in the case of a healing *shave*), but most are said to want only to dance. Although it has no special function, such a spirit is believed to have the extraordinary powers attributed to all spirits and to be able to make its influence felt on the living community. Being strangers, *mashave* are said to choose their hosts arbitrarily, but once a spirit has done so, it is expected to remain in the family and, when the original host dies, to possess a descendant or close relative of his.

In some areas, all skills are associated with alien spirits. Thus among the Ndau of the Chipinga District it is presumed that everyone has a number of secret *mashave*, which he honours in private and from which he obtains all his personal talents: such spirits simply convey skills and rarely come out by possessing their hosts. In other areas, alien spirits are associated primarily with possession dances and many (baboon spirits, for example) are said to possess their hosts only in order to dance, and to convey no real skills. In most areas, such traditional arts as hunting, playing the *mbira* (a dominant Shona musical instrument), divining and healing, are attributed to possession by appropriate *mashave*, which must be honoured occasionally and which periodically come out in possession dances.

When a person becomes host to an alien spirit that comes out in a possession trance, the preliminary signs and the initiation ceremony are the same as those of any spirit medium. The first sign that someone is to become a host to one of these spirits is some adversity followed by divination that the spirit wants the patient as its host. There appear to be no special symptoms which are particularly liable to lead to this divination, and the illness may be fairly mild: a persistent cough, stomach trouble, scabies, a child with diarrhoea and barrenness are examples of the signs received by various hosts. Often the host is claimed by the spirit while still a small child and only becomes possessed years later after further illness.

A number of factors may influence the divination, one of which is the previous mediumship of a deceased close relative. A woman with a particularly uninhibited personality is likely to become a member of a dancing spirit cult, but the cults also include retiring personalities and there are no obvious characteristics common to all members of any particular cult. It is rare for a man of high social standing to become host to a dancing spirit, but the same does not apply to women. Indeed, spirit hosts are often the wives of men of high standing and gain status through their ritual roles and the supposed powerful support of their spirits.[21]

---

21. Cf. Werbner 1972, p. 235; and 1971. The author analyses the part played by Kalanga *mazenge* possession in the social status acquired by women.

It is said that an elderly person is never chosen by a dancing spirit. Occasionally, a middle-aged woman might be divined to be required by a *shave* as its host, but as likely as not the woman will fail to become possessed and the divination will be judged erroneous. Once a member of a dancing spirit cult, however, a woman continues to become possessed at séances as long as she is sufficiently agile. Men tend to drop out of the cults as soon as they begin to feel that their senior status demands decorum incompatible with gay spirit dances.

Once a person has been initiated as a host to a dancing spirit, he or she is supposed to hold a regular dancing séance at which the spirit is honoured with millet beer. Many say that this should be an annual event, but in practice it rarely occurs spontaneously except in a season when grain is particularly plentiful, and most séances are held only at the request of the spirit made in the usual way by sickness and divination. The ceremonies are simple. Musicians are hired, and food and beer are prepared by the family of the host. The music starts late in the night and the 'owner' of the dance (the host for whose spirit the ceremony is held) is the first to become possessed, followed shortly by other members of the cult. The possessed mediums, joined occasionally by spectators, keep up their vigorous dancing throughout the night (though individual mediums may become dispossessed for short or long periods, giving them a chance to rest a little). In the early hours of the morning, the possessed 'owner' is shown the beer brewed for him and the first pot is distributed under his directions. Another pot is presented to the musicians and the rest of the beer is distributed at intervals during the morning, at least one pot being reserved for the possessed hosts who drink only water while they are possessed.

At dawn, many spectators offer token gifts to the spirits, usually joining in the dancing and presenting the gift during it. These are small coins, small baskets of grain or meal, or other items of use which the possessed mediums pass on to the musicians or others whom they wish to thank or honour. The gift giving takes place amid much laughter and is part of the night's entertainment. It also helps to defray the costs of the séance.

These séances are great social occasions. The dancing and music are highly entertaining, as are the antics of the possessed hosts, and large crowds may gather to enjoy the spectable, many bringing blankets and sleeping mats with them in order to rest themselves and their small children a little during the night.

Perhaps the most common of these possession cults is that of baboon spirits, which is found throughout Shona country. The hosts of baboon spirits form a distinct cult with an almost exclusively male clientele. Occasionally, baboon spirits are said to convey skills of healing or hunting, but usually they are concerned only with entertaining dance séances. Members of the cult meet at séances specifically for baboon spirits with their own distinctive drumming rhythms.

When the music starts late at night, the hosts go one or two at a time into the dancing area in their ordinary clothes and dance a little, or simply walk around in a circle, until they suddenly become possessed, when they strip to the waist and dance vigorously for a while. The ritual dress of the spirits is usually donned in public. It consists of a colourful cotton skirt worn over the trousers, a fur headband and usually leg rattles to emphasize the rhythm when dancing; possessed hosts also carry whisks made from animal tails. When they are first possessed, the hosts have the fixed blank expression common to all possessed mediums, but this frequently gives way to other expressions as they chat and joke with each other and with spectators. Possessed hosts speak in artificial lilting voices, quite different from their natural voices.

When they are not dancing, possessed hosts act as baboons are supposed to behave. They drink water from a plate lying on the ground; they climb trees; they go wandering off outside the homestead upturning stones, supposedly looking for scorpions and other delicacies to eat; they savagely beat any domestic dogs they come across, supposedly the enemies of baboons (but should the owner of the dogs let the possessed hosts know that he thinks they are going too far, they readily drop the pastime); and they generally mimic baboons to the amusement of all.

Although people say that a baboon spirit can bewitch a person or cause baboons to eat his crops, the possessed hosts are treated with scant respect. They are ridiculed openly and answer back jokingly. They are often egged on in their mimicry, as when during the gift-giving in the morning donors scatter their gifts of groundnuts on the ground and stand back laughing as the possessed hosts scramble for this favourite delicacy of baboons. A séance for baboon spirits is eagerly anticipated as the most enjoyable of all spirit dances.

The Shona say that although baboon *mashave* are not *midzimu* (family spirit elders), they are like *midzimu*. The spirits are presumed to have a kinship structure as people do, and the possessed hosts adopt appropriate kinship terms towards one another (although few of the mediums are in any way related). The 'spirits' hold conferences about their private affairs. They constantly exhort people not to go hunting their relatives in the veld: although the Shona are afraid the baboon spirits will take their revenge if poisoned baits are used against crop-ravaging baboons (people cite instances, as when some distant community killed a number of baboons in this way and suffered losses in return when baboons poisoned their drinking water), people do hunt baboons with dogs and guns, and many are prepared to eat the flesh of slain baboons.

Baboons, which are completely outside the realm of human social life and which nevertheless appear very human in the social behaviour of their colonies, constitute an ambiguous phenomenon which is partially resolved in the baboon spirit cult. In the entertaining baboon spirit dances, people are able to come to terms with the human attributes and possible powers of these alien creatures.

There are numerous other *mashave* and it is not my intention to give a complete list here.[22] There are various hunting spirits which possess men in exclusive cults. Ndebele spirits, whose possessed hosts act as fierce soldiers, are also common, as are spirits of neighbouring Shona groups. There are various types of spirits of white people which act various stylized roles: a district commissioner lording it over attendants, a woman meticulous over cleanliness, or continually drinking tea and perhaps speaking a little English, traits which sometimes carry over into the daily lives of the hosts. The spirits generally represent peoples on the periphery of the society in which the cult occurs, and the spirit dances enable people to meet and come to terms with the invisible powers of peripheral peoples.

Some spirits, however, appear to have no function other than entertainment and entertainment is a dominant feature of all spirit dances. Thus a host may be possessed by a blind *shave* and require to be led around by a child. Possessed women often have male spirits and mimic male roles, sometimes even taking the male part in a dance full of lewd gestures, to the amusement of spectators.

In many seances, especially in cults for women, hosts become possessed by a number of spirits in turn. Thus a peaceful spirit may leave its host, who then becomes possessed by a Ndebele spirit at which other hosts run away in terror (to the great amusement of spectators) to return only when they too are possessed by Ndebele spirits or when the first Ndebele spirit has left its host. But the spirits which take part in such a frivolous séance are said to want only to dance in order to make the people happy: more serious spirits take no part in these frivolities. Thus one woman I know has four *mashave*, three dancing spirits and one healing spirit. Although the healing spirit is regarded as the most important and powerful of the four,

---

22. Lists of *mashave* and their characteristics are given in Gelfand 1959, pp. 121 – 152; 1962, pp. 84 – 105; 1966a, pp. 91 – 106; 1977, pp. 117 – 126; 158ff., 204 – 208. Tracey 1934b.

it never comes out at a spirit dance but only at private seances held specially in order to consult it, and it is honoured with millet beer at its own special celebration when it may dance a little but at which the other three spirits make no appearance.

In the large possession dances, entertainment is the dominant aspect. In some areas, hosts of family spirit elders may gather for a possession dance which provides amusement to spectators; although on these occasions crowds gather for entertainment and may regard the spirits as equivalent to dancing *mashave*, the families of the spirits still demand that their spirit elders be treated with some respect. In any case, family spirits may always be consulted at private séances, when a more serious aspect to their cult is evident.

As there is a more serious side to family spirits, so there is also a more serious side to many *shave* spirits. This applies especially to spirits which are believed to convey the skills of divining and healing. When the hosts of such spirits meet for possession dances, the meeting may take on some aspects of clubs and associations in which men and women unrelated by family ties can meet to share their common interest.[23] The host of a healing *shave* may become renowned as a diviner and healer, in which case he or she acquires the respect due to mediums of the greater spirits.

Spirit elders in modern life

In most of Shona country, families believe in and practise their traditional religion much as they have always done. There are a number of minor variations arising from contact with European culture: thus a corpse is often buried in a coffin with straightened limbs instead of in a reed sleeping mat with legs flexed; the grave is often more elaborate than it used to be, perhaps built up with cement and with an ornamental tombstone at the head; enamelled metal utensils replace the traditional gourds and clay pots left on the grave; a Christian minister may say some prayers over the grave; but for most, the fear of the ambiguous powers of the spirit remains as does the fear of witchcraft. A *n'anga* might wear a white coat and keep a card index on his clients, but he is still expected to inform them of the spiritual causes of their troubles. Spirits of white people and spirits encouraging traits associated with whites come out in possession cults, but the rituals of possession remain much as they have always been. Spirits may

---

23. Cf. Gelfand 1959, p. 123.

now be consulted or appeased over problems in employment or difficulty in passing an examination, but this is to include new circumstances into the old religion. For the majority, religious beliefs remain much as they have always been and superficial changes are fitted into a traditional philosophy.

Some, however, have broken away from traditional beliefs, either through conversion to some new religion or because of a scepticism acquired through contact with a materialistic society (indeed, there are profound sceptics even in the most conservative and technically backward communities). For these, there are two very strong forces pushing them to return to Shona traditional religion.

One is fear in any danger or crisis. When a member of the family is seriously ill, or if a number of socially or financially adverse events take place, a man is likely to fear that the reason may be his neglect of his ancestral spirits. He may be influenced not so much by a positive belief in their powers as by a fear that these powers might be real. A return to traditional religion may thus be a kind of insurance against insecurity.

This kind of situation is more prevalent in poorer families. People living on or below the subsistence level are always in financial difficulties, causing emotional stress and giving prominence to any adverse fortune. People living on a sparse or unbalanced diet are prone to disease and are likely to be seriously affected by ailments which would be minor in a well nourished person. Since the influence of family spirits is felt most acutely in times of stress, poorer people are likely to have a stronger faith in their traditional religion.

The second force inducing a return to traditional religion is that of family ties. We have seen how a kinship group is supposed to co-operate in ritual for the benefit of all. If a member of a family of traditionalists were to stand out and refuse to take part in traditional rituals, he might easily incur strong resentment. And if the ritual were occasioned by serious illness in the family, a refusal to attend is tantamount to witchcraft and murder; it is viewed as an indication that the abstainer does not want the sick person to be cured. Thus a person who refuses to take part in traditional rituals may find himself ostracized by his kin. Clearly this is socially and emotionally extremely undesirable in a society based strongly on kinship ties, but it also has serious economic consequences: since few Shona can afford adequate insurance against unemployment, sickness and old age, most rely on their kin for sustenance in times of hardship. A man who has been ostracized by his kin is thus deprived of his principal form of social security.

This kind of sanction is regularly used against a widow who legally inherits her husband's estate. When a couple are living away from the husband's kin, and especially if both contribute economically to the household, the husband may will his estate to his widow. At his death, however, his kinsmen may insist that she hand over the estate to them according to 'tradition', threatening that otherwise they will refuse to have anything to do with her and her children: in particular, they will refuse to take any action with respect to family spirit guardians should they subsequently become ill. Few widows can withstand such a threat.

Finally, the institution of spirit mediumship provides for concrete contact with the spiritual powers that are believed to control one's environment. A spirit to whom one can speak and who answers back through a medium seems more real than a spirit from whom one receives no communication. The emphasis on empirical events (sickness and trouble) as the reason for many religious practices further provides for a very real experience of the influence of the spirits and of the relevance of religion to daily life. In traditional religion, the important spirits are family elders who are known to the living community and who understand their problems. Most Shona thus see little reason or incentive for breaking away from their traditional religion.

A meeting of a group of Apostles of John Maranke.

A gathering of Zionists.

10

Traditional Religion
at the Tribal Level

Lion spirits

The burial of a dead chief is a more public affair than the burial of a commoner, and the rituals are more elaborate. One significant custom in the burial of a chief is to leave a passage to facilitate the spirit's exit from the grave, should it wish to come out as a powerful 'lion' spirit of the chiefdom. A common practice is to place a hollow reed against the ear of the corpse leading to the surface of the grave. A leaf may be placed over the open end of the reed, and the Shona explain that if the leaf has been blown off during the course of the following night, it means that the chief's spirit will shortly reveal itself as a 'lion' spirit.

A belief that certain powerful spirits, particularly the spirits of departed chiefs, take the form of, or take possession of young lions is common to most Shona country. Such a spirit is believed at first to take the form of a lion cub, which can occasionally be seen playing near the grave from which it came, but which will quickly vanish if approached. The spirit then enters (or in some accounts grows into) a young maneless lion, which wanders about in the bush until it decides to enter a medium. The spirit and the medium are called *mhondoro*,[1] a word which can also mean a wild lion, and a possessed medium is supposed to be able to roar like a lion. It is said that lions roaring in the veld are often heard in the vicinity of a possessed lion spirit medium.

Mhondoro or lion spirits are associated with the strength and fearlessness of the lion, and particularly with its terrifying roar: 'The lion is the most renowned of all animals, at whom everybody shudders. . . . When he roars, the earth trembles.'[2] Yet lion spirits are the guardians of their people, and people say that spirit lions would never hurt their people unless they are provoked. It is said that they take the form of young maneless lions precisely in order not to frighten people away. People say that one can tell when a lion in the veld is really a spirit because it does not do any harm. But the signs are not always clear: when a lion killed an ox from the herd of an unpopular claimant to a Korekore chiefship, most people said that it was a spirit punishing him, but his supporters claimed that it must have been a wild lion since no spirit would attack their domestic cattle. On

---

1. Among the Karanga, the name *mhondoro* is not normally used for chiefly spirits. The cults of these spirits are, however, similar to the cults of lion spirits in other parts of Shona country and Professor Gelfand (1974, p. 95) states that a Karanga spirit may reside in a lion.
2. Kumbirai 1964, p. 7.

another occasion (soon after my arrival in a chiefdom) a pride of four lion walked through a populated area (and right past my camp) waking no one, not even the numerous domestic dogs in the surrounding homesteads: everyone said they were spirits (coming to warn me to behave) and were quite harmless, but few dared to leave their homesteads at night for some weeks afterwards. You can never be sure that a lion is a spirit until you meet it — and then if it attacks you, you know that it is not.

People say that anyone can become a lion spirit by taking appropriate 'medicines' during his life. In central Shona country, the spirit head of any large family who comes out in a medium is called *mhondoro*, but in the north it is very rare for a commoner spirit to acquire this title, and the lion spirit mediums keep themselves clearly apart from the family spirit cult. In any case, lion spirits of the chiefly families carry more prestige than commoners. The 'medicines' necessary for becoming a lion spirit are known to the spirit guardians of any chiefdom, who are believed to pass their secrets on through their mediums to their favourites in the chiefly family, which always has their special attention. It appears to be somewhat arbitrary precisely which members of the chiefly families reveal themselves as lion spirits. The founder of the chiefly dynasty and a sister of his usually come out as the senior lion spirits of a chiefdom, and the spirit of an influential paramount chief (such as Mutota, the legendary founder of the Korekore nation) may be thought to control a territory much larger than a single chiefdom. Lesser and later chiefs, their sisters, and occasionally their brothers, may come out as lion spirits, in some cases for the life span of only one medium, but in others the spirit acquires permanent fame and may acquire functions in the spirit medium hierarchy or possibly the care of a ward or a branch of the chiefly family.

Occasionally, there may be some conflict as to which spirits can be active as lion spirits. Thus in one Korekore chiefdom a man claimed to be possessed by the lion spirit of an ancient member of the chiefly house, who according to tradition had with his descendants been banned from the chiefship on account of a crime he had committed. When the possessed medium started campaigning for this house to be readmitted to the chiefship, people say that the senior lion spirits of the chiefdom drove the new lion spirit away, and the medium died shortly afterwards.

The spirits of a chiefly family are spirit guardians not only of their own descendants, but also of the chiefdom as a whole. They are thus associated with a territory which they 'own' rather than with a kinship group of which they are the senior members. In some areas, this territorial guardianship is emphasized, each lion spirit having its own clearly defined ward in the

254

chiefdom;[3] elsewhere territorial domains are less clearly defined or they simply coincide with chiefdom boundaries. Although it is not impossible for a dynasty to keep its lion spirit cult alive as it moves from territory to territory,[4] commonly when people are moved off their traditional land, their lion spirit cult dies, and they may become subject to the cults previously operative in their new land.[5] Certainly knowledge of the histories and legends about the territorial spirits are regarded as the private property of the residents of the land and should not lightly be passed on to strangers.

The territorial proprietorship of the lion spirits of a chiefdom is reflected in their ritual prescriptions and in their responsibilities to their people, which concern the land and its fertility rather than the care of individual persons. Thus certain days (*chisi*) are dedicated to the territorial spirit guardians (traditionally often determined according to the phases of the moon, but now usually a designated day of the week) on which no one may plough the soil in the spirit's domain. When a newcomer wishes to reside in the country, he should honour the territorial spirit guardian with a gift and invite the senior medium to a house-warming party. The permission of the spirits (through the mediums) should be obtained before major buildings are built in their country or before dams are erected to stabilize the water supply. In most areas, the territorial spirit guardians are particularly concerned with the crime of incest, which is associated with ritual power and sometimes with the fertility of the soil. When the crops of the land are threatened, particularly by drought but also by plagues of insects or birds or by such beasts as elephant, people may approach the territorial spirit guardians to obtain their help. The lion spirits of a chiefdom may also be approached when epidemic disease threatens the whole area, but generally sickness is the concern of family rather than territorial spirits. And lion spirits exercise their control over their territory by appointing and maintaining the chief of the country.

---

3. This is true of the Valley Korekore (see Garbett 1964a, pp. 141 – 144) and also of some Manyika peoples (Gelfand 1974, p. 69).
4. Thus the Mutasa dynasty has carried its lion spirit cult with it on various migrations (see Gelfand 1974, pp. 84f).
5. Thus in the Mount Darwin district, the peoples of Nembire and Noedza (see Bourdillon 1970), who were moved off land to make way for settler farms, now honour the traditional owner of the country into which they moved, and their own chiefly lion spirits have had no mediums for many years. Where the international frontier has cut through chiefdoms, people often honour the traditional spirit guardians of the land even when they have become subject to the chief of some other dynasty.

Some lion spirit mediums regularly practice as diviners and healers. Although there is a general distinction between the functions of lion spirit mediums and those of *n'anga* in that the former are associated with the concerns of a chiefdom or a comparable large community whereas the latter are approached primarily on matters which concern an individual or his immediate family, this distinction is not rigid and there is some overlap in functions.

Occasionally a *n'anga* may be consulted on public affairs when witchcraft is believed to be involved. When a community believes itself to be seriously troubled by witchcraft, or to be seriously in danger of witchcraft, a traditional healer may be asked to protect them by planting 'medicines' around their homes and by treating all members of the community with medicines, either as prophylaxis or in order to reveal any witches among them.[6] *N'anga* rather than lion spirit mediums are associated with 'medicines' which fall into the same category as witchcraft.

This is to some extent simply an aspect of the distinction between the public clienteles of lion spirit mediums and the private clienteles of traditional diviners. The moral values of the Shona are closely associated with the good of the community: what is done for the public good is morally right whereas what is done for one's own private ends, especially if it is done secretly and away from the public eye, is at least suspect. A traditional healer who deals with private affairs by means of secret medicines must always come under some suspicion.

Lion spirit mediums, on the other hand, are essentially public figures and their operations are for the most part open to the local public. Although some do deal in medicines, others maintain a taboo against such practice,[7] and in any case they emphasize spirit mediumship. One lion spirit medium I knew was told during a heated succession dispute that she was a *n'anga*, a remark that was intended and understood as an insult. Lion spirit mediums regard themselves as being above the ordinary

---

6. Gelfand 1964a, pp. 93f.

7. Professor Gelfand (1962, pp. 20f) says a medium may be a *n'anga* who uses medicines, and Kumbirai describes a lion spirit medium who is also a hereditary *n'anga* saying, 'She does not use *muti* (which normally means herbal medicines) as the ordinary *n'anga* do. She uses mysterious ways of healing. She uses for example, tobacco, or powdered charcoal etc.' (1964, p. 51). Most mediums dispense medicated snuff tobacco as a universal cure and prophylatic against all troubles and some dispense herbal medicines (including such a high ranking medium as Mutota). So it is not possible to generalize absolutely about the relationship between mediums and 'medicines' except to say that 'medicines' are not their primary concern.

herbalists; they do not have to rely on a paraphernalia of charms and medicine horns to inspire fear and awe in those who consult them, and their dress is usually simpler than that of *n'anga*. Perhaps the most significant distinction is that lion spirits are the guardians of the communities in their domains, and within their own domains their mediums accept a responsibility towards the people who come to them for help, whereas a professional *n'anga* practices only for his own gain (as a lion spirit medium might do in a foreign country).

Lion spirit mediums do, however, inspire awe with their ritual dress and general appearance. This effect is achieved mainly during seánces by chanting in a distorted voice names of great spirits of the past and by roaring like a lion; if the audience does not appear sufficiently impressed, the preliminary chanting may go on for hours before the medium comes to the business of the consultation. A medium who wants to raise his own status might increase the number of his acolytes, improve on his performance while possessed, develop his technique of assessing public opinion and making popular decisions, and, for rain rituals, learn to assess weather conditions and to predict when rain will fall. A medium might also elaborate and build up the myth about the life and past activities of his spirit and how it came to possess him. But all this is designed to emphasize the power of the spirit and its control over the medium, as opposed to a *n'anga* who may try to build over certain spirits.

Although ideally lion spirits are associated with serious and public affairs, they often do deal with private matters. Many lion spirits are also family ancestors with living descendants, and the medium of such a spirit may be approached by its descendants on such matters as inheritance, succession and troubles with the spirit world. Even people who have no mediums for their ancestral spirit may occasionally approach a local lion spirit medium over family affairs. These spirits do occasionally divine the cause of sickness, and far from charging the heavy fees of traditional healers, they may even give financial help to a person in need. Lion spirits are primarily guardians of their people.

We have seen that territorial spirit guardians are usually spirits of chiefly families, and occasionally a commoner spirit may acquire a similar status. In a few cases, recognition of a commoner spirit may have no ostensible reason apart from the popular belief that the person concerned took the appropriate medicines during his life. More often, a commoner spirit acquired status through association with the foundation of a chiefdom: thus the female slave of the legendary first chief (a woman) of one Korekore chiefdom was given her own domain within the chiefdom, over which she now presides as a lion spirit and which she controls through the senior man of her lineage who is the headman of her area.

Also the rulers and territorial spirits of a country prior to the invasion by the current chiefly dynasty may acquire high status. People coming into a new land have to face a number of difficulties: they do not know the peculiarities of the soil and the rainfall in the area; they do not know much of the vegetation, which fruits are edible and which are not; the ingredients of traditional herbal remedies may be absent; it may take some time to learn how best to hunt local game; and often they sum up all the uncertainties of the new country in a vague fear that they do not know the spirits of the land.[8] Although this may not immediately bother an invading people jubilant and prosperous after their conquest, the invaders are likely to get worried should things begin to go wrong for them. Then they may turn to the cults of surviving locals. In this way, cults of autochthonous people are liable to acquire renown above the territorial cults of more recently established chiefdoms.

One such cult is that of Dzivaguru and Karuva on the north-east border of Korekore country: these are spirits of an ancient dynasty defeated by the invading Korekore centuries ago. The renown of the two spirits for producing rain in times of serious drought is more widespread than that of any of the neighbouring Korekore lion spirits. A virgin dedicated to Karuva used to live in Karuva's sacred grove and from time to time, when there was a severe drought, a man was burnt to death for supposedly causing the drought by seducing the dedicated virgin, a practice which added to the prestige of the shrine. Although people normally honour only the territorial spirit guardians of the chiefdoms in which they live, delegations from chiefdoms over a hundred kilometres away come occasionally to the sacred grove to request from Dzivaguru and Karuva alleviation of drought at home.[9] There are other cults of autochthonous spirits, some quite well known[10] and others known only in the locality over which they are believed to have influence.

---

8. This reaction is well illustrated in Colson's description of the Tonga (who are culturally akin to the Shona) on their resettlement after evacuation of the area to be flooded by the Kariba dam (1971, pp. 49–59). Notice that a similar reaction has occured from time to time among white farmers who have recourse to traditional African cults in times of severe drought (cf. Fry 1976, p. 97 and n.7).

9. Cf. Bourdillon 1972a; 1979b.

10. Descriptions of two such cults have been published, those of the cults of Chidzere (Mitchell 1961a) and of Chimombe (Cambell 1957).

These autochthonous spirits acquire reputations particularly for producing rain, and occasionally for other aspects of fertility. They need not, however, carry much prestige outside this limited sphere of influence. Even a powerful spirit like Karuva who has acquired the status of a lion spirit, is said by the neighbouring Korekore people to be like a woman: he provides rain when they want it (as a woman fetches water for her husband) but they say that otherwise he is less significant than the founder of their own chiefly dynasty who defeated him (a view that is not shared by members of the spirit's clan). Such statements express the view that although the autochthonous people provide fertility (through the wives they provide), it is the invaders who now own the land.[11] Lesser autochthonous spirits may not be classified as lion spirits and are insignificant except on the rare occasions that they are approached to relieve a severe local drought.

In central Shona country, the most powerful lion spirits (called also *makombwe)* are said to be spirits of people who lived in the country very long ago, possibly before the present dynasties were established, and about whom nothing is remembered. The legends about such spirits are learnt only from the mouths of their possessed mediums, and the prestige and renown of such a spirit depends largely on the activities of its successive mediums.[12] Although they may be approached in time of drought or when crops are otherwise threatened, these spirits do not have strong territorial associations and their influence tends to spread over a number of chiefdoms. A more famous spirit (made famous possibly by the activities of a previous medium) is likely to have a number of claimants to its mediumship, providing cult centres in different localities. These mediums may take part in local chiefship disputes, and occasionally opposing parties to a dispute may consult opposing claimants to the mediumship of the same spirit.

Such *makombwe* spirit mediums more readily operate as professional diviners and healers than other lion spirit mediums. Since the spirits do not have definite territorial domains, and since they do not have a known hierarchical and historical place in the traditional histories of any chiefly dynasty, the principal source of status and prestige for their mediums must come from a growing clientele consulting them over personal problems.

Nevertheless, certain of the *makombwe* spirits have become so well and widely known that they form a clear apex to the spiritual hierarchy of a number of subject peoples. The most important of these are the spirits of Chaminuka and Nehanda whom we will be discussing later.

11. Cf. Lan 1983, p. 332
12. The most detailed study of Zezuru spirit mediums is Fry 1976.

Rituals to territorial spirits

The most important ritual involving territorial spirit guardians is a ceremony at the beginning of the wet season to request adequate rains[13] — either too much rain or too little can spoil the crops and lead to famine. Although the time for performing this ceremony may be as early as September or as late as February (the rainy season normally lasts from October to March), some ceremony to request good rains is an annual event throughout most of Shona country. In some places, people may delay organizing the ceremony until there is reason for anxiety because the rains are late or sparse, but the early months of the rainy season are always an anxious time, and the slightest abnormality in the weather can inspire people to hold the ceremony if it has been omitted earlier in the season.

The ceremony takes place at a shrine to the spirit guardians of the area. This is usually situated by a tall tree just outside the residential area, and takes the form of a roughly fenced shrine in which are kept small clay pots consecrated to the spirits, though some shrines consist of permanent or temporary thatched shelters in the bush, and some Manyika peoples perform the ceremony at a temporary thatched shelter built over chiefly graves.[14]

Usually the ceremony is arranged by the chief or headman of the area, who, however, has little part to play in the ritual itself. The person in charge of the ceremony collects from every village or every household in the area grain, which is then brewed into millet beer. The beer is usually brewed outside the homesteads by old women past the menopause, aided by young girls who have not yet reached puberty: women of child-bearing age are not normally allowed in the vicinity of the brewing beer since 'lion spirits do not like milk'. The grain may be germinated by rain water or water from a special well associated with the spirits.

The evening before the beer is ready, the senior acolyte to the spirit (a man descended from a woman of the spirit's clan and therefore classed as 'sister's son' to the spirit) may make a formal address to the spirit to inform it of the coming festival in its honour. The local community gathers early the following morning to sing and dance in honour of the spirit: all households should be represented and according to strict tradition no one may

---

13. Detailed descriptions of rituals in honour of territorial spirit guardians can be found in Gelfand 1959, pp. 49–73; 1962, pp. 13–16, 37–46; 1966a, pp. 18–22, 29–32; Mitchell 1961, pp. 29–33; Chitehwe 1954.
14. Kandamakumbo 1940.

dig the soil in the spirit's domain on the day the ceremony is held (though people do sometimes let their teenage children continue with the ploughing if there is any hurry over this). The mediums of local lion spirits should also be present at the ceremony and become possessed. The acolyte to the local spirit guardians pours millet beer into the consecrated pots and formally addresses the spirits on their duties in looking after their people. Other attendants may join in, and the remarks are often abusive to the spirits over their failings in the past and the various afflictions that have affected crops in the past years. Then the rest of the beer is distributed to the people who proceed with the business of drinking, singing and dancing, which may last well into the following night provided there is adequate grain from the previous harvest for plenty of millet beer: if the spirit guardians failed to provide a good harvest the previous year, they are not so lavishly honoured and the celebrations cease when the attendants have consumed what little beer they could afford to brew. Depending on local custom, a further formal address may be made to the spirit guardians in the evening or early on the following morning.

In most places a similar ritual takes place in thanksgiving after harvest, a very festive occasion, especially if the harvest has been a good one. In some chiefdoms the thanksgiving ceremony occurs only after a particularly good harvest and includes feasting on the meat of oxen killed by the chief for the occasion. At a particularly large festival, people may be asked to brew the millet beer in their homes and contribute beer on the day of the festival instead of grain before it. And the same may apply to smaller festivals arranged at the request of possessed mediums.

As in family rituals the whole kinship group gathers for the good of the community, so in these ceremonies the larger community, whether it be a small neighbourhood associated with a particular spirit or the whole chiefdom, must co-operate to obtain from the local spirit guardians what is necessary for the good of all. The chief or senior man of the spirit domain makes the arrangements for the ceremony and often decides (possibly with the prompting of the possessed senior mediums) if and when the ceremony is to be held. All heads of families in the domain must provide grain for the millet beer; if the whole chiefdom is involved, this is done through the village headmen. Long standing families in the domain have tasks to perform appropriate to their traditional relationships with the spirits: one family provides the acolyte, others provide men to perform the tasks of 'sons-in-law' and 'daughters-in-law', and other tasks may be assigned according to the details of the traditional history of the spirits. All in the domain should attend (or at least be represented) in honour of the spirits.

So territorial spirit guardians help to bring and keep local communities together.

Apart from these regular ritual festivals, the spirits may be consulted in the event of some misfortune affecting the whole community, the most common being late or insufficient rainfall. Lion spirits are also consulted when their domain is plagued by locusts or other pests, when lions or other beasts are troubling the community, when the community is threatened by epidemics of disease and, in the distant and recent past, when the people were about to become involved in war. Senior men from the neighbourhood or domain approach the medium of the guardian spirit to find out the reason for the trouble and what can be done to avert it. They may go to the homestead of the medium with a large party to the accompaniment of singing and dancing in honour of the spirit, or they may approach the medium on their own, usually after consulting the local chief or headman. At night, or early in the morning, the medium becomes possessed and the consultation can proceed.

The spirit, through its possessed medium, may announce the cause of the trouble. It might simply say that the people have been forgetting their ancestors and should honour the guardian spirits of the country with millet beer. It may name some offence as the cause of the trouble, particularly a violation of any tradition that is particularly associated with the greater tribal spirits such as incest, ploughing on their holy days, any violation of the medium or his property, quarrelling at the shrine of the spirit and so on. When such an offence is cited as the cause of the trouble, some punishment or fine is demanded from the guilty party. In the north of Shona country, the offender may be tried at a formal court in the presence of the chief and the possessed mediums of the country, who have a say in the fine or compensation to be paid to them, whereas in the south the medium may simply point out the guilty party, leaving the details of the offence and the necessary compensation for the chief or a professional diviner to decide. Sometimes the spirit is thought to be unjustified in its bad treatment of its people: although the Shona do not readily attribute events to an impersonal fate, they do believe that the spirits who control their lives can on occasion be somewhat capricious in their actions.

Sometimes the medium gives no reason for the trouble, especially if the people approach their spirit guardians when their crops are threatened rather than damaged. Thus in a Korekore chiefdom, the crops had been spoilt by corn crickets and then drought in successive years; when in the third year young corn crickets appeared in numbers early in the season, people in the various neighbourhoods approached their local mediums. The possessed mediums spoke only of evasive action: each landholder had to collect a few of the crickets from his field, and all were gathered in a large container and presented to the local medium, who treated them medicinally and kept them overnight. In the morning, the crickets were either thrown to hungry chickens (as the chickens ate them now, so would birds eat them in the fields) or scattered in the veld where two paths meet (so that the crickets would not be able to find their way to the fields). When the threat subsided and a bumper crop was harvested, the people proudly claimed that they had approached their spirits, who had looked after them and driven the crickets away.

Rituals such as these have endless local and personal variations. The more regular rituals have local variations, but fit into a common pattern. Cults of autochthonous spirits, however, often show peculiarities which clearly distinguish them from the more common Shona lion spirit cult, or indeed from all other Shona cults. Thus in one Korekore chiefdom, there is a tradition that in time of severe drought the chief should send a delegation to a lonely marsh and there leave a black dog tethered to a tree as a gift to the man who had been defeated by the founder of the chiefly dynasty.[15] In no other ritual do dogs appear: sheep or goats are normally killed in sacrifice. Offerings to the great rain spirit Karuva are usually lengths of cloth (confirming the opinion of the neighbouring Korekore that he is like a woman), and drought in his own country used regularly to result in the ritual burning of the supposed offender. Another autochthonous spirit on the borders of Korekore country is honoured in an iron figure which is unique in Shona country.[16] Thus the spirits of defeated peoples which are honoured only in specially severe circumstances preserve their identity as being quite apart from the current Shona rulers.

Lion spirit mediums

People say that when a lion spirit wishes to 'come out' and speak to the people, it chooses someone to be its medium. The medium may be of either sex, but more often than not a lion spirit picks a medium of the same sex as itself. The medium should be a devout person with a blameless past,

---

15. When I was in the field, the rite had not been performed for about ten years, since the early 1960s. People said that no rain fell when they had performed it last, and that they no longer bothered with it since the spirit had become powerless under the white man's rule. The rite was revived during the war, but was not performed to avert the 1982/3 drought.
16. Cf. Campbell 1957.

and may not be a witch or (in some areas) anyone who deals in medicines. A young person still in his teens or early twenties is preferred although an older person may be chosen. In north and central Shona country, the medium should not be of the same patrilineal clan as the chiefly spirits, and people say that the medium should be a stranger to the territory in which the spirit is active, although when the medium dies it is believed that the spirit will have a preference for a near relative of the deceased medium. In the south and east, however, the medium should be of the same clan as the spirit (and therefore usually of the chief's clan) and is often an agnatic descendant of the spirit.

Where the mediums of the senior chiefly spirits are of the chiefly clan, they are often members of the houses of the chiefly family who have become excluded from succession to the chiefship and who receive ritual office in compensation. [17] In the north, the role of the spirit mediums in settling succession disputes between members of the chiefly lineage depends on the fact that the mediums are outsiders to the chiefship and not party to any one line; hence they must not be of the chiefly clan and should ideally have come from outside the community in which they live as mediums. [18] The mediumship of a very senior spirit (such as the spirit of Mutota who is highest in the Korekore spirit hierarchy) may be inherited, or the successor may be nominated by the old medium before he dies, since there is no senior spirit to whom a new medium could appeal for recognition. In one case the medium of the most senior spirit (Musikavanhu of the Chipinga district) is traditionally the ruling chief, and very occasionally elsewhere the chief may be the medium of a senior spirit. [19]

The spirit is supposed to make the chosen person mentally ill, causing him to wander around the forest, eat raw meat like an animal, treat elders as children, and generally to behave in a strange manner. The spirit also troubles the prospective medium with dreams, often about the past life of the spirit itself. Another sign that a member of the community is wanted as the medium of a lion spirit is the presence of lions in the vicinity of his home. Finally a diviner confirms the suspicions of the sick man and his relatives when they consult him on the cause of the trouble. Having revealed its desire in this way, the spirit is supposed to lead the medium to its home country: there are stories of new mediums wandering off apparently aimlessly on foot and turning up after a journey of a week or

17. Weinrich 1971, p. 113.
18. See Garbett 1966a, pp. 166–170.
19. Garbett 1966a, p. 160; Weinrich 1971, p. 78.

more at the home of the senior medium of a country they have never before visited.

Not everyone who claims to be possessed by a lion spirit is accepted immediately, and such persons are often required to undergo some test or ordeal. A new medium normally has to be recognised and approved by an established medium, usually the senior medium of the area, but occasionally the recognition by some other diviner is accepted as decisive.[20] The principal test is that the medium in a state of possession should be able to give a credible account of the life of the spirit, where he was buried, the genealogy connecting him to the senior spirit, the boundaries of the spirit's province of influence, the ritual staff and paraphernalia of the previous medium, the favourite songs of the spirit, and other things that the spirit ought to know. This knowledge is supposed to be esoteric in that the medium himself is presumed to be ignorant of much of it, and the correct recital of the facts is often explained only in terms of the spirit itself speaking through the medium (though in fact as we shall see, the medium often has a chance of learning them through other sources).

A common test for mediums of lion spirits (and also of some family spirits) is that the medium should while possessed be able to drink the warm blood of a sacrificed ox, goat or fowl without vomiting: many Shona believe that only a genuine spirit medium can do this and live. Other signs by which a medium may be recognised include an ability to produce rain, inexplicably being able to find his way to the home of the spirit, knowledge of the graves of chiefs and other sacred places, and being able to expose an imposter. A new medium is often tested by the senior mediums and elders of the people in the presence of the ruling chief, who is the living representative of the spirits of the chiefdom. In practice none of the tests are as conclusive as the accepted beliefs suppose.

Firstly, there is the question of esoteric knowledge about the spirit, especially when the new medium comes from another country and finds his way to the home of the senior medium of a chiefdom. Even where the ideal is that a medium should come from far away, people are aware that usually, and against the ideal, mediums come from the local communities in which they practice and people expect the mediumship of a particular spirit to remain within a group of kinsmen. People insist only that no member of the chiefly clan becomes a lion spirit medium in his own chiefdom: mediums are thus all classed as *vatorwa* or foreigners (though there

---

20. Garbett 1969, p. 116; cf. also Gelfand 1959, pp. 43-46. Gelfand 1966a, pp. 10, 22f.

are occasional exceptions even to this rule[21]). Of those cases which at first sight appear to correspond to the ideal, there are often other explanations for the extraordinary knowledge of the mediums: of the two Korekore mediums I came across who came from chiefdoms far from the chiefdoms of their spirits, one had moved into the latter as a small girl before she became a medium and the other had previously married a man from the area of her spirit and could (albeit unconsciously) have obtained the necessary information from her husband and his friends. Among some peoples, a new medium stays some time with a senior established medium before he is finally recognised: during this period, when the medium is said not to be strongly possessed by his spirit, occasional mistakes in the supposed esoteric knowledge are readily condoned.[22] The conclusive criterion of the validity of the medium must therefore be found elsewhere.

The other tests which are supposed to prove that a medium is genuine are often omitted, or when they are applied, they are not always taken as conclusive. Of the two suggestions I came across that a new medium should be formally tested, one occurred when a late chief was to be buried at the sacred chiefly burial ground: it was suggested that two new mediums be asked to show their knowledge of the graves of all the past chiefs, but in the event everyone was too occupied with the funeral to bother about the test. On another occasion, the possessed senior medium appointed to each spirit a separate entrance to the main shrine of the chiefdom and said that at a forthcoming ritual the new medium would have to find hers without help: in the event the new medium did not attend the ritual (there was a conflict between her and the senior medium), and in any case she could easily have calculated her entrance from an elementary knowledge of the genealogy of the spirits. One medium was criticized by a senior medium for failing to undergo the test peculiar to his spirit in which the possessed medium is supposed to survive unscathed when shot in the chest by a muzzle-loading gun; nevertheless the medium became generally accepted and highly influential. So the tests of a new medium are often not conclusive, nor are they considered to be of vital importance.

In practice a new medium receives at least overt signs of respect if a senior medium recognises and initiates him, but people may still privately doubt his authenticity, especially if there had been any sign of disagreement among the senior mediums. Ultimately the safeguard against impostors is believed to be the power and anger of the spirit: people say that

---

21. See Garbett 1966a, p. 160; Lan 1985, pp. 119-121.
22. See Garbett 1969, pp. 115f.

the spirit will kill anyone who falsely claims to be its medium, but the cases they cite in support of this belief indicate that a medium may practise for a number of years before his early death shows him to have been an impostor. Sometimes two people may claim the mediumship of the same spirit and both practise in opposition for many years before the death of one proves the other to be the genuine medium. People also say that it is possible (though extremely rare) for an established medium to lose favour and be rejected by his spirit, in which case the medium would quickly die, possibly after a new medium has already come out. So in spite of what the Shona say about the ways in which they prove their mediums to be genuine, they have no infallible way of ascertaining that a person is a genuine medium at any particular time: if at any time a medium should give grounds for suspecting his authenticity, this does not upset the belief in mediums in general.

In order to maintain his position, a medium must behave as a medium is expected to behave: he must put on a convincing possession ritual, he must show himself above partiality of sides in a dispute and he must show soundness of judgement — and to show soundness of judgement to the satisfaction of the local community, he must express opinions compatible with popular opinion in the local community. Outside the context of possession, a medium should maintain a certain aloofness from the common people, cutting himself off by wearing appropriate dress and the observance of taboos: these usually include taboos against any proximity with anything associated with death or blood or the colour red; against proximity to lactating mothers and small infants; against 'hot' foods and strong odours, including washing with soap; perhaps an important medium may protect himself from contact with tabooed situations by living slightly apart from the community, in the bush rather than the village.

Even when nobody doubts the authenticity of a particular medium, there is a certain fluidity about his standing in the community. According to Shona belief, once a person is accepted as the medium of a particular spirit, his status is determined by the historical status of the spirit, and the powers of the medium are supposed to be determined by the powers of the spirit. Yet sometimes the medium of the senior spirit of a chiefdom plays second string to a slightly more junior medium on account of the latter's more forceful and awe-inspiring character. And an awe-inspiring spirit famous for his powers of healing can become a retiring and weak figure when the old medium dies and is replaced by a young man without experience. The behaviour of the medium affects the standing of the spirit in the community.

267

In some cases, the reputation of the spirit depends almost entirely on the medium. In central Shona country, knowledge of ancient and 'forgotten' *makombwe* depends on what their possessed mediums do and say, and the activities of the historical persons become confused with the activities of famous mediums.

Thus the most famous spirit in central Shona country is Chaminuka, renowned as a rain-maker who is beseeched in rain rituals in widely dispersed localities and whose name appears in militant nationalist songs. When asked about the history of Chaminuka, people readily tell the story of how he was captured by the Ndebele and killed at the orders of Lobengula: the popular story says that the Ndebele soldiers were unable to kill Chaminuka and he advised them to give a spear to a small boy standing by who was able to kill him without difficulty, this being the chief of a number of wonders that surrounded his life and death. [23] Few people seem aware that the man killed by the Ndebele was in fact an influential medium of Chaminuka. Similarly the fame of Dzivaguru (who has been mentioned earlier) appears to have arisen at least in part from the activities of his medium at the beginning of this century, who travelled extensively around the north-east of Zimbabwe and acquired widespread fame as a rain-maker.

Occasionally, a medium acquires a reputation independently of his spirit. One new medium in Korekore country inspired awe in all he met, although he refused to reveal the name of his spirit. He had an arrogant manner, ridiculed the possessed mediums of the chiefdom in which he first started to practise as a medium, and persuaded the people to build a shrine for him. He became possessed often and at any time, and it was not always clear whether or not he was possessed. He was said to be able to perform a number of extraordinary tricks, such as taking a gourd of millet beer mixed with water, drinking the beer and leaving clear water in the gourd. Although he shrouded himself and his spirit in mystery, all agreed he was possessed by a very powerful spirit — until things started to go wrong for him after about a year (first his shrine was destroyed by a whirlwind; then the 1969/70 drought followed his predictions of good rains; he tried to prevent the building of dams and schools; and finally he tried to discredit a local chief who had him removed).

Even an established medium can become discredited. If a medium

---

23. Cf. Gelfand 1959, pp. 30 - 33; Ncube 1962; Posselt 1935, pp. 201-204; Woollacott 1975.

loses his charisma, people may presume that the spirit has left him. Thus when the medium of a militant spirit was recently arrested by government forces and convicted of 'encouraging terrorism', the rumour quickly spread that the spirit had left the medium (or it would have saved him from arrest) and would shortly come out again in another. Or should a convincing rival claimant to the mediumship of a spirit arise, people may suspect that the spirit has left the original medium who should shortly die. The importance of playing the role of a medium in accordance with popular appeal is, of course, emphasized when more than one person claims to be the medium of a particular spirit: each must strive to make himself more convincing and popular than his opponents.

So mediums cannot normally rely for prestige solely on the renown of their spirits or the place of their spirits in the history of the people. Whether or not he is aware of it, in order to acquire and maintain the respect of the community among whom he lives, a lion spirit medium must say and do what is expected of him. To try to push unpopular ideas would incur the risk of being rejected.

Sayings of the spirits

Shona people say that once a medium is proved to be genuine, nobody can question or doubt what the spirit says when the medium is possessed. Most affirm emphatically that the spirits can never make a mistake, they can never lie and they can always enforce their will on their people. The sayings of possessed mediums certainly carry weight. Mediums are often leaders of public opinion: in one recorded case, a medium was prominant in changing local customs in accordance with new national egalitarian ideology, and started to add to legends about the past in ways to emphasize national unity.[24]

Nevertheless, in practice people find excuses to doubt inconvenient pronouncements without overthrowing the institution of spirit mediumship.

Most Shona admit that even a genuine medium can occasionally fake possession and speak his own mind while pretending to speak with the voice of the spirit. Thus after a seánce during which the lion spirits of a chiefdom advocated a change from the traditional succession pattern of the chiefship, the acting chief afterwards privately expressed his opinion that only one of the five mediums taking part was really possessed. And when

---

24. See Lan 1983, pp. 305f., 318.

on another occasion the possessed mediums showed knowledge of an event which occurred some time before the seance, doubts were expressed about the state of possession of the mediums. That people acknowledge in practice the possibility of human intervention in the supposed sayings of the spirits is further illustrated by a case in which the people readily blamed the mediums for the election of an unpopular candidate to the chiefship, although the mediums (in accordance with orthodox belief) strongly disclaimed any responsibility for the election and said it was the wish of their spirits. So although a lion spirit medium may be recognised as such, there is room to doubt any particular statement of the possessed medium and a very controversial statement is likely to fall under suspicion in some quarters.

The frequent long delays before the appointment of a new chief suggest that mediums are aware of how controversial statements can undermine their position. In practice an appointment is often delayed considerably longer than the two years officially allowed after the death of the late chief, and it is preceded by a number of meetings between the senior men of the chiefdom and their lion spirit mediums. While the people are discussing and weighing the attributes and claims of the various candidates, the spirit mediums procrastinate, saying that they must consult with other spirits before they can make a decision. In practice, they often wait until public opinion, which they help to form, crystallizes on one candidate before accepting the choice of the people: I have come across a case in which the mediums were not prepared to commit themselves finally until they had ascertained that their candidate was acceptable both to the people and to the government. And when mediums do enforce, or try to enforce, their election of an unpopular candidate, they are likely to be accused of taking bribes and to lose the respect of many in the community. So although the sayings of the possessed mediums are supposed to be the sayings of the spirits to which all must submit, in practice they often reflect, rather then control, public opinion.

Even when people do not openly doubt the possessed state of a medium, they do not always follow their expressed belief that spirits can never make a mistake. The very people who before an election say that it is the role of the spirits to elect a new chief and that in this role they can never make a mistake, may later say that the spirits were wrong in their choice and had made a big mistake, especially should drought or pests diminish subsequent harvests. In one succession debate the people only agreed to the new chief some five months after the spirits first made their appointment. During the course of the dispute the possessed mediums were often openly abused, and in the heat of one argument one of the candidates for succession called the senior spirit a liar. One medium dropped out of the debate on account of a personal insult. The mediums were persuaded to change their appointment three times and finally had their way only through the support of the administration.[25] This is probably an unusual case, but it does illustrate that beliefs concerning the sayings of the spirits do not always coincide with practice.

Apart from arguing with possessed mediums, people sometimes play mediums off against one another in order to counter an unfavourable statement. This course of action is common when two persons claim to be mediums of the same spirit and each tries to gain support by siding with one party to a succession dispute. Also when two mediums are jostling for status and control over a chiefdom, disputants may involve the conflict between the mediums in their own dispute. And the decision of a junior medium is always subject to an appeal to a more senior medium.

Occasionally, too, people oppose mediums who refuse to change with the times and in the opinion of their people are being unreasonable. Thus a medium who was at first highly respected and greatly feared lost his support and was expelled from the chiefdom when he tried to oppose the building of dams and schools in the area.[26] On the other hand, another medium had her way when she threatened severe drought if the people allowed a dam to be built which would flood a sacred well. Although the Shona belief system provides sanctions in support of the sayings of possessed mediums, the position of a spirit medium does depend to some extent on the spirit saying what the people want to hear. People do not follow blindly all the sayings of a possessed medium.

Doubts about particular statements of particular mediums in no way diminish the faith of the people in mediumship generally. Since there are ways of explaining away any unsatisfactory instances of possession, no particular failing of a medium can destroy the belief that there are some mediums who are genuinely possessed by spirits who in turn genuinely care for their people. For the most part, people accept their mediums as genuine and respect their sayings as the sayings of their spirit guardians. Doubts generally occur only in times of controversy or crisis.

---

25. Colson (1948, p. 278) cites a parallel case among the Tonga just north of the Zambezi: a conservative statement by a possessed medium was jeered down by the people on the grounds that times had changed. Colson comments that the Tonga are not slavishly obedient to the whims of the spirits speaking through their mediums.

26. This was a case I followed closely in Korekore country.

Unity across chiefdom boundaries

We have seen that the cult of territorial spirit guardians brings diverse family groups together to form a local community. We have also seen that the cult is associated with the government of a chiefdom and that the spirit mediums exert some influence on the politics of their chiefdom. The senior spirits are often associated with military prowess in the past and were responsible for protecting their people against enemies. Thus in various ways, the cult of territorial spirit guardians reinforces the chiefdom as a political and administrative unit.

The cults of the more famous spirits go beyond this and provide some unity between diverse and independent chiefdoms. They achieve this in various ways. At the simplest level, the common pattern of territorial cults, which include spirit mediums of the guardian spirits and rituals in their honour consisting of offerings of millet beer all over Shona country, allows strangers from a distant Shona people readily to fit into the community they have joined. The numerous local peculiarities may be ignored by people moving from one territory to another, who see only the familiar cult serving familiar functions everywhere.

At a more concrete level, spirit guardians often have traditional associations with the spirits of neighbouring chiefdoms. These may involve some form of kinship, an ancient marriage between the two chiefly families or simply friendship. The mediums from neighbouring chiefdoms may come together when their spirits are honoured, in which case they may help to maintain friendly relations between their chiefdoms. This kind of permanent spiritual basis to an alliance between two chiefdoms has little relevance now except when one claims paramountcy over the other, but it was important in the past when chiefdoms were responsible for their own military defence.

A few cults, such as that of Dzivaguru and Karuva in Korekore-Tavara country, involve people from many and diverse chiefdoms. Thus the virgin dedicated to Karuva had to come from Chief Gosa some thirty kilometres to the north of the cult centre. If she was defiled, the neighbouring Chief Chizwiti was involved in the reprisals. Tribute used to come to the cult centre from people as distant as the Tavara Chief Chioko eighty kilometres to the east of the centre, and the people of Pfungwi some fifty kilometres to the south-east. Even today delegations arrive from a number of Korekore and Tavara chiefdoms who thereby have a common cult centre.

The contact of the various peoples with the cult centre was strengthened by the wandering medium of Dzivaguru who travelled so extensively that many people say the spirit has no home: they say he owns all the land and wanders about making rain where he wills. Even today, a spirit medium often establishes a clientele spreading over a number of chiefdoms, which may depend partly on his own travelling. The activities of a medium may thus provide a common focus of interest for diverse communities.

Occasionally, a lion spirit may provide unity because of its place in the traditional history of the people. Mutota appears in myths and legends throughout much of Korekore country as the founder of the Korekore peoples; and many chiefdoms claim to have some connection with him, whether because in the legends they travelled with Mutota or he gave them their land, or through some (probably fictional) kinship link. Many from chiefdoms in the vicinity, and some from more distant places, used to consult the medium of Mutota, both as a diviner and healer and on public issues such as a chiefly succession dispute or the recognition of a new lion spirit medium. The widespread reputation of the spirit was undoubtedly affected by the aged and talented medium who had held the position for half a century when he died in the late 1970s; but the supremacy of Mutota as the head of all Korekore peoples is recognised by many who had no direct contact with the cult of the spirit.[27]

A local territorial spirit is considered the owner and ruler of its territory, providing its inhabitants with a group identity. The greater spirits whose influence is not limited to a defined territory are thought in some vague way to rule over all in the country under their influence. Thus people from a collection of chiefdoms submit themselves to Mutota or to Chaminuka or to Musikavanhu, and in each case they believe in a common spiritual power that cares for all and controls their well-being. It is through these greater cults that the Shona people have always been more than a collection of petty chiefdoms.

The cultural unity provided by these spirit cults has occasionally found practical significance. One of the most renowned incidents in which spirit mediums appear to have provided a practical unity across chiefdoms was the Shona rising of 1896/97. The rising seems to have comprised a chain of

---

27. The cult is discussed in Garbett 1977 and Lan 1983. Lan argues that Mutota, originally a mythical symbol of the source of life, only became thought of as an historical person (with a medium and a cult) at the end of the nineteenth century, when the first medium of Mutota successfully altered Korekore perceptions of their history.

spontaneous revolts against malpractices by the whites,[28] frequently encouraged by important spirit mediums, with the result that the Shona resistance persisted months after the defeated Ndebele had come to terms with the settlers. Chaminuka had no established medium at the time, but mediums of spirits subordinate to him were active in goading the fighters on.

Two of the most active mediums were the mediums of Kagubi and of Nehanda. Kagubi appears to have been a relatively unimportant spirit who acquired some fame through his activities in the uprising,[29] but Nehanda is a female spirit renowned throughout central Shona country and on a par with Chaminuka. There is also a Nehanda, the daughter of Mutota, who is an influential lion spirit in Korekore country and who is vaguely associated with Nehanda of the Zezuru: the Korekore say that it is the same spirit, the Zezuru medium on the plateau being the head and their own in the Zambezi Valley the feet, but the relationship between the two is vague and historically the two spirits were probably separate. What is important is that Nehanda, Kagubi and various other mediums were able to claim the allegiance of a number of chiefs and to co-ordinate their resistance to the European settlers.

When a new medium of Chaminuka appeared in 1903, eleven paramount chiefs are known to have paid their respects to him, either personally or by sending gifts, in spite of the dangers of incurring the suspicion of the administration so soon after the war. These were the successors of men who had united to fight the settlers, but who had been locked in bitter rivalries a decade before.[30]

The unity was not perfect. Many chiefs did not join the revolt and some used the war to exact vengeance on traditionally hostile neighbours. Occasionally a chief who joined the fighters found himself opposed by a rival to the chiefship who joined the settlers.[31] Nevertheless, the senior spirit mediums provided a cohesive focus to the revolt in a way that no secular authority could have done.

Later, spirit mediums in the north-east played a similar role in the

---

28. Ranger (1967, pp. 206-226) gives a central place to religious authorities as co-ordinators of the war. Recently Beach (1979) has pointed out that there was in fact little co-ordination between chiefdoms, and that the mediums consequently had had very limited influence as organizers.
29. Ranger 1967; p. 215.
30. Ranger 1967; pp. 208f.
31. Ranger 1967, pp. 196f.

Mapondera revolt in 1901 and the Makombe war against the Portuguese in 1917. These involved some Korekore and Tavara peoples, who had not been involved in the earlier wars, and among others, the medium of Dzivaguru.[32]

This is not to suggest that the mediums have absolute sway over the Shona population. There are enough ways to discredit a medium who tries to persuade the people to do something they do not want to do. There were a number of factions which did not join the rebellion of 1896/7, indicating that people could ignore the call of the spirits if they had sufficient motive. In all the cases of incitement to war, the unrest and the desire to fight the white rulers were widespread. The spirit mediums provided a focus for a common feeling.

With the rise of nationalism among the Shona, the status of spirit mediums increased. The famous spirit mediums provide a connection with the glories of the Shona past, be they real or mythical, and names like Chaminuka are invoked in militant nationalist songs. The political movement was accompanied by a cultural nationalism which included a movement away from Christian churches back to the traditional religion of the Shona, and some spirit mediums involved themselves in the movement by becoming openly political. After the suppression of African nationalist parties in 1964, spirit mediums remained on the whole unmolested, partly because they enjoyed the respect of black employees in the government administration and in the police force, and partly because government policy respects the more traditional elements of Shona culture. Those mediums who took an interest in politics thus became the only focus for nationalist sentiments.[33]

Not all mediums involve themselves in politics, and many clearly opt to maintain the status quo. In some relatively backward areas, the lion spirits remain aloof from the whites and some mediums refuse to have any contact with their culture,[34] which does not necessarily involve opposition to

---

32. See Ranger 1963. Also Isaacman 1976.
33. Cf. Fry 1976, pp. 107 − 123.
34. The absolute taboo on the white man and his culture by some spirit cults is illustrated in Holleman 1958, pp. 226 − 240, where the author describes the problems he encountered in his dealings with an aged medium whom he was not allowed to meet. (The old woman has since received white visitors − cf. Berlyn 1972, where it is claimed that although closely connected with a spirit cult she is not in fact a medium). In my own experience in the north-east, it took some time before friends dared to ease me into seances of possessed mediums, and certain spirit mediums in neighbouring chiefdoms maintained their taboos against contact with whites (at least when possessed).

white rule. Although some mediums may mix and travel with the most westernized of the Shona, wearing smart western suits when not possessed and taking an active part in politics, others remain unsophisticated persons who wear only their ritual blue and white cloths, live in remote pole and mud thatched huts and desire only life without want and trouble for their people. And between these extremes there are infinite variations in the sophistication and the religious and political attitudes of spirit mediums. Whatever the political and religious role a particular medium may play, the Shona belief in lion spirits and their mediums remains strong in all strata of Shona society.

The role of spirit mediums in the recent war shows that they are still able to function as co-ordinators in military activities. When the war broke out in the early 1970s, months after the nationalist forces had infiltrated into the country, it became apparent that the cults of lion spirits had been influential in rallying support for the guerrillas, and in keeping a veil of strict secrecy over their operations. Mediums throughout the country were regularly consulted by guerrillas, who wished to receive the protection of the spirits, and who wished to have through the mediums secure and trusted ties with local populations. Indeed, it can be argued that through the mediums, the guerrillas acquired political legitimacy in the place of chiefs who had become compromised by their enforced service to the white administration.[35] The mediums served in some cases as co-ordinators between civilians and guerrillas, and were able to act as centres of information on military activities. The fame of Nehanda, and others involved in the 1896 war, was revived: such spirits are symbols of native African power against the dominating the rule and culture of the whites. Although spirit mediums had no say in the overall conduct of the war (demands by a spirit that no blood be spilled in its domain were lightly brushed aside), they played a significant role in maintaining morale and effective unity in their various domains throughout Shona country.

Again, not all mediums took on this role. In the event some mediums were killed by forces of both sides in the war, allegedly for supporting the other. The point is that their position in Shona society lends itself to playing a prominent part in war.

---

35. See Lan 1983.

The high god

As do many African peoples, the Shona believe in a remote high god. He is known by various names[36] including: Nyadenga or Dedza (Lord of the sky), Musikavanhu (Maker of the people), Chikara (One inspiring awe), Dzivaguru (The great pool), Chirazamauva (The one who provides for good and bad), Mutangakugara (One who existed at the beginning) and Mwari (a personal name). Mwari is now the most common name for the high god, spread by Christian missionaries from the cult in southern Shona country and explicitly associated by many with Christianity. The Shona rarely speak about the high god and in most of Shona country no attempt is made to communicate with him or to influence his actions either by imprecation or ritual. The high god is, however, believed to be some personal being above and more powerful than the lion spirits; even such spirits as Chaminuka are ultimately subject to the high god.

Traditional beliefs are unclear about the nature of the high god and his relevance to the origins of the world. People believe that he is in some way ultimately responsible for all that happens. He knows everything and sees everything, and is ultimately responsible for the weather, the fertility of the land, the wild forests, character traits of men, and so on. Myths or legends about Mwari are rare — certainly less common and less well known than those about lion spirits. Mwari was not a man and nobody has ever seen him.

Although Mwari is known under different names, he is believed to be the God of all men. Thus the things which 'belong' to him, such as wild fruit and honey and sometimes game, cannot be withheld even from a complete stranger, and the rain he provides falls on all alike. He is considered to have made the white people as well as the black. Far removed from the family spirit elders who are intimately concerned with the private affairs of their descendants, the high god is too remote and his interests are too broad for him to concern himself with private individuals and their problems. He can be ill-tempered and is sometimes believed to 'cheat' his people for no justifiable reason.[37] Nevertheless, in time of extreme emotion, especially at death in the community, people may voice their complaints directly to Mwari; and his name is commonly used as an oath.

Mwari is believed to be too remote to be concerned even with the spirit

---

36. See Murphree 1969, p. 49; van der Merwe 1957, pp. 41-45.
37. Cf. Howman 1914.

elders of a family, but the Shona believe that the more important lion spirits can communicate with him. In the manipulation of natural phenomena, particularly of rain, lion spirits are believed to work in co-operation with the high god. Thus one man explained a widespread drought by saying that Dedza and all the lion spirits had held a meeting in the sky at which they decided for some unknown reason to stop the rain everywhere. It is thought that a powerful lion spirit on good terms with his people should normally be able to persuade Mwari to allow rain to fall on his chiefdom. Also, senior lion spirits are believed to be able to call support for themselves from the high god. Thus in a chiefship dispute a possessed medium may try to threaten recalcitrant disputants into submission with the words, 'You know Dedza when the lightning strikes.'

Three types of events are especially attributed to the high god. The first comprises events with an effect more wide-spread than the territorial domain of even the most powerful lion spirits. Thus the drought of 1970 was attributed to Mwari rather than to the territorial lion spirits on the grounds that it affected crops throughout Zimbabwe and even beyond its boundaries.

Secondly, those events are attributed to the high god which are in the natural order of things in the sense that they are expected and do not require further explanation in terms of a personal agent. Thus occasionally, when no evil influence is suspected, the death of a very old person may be said to have been caused only by Mwari, and the same is sometimes said of mild illnesses when no diviner is consulted.

Thirdly, thunder and especially lightning are usually understood to come from the high god. These reveal occasional and unusual power coming from the heavens which is terrifying, unpredictable and inexplicable in terms of the ordinary events of social life.

The high god appears to be relevant to the thought of most traditional Shona only in order to explain events which fall outside the domain of the usual spiritual causes, whether because they are too widespread, too trival or common, or too terrifying. Outside the context of such events, the high god remains unknown and unknowable, and too remote to be interested in the troubles of men or to be influenced by their imprecations.

Since the Shona lack a systematic theology, their ideas about their spirits are expressed primarily through the activities in which the spirits are concerned. Since regular rituals normally concern only the more intimate and local spirits, Shona ideas about the high god naturally tend to be somewhat nebulous. For most Shona, belief in the high god is operative only on the rare occasions that other beliefs are inadequate. And although the influence of the high god is supposed to extend beyond the limits of tribe or race, the Shona rarely consider Mwari's relationship with other peoples: the question simply does not arise in the context of Shona society.

Certain of the greater lion spirits merge and are confused with the concept of the high god. Thus the possessed medium of Mutota acknowledged no spirit greater than himself and was confused and evasive when asked about his origins and his ancestry: he claimed to be the highest of all spirits and the father of all peoples, thus taking some of the attributes of a high god. In some areas, Dzivaguru, the high god, is said to have a home in Korekore country, clearly associating the high god with the famous lion spirit; but others use Dzivaguru as a praise-name for the high god with no reference to the Korekore-Tavara lion spirit cult. The Manyika use Karuva as a name for the high god[38] which may be associated with the Korekore-Tavara cult of the Karuva. And the distinction is often obscure between the high god and Chaminuka, who is clearly the most important spirit to many Shona peoples.

Among the Karanga, however, in the south of Shona country and probably under the influence of neighbouring Venda peoples, there is an organized cult of Mwari, the high god. Mwari is a common personal name for women, and Mwari is the name of the lion spirit of an ancient ancestor in the more central Wedza district[39] — it is possible that the southern cult of Mwari originated historically from this lion spirit cult. But the Mwari of the southern cult is identified with the high god, and it was from early contact with this use of the name that Christian missionaries spread it throughout Shona country as the name for the high god of all.

The cult is centred on a number of shrines in and south of the Matopo hills in what is now Ndebele country.[40] Some of the various shrines clearly cohere in an established hierarchy with regular communications between them, and between others there is a certain amount of competition and rivalry. Currently the most influential and well-known shrine is at Matonjeni in the Matopo hills:[41] the officials at this shrine maintain communications with all surrounding chiefdoms and spread its network up to four hundred kilometres to the east and the south. This is the most influential

---

38. Gelfand 1974, p. 68.
39. Professor Fortune (1973) discussed the origins of the name Mwari.
40. The various shrines are discussed in Cockroft 1972 and Schoffeleers and Mwanza 1979. See also Werbner 1977
41. This shrine is discussed in detail in Daneel 1970a, from which much of my material comes; also in Gelfand 1966a, pp. 33 — 42.

of all Shona shrines and has received tribute from the invading Ndebele, who occupied the surrounding country, and even from neighbouring white farmers (who are as anxious as any about rainfall) apart from many Karanga chiefdoms.

The shrines are served by hereditary officials (with the usual disputes arising over succession) and various messengers, many of whom are hosts to appropriate spirits. At the Matonjeni shrine, the principal officials are a high priest and priestess (a brother and sister who inherit their positions and who communicate directly with the oracle), a keeper of the shrine (a senior man from a lineage related to the high priest's family) and the 'voice' (an elderly woman married into the high priest's family). The shrine is a cave from which the voice of Mwari speaks its oracles.

Delegations from surrounding chiefdoms come to consult the 'voice' over matters of public importance, such as the appointment of a new chief, the acceptance of a new spirit medium, drought or some other communal disaster. For such consultations, the delegation should have some authority, either from the chief or senior spirit medium, or on the grounds of holding the inherited position of messenger to the oracle.[40] A party may occasionally arrive to consult the oracle on private affairs and may receive some advice from it, but the oracle is more likely to refer private individuals to a lesser diviner.

The party arrives at the hamlet below the shrine where the officials live, and states its business at a formal meeting of all the officials with the keeper of the shrine presiding. The party is then conducted to the shrine (after the 'voice' has had time to reach it secretly) and sits at the mouth of the cave. The high priestess is closest to the cave and is the first to address the oracle; next to her is the high priest, who takes the initiative in communicating with the oracle, and who is responsible for mediating between the oracle and the clients; then there is usually a junior priest (a younger brother of the high priest); beyond them sit the clients. The delegation which has come to consult the oracle brings a gift for Mwari, which is pass-ed from hand to hand to the mouth of the cave. The clients are not allowed to look to see what happens to the gift or to look inside the cave under pain of severe penalties;[43] all sit with their backs to the cave. Questions put to the 'voice' are asked through the high priest and the 'voice' answers in an

---

42. Franklin 1932, p. 81; Gelfand 1966, pp. 14f.
43. Van der Merwe 1958, p.54. Professor Gelfand was taken inside the cave but he was observing as an outsider and not at a consultation with the oracle.

ancient dialect which must be translated into the language of the clients. Besides deciding on the matter of the consultation, the oracle often exhorts the people to remember the traditions of their ancestors and not to drop them for some new religion.

Apart from consulting the oracle, subject chiefs contribute to rituals at the shrine in honour of Mwari; for these, as for ceremonies for territorial spirit guardians elsewhere, they collect contributions from all households under their jurisdiction through ward and village headmen. These rituals involve the usual millet beer with singing and dancing in honour of the spirit and sometimes the sacrifice of black oxen. They take place at the beginning of the rain-season to implore good harvests from Mwari, and after harvesting in thanksgiving. In this respect the cult is similar to the territorial lion spirit cults.

In other respects too the cult of Mwari in the south serves the functions of lion spirit cults elsewhere, and the cults of local spirits with their mediums are not as dominant among the Karanga as they are in the north of Shona country. Mwari is honoured as the provider of rain. Troubles over crops are referred to his oracle, as elsewhere they are referred to lion spirit mediums. Chiefly succession disputes are referred to the oracle, and chiefs pay tribute to Mwari, as elsewhere they pay tribute to a senior lion spirit medium. Like lion spirit mediums, the oracle may also be consulted over private troubles with the spirit world. The Mwari oracles bring diverse chiefdoms together as do the greater lion spirit mediums. Mwari oracles were involved in the 1896 war and have since associated themselves with nationalist politics.

The mediums of senior tribal spirits in subject chiefdoms have often had previous close contact with the shrine. Some girls and boys, usually children of cult messengers, are in their youth dedicated by their parents to Mwari and they grow up at one of the shrines. These persons have chores to perform in connection with the care of the shrines, but their main official function is to dance in honour of Mwari on ritual occasions. While in the service of the oracle, they observe a number of taboos, including sex taboos, but they do eventually leave the shrine and marry under the direction of the oracle. Many become mediums to senior spirits of surrounding chiefdoms, and others become hosts to *jukwa* spirits, which are especially associated with the cult and its messengers. The cult thus acquires in subject chiefdoms a network of religious functionaries who maintain its widespread influence.

The oracle at Matonjeni has shown itself antagonistic to Christianity, both to mission churches and to the new independent churches that have grown up in Karanga country, on the grounds that these turn people away from honouring their ancestors in the traditional way. Clearly many of the population have rejected the cult in favour of these new religions. Nevertheless, the cult with its network of spirit mediums to support the Mwari oracle retains a strong hold in southern Shona country, and its officials can occasionally demand the obedience even of Christians through threats of drought and death.[44] Modern communications have spread its fame, if not its influence, throughout most of Shona country. The remote high god of the central and northern Shona is thus becoming more accessible as the Mwari of the Christian missionaries and as the Mwari of the oracles in the Matopo hills.

---

44. Cf. Weinrich 1971, p. 86.

GUTA RA JOHOVA
RAKATANGA. 12/6/54.

MURAWU WE GUTA HAUBVUMIRE
MUNHU ASATI ARE URURA KUPINDA
MUGUTA KANA ACHIDA TANGA
WAWONA VAKURU VE GUTA

CITY OF GOD
STARTED ON 12/6/54
THE LAW FOR SOCIETY IS NO
PERSON IS PERMITED TO COME
OR ENTER IN TO CITY OF-
GOD ANY ONE WISHES TO JO
IN US SHOULD SEE SENIOR MEMBER

Sign at the entrance to the City of God (Guta raJehova), the church of Mai Chaza, the famous woman faith-healer.

Many Shona have joined the various mission churches. Today about 16% claim some affiliation to one or the other or them. Picture shows RC Church at Serima.

11

New Religions

Mission churches

Some Shona first came into contact with Christianity even before the occupation of the land by the British South Africa Company in 1890, partly through contacts while they were working in the mines of South Africa and partly through the early evangelization by Protestant Mission Churches of southern Shona country.[1] Most, however, met Christianity later, after the expansion of missionary activity following colonial settlement. Different missionary bodies have always varied considerably in their attitudes, their methods and their religious practices. Some missionaries teach the Bible as they understand it with little knowledge of, and little consideration for, traditional religious beliefs; others take great care to study the traditional culture to see how much of it they can incorporate into the Christianity they preach. Some mission churches conduct austere services involving only Bible readings, preaching and formal prayer; others have an elaborate ritual with colourful vestments or uniforms and much singing. Some missionaries have strict rules to be observed as conditions of church membership, and readily punish breaches of them with excommunication; some demand long periods of instruction prior to reception into the body of the church; and some require little more than a simple of profession of faith. So there are a wide variety of mission churches operating in Shona country and the brief and general comments we make about them must be treated with some caution.[2]

All Christian mission churches offer to the common people means of directly approaching the high god. Instead of the high god of traditional Shona religion who is too great and too remote to be concerned with the personal problems of individuals, Christianity presents the high god as someone intimately concerned with the welfare of all his children, someone to whom all and any can pray, and who has provided a mediator in his son, Jesus Christ. The God of Christianity is concerned with the details of the lives of all men and dictates a moral code that all must obey, whatever their race or tribe. Christianity thus provides a religion that stretches beyond the limiting boundaries of kinship group or chiefdom.

This is a significant change from traditional religion which was little concerned with what we would call ethics. It is true that traditional

---

1. Pre-colonial contact of the Shona with Christianity is discussed in Beach 1973a. For a very good study of the introduction of Christianity to Western Zimbabwe, see Bhebe 1979.

2. Case studies of missionary activities are given in Murphree 1969, pp. 60 – 91; Daneel 1971, pp. 185 – 281.

religion reinforces the observance of the traditions of ancestors and demands the observance of certain taboos, against incest, for example, or ploughing on holy days. Traditional religion also demands a certain co-operation and concord within a community, be it a gathering of kin for a ritual in honour of a family spirit elder or a neighbourhood community honouring a territorial spirit guardian. But traditional religion is concerned primarily with respect for spirit guardians, and has very little to say on people's relations with strangers or anyone outside their communities. As the Shona break out of their small local communities and have dealings with an ever widening society, it is advantageous to find an overall religious view, which incorporates all the people they may meet and which implies universal ethical norms.[3]

Many have joined the various mission churches, to the effect that in 1974 about seventeen per cent of the black population of Zimbabwe claimed some affiliation to one or other of them[4] and a further eight per cent belonged to the numerous new independent churches.[5] Of course the proportion varies from area to area: in strongholds of a particular church the majority of the local population may be church members, whereas in outlying districts there may be few if any Christians. Nevertheless the overall figures show that Shona religion has been significantly affected by the advent of Christianity. Some families have now been Christian for a number of generations.

There are a number of reasons in favour of joining a Christian church apart from religious conviction. One is education. In the early days of education in Zimbabwe, the Shona saw it as a means of obtaining the white man's knowledge and ultimately the white man's wealth. In practice, education is still the principal means for obtaining better paid employment. Education of the Shona, both in academic and technical fields, has until recently been largely the work of missionary bodies, some of which demanded church membership for attendance at their institutions and many of which gave preference to their own church members even when they did not exclude others. Religious practices and indoctrination were often compulsory features of church controlled schools, encouraging to conversion those who were not church members prior to their admittance.

3. This point is argued more fully in Horton 1971, 1975.
4. The *News Sheet of the Rhodesia Catholic Bishops' Conference*, No. 43, February 1974, (Mambo Press) lists membership estimates for the major denominations (p. 13) which form the basis for the figure of seventeen per cent of the total black population.
5. This comes from the figure of half a million in Barrett 1968, p. 78, which, however, is based on impressions.

The highly paid (relative to average incomes) teaching posts in church schools were often reserved for church members. So many Shona have become at least nominal Christians, either through education or in order to be able to profit financially from it. Although most primary schools have now been taken out of the hands of mission churches and placed instead under the control of local councils, the more desirable secondary schools and some of the better primary schools remain church schools. Education thus remains, though to a lesser degree than in the past, a motive for adherence to Christianity.

Another attraction of mission churches has been the benefit of their medical facilities. There are mission hospitals and clinics scattered throughout the Shona country, and the Shona appreciate that the European medicine they bring is on the whole superior to the arts of traditional Shona healers. Although the contact of missionaries with their patients is less prolonged than that with pupils at a school, visits to a mission hospital do provide an opportunity for contact with Christianity, and a few missions have insisted on church attendance as a condition for receiving treatment. Some traditional rituals in honour of family spirit elders are often motivated by the anxiety of serious illness, the ability of the mission to reduce this anxiety reduces the hold of traditional religion, and a church which brings superior powers of healing readily suggests itself as an alternative to traditional religion.

The emphasis of some missionaries on the nuclear family of a husband, his wife and their children has proved an attraction to some wealthy or ambitious men who wish to free themselves from the burden of dependent kinsmen. Besides, the religion taught by the white people is one aspect of the culture which gives prestige to the wealthy who wish to show themselves more advanced than their neighbours. Associated with the status of Christian churches is the fact that their members tend to be better educated and hence financially better off than traditionalists. This perhaps gives some prestige to being a church member and is the reason why many claim to belong to a mission church on such grounds as occasional attendance at one of its schools, grounds that the church authorities do not regard as constituting church membership.

Members of mission churches are generally better off economically than their traditionalist counterparts.[6] Christians tend to be more successful farmers than non-Christians. The precise reasons for this are not always

6. For a discussion of this point, see Bourdillon 1983.

clear, and usually combine a number of factors. Many mission churches have provided agricultural extension services. Education through mission schools, and the resultant literacy, made government extension services more accessible. Education also makes possible greater earnings for initial investment in agriculture. Perhaps those who improve their incomes through improved agriculture find Christianity an aid to reducing their economic obligations to their extended families. In some cases, Christian churches provide tightly-knit, mutually supporting communities which help members to cope with social and economic changes. Perhaps, too, those who are more open to a changing technology are also those who are ready to change their religion. Whatever the reasons, there is a correlation between Christianity and economic success in the rural areas, and this provides a further incentive for conversion to Christianity — or at least associates Christianity generally with success and progress.

In the urban situation, churches serve the function of bringing people together from a specific rural area. The Rhodesian government pursued a policy of keeping mission denominations apart in the rural areas to avoid conflict and confusion. As a result, Christians from any one locality tend to belong to the same mission church. When a man leaves home to live, perhaps temporarily, in one of the larger townships, weekly services at a church of his denomination are likely to attract others from the same rural area. Church services provide an opportunity for meeting relatives and friends scattered widely in the dense urban population and for catching up on news from home.

In spite of these advantages offered by the Christian churches, adherence to orthodox Christianity poses a number of serious problems. The most significant arise from the fact that most missionaries either ignore or deny the powers of ancestral spirits and of witchcraft. When a man and his family are in good health, spirit elders and witches may be forgotten in the face of a new religion, especially if its preachers show themselves capable of rapidly curing minor ailments. But should the new medicine fail, or should some serious or permanent trouble his the family, traditional spiritual powers are not so easily put out of mind and a new Christian may readily fear that the he has incured the displeasure of his ancestors. It is difficult in such a situation to refrain from reverting, at least temporarily, to traditional religious practices

The pressures to conform with the demands of traditional religion are even greater when territorial spirits are concerned and the whole community believes itself threatened by drought. Dr Weinrich cites a case in-which a Christian family was unable to prevent two daughters from being taken away to the Mwari cult centre to be trained as assistants or companions for the local tribal medium.[7]

Even when there is no crisis, traditional family piety demands that spirit elders be honoured. The Shona often remark that their rituals in honour of deceased relatives are essentially similar to the European practice of putting flowers on a grave on, for example, the anniversary of the death of a close relative. Some missionaries appreciate this point and have made attempts to incorporate traditional respect for deceased ancestors into their Christian rituals,[8] but most regard traditional religion as the antithesis of Christianity and adamantly refuse to admit any influence from the traditional reverence of ancestral spirits. This attitude encourages a neglect of one's ancestors which might disturb a man who respects his deceased parents and grandparents, and his unease is likely to be intensified should his family be troubled by illness or other misfortunes.

In practice, many Christians believe in the power of witchcraft and of their ancestral spirits and see no conflict between these beliefs and official church doctrines, though they may accept that church discipline prevents them from meddling with these powers and prudence may dictate that they do not speak about them to church authorities. Indeed an exclusively orthodox body of belief seems relatively unimportant to the Shona and one often finds a casual mixing of the tenets of different faiths. They do not find it extraordinary to find a professed Christian who claims to heal by the power of God and who also obtains help and advice from a traditional spirit medium.[9] As one traditionalist who also believed in Jesus and in the Holy Spirit explained, 'It is best to believe it all.'[10]

Apart from the personal doubts and anxieties a new Christian may feel in times of trouble, he is likely to find himself under family pressure to revert to traditional Shona religious practices. Even though the Christian may be firm in his faith in the providence of God and firm in his conviction that ancestral spirits and witches are powerless against faith in God, his heathen relatives are unlikely to accept this view. If someone in the family

7. Weinrich 1971, p. 86.
8. An example of this kind of blending between old and new is given in Daneel 1971, pp. 270f.
9. Cf. Gelfand 1968, pp. 146-158; 1971b.
10. Murphree 1969, pp. 132ff.

is seriously ill, it seems to them tantamount to witchcraft for a Christian member of the family to refuse to co-operate in the necessary appeasement rituals, especially if the Christian is the family head who is responsible for honouring the spirits believed to be the cause of the trouble. A parallel situation arises when a Christian becomes a chief or headman and finds himself responsible for rituals in honour of territorial spirit guardians: to refuse to perform these would appear as a gross failing in his care for his people.

One of the difficulties here is that mission churches tend to emphasize the individual rather than family or neighbourhood groups. Prior to the advent of Christianity, there was only one religion with a single system of belief working to keep communities together. Initially, the basis of conversion to Christianity was a personal decision, ideally based on personal conviction and without overt reference to other members of the community. Christian rituals thus tend to break down rural communities and the social and communal aspects of traditional religion are impaired.

Christian views on marriage have provided another stumbling block for many would-be Christians. Firstly, there is the problem of understanding the nature of Christian marriage. White missionaries usually regard marriage as a sacred union between husband and wife, in some cases an indissoluble union, which is enacted through a religious rite. This rite creates the union with all the rights and duties it involves: in particular, sexual intercourse is licit only after the marriage ceremony. Central to Shona marriage is the payment of bride-price for the right to children, negotiated possibly over a number of years. Many Shona are not prepared to go into a monogamous marriage, especially if there is no possibility of subsequent divorce, without first ascertaining that the proposed wife can bear children. The result is that many enter a church marriage only after the birth of the first child, a practice that conflicts with the morals taught by the churches. Some missionaries have tried to give young Christian couples more independence from their families (particularly from the bride's parents) by insisting that marriage payments be made before the church wedding, with the result that a prior unofficial union becomes yet more likely. Instead of being central to marriage, a church ceremony is to the Shona often merely an extra rite in the long process of marriage, the central feature of which remains the negotiation of bride-price payments.[11]

---

11. The relationship between Christian marriage and traditional Shona marriage is discussed in Weinrich 1963 & 1982, and Hatendi 1973; cf. also Chavunduka 1979a, pp. 43-49, and 1979b, for discussion of polygamy among Christians.

Then there is polygamy. A man may want a second wife simply for status, or because a single aging wife is not sexually satisfying, or to provide more labour for his farm. At the death of a brother he may find himself under obligation to take responsibility for the deceased's widow and family, in which case in Shona eyes she becomes a second wife to him. Whatever the reason, many men find the insistence of Christian missionaries on monogamy too restrictive.

Apart from the chronic difficulty facing Shona Christians of balancing the beliefs and practices preached by missionaries against more traditional Shona values, there are other forces which have recently induced a general disillusionment with mission churches. One is that the expensive process of missionary education did not lead to equality with whites in the wider Rhodesian society. Even in some of the churches, there have been discriminatory practices and it was very difficult for a black man to acquire a position of leadership on a par with white authorities. Then came the African nationalist movement which gloried in the Shona past with its traditional heroes. Mission churches were European in origin and had detracted from the heroes of the past (now the great tribal spirits); consequently they became the focus of much hostility and lost many of their members.

During the recent war, hostility to the mission churches was in some places intensified by the propaganda of guerrillas trained in countries hostile to religion. The campaign against missionaries and their teachings was part of the nationalistic pride in traditional religious leaders. The historical link between missionaries and the colonial settlement of the country is symbolized in the accusation that the God of the Christians was silent while the people suffered. Nevertheless, many nationalist leaders appreciate the education and the support they received from missionaries, who were often openly opposed to the white governments of the past. In some areas, missionaries were able to remain at their posts until the closing stages of the war, and in many places now there is close co-operation between political leaders and the churches.

In spite of difficulties, many Shona retain their membership of Christian missionary churches through deep conviction and staunch faith. Others have foregone attractions held out by missionary bodies to maintain piously the traditions of their ancestors. And there are those who retain their church membership for reasons of convenience and prestige, and many others after dabbling in Christianity have returned to their traditional religion. Others still have found an intermediate form of religion in the new independent churches.

New independent churches

Shona labour migrants working on the mines in South Africa in the early years of this century met new African independent churches which were growing out of contacts with similar movements among American negroes. On their return to Zimbabwe, some founded independent churches in their home communities, mostly in southern Shona country. The movement did not gain much momentum until the 1930s when the independent churches, which had acquired by now a character distinct from that of their South African counterparts, began to multiply and to spread throughout Shona country.

As a church acquires a following and grows in size, fission is likely to take place with sections hiving off to found new churches. Fission is often the result of conflicts over leadership, which become most acute at the death of the founder of a church, when his principal assistants are likely to vie with each other and with the sons of the founder to succeed to his position of leadership; but at any stage a church official with a large personal following might break away from the church to which he belongs and start his own sect. Now there are over a hundred independent churches or sects in Zimbabwe with a total following in the order of half a million.[12]

The churches vary considerably in size. The largest is the African Apostolic Church of Johane Maranke (whose members are commonly known as *Vapostori* — 'Apostles') with over fifty thousand members in Zimbabwe and half as many again in neighbouring territories.[13] A smaller church may extend no further than the neighbourhood of its founder.

The churches also vary in kind. The most common and most popular are the 'spirit-type'[14] churches, which emphasize inspiration and revelation by the Holy Spirit. Prophecy under the inspiration of the Holy Spirit is a dominant feature in these churches and the phenomenon of speaking in tongues is common. Another central feature in most spirit-type churches is faith-healing, which we shall discuss later. Historically, these churches are related to the 'Zionist' movement in South Africa and ultimately to Zion City, Illinois, in the United States of America. The names of the spirit-

---

12. See Barret 1968, p. 78.
13. See Daneel 1971, p. 331. This estimate is probably very conservative.
14. I am using the typology elaborated in Daneel 1971, which is the source of much of the material in this section. For a brief description of practices of spirit-type churches, see Weinrich 1969.

type churches usually refer to Zion or to the Apostles in order to establish an ideological association between the new independent churches and the founding of Christianity.

Secondly, there are churches which lay no claim to manifestations of the Holy Spirit. Their services tend to be less emotional than those of spirit-type churches and they follow closely Protestant missionary denominations in organization and ritual. These churches often claim a connection with the first Christians through the Church in Ethiopia (which links Africa to the earliest Christian communities) and 'Ethiopian' occurs frequently in the names of the churches. They have consequently been classified as 'Ethiopian-type' churches.

Even within these two broad types there are wide variations. Nevertheless, there is a common feature in all in the interpretation of the Christian Bible independently of white overseers. All churches stress the reading of the Bible and its exegesis in sermons, though in the Ethiopian-type churches exegesis is more systematic and closer to the teachings of mission churches.

The reasons for the rapid growth of independent churches are many.[15] They offer material advantages in the supposed powers of healing of many of their ministers. Community co-operation within the churches often extends to the formation of economic co-operatives which can share expensive equipment and pool surplus agricultural produce for more economical transport to market centres. As a result independent church communities are often more wealthy than their neighbours in rural areas.[16] One church, Johane Masowe's *Apostolic Sabbath Church of God*, is renowned in Zimbabwe and in its neighbouring territories for basket-making and other crafts, the products of which are sold on a co-operative basis, providing an income for church members.[17]

But there are also ideological reasons for the growth of independent churches. One is conflict between white missionaries and their black congregations. A number of independent church leaders broke away from the mission churches to which they had belonged after a clash with mission

---

15. This is discussed at length in Daneel 1974.
16. Cf. Daneel 1973, p. 179. This corresponds with my own experience in Korekore country. Cheater (1981) points to the importance of polygamy and the exploitation of female labour in the acquisition of wealth by some male *Vapostori*. See also Bourdillon 1984.
17. This church is discussed in detail in Dillon-Malone 1978. Cf. also Daneel 1971, pp. 339-344.

authorities or on account of frustrated ambition to positions of leadership within the mission churches. A situation favourable to conflict and independence is created by the contradiction between love for all men taught by the missionaries and the poor treatment that their African congregations received from the white community as a whole. The realization that the expensive education of the missions does not bring rapid advancement and the occasional practices of racial discrimination on the part of missionaries themselves reinforced the climate of opinion favourable to independent churches.

From this it is evident that some of the independent churches were created and supported out of racial hostility. But not all independent churches are initially hostile to white missionaries, and the antipathy of those that are is usually short lived. Generally the independent churches are friendly towards mission churches, and would like to be accepted by them as members of the Christian body. Most independent churches also seek and acquire government recognition as religious organizations authorized to preach.

As the Bible became readily available to the Shona in their vernacular, and as more and more of the Shona learnt to read, they became less dependent on the white missionaries for a knowledge of the Bible. Most Shona are now able to work out their own interpretations of the Bible and to put their own emphases on the different books in it. In particular the accounts of many of the Old Testament figures with their numerous wives and concubines appear to belie the insistence of white missionaries on monogamy. A desire to preach and apply interpretations more in accordance with traditional Shona values is another reason for the rise of independent churches.

Another factor which attracts followers to independent churches is their ritual. This applies particularly to spirit-type churches with their music, the emotional out-pourings of the Holy Spirit and their colourful uniforms for the different ranks of members, all of which contrast sharply with the austere services of some of the Protestant denominations.[18]

The attraction of the gift of prophecy in these churches can be understood in terms of the parallels between prophets and traditional Shona

---

18. Dr Daneel (1971, p. 264) suggests the liturgical difference between the Roman Catholic Church and the Dutch Reformed Church as one of the explanations of the greater defections from the latter to independent churches. He suggests, however, that the main reason is to be found in the Roman Catholic Church's more accommodating attitude to traditional customs and religious practices (p. 248).

spirit mediums. Some prophets borrow much from traditional rituals of spirit possession, speaking in the lilting voice typical of lion spirit mediums and uttering groans, sighs and other sounds associated with lion spirits. A prophet when possessed by the Holy Spirit may twitch and shake as possessed mediums do. When he begins his prophecy, a prophet may utter an incomprehensible jumble of names and phrases from the Bible just as a medium at the beginning of a séance may utter a jumble of names from the traditional history of the chiefdom to which he belongs. It is true that there are differences: a possessed medium claims to speak with the voice of his spirit whose identity he adopts during the course of a séance, whereas a prophet claims only to be inspired by the Holy Spirit and retains his own name and identity throughout. After a séance there is nothing against a prophet remembering what he said in prophecy and why, whereas an unpossessed medium is supposed to be conscious of none of the doings or sayings of his spirit. Nevertheless, in the institution of prophecy the Shona find something closely allied to, and a substitute for, their traditional spirit mediumship.

Apart from the ritual surrounding prophecy, the activities of some prophets closely parallel those of traditional spirit mediums. As one aspect of communicating with the spirit world, some prophets acquire a reputation for divining. Their field is more limited than that of traditional diviners since they do not co-operate with communications from ancestral spirits. But many claim to be able to discern witches, and occasionally a prophet may be called into a hamlet or village to expose all witches in it and to seek out and destroy their secret medicines. Sometimes too a party may consult a prophet of repute to decide on a case of suspected adultery. The prophet becomes possessed by the Holy Spirit through whose power he is supposed to be able to see the miscreant. A number of prophets also acquire reputations as faith-healers together with the large clienteles which a reputation for healing naturally brings.

Akin to prophecy, the Holy Spirit is believed to bestow on certain people (including most prophets) the gifts of 'speaking in tongues'. At the services of spirit-type churches, a number of people may enter into a kind of trance, partly induced by the rhythmic singing and the emotional preaching and praying of the assembly, in which they jabber in incomprehensible 'tongues'. The phenomenon to some extent replaces spirit possession on such traditional occasions as a dance in honour of alien *mashave* spirits, when a number of people may become possessed without any serious mediation from the spirit world.

Perhaps the most significant attraction of the new independent churches is their attitude to traditional beliefs in the power of spirits of the dead and in the power of witchcraft. Some of the Ethiopian-type churches cover the range of attitudes found among white missionaries, varying from a tolerance of traditional religion to an outright rejection of all its beliefs and practices. But among the more popular churches, we find an acceptance of the basic beliefs behind traditional religion, together with a total rejection of traditional religious practices.

These churches accept that the spirits of the dead can influence the physical world, especially to cause sickness, and they certainly accept the belief in the evil influence of witchcraft. But they maintain that spirits which cause sickness are evil spirits whose power can be overcome by faith in God. Thus if a man believes himself to be troubled by a spirit which wants to possess him and accordingly he asks for help from the church officials, they do not deny his explanation of his trouble as a white missionary is likely to do; instead they accept his understanding of the situation with all the implied anxieties, and they perform a rite to exorcise the spirit by the power of the Christian God. Similarly, when a person believes himself to be troubled by his family spirit elders, spirit-type churches offer understanding and ritual healing, accepting the power of the troubling spirit but calling on a greater spiritual power to overcome it. They offer a way of coping with sickness and trouble that is in accordance with the traditional Shona understanding of the world and yet purports to transcend it.

In the case of witchcraft, popular independent churches are more explicitly traditional. We have mentioned that prophets are sometimes invited to detect witches in a community and to exorcise them, and they even perform these functions for traditionalists who have no connection with Christianity. In church penitential rites, witchcraft is regarded as a sin which must be confessed or exposed. It is believed to be common, and certain people are believed to relapse repeatedly into witchcraft, from which they require repeated purification. Spirit-type churches try to overcome the acknowledged evil of witchcraft, an important function for any institution claiming to promote morality among those who are convinced that witches exist — and most Shona are so convinced, including most members of orthodox mission churches. As one man who lived in the vicinity of a Roman Catholic mission remarked, 'The "Apostles" are better than Roman Catholics: you can be a Catholic and at the same time a witch, but you cannot be an "Apostle" and a witch.'

The beliefs of the more popular independent churches incorporate traditional explanations of events, and specially of misfortune. Yet the

296

members of these churches are often even more convinced than members of mission churches in those Christian beliefs which replace parallel traditional beliefs: thus the 'Apostles', for example, hold most strongly that God, and not the tribal spirits, is responsible for drought; that the soul of a good man goes to heaven and does not become a *mudzimu* (spirit elder); that God speaks through the Bible and not through the tribal spirits; that at least some sickness can be healed only by prayer to God.[19] They utterly reject all traditional religious practices, which they regard as giving honour to evil spirits: any church member who takes part in these practices must confess and be forgiven before he is allowed back as a full member of the congregation.

This does not mean that members of independent churches are necessarily harsh on those who temporarily revert to traditional religious practices: such have given in to an understandable weakness and are readily forgiven. Professor Murphree describes one church leader who absented himself from the congregation for a period while he arranged the traditional treatment of his wife's illness on the persuasion of her parents: although other church members spoke of him as a 'backslider', no one attempted to usurp his position of leadership and when the treatment was over he confessed his sin and was reinstated as a leader.[20] Although such action is vehemently and explicitly condemned by members of the church, they tacitly condone it.

The popular independent churches have managed to combine traditional ways of thinking and acting with the new international religion based on a high god who cares for all people and who can be approached by anyone. They are thus well able to cope with the transition from traditional tribal communities to contact with the wider international world.

The African Apostolic Church of Johane Maranke

We have spoken in general terms about independent churches. One of these stands out as the most popular and widespread in Zimbabwe, namely, the *African Apostolic Church* of Johane Maranke, also known as the Church of the Apostles, whose members are commonly known as *Vapostori* ('Apostles'). Although we should beware of generalizing from

---

19. See the survey responses of the various religious groups to question 1, 2, 3, 14 and 15 in Murphree 1969, pp. 179ff., 186.
20. Murphree 1969, p. 140.

one example, some comments on the history, organizat'on and ritual of this church will serve to illustrate how an independent church can operate.[21]

The founder of the church, Johane Maranke, was born in 1912, the grandson (on his mother's side) of a chief. Johane attended four years of schooling at a Methodist mission, where he was baptized into the church. While still a boy, he started having dreams and visions, the most important of which are recorded in the *Umboo utsva hwavaPostori*,[22] regarded by the 'Apostles' as a canonical addition to the Bible. In 1932, when Johane was twenty, he had a vision which marked the beginning of his work of preaching baptism and conversion from sin: he returned home in a dazed trance so that his family thought he was mad until one (a member of another spirit-type church) recognised the out-pourings of the Holy Spirit. In the book of his visions, Johane claims to have received a full charter for his church with all its rules and practices through the direct inspiration of the Holy Spirit.

The news of his revelation spread rapidly through his extended family to others in the neighbourhood and at the first sabbath meeting, only three days after the revelation, about one hundred and fifty people were baptized into the church at a nearby river. The ceremony took place amid chanting, speaking in tongues, exorcisms and, as one of the leaders remembers, much thunder and lightning. Some of the new members were consecrated to the offices of the Holy Spirit: evangelists, prophets, healers and an elderly judge (Johane's father) to settle the domestic disputes of church members. A secretary was also appointed. The key positions were given to relatives of Johane who became senior figures in the more detailed hierarchical structure of the church which was elaborated (reputedly under directions of repeated revelations to the founder) as the church grew in size.

The new church quickly came out against traditional religious practices, associating ancestral spirits with evil demons. Johane's father killed without ritual the bull dedicated to his spirit ancestors, and his mother, a senior spirit medium, burnt her regalia. The latter, however, after some oscillation between traditional religion and her son's church, finally broke

---

21. The historical material in this section comes mainly from Daneel 1971, pp. 315 — 339; material on religious beliefs and practices comes primarily from Murphree 1969, pp. 92-110; Weinrich 1967b also has some material on this church. Cf. also Cheater 1981.
22. An English version, *New Testament of the Apostles*, has been published by Peter Nyamwena of The Church of the Apostles, Salisbury.

with the church to continue to practice as a diviner and the medium to a senior spirit of her father's chiefdom.

In the early days there was an abortive effort by the leaders of the new church to receive recognition from, and to join forces with, an established spirit-type church. But no agreement could be reached and the rapid successes of the travelling preachers of the new church soon rendered recognition by an established body unnecessary. Johane himself travelled to South Africa, Mozambique, Malawi, Zambia and even to central Zaire where the church today has a large following.

There were two early schisms within the church. One of the earliest evangelists broke away with a small personal following, and later a senior prophet-healer broke away with some local support after a conflict over the use of church funds. A more serious schism took place in 1963, shortly after the founder's death. There followed a struggle between Johane's elder brother and his maternal relatives who had held positions of leadership within the church. One of the latter, Simon, who claimed he had always been second to Johane in the church hierarchy, was suspected by some people of ensorcelling the founder in order to take over his position in the church (the two were travelling together immediately before the founder's death). In the end, the traditional rule of inheritance won the day and Johane's sons succeeded to the key positions in the church with Johane's elder brother (their 'great father') maintaining his influence. The two senior sons also inherited two Landrovers for their official church visiting, an arrangement which Simon's followers opposed on the grounds that they were church property and not part of Johane's personal estate. When the elder brother tried to manoeuvre Simon and his son out of office and ordered a change of venue of the annual *Paseka* ceremony from its traditional site near Simon's home, Simon took his grievances to the chief's court. The chief evaded the issues by allowing Simon to found his own church, which he did reluctantly; it became a refuge for any who were dissatisfied with the organization of the principal body.

The 'Apostles' set themselves apart from their neighbours in many ways. On Saturday afternoons they don their church uniforms for the sabbath service. For girls and women this is usually simply a white veil tied to the head with a red ribbon. The men wear white tunics, each with an embroidered decoration including a badge indicating the person's office in the church; men also carry long wooden staffs, wear their beards long and shave their heads. All go barefooted at a service: they must take their shoes off on ground that is holy. 'Apostles' may not drink alcohol, nor smoke tobacco, nor may they eat pork. They may take no part in the rituals of traditional Shona religion and they taboo traditional musical instruments which are used at these. They may not use any medicines, neither traditional nor European; some would rather die than receive medicinal treatment, though a temporary lapse from the church in order to receive medical treatment in times of severe sickness may be readily condoned. When an 'Apostle' dies, church members take responsibility for the burial, taking over from the deceased's relatives if they do not belong to the church: all rites associated with the traditional veneration of spirit elders are omitted, and the corpse is buried in the proximity of the graves of other 'Apostles'. When 'Apostles' have functions to perform at traditional rituals by virtue of kinship or friendship, they usually find pagan acquaintances to stand in for them.

Every Saturday, the small local congregation of 'Apostles', perhaps forty in number, gathers for the sabbath service. This opens with a public confession of faults. At least before the greater ceremonies, all members of the congregation must pass through a 'gate' between two prophets. As each does so, he is supposed to mention all his sins of the previous week, and the prophets may add to the list if they 'see' faults the penitent fails to mention. A fairly common fault, confessed either by penitent or prophet, is witchcraft: this and other serious faults must go before the informal court of elders who decide what is required to cleanse the sinner. The procedure accepts and exposes quarrels and other forms of malevolence in the community and shows a public effort to improve the situation.[23]

The sabbath service consists mainly of Bible reading and preaching. Each preacher has a lector who reads from a chosen passage of the Bible a verse at a time, each verse followed by comment from the preacher. The preaching may from time to time be interrupted by the women breaking out into rhythmic singing. Some present may fall into a trance and prophesy or speak with tongues, but they are generally ignored except by those individuals to whom a prophet may speak directly. The service, which may last for a couple of hours, ends when all kneel facing east and pray aloud their own spontaneous prayers.

After the service, water may be consecrated for healing purposes and healers of repute may lay their hands on any sick who are brought to them,

---

23. In the view of some, this contrasts favourably with, for example, the Roman Catholic confessional, the secrecy of which accords with the sinister secrecy of witchcraft. Many, nevertheless, appreciate secret confession.

praying for their recovery. Baptisms in a nearby river 'Jordan' and exorcisms may also be conducted when necessary or convenient.

Since the first *Paseka* (Paschal service) two years after the founding of the church, there has been an annual ceremony near the home of the church's head. This is attended by any who can make the journey and the annual attendance now is in the order of twenty thousand.[24] Nominees for positions of leadership in local churches should attend to be approved and consecrated; local church leaders (who sometimes call themselves bishops, although this is not an official church title) are also likely to attend. There are also numerous smaller centres at each of which an annual *Paseka* ceremony is conducted by the head of the church or one of his immediate assistants: for these a number of local congregations combine to form a local church with a well defined hierarchy.

The *Paseka* involves a camp lasting up to two weeks. Most of the days are filled with services similar to the normal weekly services. Rhythmic singing late into the night may induce possession by the Holy Spirit, and possibly also the exorcism of evil spirits. During this time seniors in the church, or the visiting dignitary to the local centres, judge cases which could not be solved by local church elders. But the climax of the *Paseka* is the communion service which takes place on the last Sunday of the camp.

For this, virgins in the congregation are selected some days before to prepare the unleavened bread and fruit juice 'wine'. On the last Saturday evening there is a confession service after which each member of the congregation has to pass through a 'gate' of two prophets into the prepared communion enclosure. Some may be refused entry at their first attempt on the grounds of offences they are supposed to have committed, perhaps involving a quarrel, or some sexual offence, or more seriosly witchcraft; these must be dealt with and settled by the 'judges' of the church before they can enter the sacred enclosure. The penitential service is likely to last all night, though those who have once gained entry to the enclosure may leave until the communion service the following morning. This includes a footwashing ceremony, an address by the senior man present, and then all file past the communion table to receive the bread and 'wine'. After they have received communion, they may leave.

Members of the church may aspire to one of the four principal offices of baptizers (who alone may perform the rite of baptism), evangelists (the

---

24. Daneel 1971, p. 331.

principal preachers), prophets and healers; women are confined to the last two offices. The office is supposed to be a gift of the Holy Spirit. In practice, a person may receive a call to one of the offices through dreams or on the inspired announcement by a prophet: in either case, the call normally accords with the character and abilities of the person concerned. Junior members of the congregation may also be official singers, who are supposed to lead congregational singing and who may at the same time hold one of the offices given by the Holy Spirit. Older men may, besides holding one of the regular four offices, acquire the office of judge to decide on cases sent to them by prophets and to give advice to members of the church where it is deemed necessary.

Leadership in the local church is usually acquired through ability in one of the offices and fidelity to the values of the church. It is exercised without ostentation and in practice is most noticeable during the informal court sessions to discuss confessed faults before weekly services: the leader presides, summing up the opinion of the court and finally giving his judgement on the case. Leaders of local congregations are also very active in the considerable organization required for a *Paseka* service.

Apart from church services, members of a local congregation cooperate in a number of secular activities. A local congregation may, for example, form a farming co-operative or in other ways pool their knowledge and resources for the benefit of the community. They may pool contributions for the help of someone in need, perhaps for the support of a cripple in the neighbourhood who may not even be a church member.[25] The 'Apostles', as do members of most independent churches, tend to form united and cohesive local communities.

Faith-healing

We have remarked that the 'Apostles' are not allowed to use any form of medicine, that the office of healer is one of the principal offices in the church, and that healing rites follow most weekly services. Faith-healing is commonly practised in most spirit-type churches and reputedly with remarkable success. The healing activities within the independent churches find a charter in the healing activities of Jesus recounted in the

---

25. See Murphree 1969, p. 100.

Christian New Testament; in the eyes of his followers, a prophet or founder of a new church shows himself to be inspired by the Holy Spirit promised by Jesus through his power to perform the healing wonders that Jesus performed.

Faith-healing is an important aspect of the fight against traditional religion, the ceremonies of which focus on the need for obtaining the good-will of ancestral spirits in times of sickness and trouble. The healing ritual of faith-healers supplies a replacement for the traditional appeasement of the spirits supposedly causing the sickness. Also important in this respect are rites of exorcism by which troubling spirits and spirits of witchcraft are driven out of a person.

The healing rites are usually associated with church membership. Although there are occasional cases of a prophet of the 'Apostles' being called in to cleanse a pagan homestead of witches and witchcraft, and although a traditionalist may occasionally be cured by a famous faith-healer, the cures and exorcism normally depend on faith in the Holy Spirit, a faith which the patient should share. The cure may depend on the patient's continual attendance at church services, or possibly on the rite of baptism. We have mentioned a reluctant spirit medium who was baptised into the Church of the Apostles in an attempt to have his spirit exorcised, but who left the church to become a spirit medium when the attempt at exorcism failed and the bad health attributed to the spirit continued.

Sickness and its cure is a common reason for religious mobility. We have mentioned that mission hospitals and clinics have been one of the influences converting Shona to Christianity. We have also remarked that when medicinal treatment fails to cure sickness in a family, this is a strong incentive for a Christian to revert to the practice of his traditonal religion. 'Apostles' may temporarily leave their church while seeking treatment for disease, whether from a mission hospital or from a traditional healer, and a person may become a temporary member of a spirit-type church while seeking a cure. Although conviction and piety are important to Shona religion, coping with disease has traditionally been a central feature in Shona religious practice and remains a focus for Shona religion in its various contemporary forms.

Dr Daneel points out that healing is the most specific power of attraction of Zionist (spirit-type) churches for the indigenous population.[26] The headquarters of the Zionist Christian Church of Bishop Mutendi (a

---

26. Daneel 1970b, p. 11. Much of my material on faith-healing comes from this short work.

large church with over ten thousand members spread all over Zimbabwe) had in 1965 two hundred huts, explicitly called 'hospitara' (hospital), built for the accommodation of visitors. A newcomer to the headquarters is first sprinkled with sanctified water to remove all impurity and expel any evil spirits. If his case is serious and he intends to stay for some time, his name, address and the particulars of his complaint are noted down in the sick register. He is assigned a house and a prophet to diagnose his case in due time.

Diagnosis by a prophet follows closely the patterns of diagnosis by traditional diviners, although the insight of the prophet is supposed to come from a different source than that of a traditional diviner. Both types of diviner attribute disease to conflict with spiritual powers or to conflicts within the community supported by witchcraft. But the two types differ radically in their prescriptions for a cure: whereas traditional diviners recommend appeasement of the spiritual powers, prophets base their therapy on the belief that the power of the Christian God can overcome all other powers.

Apart from appeasing the cause of illness, traditional healers provide medicinal treatment to remove the symptoms. Prophets generally reject all medicines and claim to rely solely on the power of the Holy Spirit for their cures. They do, however, use symbolic instruments which find parallels in the traditional treatment of disease. Thus a patient may be instructed to inhale the smoke from burning shreds of sanctified paper in order to drive out a spirit; sanctified needles may be used to remove evil blood from a patient; sanctified strips of linen cloth may be worn to stimulate fertility or to keep away evil spirits; and sanctified water is a general protection against evil.

Another way in which faith-healers borrow from traditional Shona religion is in the exorcism of a possessing spirit. An alien *shave* spirit which is not very dangerous may be exorcised simply by baptism. If it returns after the first exorcism (as a more powerful healing spirit is likely to do), further rituals may be necessary: in some churches the congregation induces the patient to become possessed through rhythmic singing and dancing, and assembled prophets then chide the spirit and drive it away. An avenging spirit is treated extremely seriously, and the entire family must undergo repeated cleansing rituals to ensure that the dangerous and angry spirit does not leave one member of the family only to attack another.

Conversion to the church of the healer is not essential to all treatment, but it is encouraged. A patient at Bishop Mutendi's 'hospital' who is not Zionist is likely to be advised to wait a few days in order to have direct contact with the Bishop, during which time he is totally taken up into the community. He attends two daily prayer meetings, each ending in the laying on of hands and prayers for the sick. There are almost always church leaders present to give a patient personal counsel should he require it. Serious patients receive free food subsidized by contributions from outlying congregations of the church. They thus become indebted to the church and are made aware of its pride in its organization and achievements. Besides, the prophets make their opinion clear that the best chance of a cure lies in being purified by baptism in the 'Jordan'. In these circumstances, few can resist becoming at least temporarily identified with the community and the church: a strong sense of community provides an attraction to this as to many independent churches.[27]

Interrelations between religious groups

We have seen that roughly a quarter of the black population in Zimbabwe are affiliated to some Christian body. So in any Shona community, we can expect to find significant numbers of Christians mingling with those who adhere to their traditional religions. The most notable characteristic of relations between adherents of different religions is mutual tolerance and a certain inter-dependence.[28] Dividing the religions operating in Shona society into three broad categories of mission churches, independent churches and traditionalists, we find that each category provides services utilized by members of the other categories.

Mission churches provide hospitals and clinics which are utilized by traditionalists, and less frequently, by members of independent churches. They also provide education for all (which is, however, boycotted by some spirit-type churches)[29] and contact with the white man's culture. Mission churches are also a source of enrolment for independent churches: although these receive over half their converts from among the traditionalists, many of their members are men who, after joining one of the mission churches and learning its doctrines, contracted polygamous marriages: these find a welcome for themselves and their families in most in-

27. Cf. also Daneel 1973, p. 162.
28. Professor Murphree (1969, pp. 137 – 151) brings out in some detail the interrelations and inter-dependence of religious groups among the Budya (north-eastern Shona). Cf. also Murphree 1971.
29. For attitudes of independent churches towards education, cf. Daneel 1973, pp. 168 – 174.

dependent churches. From this it follows that the religious teaching of the mission churches is influential in forming the beliefs of independent church members. Certain Christian teachings influence the beliefs even of traditionalist: the name Mwari for the high god has spread throughout Shona country under the influence of the missions, and there is a wide spread belief in the sacred inspiration of the Christian Bible.[30]

The independent church prophets are consulted by members of all religious groups, particularly for divining witches and eradicating witch-craft. Traditionalists, and occasionally members of the mission churches, sometimes resort to the faith-healers of independent churches.

Traditionalists provide diviners and healers whom anxious church members may consult. Traditional religion also provides the basis of the family and political structures of rural society since few church members have totally rejected the belief in the power of ancestral spirits to cause trouble.

We do not need to elaborate on the fact that people with troublesome diseases may move from one group to another in search of a cure, giving to the group from whom a cure is sought temporary allegiance which may become permanent if the treatment is successful. There are other reasons for changing religious affiliation. We have mentioned the desire for educa-tion and polygamy. A person may also change his religious affiliation to acquire status, whether by joining a mission church to associate himself with the prestige of the white man's culture, by leaving a mission church to acquire a position of leadership in an independent church, or by leaving Christianity in order to take up a position of leadership in a traditional neighbourhood or chiefdom which requires the performance of rituals in honour of ancestral spirit guardians. And many Shona convert from one religion to another through genuine conviction that the new religion is more true than the old, a conviction which may be based partly on success in healing. The tolerance common to most Shona communities gives little stigma to changes of religion.

Although it is true that members of mission churches tend to have more education than others and consequently to be financially more affluent, there is no clear class structure between the religious groups.[31] Members of

---

30. See the replies to question three in Murphree 1969, p. 181. In the survey of different religious groups in the Budya community, forty-seven per cent of non-Christian said that God speaks to his people through the Bible.
31. Weinrich's analysis (1966, pp. 11-13) is not valid for all parts of Zimbabwe. Cf. Daneel 1973, p. 179.

mission churches may pride themselves in the international nature of the bodies to which they belong, in the size and efficiency of their organizations, in the greater education of their members and in their greater adaptation to European culture. Members of independent churches, however, do not necessarily think very highly of European culture and sometimes openly oppose it; they are often wealthy relative to the neighbourhoods in which they live, but do not display their wealth by trying to ape the white people. Members of independent churches pride themselves on their independence of all white people, in the powers of their prophets, often in the size of their organizations (which occasionally rise to running their own schools) and in greater knowledge of the contents of the Bible than most members of mission churches. Traditionalists usually hold established positions of leadership. They pride themselves in upholding the traditions of their ancestors and readily blame troubles concerning family or crops on Christians who refuse to honour their spirit guardians.

This brings us to a realm of conflict between traditionalists and Christians. When a man has an essential function in a traditional ritual, he is expected to fulfil it regardless of whether he belongs to some Christian church. Thus a ward headman or chief must organize ceremonies in honour of the territorial spirit guardians, and a family head should arrange ceremonies in honour of family spirit elders. The senior 'sister's son' of a family may be expected to address the family spirit elders even if he is a Christian. Various functionaries may have tasks to perform at a traditional funeral. Refusal creates conflict. So many Christians surreptitiously accede to the wishes of the rest of the community, or at lest find among their relatives or acquaintances a suitable traditionalist to take their place.

More hostility may be shown by the religious leaders of the various groups. Lion spirit mediums are sometimes hostile to Christian practices, and the Mwari oracle strongly opposes those who break from their traditional obligations to the cult, including the independent churches in the area of the cult's influence. Official church teachings strongly oppose all traditional religion in a way that does not accord with the casual tolerance of many church members. Some independent church leaders are hostile to the mission bodies from which they broke away, and even hostile to each other. Some missionaries are hostile to other denominations and totally repudiate the independent churches. But even where there is hostility at the level of leadership, the rank and file of the various religious groups are usually able to co-exist in peaceful toleration.

Common scene in one of the modern hotels in Harare's high density Suburbs.

TV too has come to some of the African urban homes.

A family finds time to share a meal. Urban living has greatly reduced the occasions when families can be together.

African urban weddings often display Western style and custom.

12

Becoming Urban

Modern shopping is done in the Supermarket

Seniors and Juniors are becoming fashion-conscious

The attraction of town life

We have already mentioned in passing how various Shona institutions are affected by life in the big towns and cities. Increasing numbers of Shona are moving into Zimbabwe's towns and cities,[1] many on a permanent basis. While a study of these towns and cities would provide more than enough material for a book in itself, and although the proportion of Shona permanently committed to urban life remains small, it is fitting to end this study of the Shona with a brief look at urban life.[2]

In the black townships of the cities and towns in Shona country, different peoples from inside and outside of Zimbabwe gather together.[3] Nevertheless, the Shona are by far the most numerous and the Shona language is widely spoken — or rather *chitaundi*, the language of town, which is basically the Shona language with the addition of a large extraneous vocabulary taken from English and other tongues.

'*Chitaundi*' can refer to the culture and customs of the towns as well as to language. The language, which is clearly Shona in structure and style though half the words may be English, typifies the many changes that have taken place as Shona culture adapts itself to town life: new institutions and new ways of life fit themselves into the older social patterns, with which the new town dwellers are familiar and which they adapt appropriately to produce a culture which is neither western nor traditionally Shona.

There are in the towns many obvious innovations to the Shona way of life. Electricity in most town homes provides lighting late into the night and heat for warmth in the winter and sometimes for cooking. Paraffin and electric stoves are easier to cook on than wood fires, and do not fill the room with the unpleasant wood smoke that commonly fills rural kitchens — or any rural room in the winter. Running water to most homes[4] obviates the necessity of women fetching water from some distant supply and allows more convenient washing facilities than are available in most rural homes. Brick houses with corrugated iron roofs are proof against rain, wind and dust, and are more readily defended against bats, mice and other

---

1. According to the 1969 population census of Rhodesia, the black population of urban areas was 801 760, or 16,5 per cent of the total black population of the country of just under five million. This proportion had been roughly static over the previous decade. A good brief study of the main features of African urbanization in Zimbabwe is Gargett 1977.
2. My material for this section refers particularly to the townships around Harare, and especially to Highfied, since this is where much research has taken place.
3. A survey of highfied African Township showed that 15 per cent of its population came from outside Zimbabwe (Stopforth 1971, p. 8).
4. Some poorer homes have to share a communal water supply.

creatures, all of which can make life very uncomfortable in traditional rural huts. It is true that some town dwellers can find accommodation only in rough shacks made from plastic and cardboard and corrugated iron fixed onto a rough wood framework, but these are a minority and they normally aspire to the better style of dwelling that they see about them.

Access to monetary incomes and close contact with markets allow for furniture that provides some comfort and a smart appearance to a town home, and for radios and gramophones for entertainment. In the towns people dress as smartly as they can according to their incomes and occupations. Most people have fixed hours of work during the day and fixed times for relaxation, when they can drink at beer halls or shebeens and enjoy cinemas, night-clubs, and football and racing at weekends. All this contrasts sharply with the rural areas where families survive on their own with a minimum of outside help or interference and a minimum of expense.

Many inhabitants of the towns have been born and brought up in an urban environment[5] and many others have spent over half their lives in the towns. It is hard for these to give up the comforts of town life to revert to the more primitive rural life, and few have any intention of doing so if they can possibly avoid it. Some have no real ties with rural relations and would find it impossible to find a rural home even if they wished to.[6] They are town or city people who would find themselves at a loss in the country: town is their home and they have no other.

Nevertheless, there are a number of difficulties in living permanently in the towns, particularly those concerned with the lack of social security.[7] Since accommodation in towns cannot be based on patterns of kinship, people tend to live away from close kin, and may have no one on whom they can rely should they fall sick or find themselves unemployed or when they grow old; and those relatives who may wish to help are likely to find themselves barely able financially to support their wives and children, let

5. A survey of Highfield African Township showed that 15 per cent of the adult population of the township and 68 per cent of the pre-adult population were born in a town (Stopforth 1971, pp. 18f). In a survey of Mbare African Township, 26 per cent of adult males were born in the town (see May 1973, p. 3).

6. In a survey of adult males in Mbare, 10 per cent of the sample claimed to have no connection at all with any rural area and 29 per cent had not visited the homes from which their families came for ten years or more (may 1973, p. 4) The point that many blacks have no rural home was ignored by past white administrators who did not wish to have to cope with a permanent black urban population. It is also ignored by some current administrators: it is not always accepted that a black may have no chief, and may be identified with no rural area.

7. For a concise account of these, see Gargett 1977, especially chapters 3 and 4. Cf. also Stopforth 1977.

alone other kin in need of sustenance, which is ever more expensive in the towns. In the rural areas, one can always find *some* food from a plot of land; not enough to keep healthy, perhaps, but at least enough to keep alive. In the towns everything costs money: food, accommodation, entertainment, all of which can be had relatively cheaply or for nothing in the rural areas, even though there the quality may be inferior.

Accommodation in the towns is particularly problematic. Many town dwellers lodge in hostels or illegally in the homes of others, neither of which is satisfactory on a permanent basis. Others live in houses owned, or at least supplied, by employers and they have to move when they lose their employment, be it through old age or for any other reason. Of those who rent their own accommodation few receive pensions in old age adequate to meet this cost and few earn salaries sufficiently large to enable them to save for old age or other times of need. Some own their urban homes which they have built for themselves,[8] but there are still rates to pay and people believe they can be, and are likely to be, evicted for any of numerous minor offences: although they are not entirely justified in this belief, only a few of the wealthiest black people have freehold rights to property in the townships. Until independence, township residents generally felt themselves to be completely at the mercy of their white rulers, and since the establishment of black government in Zimbabwe, the administration of townships is changing but slowly. So a home in an urban area rarely provides the householder with a sense of security.

Then there is the need for physical care in old age. Since social services are not adequate to care for all the urban aged,[9] they must rely on kin, who in the urban situation rarely have room in their cramped housing to take in any extra persons, and who are usually financially unable to support aged parents or relatives. It is often difficult for adult children even to visit aged relatives to do their chores: the aged are concentrated in the oldest townships, while married sons and daughters have had to take accommodation in the newer townships, many miles from the homes of their parents. Sometimes a married son occupies the house of his aged parents while they are still alive and living in it; although this may save him years of waiting for accommodation on the ever growing waiting lists, the arrangement lacks permanence where the house is rented, since the son might be

---

8. In some of the township none of the houses are privately owned, while in others (St Mary's and Kambuzuma near Harare) all householders can own their homes. The supply of both rented and privately owned homes around Harare is a long way short of the demand for them.
9. For an account of the economics of old age, see Clarke 1977b. See also Hampson 1982.

evicted when his parents, in whose name the house is let, die. So in old age, many are forced to leave their urban homes and to search for a new home in a rural area where they can hope for a little support.

Most urban residents maintain some contact with rural relatives, both for social reasons and as a security against old age or unemployment. But this does not mean that they regard the rural area as their home, nor does it mean that they will go to live in a rural area if they can possibly avoid it. Even elderly townspeople may try to keep going in the towns by obtaining a small income through petty trade (often illegal) and taking in lodgers, before going to a rural area as a last resort to keep alive.

With the various forces pushing people to the towns and then back into the country, a number of factors are influential in making people clearly urban in orientation, and increasingly stabilized in the urban environment.[10] Income level is one: the higher a family's income, the more likely is that family to settle permanently in a city. The security of home ownership is another. And the longer a person lives in an urban centre, the less likely he is to return to a rural area. Associated with greater commitment to urban areas are a decreased reliance on kin, a weakening of the social networks derived from the rural areas, and a greater involvement in urban social institutions.

Family life in the towns

The most fundamental change brought about by the urban situation on Shona social life is in their family structure. In the towns, one has to take accommodation where one can find it, which is usually away from family and kin. Also, where houses cater for families at all, they are designed for small elementary families each consisting of simply the husband, his wife and their children, and the accommodation is often very cramped even for these. Where an elementary family does have outsiders staying with them, these are likely to be unrelated lodgers or more distant kin who can be expected to pay for their accommodation to help the family defray the expenses of town life. As a result, the rural system of extended families living together must break down. A man is rarely able to live with a polygamous family in a town: apart from the problem of cramped accommodation, an extra wife in the towns is not able to cultivate her own field and, instead of being the economic asset she is in the country, she becomes a further burden on strained family resources. So in the towns, the most common household unit is an elementary family.

---

10. Cf. Moller 1978, esp. pp. 390ff.

Nevertheless, extended kinship obligations are maintained and, since accommodation is usually short in the towns, most families have one or two kinsmen staying with them, at least on a temporary basis while they seek employment and alternative housing.[11] But such arrangements are usually temporary, and one does not find whole families living together as happens in the rural areas.

Since in a traditional rural home a man lives with his close kin and is partly dependent on them, these are able to apply considerable pressure on his behaviour. The social control of kinsmen maintaining customary standards of behaviour is absent in the towns, and one of the effects of this is seen in a changing system of marriage. Marriages now are usually arranged by the couple concerned, their relatives having very little say in the choice of spouses. The bride-price payments are made by the prospective husband to his bride's father (or to his successor if the father is dead), and they concern no one but these two men. Often the two families are completely unknown to each other, and may even be from different tribes: neither family has the traditional vested interest in bride-price cattle. Since the traditional controls of kinship and village communities are absent, the father-in-law may decide that the only way to ensure the payment of the bride-price without undue delay is by insisting that it is all paid before he gives his consent to the registration of the marriage (a necessary procedure before the husband may apply for married accommodation). Perhaps a more fundamental reason for this practice is the protection of his daughter. Once the husband is independent with a home of his own, he is able to reject his wife and take in any woman that meets his fancy; he may be prepared to do this if he has paid only a small portion of his bride-price which he can waive, but he would be more reluctant if he has paid the full marriage consideration. Whatever his reaons, the father-in-law is unlikely to forbid the couple living together once payments have started (in accordance with traditional practice); he simply prevents the registration of the marriage until the husband is able to pay the full consideration, which with the current practice of demanding very high bride-price may take some years.

This encourages loose informal unions, already common on account of the unstable urban populations and the preponderance of men among young adults. But when the couple are serious about their marriage, they may live in the home of either parents until the husband has been able to pay the full bride-price and find a home of his own. Thus a return to the

---

11. For family structures in Highfield homes, see Stopforth 1971, pp. 38–41.

pattern of residential extended families is beginning to appear in the poorer township circles, but on a temporary basis and in extremely cramped circumstances: one may find in a small three-roomed house the house-holder and his wife, a couple of children with their unofficial spouses, a number of younger children, and perhaps some very young grandchildren.[12] This arrangement is explicitly temporary and does not yet typify the family structure in the towns, in which the elementary family unit is dominant.

The dominant residential pattern of elementary families living among strangers has brought about changes in lifestyle. Young wives gain a certain independence in the management of their households, which they could never have living within their husbands' extended families; though against this, they lose the help of relatives, especially to look after young children while they do their chores. The traditional relationships between men, women and children sometimes become less formal as a result of the family being isolated among strangers; it is now not uncommon to find in an urban area a man eating together with his wife and children, something that would never happen in a more traditional setting.

But it does not follow that members of an elementary family necessarily come closer together in an urban situation. The contrary seems usually to be the case. The reason for the dominance of the elementary family is the absence of kin rather than any strengthening of ties within the family. It is true that the isolation of the family can and often does strengthen its internal bonds, but this does not always happen.

We have seen the difficult position in which women find themselves in the towns, and it is clear that the traditional Shona relationship between husband and wife does not easily adapt itself to the urban environment. Since a woman in a public place may readily be taken for a prostitute, few husbands are prepared to take their wives out in public. Yet there are no restraints on the men who (in accordance with traditional ways) prefer the company of other men to that of women, and who may spend much of their time with their mates in beer halls and other places of entertainment or relaxation. Thus, although the wife is isolated from her own and her husband's kin, she does not necessarily see more of her husband than she would in a traditional rural setting.

The weakness of the relationship between husband and wife in urban families becomes clear when the husband's family visit the home for any length of time. The husband's parents, brothers and sisters regard their kinsman's home as their own, and his wife as the outsider she would be in a

12. May 1973.

316

rural homestead. The urban wife's status as lady of the house is dependent not on any new relationship with her husband, but simply on the absence of more traditional contenders for the title.

This attitude is illustrated in an extreme form in the system of inheritance of a dead man's estate that has become common among Shona in the towns. Although any man can will his property to his wife, few in fact do so: some are ignorant of the procedures, some do not bother with them, and many do not trust women with their estates on the grounds that a widow can always marry again and squander her late husband's wealth on another family (ignoring the fact that kinsmen are equally likely to squander the savings of a late relative without taking proper care of the deceased's own children). And even should a man will his property to his widow, he cannot, if his marriage is registered as a customary marriage, give to his wife the custody of his children after his death. In practice, on the death of the husband, his family has no control over his widow, who lives on her own some distance from them, and they suspect that she will try to remove some of her late husband's property for her own use. At the same time, the husband's kin are not constrained by the traditional social sanctions to see that due respect is paid to the dead man's property, and that his widow and children are properly cared for. So immediately on the death of a man, his brothers are likely to come in to strip the homestead of all but the widow's personal property, leaving her with a bare home and no one to help her pay for food and rent.[13]

Neither are the bonds between parents and children necessarilly strengthened in the elementary families of the towns. The fact that there are no kin of the children's generation in the vicinity of their home does not necessarily drive the children to their parents: children are likely to associate with school mates or gangs of their own age, who are less under the control of their parents than are kin in the rural homesteads. Parents often fail to take over the roles of absent kin like the father's sister and the grand-parents, who in traditional society have important parts to play in the education of children. The children learn town ways and receive little education in Shona customs, resulting in a substantial generation gap which is recognised by all.[14]

---

13. My information comes from conversations with Joan May, who says that the question of inheritance is one of the major worries of township women. Recent research by J.R. Folta and E.E. Deck, as yet unpublished, indicate that insecurity over inheritance is a major problem for rural women as well. In the early 1970s, the courts began to drop their previous legal support for 'custom', absurdly applied in a context for which it was never intended; but little became of thhe move, and the situation remains in dire need of change.

14. Cf. Stopforth 1972, p. 69.

One result of the weakening links between parents and children, and between children and traditional society, is that people born and brought up in town often do not know how to behave correctly when they visit relatives in the country. They have not learnt the details of traditional social patterns or the formal greetings due to different senior kin or affines. Besides, they are likely to have a higher standard of living than rural kin and children in the towns are more aware of wealth differentials than absent patterns of kinship: parents of such children may find it difficult to persuade them to pay due respect to rural elders which may involve sitting on the ground and soiling their smart town clothes. Even adults often find it difficult to sit down and talk to kinsmen from a social stratum lower than their own.[15] Many urban families try to overcome this problem by sending their children to stay with rural kin for a while. In a survey of children at a secondary school in Highfield, Salisbury, all of the 103 children interviewed had been brought up in urban areas; yet ninety per cent of the girls and eighty-two per cent of the boys had spent some time staying with a grandmother in the rural areas, and the majority said that they had been taught their manners by grandmothers and fathers' sisters (*vatete*).[16] But this kind of education serves only further to hide the growing divergence between the traditional ideals of kinship to which nearly all Shona give at least notional assent, and the new patterns of relationships necessitated by urban life.

Difficulties about behaviour and lifestyle also arise on the other side. Rural dwellers visiting kin in town may not find it easy to fit into town ways, and may not understand the financial constraints against extending in towns the lavish hospitality mutually expected by kin in rural areas. People who move permanently into urban areas inevitably find their numerous kinship ties weakened.

One way in which this is reflected is in a lowering of reliance on kin. In rural areas, and even among transitory labour migrants, the Shona normally rely largely on kin for help when they are in difficulty or in need. In the towns there is still a tendency to rely on kin for more traditional needs, such as help in sickness or to pay a fine or for care of one's property in one's absence. For new needs, however, such as money for rent or school fees or to buy some specified article, townspeople tend to rely more on friends, neighbours, co-workers, welfare institutions and others who are not kin.

---

15. See Lukhero 1966, p. 133.
16. Cf. Gelfand 1979, p. 75.

And this independence of kin spreads to more traditional needs as people become more committed to town ways.[17]

The weakening of ties does not usually mean that these ties are broken off completely. Many people have settled permanently in a city, have rejected the traditional way of life in favour of a more westernized culture, and are financially secure and independent of kin; even these are likely to keep in touch with more backward rural kin. This may be partly an insurance against financial or other catastrophe, particularly if the urban day require the help of kinsmen to appease family spirit guardians. But it is also due to natural social ties, which may be modified to meet new circumstances, but which few would wish to destroy entirely.

New forms of union

The definition of marriage in urban situations has become somewhat confused. In many cases, there are unions in which all customary rights and conditions have been fulfilled, yet which have not been registered in any way: such unions are socially recognized as marriages, but have little legal status. In some cases husband and wife are living together according to custom, while the father of the wife refuses to give his formal consent, to the marriage, perhaps because he is holding out for further payments from his son-in-law. In the past, this consent was necessary for the registration of the marriage: although now legally a girl over the age of eighteen has full adult status and is no longer dependent on parental permission[18], it is socially difficult for her to assert her rights against her family, on whom she may become dependent in times of trouble. In practice, the status of any union which does not have the parental consent of the women, and the rights of the two parties to it, are somewhat tenuous. There are marriages in which bride-price as been agreed and promised, but not paid: these may have full legal status, while they are less secure from the social point of view. Yet another variety of marital types appears in *mapoto* unions.

These comprise a new form of union in urban situations, in which a man and a woman live together although no bride-price is paid.[19] Many Shona reject the idea that such unions are properly to be called marriages: they are referred to as *mapoto* (pots), suggesting simply a convenient sharing of cooking arrangements. Indeed, sometimes the union is a short-term, temporary convenience for both parties. Nevertheless, many *mapoto* unions are

---

17. Cf. Stopforth 1972, pp. 64f; Moller 1973, pp. 83f.
18. As a result of the Legal Age of Majority Act (No. 15 of 1982).
19. See Chavunduka, 1979a, pp. 42-56; also 1979b.

relatively stable, lasting ten years and more, and involve a contractual arrangement which has been partially recognised by a Shona urban court. The man takes responsibility to provide for the woman and her children; and the woman looks after the man's home and she agrees to sexual fidelity towards him. It is legitimate, therefore, to speak of *mapoto* unions as a type of marriage.

The reasons a man may have for entering into a *mapoto* union are various. One is the domestic need of a migrant worker who has left his wife and family at his rural home. A stable union with a woman in town can solve the problem, without creating complications when the migrant eventually returns home. A man may enter into a union with a salaried woman in order to alleviate financial difficulties.

A number of Christian men, whose legal wives are barren or bore no sons, have entered into secret *mapoto* marriages with other women until such time as the desired children can be adopted by the legal wives. In all cases, the legal wife may or may not have prior knowledge of the union: often, but not always, the husband has her sympathy and the union her approval. In all these cases, the attraction of a *mapoto* marriage is its relative stability on the one hand, and, on the other, its lack of formality, making it easy to dissolve and possible to be kept clandestine.

Women who enter *mapoto* marriages usually have little hope of a more formal marriage, either because they have been previously married and divorced or widowed, or because they already have illegitimate children to care for. For such women in an urban area, a man can provide the security of a home and maintenance. Some women regard the equality and relative independence they maintain in a *matopo* marriage as preferable to the subordinate position they are forced to accept in a formal marriage. This is especially true of divorcees, who have been made aware that formal marriage does not guarantee security.

The family of a girl who has entered a *mapoto* marriage is usually presented with a *fait accompli*. Some families may resent the union, and try to break it up or exact bride-price payments from the husband. But in practice, usually the girl is not readily marriageable before entering the union, and is less so afterwards. The loss to the family is minimal, and often the husband is accepted as a traditional son-in-law, who presents his wife's parents with occasional gifts.

One establishment Shona urban court, which was conducted on traditional lines and reflected the thinking of respected elders, had by the late 1970s begun to recognise *mapoto* unions as marriages. In one case, the husband of such a union was enjoined to give his name to children of the union, thereby taking responsibility for them and giving them legitimacy. When a family of a *mapoto* wife tries to break up the union, it gets little sympathy from the court, especially if any gifts have been received from the husband. Nevertheless, the court did try to make *mapoto* marriages more stable by insisting on some bride-price payment being made.

Although many Shona think of *mapoto* unions as similar to prostitution, and although both are relatively new to Shona society, brought about largely by urban environments, the two are very different. There are a number of factors that encourage prostitution in urban areas.[20] One is the desire of relatively poor women to acquire a certain economic independence from their husbands, which may result in limited clandestine prostitution. Another is the desire of girls to be free of kin and of unpleasant domestic service. Certainly a girl can, through prostitution, earn an income which allows her to live in a style far beyond the means of most women. Prostitutions are usually shunned by married women, but there is little stigma attached to the profession, and professional prostitutes are usually quite open about the way in which they make their living. A Shona girl who earns a good living through prostitution in towns may be received well by her family in the rural area, which will adopt any children she may have.

A further factor which encourages prostitution are conditions which make any kind of family life impossible. I have mentioned the living conditions of many domestic servants in this respect. Another instance are the hostels in some of the old townships, which housed single men in very cramped conditions — as many as five to a room, with communal kitchens and mess rooms. A study of hostels in Mbare,[21] Harare, revealed that half the residents were married men, and that their everage age was just under thirty. The bachelor accommodation for most of them was consequently inappropriate to their age and status. The hostel dwellers were largely rurally orientated, with little stake in urban life. Some (13 per cent) commuted weekly from their rural homes, where their wives and families lived; but the majority only went home once a fortnight (30 per cent) or once a month (53 per cent). In spite of attempts to provide recretional facilities for hostel dwellers, large numbers of men[22] living in these conditions represent a significant disruption of normal family life. This is confirmed by the fact that during the war years, when authorities became more

20. Cf. Weinrich 1976, pp. 412f.
21. Moller 1973; 1978, pp. 303-349.
22. 24 000 in Harare in 1973.

lenient concerning lodgers in township dwellings and 'squatters' in make-
— even amid the hardships of a squatter settlement. As a result of vacan-
cies in hostel accommodation in Harare, some has now been converted into
family accommodation.

Voluntary associations

One of the consequences of leaving rural areas, where social life revolves
around kinship and local communities, is that people have to find companionship through other associations. Since an urban population is large
and heterogeneous, physical proximity is not an adequate basis for choosing one's companions. I have mentioned the growth of women's clubs in
towns, in which women can gather for companionship and mutual help in
running their urban homes; there are numerous other voluntary associations in which men, women or children with some common interest can
meet and find companions. Most common among men are the informal
clubs in which members pool their wages, and take it in turn to keep the
pool to buy some expensive item. Many men are also members of football
clubs, where they find their weekend entertainment. Another common
financial type of club are burial societies, which for a small regular
subscription provide donations and support immediately after a death in a
family, and guarantee funds for a good burial, often including transport of
the corpse to the rural home; burial societies also provide various other
benefits, including social activities for their members, who gather from
time to time for music, feasting and dancing. And there are associations
for different professions, co-operative societies, clubs for dancing and for
various sports, numerous religious groups and societies, youth clubs,
charitable organizations, and even occasional drinking clubs.[23]
   Some of these bring together co-workers or strangers with common
interests. But some are dominated by people from a particular area: this
applies particularly to many religious associations, since different
denominations have defined territorial spheres of influence in the rural
areas. Thus by joining a voluntary association connected with the mission
church operative in his home rural area, a man in town is likely to meet
others from the same area, and to keep up with news of relatives in the
country. Although it may not be possible in the towns to keep contact with
a large group of kin, people still try to keep in touch with others from their
area or tribal group.

---

23. For a list of voluntary associations in Highfield, see Stopforth 1971, pp. 45ff.

Indeed, the churches themselves perform the functions of voluntary associations. Even in the larger churches, people are likely to meet friends and associates at Sunday services, which, together with the enjoyable singing, makes them important social events. The smaller churches provide more closely knit communities, in which people are able to acquire special roles — an identity in an anonymous urban society. In such communities, mutual co-operation can help to provide security against the vagaries of urban life.

Religious affiliation and practice in towns provide a good illustration of how people can combine old and new. In the towns, most people claim affiliation to some Christian denomination. These provide a broader range of social contacts than the kinship groups or local communities which gather for the practice of traditional religion, and the many associations within the various denominations (particularly women's associations) help in the transition to town life. But of those who claim affiliation to Christian denominations, most continue to practice their traditional religion,[24] and we have remarked that traditional diviner-healers can make a lucrative living in the towns. The old must change to meet new circumstances and ideals, but there remain basic patterns of thought and behaviour that govern change.

One type of voluntary organization which has grown up over the years in urban centres comprises the workers' unions.[25] The emergence of workers' unions dates back to the unrest arising from high inflation after the second world war, and they have over the years been instrumental in gaining improvements in salaries and working conditions for black industrial workers, occasionally in co-operation with white controlled unions. A united black trade union movement, however, never fully developed. As late as 1971, only 11,4 per cent of employees (not counting those in domestic service or agriculture, among whom concerted industrial action is virtually impossible) were paid up members of workers' unions, with a further 6,5 per cent of nominal members.

The reasons for the weakness of the unions are various. One is legisla-

---

24. In a survey of Highfield township, 78, 1 per cent informants claimed affiliation to some Christian denomination, 20,4 per cent practised their traditional religion only and 1,5 per cent practised no religion. Of those who claimed affiliation to Christian denominations 76,3 per cent admitted to practising their traditional religion as well and there were no doubt more who would revert to traditional religion in an emergency (calculated from table 20, Stopforth 1971, p. 26).

25. For a brief account of African trade unions in Zimbabwe, see Brand 1976. Brand 1971 gives a more detailed history of the unions, and Brand 1975 examines their political implications.

tion, introduced mainly in the 1950s, which effectively curtails the powers of trades unions, and which makes a legal strike virtually impossible.[26] Another reason for the weakness of the unions is the insecurity of African workers in the towns, who often depend on their employers even for a place to live, and who could readily be replaced from the large pool of unemployed persons, many coming from neighbouring countries. A third reason for the weakness of black trades unions has been the rivalries within nationalist politics with which the unions have been associated. Any movement concerned to improve the lot of black workers in a society dominated by whites, must inevitably become involved in the politics of opposition to this domination. From the time of the institution of workers' unions, there have rarely been periods in which African nationalism in Zimbabwe has not involved conflicts between rival parties; as a result, black trade union leadership has usually been divided between supporters of the rival political parties.

At a different level, the nature of leadership in workers' unions has been a source of weakness. Among a largely uneducated pool of workers, the men who were able to put an effective case to employers, and who attained official status of leadership in the unions, were the educated elite. These were mainly white collar workers, whom unskilled workers were liable to suspect of serving simply their own interests. Indeed, the insecurity of African urban life meant that in many cases a union official derived from his office an income (possibly deriving from international aid) and status which he had no hope of emulating outside the unions. The result has been that leaders have not been prepared to risk their posts in any way, and have been ready to form splinter unions rather than to give way to a successor. Industrial action has for the most part been spontaneous, or organized on the shop floors, ignoring the official union leadership, which consequently gives the appearance of being more concerned about persuading workers to accept a compromise and to go back to work, than about supporting the workers' grievances.

Strikes in practice have always been illegal, and have been rare except in times of political unrest, such as at the visit of the Pearce Commission in 1971 and 1972, and at the outbreak of the guerrilla war. In times such as these, the oppressive economic structure of Rhodesia appeared not totally

---

26. See Harris 1974b.

impregnable. Similarly, when the government of Zimbabwe was established, workers all over the courntry ignored the official union structures and
came out in a series of strikes to ensure that they received a share of the
fruits of majority rule.

Social control

In the towns, associates from a man's rural place of origin may serve not
only as companions with interests common to his own, but also to provide
some other functions of a traditional local community, particularly an element of social control. At the simplest level, they can report on his
behaviour to the rural community, whose goodwill he must preserve should
he ever need to return to it. Also, senior men from a particular tribal
group often hold an informal court in a town to solve along traditional
lines any disputes that may arise within the group. This kind of institution
is especially popular among those who through preference or necessity
regard their stay in town as temporary.

In the past, those who became more committed to town ways preferred
to traditional tribal courts the district commissioners' courts, which often
combined a sympathetic understanding of Shona custom with an impartiality that was not always found in chiefs' courts. Townspeople had more
confidence in a district commissioner's ability to understand the complications of modern life, and most were against the white government's policy
of increasing the powers of the chiefs' courts.

But even these had the disadvantage that they applied customary law
which was often unsuited to the urban sistuation, and which was often out
of harmony with the new ideas, and the ways of living, which urban people
had adopted. Although they are not always able to avoid the jurisdiction.
Of customary law, many prefer magistrates' courts and the High Court,
which normally judge according to the Roman-Dutch Law of Zimbabwe
rather than customary law: people claim that these courts are more competent than either tribal courts or district commissioners' courts, and that
they are fair, without bias. This preference applies especially to the more
wealthy and westernized people in the black townships.[27]

27. See Stopforth 1972 and 1973a, tables 44-48c, 59; 1973b, pp. 74-78.

The establishment of the urban courts run on traditional lines has not been a frequent phenomenon in Zimbabwe, but one, the Makoni court,[28] established in St Mary's township near Harare in 1962, proved popular, with a growing clientele from a number of neighbouring townships. This was established by elderly township residents who felt the need for a traditional court to settle disputes which, in their view, were not being settled — or not satisfactorily settled — by district commissioners' courts. The court received official approval, and held regular weekly sessions on Sundays, and attracted a clientele even from distant townships. The conduct of the court ran along lines similar to those of any chief's court in the rural areas. The need that the popularity of the Makoni court showed, has now been filled by the establishment of primary courts, with elected officials, and community courts in all the townships.

Such a court has a number of attractions. Since it is conducted by members of the township community rather than by outsiders, it can take into account changes in life style and expectations of behaviour which are known instinctively by the townsmen concerned, but which are not documented in any account of customary law. A clear example is the way the Makoni court deal with *mapoto* marriages, which I have already commented on.

Over half the cases brought to the Makoni concerned marriage disputes, usually between husband and wife, but in 40 per cent of the cases between in-laws. In these, and in other cases between neighbours and friends, the Makoni court was not simply required to decide on who was at fault and what compensation should be paid, but the court was also expected to lay down norms of conduct which could bring about a reconciliation between the quarrelling parties. The informal character of all traditional courts allows for advice to be freely sought and given, and the court officials can exhort miscreants in a way that puts pressure on them to adopt attitudes appropriate to reconciliation.

Such a court has the advantages and disadvantages of all traditional courts. That the officials are thoroughly familiar with the current urban environment makes it more likely than the chiefs' courts to give satisfaction to those who are accepting urban ways.

Townsmen generally have less respect for the position of chiefs than do their rural counterparts. Although in the 1970s townsmen recognised that chiefs had a place in the rural areas to conduct their courts and to control

28. This is described in Chavunduka 1979a. It was officially recognized by past governments; its status, and that of similar institutions, under the present government is not yet certain.

the land through their headmen, few townsmen wanted the chiefs to have any authority in the towns, which would allow these old-fashioned rural elders to interfere in fields of which they were ignorant. Although the majority agreed that the interests of chiefs should be represented in government, many said that chiefs should be represented by educated blacks, who would be more able to understand the procedures of government, and who would be better able to argue a case in parliament, than their elderly and more backward chiefs.[29]

The policy of community development, according to which rural communities were to become responsible for local government through their own rural councils, was never applied by the white Rhodesian government to the urban areas. Moves in the late 1950s and early 1960s to give the black townships of Salisbury a degree of autonomy were reversed in 1969 and 1970. when all were brought under the control of the Greater Salisbury Council, in which black representation was precluded. 'Advisory boards' had been established in the townships as elected bodies to advise government on township affairs; but they had no real power, and in Salisbury little influence. Neither their elections nor their conduct inspired much interest.[30] Now township residents have a say in local government, and city councils in Shona country have a majority of Shona members: we can expect elections to provoke interest and enthusiasm.

Stratification

Achievements in education, professions and wealth receive more recognition in the towns than does status due to noble birth or kinship relations. Thus an emerging class structure in the towns replaces the old structure based entirely on wealth. One may meet a very wealthy entreprenuer, who continues to eat stiff porridge with his fingers as the principal ingredient of his diet, who speaks only a little broken English, who keeps a polygamous family and upholds the traditional relationships between men, women and children within the family; such a man is not likely to be wholly acceptable in the upper class of professional men, although the standards of these

29. See Stopforth 1972 and 1973a, tables 51, 55-60a; 1973b; 1973b, pp. 80ff.
30. For an account of local government in black urban areas under white Rhodesian governments, see Gargett 1977, pp. 83-102.
31. Cf. Schwab 1961, who points out that the social stratification in African towns does not at present correspond exactly with a 'class' structure with its clear divisions and political overtones.

depend on their being significantly more wealthy than most townsmen. The kind of work a man does, as well as his way of life and his wealth, is relevant to his social class.

Professional men have normally received long formal education in western oriented institutions. They tend to live in select, upper class localities in the towns (previously in select 'African' areas, now usually in what used to be the white suburbs). Men in this class usually marry educated wives who are comparatively emancipated. The family is likely to base its life style, including housing, dress, eating arrangements and entertainments, on western society, and they often speak English rather than Shona when they meet. They usually look down on, and discourage approaches from, people (and even sometimes kin) whom they regard as socially below them.[32]

This does not mean that even upper class Shona become simply European in their outlook and way of life. Much from Shona culture always remains. No respectable Shona man would, for example, regard his father's brother's son as a cousin rather than a brother. In numerous ways, any person's cultural background is bound to affect his thinking and behaviour. But much time spent in alternative environments, during formal education and at work, results in professional people being less tied to traditional culture than are most other Shona.

Although, as I have pointed out, there have always been differences between rich and poor in Shona society, in the modern urban situation, these are greatly increased and have developed into clear divisions. In cities, the rich are able to separate themselves off from the rest in upper class residential areas, especially now that racial restrictions on residence have been lifted. In these exclusive areas, the clothes they wear, the food and drink they consume, the education they arrange for their children, are all way beyond the means of the majority of Shona. The result is that from childhood onwards, different urban strata become separated from each other, creating the modern Shona society with its unlimited variations.

At the lower end of urban strata are 'squatter' camps, in which homeless people live in makeshift shelters of polythene sheets and various scraps of wood, cardboard, iron sheeting and anything else that can be found lying about. Such settlements are liable to grow in urban areas everywhere, and under past white governments periodically grew and were demolished by authorities. Against popular misconceptions everywhere, the settlements do not accommodate only destitute newcomers to cities. A

---

32. See Lukhero 1966, pp. 130–133.

survey of one squatter camp near Harare[33] showed that four fifths of household heads had been living in Harare for six years or more (some had been living in the settlement for eighteen years before they were moved), and less than one fifth were unemployed. Most of these, together with the majority of wives, are likely to be employed in some kind of informal trade. They are people who for various reasons — income, nationality, lack of employment, marital status, and others — have not been able to acquire more satisfactory accommodation. The number of homeless people in the cities grew dramatically during the war years, as families fled the insecurity and violence of the rural areas, and government began to provide communal water and toilet facilities for people who would rent small plots for their rough shelters.

The way of life of townspeople is not simply determined by the economic strata in which they live. Not every wealthy or professional person makes a radical break with his or her past. In no area of change is there a strict uniformity, common to all Shona society. A wealthy professional man may be conservative in his way of life, keep his family arrangements in accordance with traditional patterns, and religiously maintain his respect to his spirit elders to the exclusion of newer religious practices. A poor couple in their traditional rural home, who have not the means to change much in their lives, may nevertheless place their marriage and their nuclear family above all the traditionally stronger kinship ties. Although we find patterns of life and patterns of change common to most, we cannot with any certainty predict how any individual will react to a new situation. Any stereotype of the black man in Zimbabwe today is bound to be false, and there is no such person as the 'typical Shona'.

Phrases such as 'knowing the African' or 'the African way of life', so common among white Zimbabweans, dangerously obscure the immense diversity in contemporay African society. Indeed, among the Shona themselves, it is all too easy to assume that one knows one's people and one's culture, without being fully aware of the plurality that has developed. A broad common language often blinds people to the diversity of local traditions: it is much more likely to obscure the diversity that is developing in the modern plural world.

The Shona peoples today are not the Shona peoples of pre-colonial times, not even the peoples of thirty years ago. The Shona are involved in a process of change from a culture without literature and with little technology and little centralization, to a culture which incorporates a growing knowledge derived from literature, and dense population centres

---

33. Seager 1977. Cf. also Seager 1979.

to meet the growth of industry. This change leads people in divergent directions, but all are caught up in it and all must adapt to it. Although some may hanker after the simplicity and surety of an idealized past, the Shona past was a response to an environment which, both physically and socially, has been surpassed and can never return.

ABRAHAM, D.P.
1959   'The Monomotapa Dynasty.' *Nada*, No. 36, pp. 58 – 84.
AQUINA, Sister Mary
          See WEINRICH, A.K.H.
BARRETT, D.B.
1968   *Schism and Renewal in Africa*. Oxford University Press, London.
BAZELEY, W.
1940   'Manyika Headwomen.' *Nada*, no. 17, pp. 3 – 5.
BEACH, D.N.
1970   'Afrikaner and Shona Settlement in the Enkeldoorn Area, 1890 – 1900.'
          Zambezia, vol. 1, no. 2, pp. 25 – 34.
1971   'The Adendorf Trek in Shona History.' *South African Historical Journal*, no. 3,
          pp. 30 – 48.
1973a   'The Initial Impact of Christianity on the Shona: the Protestants and the
          Southern Shona.' In A.J. Dachs (ed.), *Christianity South of the Zambezi*. Vol.
          1, Mambo Press, Gwelo, pp. 25 – 40.
1973b   'The Shona and Ndebele Power.' Henderson Seminar, no. 26. Department of
          History, University of Rhodesia. (Mimeo)
1979   ' "Chimurenga": The Shona Rising of 1896 – 97.' *Journal of African History*,
          vol. 20, no. 3, pp. 395 – 420.
1980   *The Shona and Zimbabwe, 900 – 1850*. Mambo Press, Gwelo.
BERLINER, P.F.
1978   *The Soul of Mbira: Music and traditions of the Shona people of Zimbabwe*.
          University of California Press, Berkeley, etc.
BERLYN, P.
1972   'The Keeper of the Spirit of Nehoreka.' *Nada*, vol. 10, no. 4, pp. 55 – 59.
BERNARDI, B.
1950   *The Social Structure of the Kraal among the Zezuru in Musami, Southern
          Rhodesia*. Communications from the school of African Studies, no. 23. Univer-
          sity of Cape Town.
BOAS, F.
1922   'The Relationship System of the vaNdau.' *Zeitschrift für Ethnologie*, vol. 54,
          pp. 41 – 51.
BOND, G.C.
1975   'New Coalitions and Traditional Chieftainship in Northern Zambia: the
          Politics of Local Government in Uyamba.' *Africa*, vol. 45, no. 4, pp. 448 – 462.
BOURDILLON, M.F.C.
1970   'The Peoples of Darwin: An Ethnographic Survey of the Darwin District.'
          Nada, vol. 10, no. 2, pp. 103 – 114.
1972   'The Manipulation of Myth in a Tavara Chiefdom.' *Africa*, vol. 42, no. 2, pp.
          112 – 121.
1974a   'A Note on Shona Court Procedures.' *Nada*, vol. 11, no. 1, pp. 11 – 14.
1974b   'Spirit Mediums in Shona belief and practice.' *Nada*, vol. 11, no. 1, pp.
          30 – 37.

1974c   'Social Relations in the Understanding of Physical Events among the Eastern Korekore.' *Zambezia*, vol. 3, no. 2, pp. 61 – 70.

1975a   'Is "Customary Law" Customary?' *Nada*, vol. 11, no. 2, pp. 140 – 149.

1976   *Myths about Africans*. Mambo Press, Gwelo.

1977   'Korekore Labour Migrants.' *Zambezia*, vol. 5, no. 1, pp. 1 – 29.

1977   (ed.) *Christianity South of the Zambezi, vol 2*. Mambo Press, Gwelo.

1979a   'Religion and Authority in a Korekore Community.' *Africa*, vol. 49, no. 2, pp. 172 – 181.

1979b   'The Cults of Dzivaguru and Karuva amongst the North Eastern Shona Peoples.' In M. Schoffeleers (ed.), *Guardians of the Land*. Mambo Press, Gwelo, pp. 235 – 255.

1979c   'Religion and Ethics in Korekore Society.' *Journal for Religion in Africa*, vol. 10, no. 2, pp. 81 – 94.

1981   'Suggestions of bureaucracy in Korekore religion: putting the ethnography straight.' *Zambezia*, vol. 9, no. 2, pp. 119-36.

1982   'Freedom and constraint among Shona spirit mediums.' In J. Davis (ed.), *Religious Organisation and Religious Experience*. Academic Press, London. pp. 181-94.

1983   'Christianity and wealth in rural communities in Zimbabwe.' *Zambezia*, vol. 11, no. 1, pp. 37-53.

1984/5   'Religious Symbols and Political Change.' *Zambezia*, vol. 12, pp. 39-54.

BRAND, C.M.

1971   'Politics and African Trade Unionism in Rhodesia since Federation.' *Rhodesian History*, vol. 2, pp. 89 – 109.

1975   'The Political Role of Unions in Rhodesia.' *South African Labour Bulletin*, no. 1, pp. 29 – 35.

1976   'Race and Politics in Rhodesian Trade Unions.' *African Perspectives: White Minorities, Black Majorities*. Afrika-Studiecentrum, Leiden. pp. 55 – 80.

BRODERICK, G.

1956   'Description of a Pagan Funeral.' *Nada*, no. 33, pp. 60 – 62.

BUCHER, H.

1980   *Spirits and Power: an analysis of Shona cosmology*. Oxford University Press, Cape Town.

BULLOCK, C.

1913   *Mashona Laws and Customs*. Salisbury.

1928   *The Mashona*. Juta & Co, Cape Town.

1931   'Totemism among the Mashona Tribes.' *Man*, vol. 31, paper 185.

1950   *The Mashona and the Matabele*. Juta & Co, Cape Town.

1951   'The Origin and Nature of Totemism among the Mashona.' *Nada*, no. 28, pp. 45 – 51.

BURBRIDGE, REV. A.

1923   'How to Become a Witch Doctor.' *Nada*, no. 1, pp. 94 – 100.

CAMPBELL, A.C.

1957   'Chimombe.' *Nada*, no. 34, pp. 31 – 37.

CHAVUNDUKA, G.L.

1967   'The Study of the Social, Economic and Political Role of Urban Agglomerations in the New States. Southern and Central Africa.' In *Urban agglomerations in the States of the Third World*. Report of the 34th Study Session of Incidi. Editions de l'institut de sociologie, Université Libre de Bruxelles.

1970a   *Social Change in a Shona Ward*. Occasional Paper no. 4. Department of Sociology, University of Rhodesia, Salisbury.

1970b   'Agents of Change in the Tribal Trust Lands of Rhodesia with Particular Reference to Extension Education.' Lecture delivered to the Vacation School, University of Rhodesia, August, 1970. Privately circulated by Department of Sociology.

1971   'Agents of Change in the Tribal Trust Lands.' *Geographical Society Magazine* (University of Rhodesia), no. 1, pp. 9 – 13.

1972a   'Farm Labourers in Rhodesia.' *Rhodesian Journal of Economics*, vol. 6, no. 4, pp. 18 – 25.

1972b   *Interaction of Folk and Scientific Beliefs in Shona Medical Practice*. Ph.D. Thesis, University of London.

1973   'Paths to Medical Care in Highfield, Rhodesia.' *The Society of Malawi Journal*, *vol. 26, no. 2, pp. 25 – 45*.

1976   'Rural and Urban Life.' *Zambezia*, vol. 4, no. 2, pp. 69 – 78.

1978   *Traditional Healers and the Shona Patient*. Mambo Press, Gwelo.

1979a   *A Shona Urban Court*. Mambo Occasional papers — Socio-Economic Series, no. 14. Mambo Press, Gwelo.

1979b   'Polygamy among Urban Shona and Ndebele Christians.' *Nada*, vol. 12, no. 1. pp. 10 – 20.

1980   *Witchcraft and the Law in Zimbabwe*. Inaugural lecture delivered at the University of Zimbabwe. To be published in *Zambezia*.

CHEATER, A.P.

1974a   *Agricultural Production in Msengezi African Purchase Land, Rhodesia: Sociological Aspects*. Research Report to the Faculty of Social Studies, University of Rhodesia. (Mimeo)

1974b   'Aspect of Status and Mobility among Farmers and their Families in Msengezi African Purchase Land, Rhodesia.' *Zambezia*, vol. 3, no. 2, pp. 51 – 59.

1978   'Bond Friendship among African Farmers in Rhodesia.' In J. Argyle and E. Preston-Whyte (eds.), *Social System and Tradition in Southern Africa*. Oxford University Press, Cape Town.

1979   *The Production and Marketing of Fresh Produce among Blacks in Zimbabwe*. Supplement to *Zambezia*. University of Zimbabwe, Salisbury.
        (forthcoming) 'The Social Organization of the Vapostori weMaranke.' *Social Analysis*.

1981   'The social organization of the Vapostori weMaranke.' *Social Analysis*, vol. 7, pp. 24-49.

1981   'Women and their participation in commercial agricultural production: the case of medium scale freehold in Zimbabwe.' *Development and Change*, vol. 12, no. 3, pp. 349-377.

1982   'Formal and informal rights to land in Zimbabwe's black freehold areas: a case study from Msengezi.' *Africa*, vol. 52, no. 3, pp. 77-91.

1983   'Cattle and class? Rights to grazing land, family organisation and class forma-
        tion in Msengezi.' *Africa*, vol. 53, no. 4, pp. 59-74.

1984   *Idioms of Accumulation: Rural Development and Class Formation among
        Freeholders in Zimbabwe*. Mambo Press, Gweru.

CHIDZIWA, J.
1964   'The History of the vaShawasha.' *Nada*, vol. 9, no. 1, pp. 16 – 33.

CHIGWEDERE, A.S.
1980   *From Matapa to Rhodes, 1000 to 1890 A.D.* Macmillan, London, etc.

CHILD, H.C.
1958   'Family and Tribal Structure and Status of Women.' *Nada*, no. 35, pp.
        65 – 70.

1965   *The History and Extent of Recognition of Tribal Law in Rhodesia*. Rhodesia
        Government, Salisbury.

CHITEHWE, S.S.M.
1954   'Rain-Making in Mashonaland.' *Nada*, no. 12, pp. 24 – 26.

CHIZENGENI, S.
1979   *Customary Law and Family Predicaments*. (Mimeo.) Centre for Applied Social
        Studies, University of Zimbabwe, Salisbury.

CLARKE, D.G.
1974   *Domestic Workers in Rhodesia: The Economics of Masters and Servants*.
        Mambo Occasional Papers — Socio-Economic Series No. 1. Mambo Press,
        Gwelo.

. 1977a *Agricultural and Plantation Workers in Rhodesia*. Mambo Occasional Papers
        — Socio-Economic Series, No. 6. Mambo Press, Gwelo.

1977b   *The Economics of Old Age Subsistence in Rhodesia*. Mambo Occasional
        Papers — Socio-Economic Series, No. 10. Mambo Press, Gwelo.

COCKCROFT, I.G.
1972   'The Mlimo (Mwari) Cult.' *Nada*, vol. 10, no. 4, pp. 83 – 92.

COLEY, D.M.
1927   'The Fate of the Last Bashankwe Chief.' *Nada*, no. 5, pp. 65 – 66.

COLSON, E.
1948   'Rain-Shrines of the Plateau Tonga of Northern Rhodesia.' *Africa*, vol. 18, no.
        4, pp. 272 – 283.

1963   'Land Rights and Land Use among the Valley Tonga of the Rhodesian Federa-
        tion.' In D. Biebuyck (ed.), *African Agrarian Systems*. Oxford University Press,
        London. pp. 137 – 156.

1971   *The Social Consequences of Resettlement*. Kariba Studies IV. Manchester
        University Press.

CRAWFORD, J.
1967   *Witchcraft and Sorcery in Rhodesia*. Oxford University Press for the Interna-
        tional African Institute, London.

CUBITT, V.S.
1979   *1979 Supplement to The Urban Poverty Datum Line in Rhodesia: A Study of
        the Minimum Consumption Needs of Families (1974)*. Faculty of Social
        Studies, University of Rhodesia, Salisbury.

336

CUBITT, V.S., and
RIDDELL, R.C.
1974   *The Urban Poverty Datum Line in Rhodesia: A Study of the Minimum Consumption Needs of Families.* Faculty of Social Studies, University of Rhodesia.

DANEEL, M.L.
1970a   *The God of the Matopo Hills.* Mouton, The Hague.
1970b   *Zionism and Faith-healing in Rhodesia: Aspects of African Independent Churches.* Mouton, The Hague.
1971   *Old and New in Southern Shona Independent Churches.* Volume 1: *Background and Rise of the Major Movements.* Mouton, The Hague.
1971a   'Shona Independent Churches and Ancestor Worship.' In D.B. Barrett (ed.), *African Initiatives in Religion.* East African Publishing House. Nairobi. Pp. 160 – 170.
1973   'Shona Independent Churches in a Rural Society.' In A.J. Dachs (ed.), *Christianity South of the Zambezi.* Vol. I. Mambo Press, Gwelo. Pp. 159 – 188.
1974   *Old and New in Southern Shona Independent Churches.* Volume II: *Church Growth — Causative Factors and Recruitment Techniques.* Mouton, The Hague.

DAVIES, C.
1931   'Chikwambo and Chitsina.' *Nada,* no. 9, pp. 41 – 43.

DAVIES, R.J.
1974   'The Informal Sector in Rhodesia: How important?' *The Rhodesia Science News,* vol. 8, no. 7, pp. 217 – 220.

DENG, F.W.
1972   *The Dinka of the Sudan.* Holt, Rinehart and Winston, New York, etc.

DILLON-MALONE, C.
1978   *The Korsten Basketmakers.* Manchester University Press for the Institute for African Studies, University of Zambia.

DICKE, B.H.
1931   'The Lightning Bird and other Analogies and Traditions Connecting the Bantu with the Zimbabwe Ruins.' *South African Journal of Science,* vol. 28, pp. 505 – 511.

DOKE, C.M.
1931   *Report on the Unification of Shona Dialects.* Government of Southern Rhodesia, Salisbury.

DUNLOP, H.
1970   'Efficiency Criteria in Primary Marketing: an Analysis of African Marketing Policies in Rhodesia.' *The Rhodesian Journal of Economics,* vol. 4, no. 3, pp. 10 – 20.
1972   'Land and Economic Opportunity in Rhodesia.' *The Rhodesian Journal of Economics,* vol. 6, no. 1, pp. 1 – 19.
1974   'Land Policy in Rhodesia 1945 – 69.' Political Economy Research Seminar paper no. 2. University of Rhodesia. (Mimeo.)

EDWARDS, W.
1926   'The Wanoe: A Short Historical Sketch.' *Nada,* no. 7, pp. 16 – 42.
1928   'Sacred Places.' *Nada,* no. 6, pp. 23 – 27.
1929   'From Birth to Death.' *Nada,* no. 7, pp. 16 – 42.

EPSTEIN, A.L.

   1958   *Politics in an African Urban Community.* Manchester University Press, Man-
               chester.

ESSEX-CAPELL, A.

   1946   'Tales of the Makorrie-Korrie.' *Nada,* no. 23 pp. 67 – 71.

EVANS-PRITCHARD, E.E.

   1937   *Witchcraft, Oracles and Magic among the Azande.* Clarendon Press, Oxford.

FELDMAN, R.

   1974   'Custom and Capitalism: Changes in the Basis of Land Tenure in Ismali, Tan-
               zania.' *Journal of Development Studies,* vol. 10, no. 3, pp. 305 – 320.

FLOYD, B.N.

   1963   *Changing Patterns of African Land Use in Southern Rhodesia.* (3 vols.)
               Rhodes-Livingstone Institute, Lusaka.

FORTUNE, G.

   1973   'Who was Mwari?' *Rhodesian History,* vol. 4, pp. 1 – 20.

FRANKLIN, H.

   1927   'A Selection of Notes on Manyika Customs.' *Nada,* no. 5, pp. 56 – 60.

   1932   'Manyusa (Amanxusa).' *Nada,* no. 10, pp. 77 – 83.

FRY, P.

   1976   *Spirits of Protest.* Cambridge University Press, Cambridge.

GARBETT, G.K.

   1960   *Growth and Change in a Shona Ward.* Occasional Paper no. 1. Department of
               African Studies, University College of Rhodesia and Nyasaland, Salisbury.

   1963a   *The Political System of a Central African Tribe with particular reference to the
               Role of Spirit Mediums.* Ph.D. Thesis, University of Manchester.

   1963b   'The Land Husbandry Act of Southern Rhodesia.' In D. Biebuyck (ed.),
               African Agrarian Systems. Oxford University Press, for International African
               Institute. London. Pp. 185 — 202.

   1966a   'Religious Aspects of Political Succession among the Valley Korekore (N.
               Shona).' In E.T. Stokes and R. Brown (eds.), *The Zambezian Past,* Manchester
               University Press. Pp. 137 – 170.

   1966b   'The Rhodesian Chief's Dilemma: Government Officer or Tribal Leader?'
               Race, vol. 8, no. 2, pp. 113 – 128.

   1967   'Prestige, Status and Power in a Modern Valley Korekore Chiefdom,
               Rhodesia.' *Africa,* vol. 37, no. 3, pp. 307 – 326.

   1969   'Spirit Mediums as Mediators in Valley Korekore Society.' In J. Beattie and J.
               Middleton (eds.), *Spirit Mediumship and Society in Africa.* Routledge &
               Kegan Paul, London. Pp. 104 – 127.

   1977   'Disparate Regional Cults and a Unitary Field in Zimbabwe.' In R.P. Werbner
               (ed.), *Regional Cults.* A.S.A. Monograph 16. Academic Press, London, etc.

GARGETT, E.

   1977   *The Administration of Transition: African Urban Settlement in Rhodesia.*
               Mambo occasional papers — socio-economic series, no. 5. Mambo Press,
               Gwelo.

GARLAKE, P.S.

   1973   *Great Zimbabwe.* Thames and Hudson, London.

GELFAND, M.
1944   *The Sick African.* Juta & Co., Cape Town.
1956   *Medicines and Magic of the Mashona.* Juta & Co., Cape Town.
1957   'Chitsina.' *Nada,* no. 34, pp. 6f.
1959   *Shona Ritual.* Juta & Co., Cape Town.
1962   *Shona Religion.* Juta & Co., Cape Town.
1964a   *Witch Doctor: Traditional Medicine Man of Rhodesia.* Harvill Press, London.
1964b   *Medicine and Custom in Africa.* E. & S. Livingstone, Edinburgh.
1964c   'Psychiatric Disorders as Recognized by the Shona.' In A. Kiev (ed.), *Magic, Faith, and Healing.* Free Press of Glencoe, New York. Pp. 156 – 173.
1965   *African Background: the Traditional Culture of the Shona-speaking people.* Juta & Co., Cape Town.
1966a   *An African's Religion: The Spirit of Nyajena.* Juta & Co., Cape Town.
1966b   'The Great Muzukuru: His role in the Shona Clan.' *Nada,* vol. 9, no. 3, pp. 38 – 41.
1967a   *The African Witch.* E. & S.,Livingstone, Edinburgh.
1967b   'The Shona Attitude to Sex Behaviour.' *Nada.* vol. 9, no. 4, pp 61 – 64.
1968   *African Crucible.* Rustica press, Wynberg.
1969   'The Shona Mother and Child.' *Nada,* vol. 10, no. 1, pp. 76 – 80.
1971a   *Diet and Tradition in an African Culture.* E. & S. Livingstone, Edinburgh.
1971b   'A Nganga Who Has Adopted Two Faiths.' *Nada,* vol. 10, no. 3, pp. 73 – 76.
1973a   *The Genuine Shona.* Mambo Press, Gwelo.
1973b   'The Shona Woman.' *Nada,* vol. 10, no. 5, pp. 41 – 50.
1974   'The Mhondoro Cult among the Manyika peoples of the Eastern region of Mashonaland.' *Nada,* vol. 11, no. 1, pp. 64 – 95.
1975   'Upombwe: Adultery in Shona Law.' *Nada,* vol. 11, no. 2, pp. 192 – 199.
1977   *The Spiritual Beliefs of the Shona.* Mambo Press, Gwelo.
1979   *Growing up in Shona Society.* Mambo Press, Gwelo.

HAMPSON, J.
1982   *A Study of Aging in Zimbabwe.* Mambo Occasional Papers — Socio-political series no. 16. Mambo Press, Gweru.

HAMUTYINEI, M.A. and
PLANGGER, A.B.
1974   *Tsumo—Shumo.* Shona Proverbial Lore and Wisdom (Shona Heritage Series: Vol.2). Mambo Press, Gwelo.

HARRIS, P.S.
1972   'Some Aspects of Apprenticeship Training in Rhodesia.' *Society.* Magazine of the Social Studies Association, University of Rhodesia. No. 3, pp. 16 – 21.
1974a   *Black Industrial Workers in Rhodesia.* Mambo Occasional Papers — Socio-Economic Series No. 2. Mambo Press, Gwelo.
1974b   'Industrial Relations in Rhodesia.' *South African Journal of Economics,* vol. 42, no. 1, pp. 65 – 84.

HATENDI, REV. R.P.
1973   'Shona Marriage and the Christian Churches.' In A.J. Dachs (ed.), *Christianity South of the Zambezi.* Vol. 1. Mambo Press, Gwelo. Pp. 135 – 150.

HODZA, A.C. and FORTUNE, G.

1979   *Shona Praise Poetry.* Clarendon Press, Oxford.

HOLLEMAN, J.F.

1949   *The Pattern of Hera Kinship.* Rhodes-Livingstone Paper no. 17. Oxford University Press, Cape Town.

1952a   *Shona Customary Law.* Oxford University Press for the Rhodes-Livingstone Institute, Cape Town.

1952b   'Hera Court Procedure.' *Nada,* no. 29, pp. 26 – 42.

1953   *Accommodating the Spirit amongst some North-Eastern Shona tribes.* Rhodes-Livingstone Paper no. 22. Oxford University Press, Cape Town.

1955   'Indigenous Administration of Justice.' *Nada,* no. 32, pp. 41 – 47.

1958a   *African Interlude.* Nationale Boekhandel Bpk, Cape Town.

1958b   'Town and Tribe (Southern Rhodesia).' In P. Smith (ed.), *Africa in Transition.* Max Reinhardt, London. Pp. 62 – 70.

1958c   'The Changing Roles of African Women (Southern Rhodesia).' In P. Smith (ed.), *African in Transition.* Max Reinhardt, London. Pp. 71 – 78.

1969   *Chief, Council and Commissioner.* Oxford Univerity Press, London.

1974   *Issues in African Law.* Mouton, The Hague.

HORTON, R.

1971   'African Conversion.' *Africa,* vol. 41, no. 2, pp. 85 – 108.

1975   'On the Rationality of Conversion.' *Africa,* vol. 45, no. 3, pp. 219 – 235, and no. 4, pp. 373 – 399.

HOVE, M.M.

1943   'Notes on the Vangowa Tribe.' *Nada,* no. 20, pp. 41 – 45.

HOWMAN, E.G.

1914   'Native Tribes of the South: A Superstitious Race: The Fate of a Rain-maker.' *The Times,* London, 25th May. Reprinted in *Nada,* vol. 11, no. 3, pp. 33 – 37.

HOWMAN, R.H.G.

1948   'Witchcraft and the Law.' *Nada,* no. 25, pp. 7 – 18.

1956   'African Leadership in Transition.' *Nada,* no. 33, pp. 13 – 25.

1959   'Chiefs nd Councils in Southern Rhodesia.' In R. Apthrope (ed.), *From Tribal Rule to Modern Government.* Proceedings of the thirteenth conference of the Rhodes-Livingstone Institute, Lusaka. Pp. 37 – 48.

1961   'The Matri-Estate.' *Nada,* no. 38, pp. 38 – 48.

1966   'Chieftainship.' *Nada,* vol. 9, no. 3, pp. 10 – 14.

HUFFMAN, T.N.

1972   'The Rise and Fall of Zimbabwe.' *Journal of African History,* vol. 13, no. 3, pp. 353 – 366.

1974   'African Mining and Zimbabwe.' *Journal of the South African Institute of Mining and Metallurgy,* vol. 74, no. 6, pp. 238 – 242.

HUGHES, A.J.B.

1974   *Development in Rhodesian Tribal Areas.* Tribal Areas of Rhodesia Research Foundation, Salisbury.

HUGO, H.C.

1935   'The Mashona Spirits.' *Nada,* no. 13, pp. 52 – 58.

HUNT, N.
1950   'Some Notes on Witchdoctor's Bones.' *Nada*, no. 27, pp. 40—46.
1954   'Some Notes on the Witchdoctor's Bones.' *Nada*, no. 31, pp. 16—23.
1962   'More Notes on the Witchdoctor's Bones.' *Nada*, no. 39, pp. 14—16.
1963   'Age and Land in a Native Reserve.' *Nada*, no. 40, pp. 108—112.
ISAACMAN, A.
1973   'Madzi-Manga, Mhondoro and the Use of the Oral Traditions — a Chapter in Barue Religious and Political History.' *Journal of African History*, vol. 14, no.3, pp. 395—410.

1976   *The Tradition of Resistance in Mozambique: anti-colonial activity in the Zambezi Valley 1850-1921.* Heinemann, London.

JACKSON, A.
1950   'Native Hunting Customs.' *Nada*, no. 27, pp. 39—40.
JONES, G.I.
1949   'Ibo Land Tenure.' *Africa*, vol. 19, no. 4, pp. 309—323.
KAHARI, G.P.
1972   *The Novels of Patrick Chakaipa.* Longman, Salisbury.
1975   *The Imaginative Writings of Paul Chidyausiku.* Mambo Press, Gwelo.
1980   *The Search for Zimbabwean Identity.* Mambo Press, Gwelo.
'KANDAMAKUMBO'
1940   'Mamwe Matsika.' *Nada*, no. 17, pp. 53f.
KAY, G.
1970   *Rhodesia: a Human Geography.* University of London Press, London.
KAUFFMAN, R.A.
1970   *Multipart Relationships in the Shona Music of Rhodesia.* Unpublished Ph.D. Thesis, University of California, Los Angeles.
KILEFF, C.
1975   'Black Suburbanites: An African Elite in Salisbury, Rhodesia.' In C. Kileff and W.C. Pendelton (eds), *Urban Man in Southern Africa.* Mambo Press, Gwelo. Pp. 81—98.
KROG, E.W.
1966   (ed.) *African Literature in Rhodesia.* Mambo Press, Gwelo.
KUMBIRAI, J.
1964   *Shona Beliefs of the Dead.* Unpublished cyclostyled notes distributed by the General Secretariate, Catholic Bishops' Conference, Salisbury, Rhodesia.
1966/7   *An Outline of Traditional Shona Belief.* A series of articles published in the newspaper *Moto* (Gwelo), March, 1966 to February, 1967.

KUPER, A. and
GILLETT, S.
1970   'Aspects of Administration in Western Botswana.' *African Studies*, vol. 29, no. 3, pp. 169—182.

LAN, D.M.
1983   *Making History: spirit mediums and the guerilla war in the Dande area of Zimbabwe.* Ph.D. Thesis, London School of Economics and Political Science.

LANCASTER, C.S.

1974   'Bride Service, Residence, and Authority among the Goba (N. Shona) of the Zambezi Valley.' *Africa*, Vol. 44, no. 1, pp. 46–64.

1981   *The Goba of the Zambezi*. Oklahoma University Press, Oklahoma.

LONG, N.

1968   *Social Change and the Individual*. Manchester University Press for the Institute of Social Research, University of Zambia.

LUKHERO, M.B.

1966   'The Social Characteristics of an Emergent Elite in Harare.' In P.C. Lloyd (ed.), *The New Elites of Tropical Africa*. Oxford University Press, London. Pp. 126–138.

MACKENZIE, J.M.

1975   'A Pre-Colonial Industry: The Njanja and the Iron Trade.' *Nada*, vol. 11, no. 2, pp. 200–220.

'MAPANABOMVU'

1924   'Fragments of an Conversation with Macebo.' *Nada*, no. 2, pp. 83f.

MARR, F.

1962   'Some Notes on Chief Sileya.' *Nada*, no. 39, pp. 81–84.

MARTIN, M.-L.

1971   'The Mai Chaza Church in Rhodesia.' In D.B. Barrett (ed.), *African Initiatives in Religion*. East African Publishing House, Nairobi. Pp. 109–121.

MARWICK, M.G.

1950   'Another Modern Anti-Witchcraft Movement in East Central Africa.' *Africa*, vol. 20, no. 2, pp. 100–112.

MAY, J.

1973a   *Drinking in Harare*. Institute for Social Research, University of Rhodesia. (Mimeo.)

1979   *African Women in Urban Employment*. Mambo Press, Gweru.

1983   *Zimbabwean Women in Customary and Colonial Law*. Mambo Press, Gweru.

1973b   'Changing Patterns of Family Life among Urban Africans.' Unpublished vacation school lecture.

1980   *Social Aspects of the Legal Position of Women in Zimbabwe Rhodesia*. Unpublished M. Phil. Thesis, Faculty of Social Studies, University of Zimbabwe.

'MBIZO'

1924   'The Lightning Doctor.' *Nada*, no. 2, pp. 60–62.

MEREDITH, L.C.

1925   'The Rain Spirit of Mabota Murangadzwa, Melsetter District.' *Nada*, no. 3, pp. 77–81.

MILLER, N.

1968   'The Political Survival of Traditional Leadership.' *Journal of Modern African Studies*, vol. 6, no. 2, pp. 183–198.

MITCHELL, J.C.

1959a   'The Woman's Place in African Advancement.' *Optima*, vol. 9, no. 3, pp. 124–131.

1959b 'Migrant Labour in African South of the Sahara: the Causes of Labour Migration.' *Inter-African Labour Institute Bulletin*, vol. 6, no. 1, pp. 12 – 47.

1960a 'The African Peoples.' In W.V. Brelsford (ed.). *Handbook to the Federation of Rhodesia and Nyasaland.* Cassell and Co., London. Pp. 117 – 181.

1960b *Tribalism and the Plural Society.* Oxford University Press, London.

1961a 'Chidzere's Tree: a Note on a Shona Land-Shrine and its Significance.' *Nada*, no. 38, pp. 28 – 35.

1961b *An Outline of the Sociological Background to African Labour.* Ensign Publishers, Salisbury.

1969 'Structural Plurality, Urbanization and Labour Circulation in Rhodesia.' In J.A. Jackson (ed.), *Migration.* Cambridge University Press. Pp. 156 – 180.

MOLLER, V.

1973 *Mobility of Migrant Labour in a Salisbury African Township.* Research Report no. 6. Harare Hostels Study 1973. Institute for Social Research, University of Rhodesia, Salisbury. (Mimeo.).

1978 *Urban Commitment and Involvement among Black Rhodesians.* Centre for Applied Social Sciences, University of Natal, Durban.

MUCHENA, O.N.

1979 'The changing position of African women in rural Zimbabwe.' *Zimbabwe Journal of Economics*, vol. 1, no. 1, p. 61.

1980a *Women in Town.* Litho Services, Harare.

1980b *Women's organizations in Zimbabwe.* University of Zimbabwe, Centre for Applied Social Sciences, Harare.

MSWAKA, T.E.

1974 'Rural Area Subsidies to Wage Employment in Rhodesia.' *The Rhodesia Sciences News*, vol. 8, no. 7, pp. 221 – 224.

MURPHREE, B.J.

1974 'Environmental Factors Influencing the Occupational and Educational Aspirations, Academic Achievement and Post School Employment of African Secondary School Pupils in Rhodesia.' Paper presented to the second World Congress of Comparative Education Societies. (Unpublished)

MURPHREE, M.W.

1969 *Christianity and the Shona.* Athlone Press, London.

1970 'A Village School and Community Development in a Rhodesian Tribal Trust Land.' *Zambezia*, vol. 1 no. 2, pp. 13 – 23.

1971 'Religious Interdependency among the Budjga Vapostori.' In D.B. Barrett (ed.), *African Initiatives in Religion.* East African Publishing House, Nairobi. Pp. 171 – 180.

NCUBE, R.M.M.

1962 'The True Story re Chaminuka and Lobengula.' *Nada*, no. 39, pp. 59 – 67.

OTITE, O.

1973 'Relationships between Traditional Rulers and Government in Nigeria's Midwestern State.' *Current Anthropology*, vol. 14, no. 3, pp. 263 – 264.

PALLEY, C.

1966 *The Constitutional History and Law of Southern Rhodesia 1888 – 1965.* Clarendon Press, Oxford.

PALMER, R.H.

1968   *Aspects of Rhodesian Land Policy 1890 – 1936.* Central Africa Historical Association, Salisbury.

1977a   *Land and Racial Domination in Rhodesia.* University of California Press, Berkeley.

1977b   'The Agricultural History of Rhodesia.' In R.H. Palmer and N. Parsons (eds.), *The Roots of Rural Poverty in Central and Southern Africa.* Heinemann, London, etc. Pp. 221 – 254.

PASSMORE, G.C.

1971   *Theoretical Aspects of Local Government and Community Action.* Monographs of Political Science, no. 3. University of Rhodesia, Salisbury.

1972   *The National Policy of Community Development in Rhodesia.* Department of Political Science, Source Book Series no. 5. University of Rhodesia, Salisbury.

PHILLIPS, J., HAMMOND, J.,

SAMUELS, L.H. and SWYNNERTON, R.J.M.

1962   *The Development of the Economic Resources of Southern Rhodesia with particular reference to the Role of African Agriculture.* Report of the Advisory Committee. Government of Southern Rhodesia, Salisbury.

PONGWENI, A.J.C.

1983   *What's in a name.* Mambo Press, Gweru.

POSSELT, F.W.T.

1929   *Fables of the Veld.* Oxford University Press, London.

1935   *Fact and Fiction.* Rhodesian Printing and Publishing Co., Bulawayo.

POWELL, R.J.

1953a   'Notes on the "Kutaya", "Kukomba" and "Kugara Nhaka" Ceremonies of the Vashankwe.' *Nada*, no. 30, pp. 14 – 21.

1953b   'Notes on Burial Customs in the Bushu Reserve.' *Nada*, no. 33, pp. 6 – 10.

RANGER, T.O.

1963   'The Last Days of the Empire of Mwene Mutapa, 1898 – 1917.' In *The History of the Central African Peoples.* 17th conference of the Rhodes-Livingstone Institute. Lusaka.

1966   'Traditional Authorities and the Rise of Modern Politics in Southern Rhodesia, 1898 – 1930.' In E.T. Stokes and R. Brown (eds.), *The Zambesian Past*, Manchester University Press. Pp. 171 – 193.

1967   *Revolt in Southern Rhodesia, 1886 – 1897.* Heinemann, London.

RICHARDS, A.I.

1935   'A Modern Movement of Witch-Finders.' *Africa*, vol. 8, no. 4, pp. 448 – 461.

ROBERTS, J.G.

1938   'Totemism and Sexuality.' *Nada*, no. 15, pp. 44 – 61.

1947   'Totemism, Zimbabwe and the Barozwi.' *Nada*, no. 24, pp. 48 – 52.

RODEL, M.G.W. and

HOPLEY, J.D.H.

1973   'Investigations into Systems of Farming Suitable for Tribal Trust Land.' Paper presented to Symposium on Influx and Urbanization Problems. University of Rhodesia, Salisbury.

RODER, W.

1964   'The Division of Land Resources in Southern Rhodesia.' *Annals of the Associa-*

               tion of American Geographers, vol. 54, no. 1, pp. 41 – 58.

1965   *The Sabi Valley Irrigation Projects*. University of Chicago, Department of Geography. Research Paper no. 99. Illinois.

SACHS, W.

1937   *Black Hamlet*. Geoffrey Bles, London.

SADZA, D.

1954   'Digma.' *Nada*, no. 31, pp. 38 – 39.

SCHOFFERLEERS, J.M. and R. MWANZA

1979   'An organizational Model of the Mwari Shrine,' In J.M. Schoffeleers (ed.), *Guardians of the Land*. Mambo Press, Gwelo. Pp. 297 – 310.

SCHWAB, W.B.

1961   'Social Stratification in Gwelo.' In A. Southall (ed.), *Social Change in Modern Africa*. Oxford University Press. London. Pp. 126 – 144.

SEAGER, D.

1977   'The Struggle for Shelter in an Urbanizing World: A Rhodesian Example.' *Zambezia*, vol. 5, no. 1, pp. 83 – 90.

1979   'War Refugees in Harare Musika.' (*Mimeo.*) Dept. of Sociology, University of Rhodesia.

SEED, J.H.

1932   'The Kinship System of a Bantu Tribe.' *Nada*, no. 10, pp. 65 – 73.

1933   'The Kinship System of a Bantu Tribe (continued).' *Nada*, no. 11, pp. 35 – 56.

SHROPSHIRE, D.W.T.

1928   'The Medical Outfit of a Wamanyika Doctor.' *Nada*, no. 6, pp. 27 – 30.

1931   'The Burial Customs of the Wamanyika Tribes.' *Man*, vol. 29, no. 4, pp. 270 – 272.

1938   *The Church and Primitive Peoples*. The Society for the Promotion of Christian Knowledge, London.

STEAD, W.H.

1946   'The Clan Organisation and Kinship System of Some Shona Tribes.' *African Studies*, vol. 5, no. 1, pp. 1 – 20.

STOPFORTH, P.

1971   *Survey of Highfield African Township*. Occasional Paper No. 6. Department of Sociology, University of Rhodesia, Salisbury.

1972   *Two Aspects of Social Change, Highfield African Township, Salisbury*. Occasional Paper No. 7. Department of Sociology, University of Rhodesia, Salisbury.

1973a   *Comparative Data for the Assessment of Problems of Social Change among Urban Africans, Salisbury*. Research Report No. 4. Institute of Social Research, University of Rhodesia, Salisbury. (Mimeo.)

1973b   *Comparative Differential Social Change: Highfield African Township and Chitepo Road, Salisbury*. Research Report No. 5. Institute of Social Research, University of Rhodesia, Salisbury. (Mimeo.)

1977   'Some Local Impediments to Social Change among Urban Africans.' *Zambezia*, vol. 5, no. 1, pp. 31 – 40.

SUMMERS, R.

1958   *Inyanga*. Cambridge University Press.

1969   *Ancient Mining in Rhodesia and Adjacent Areas.* Trustees of the National Museums of Rhodesia, Salisbury.

TAGWIREYI, J.H.

1950   'Origin of the Vamari Clan.' *Nada*, no. 27, pp. 63 – 65.

THEISEN, R.J.

1976   'Development in Rural Communities.' *Zambezia*, vol. 4, no. 2, pp. 93 – 98.

1979   'Religion and Attitudes to the Livestock Extension Service.' *Nada*, vol. 12, no. 1, pp. 48 – 51.

TRACEY, A.

1970   'The Matepe Mbira music of Rhodesia.' *African Music*, vol. 4, no. 4, pp. 37 – 61.

TRACEY, H.

1934a   'The Bones.' *Nada*, no. 12, pp. 23 – 26.

1934b   'What are Mashawi Spirits?' *Nada*, no. 12, pp. 39 – 52.

1963   'The Hakata of Southern Rhodesia.' *Nada*, no. 40, pp. 105 – 107.

UNITED NATIONS

1984   *Women and development in Zimbabwe: an annotated bibliography.* United Nations Economic Commission for Africa, Addis Ababa.

VAN DER MERWE, W.J.

1957   'The Shona Idea of God.' *Nada*, no. 34, pp. 39 – 63.

VANSINA, J.

1961   *Oral Tradition.* Routledge and Kegan Paul, London.

VON SICARD, H.

1946   'The Tree Cult in the Zimbabwe Culture.' *African Studies*, vol. 5, no. 4, pp. 257 – 267.

1950   'The Derivation of the Name Mashona.' *African Studies*, vol. 9, no. 3, pp. 138 – 143.

1959   'The Hakata Names.' *Nada*, no. 36, pp. 26 – 29.

1966   'Karanga Stars.' *Nada*, vol. 9, no. 3, pp. 42 – 65.

WATSON, W.

1958   *Tribal Cohesion in a Money Economy.* Manchester University Press.

WEINRICH, A.K.H.

(AQUINA, Sister Mary)

1960   'A Study of the Vatavara Kinship System.' *Nada*, no. 37, pp. 8 – 26.

1963   'A Note on Missionary Influence on Shona Marriage.' *Human Problems in British Central Africa.* The Rhodes-Livingstone Journal, vol. 33, pp. 68 – 79.

1964   'The Social Background of Agriculture in Chilimanzi Reserve.' *Human Problems in British Central Africa.* The Rhodes-Livingstone Journal, vol. 36, pp. 7 – 39.

1965a   'The Tribes in the Victoria Reserve.' *Nada*, vol. 9, no. 2, pp. 6 – 15.

1965b   'The Tribes in the Chilimanzi Reserve, and their Relation to the Rozvi.' *Nada*, vol. 9, no. 2, pp. 40 – 51.

1966   'Christianity in a Rhodesian Tribal Trust Land.' *African Social Research*, no. 1, pp. 1 – 40.

1967a   'The Group Aspect of Karanga Marriage.' *Nada*, vol. 9, no. 4, pp. 28 – 38.

1967b   'The People of the Spirit: an Independent Church in Rhodesia.' *Africa*, vol. 37, no. 2, pp. 203 – 219.

1968	'Mutumwi: A Note on the Waist Belt of the Karanga.' *Nada*, vol. 11. no. 5, pp. 3f.

1968   'Mutumwi: A Note on the Waist Belt of the Karanga.' *Nada*, vol. 11. no. 5, pp. 3f.

1969   'Zionists in Rhodesia.' *Africa*, vol. 39, no. 2, 113 – 136.

1971   *Chiefs and Councils in Rhodesia.* Heinemann, London.

1973   *Black and White Elites in Rural Rhodesia.* Manchester University Press.

1975   *African Farmers in Rhodesia.* Oxford University Press for International African Institute, London.

1976   *Mucheke: Race, Status and Politics in a Rhodesian Community.* Unesco, Paris.

1982   *African Marriage in Zimbabwe.* Mambo Press, Gweru.

WERBNER, R.P.

1964   'Atonement Ritual and Guardian-Spirit Possession among Kalanga.' *Africa*, vol. 34, no. 3, pp. 206 – 223.

1971   'Symbolic Dialogue and Personal Transactions among the Kalanga and Ndembu.' *Ethnology*, vol. 10, no. 3, pp. 311 – 328.

1972   'Sin, Blame and Ritual Mediation.' In M. Gluckman (ed.), *The Allocation of Responsibility*. Manchester University Press. Pp. 227 – 256.

1973   'The Superabundance of Understanding: Kalanga Rhetoric and Domestic Divination.' *American Anthropologist*, vol. 75, no. 5, pp. 1414 – 1440.

1977   'Continuity and Policy in Southern Africa's High God Cult.' In R.P. Werbner (ed.), *Regional Cults*. A.S.A. Monograph 16. Academic Press, London, etc.

WIESCHOFF, H.

1937   'Names and Naming Customs among the Mashona in Southern Rhodesia.' *American Anthropologist*, vol. 39, no. 3, pp. 497 – 503.

WOOLLACOTT, R.C.

1975   'Pasipamire — Spirit Medium of Chaminuka, the "Wizard" of Chitungwiza.' *Nada*, vol. 11, no. 2, pp. 154 – 167.

YUDELMAN, M.

1964   *Africans on the Land.* Oxford University Press, London.

INDEX

Adultery, and child birth 139, 158, 185; as crime 34; damages for 41, 48, 137; medicines against 180, 183; responsibility for 52; suspicions of 151, 295; of widow 213; with wife of kinsman 48

African Apostolic Church 292, 297-302

African Land Husbandry Act 59, 75

African Law and Tribal Courts Act 113, 127, 139

African Marriages Act 44, 45

America 292

anteater 68

antbear 175

Apostolic Sabbath Church of God 293

apprentices 99

archeology, archeologists 3, 4, 7f.

baba 25, 30, 33; father-in-law 37; headman 60; chief 114

baboon 242-6

barren, barrenness 320; as failure in marital obligations 46, 134; and witchcraft 178, 185; and alien spirits 243

Barwe 11f., 15, 17, 19

Bible, missionaries' teaching of 285; in independent churches 294, 297, 300, 307; widespread belief in 306

bona 209

bride-price 28, 41f., 56; and family relations 30, 34, 36, 38, 217; individual payment of 51, 315; inflation of 81, 103; status of wife 45, 50; in child marriage 44; in elopement marriage 43; service in lieu of 28, 44, 60, 98; marriage without 55, 116; return of 45, 133-5; and labour migration 91; and cattle 46, 75; as compensation 207; arousing angry spirit 234

British 4, 5, 14, 15

Budya 75, 305

bull 42, 61; dedicated 27, 232, 298

burial societies 218, 322

Bushmen 6

cannabis 144, 238

cattle, bride-price 28, 34, 36, 38, 41, 77, 315; family herd 29; in history 7; trade 13; in farming 74-84; as investment 76, 91; as wealth 41, 63, 76f., 104; as fine 137, 233f.; as compensation 47; like people 78; owned by women 53; symbolism of 41f.; in sacrifice 77, 211, 217, 234; in relation to spirits 232, 234, 253; scarcity of 44; and distance 71

Chaminuka 259, 267f., 273f., 276, 278

Changamire 10, 12, 14

Chaza, Mai 195

Chesa 110, 212

chickens 98, 262

chidao (pl. zvidao) 24f.

Chidzere 258

Chikanga 10

inheritance *29*, 34, 51, 73, 82, 85f., 106, 145, 209f., 249; in customary law 136, 142; in in
    dependent churches 299; in towns 142, 317; ceremony 204, 208, *214-6*, 223
irrigation schemes 54, 79, 86

Jesus 285, 289, 302f.
jukwa 281

Kagubi 274
Kalahari 6, 11
Kalanga 8, 17, 156, 231, 243
Kambuzuma 313
Karanga 14, 17, 59, 103, 158, 199; historical 7, 9f.; chiefs 68, 109; spirits 253, 281; high god
    cult 117, 279-81; independent churches 195, 281
Karuva 258f., 263, 272, 279
Khami 3, 9, 12
Khoisan 6f.
Korekore xiv, 10, 17f; village structure 57; kinship relations 35, 38, 217; oral traditions of 4f.,
    53; family spirits 48, 233; rituals 68, 110, 211, 217, 228; disease and death 156, 158, 205;
    spirit domains 69, 116, 255, 257f.; cults 258, 259, 263f., 272, 279; medium 238, 268, 271,
    272, 273; attitudes to towns 90
kutonga 112
kubuda 220f.
kugadzira mudzimu 209
kurova guva 209
kutamba n'ombe, mudzimu 209
kutya 30
kwami 155

labour migrations 55, 74, 86, *87-97*, 292, 318
land 5, 23, *67-71*, 82, 105, 201, 258, 263, 277, 285; relation to chiefs 92, 110-23,
    326; retirement to 90, 92; spirit guardians of 104, 109f., 255; tenure 59, 67, 72f.; use of
    15f., 62, 74f., .78, 97; shortage of 28, 57, 59, 60, 75, 79
Legal Age of Majority Act 56
libation 166, 207-13, 229
lighting 175, 278, 298
Limpopo 6, 7
lineage 5, 25-7, 29, 77, 186; chiefly 107, 264; kinship relations determined by l. 25f., 47;
    affined 37f.; of mother 31-4; of spirit 258; of village headman 57-60
lion 68, 162, 262; associated with spirits 222, 253f., 257; see also spirits, lion
liquor 144
Lobengula 268
lobola 36; see also bride-price
locusts 151, 262
Lozi 137

magistrates 138, 143f., 325
mai 31-3, 38
Makombe 11, 275

makombwe 259, 268

Makuni xix, 103

Malawi 84, 194, 299

Malawian 103, 186

Mambo 12, 106

mana 27

Mangwende 119, 121f.

Manyika 10, *18;* marriage 38; chiefs 54f., 106; funerary rituals 209, 212, 213, 255, 260, 279

Mapondera 15, 275

mapoto 319-21, 326

Maranke, Johane 292, *297-302*

Mari 103

marriage *26-49,* 319-321, 326; normal procedures 40-3; child m. 44; church m. 43, 46, 290; elopement m. 43; service m. 44; registration, solemnisation of 44f., 133, 315, 317, 319; M. without bride-price 55; group aspects of 36-8, 46; relations between groups 37f.; in ritual 217; strengthening brother-sister relationship 31; cattle in marriage 9, 36, 41, 77; cash payments 89, 95; emphasis on individual 45f., 95, 315f., 329; Christian 290f., 320; in chiefly families 116, 272; of spirit medium 242; dissolution of, divorce 37, 41, 45, 47, 48, 49, 53, 115, 133-5, 208, 280

Masowe, Johane 293

master farmer 80

Masvingo 176

Matonjeni 280f.

Matopo Hills 12, 279-81

mazengi 243

Mazowe River 173

Mbare (formerly Harare) 168, 312, 321

mbira xv, 13, 88, 229, 243

Mchape 194f.

medicines 54, 160f.; associated with chiefship 103f.; 116; divining 153, 156; and fortune 81; in death and burial 199, 204, 218; herbal 159f., 165, 241; in independent churches 169, 295, 303, 304; protective 158, 192, 256; and spirits 159, 163, 241, 254, 257, 264; associated with witchcraft 62, 81, 173-84, 190, 195, 295; western m. 150, 166-9, 174, 287; limits of western m. 149, 160, 187m 238

mediums 263-76; initiation of 166, 238-42, 266; testing of 265-7; associations with chiefs 68, 116f,; role in trial of crime 137; women as mediums 52, 54

mhepo 184

mhondoro 234f.; see also spirits, lion

millet beer, at chiefly succession 110; in family spirit rituals 27, 30, 32, 158, 162, 122, *227-33;* at funerary rituals 207-14; in inheritance ceremonies 215; for Mwari 280; at possession sèances 166, 240, 244, 247; for territorial spirits 69, 116, 260-2, 272; in work party 74

mining 3, 7, 9, 14, 15

missionaries 4, 11, 285-91; God of 242, 277, 279, 281; and independent churches 292-4, 307; and witchcraft 194, 289f., 296

mombe 78; see also cattle

Monomotapa 10

mother's brother 34, 218

Mount Darwin xi, xix, 212, 255

Mount Selinda 88

Mozambique 14, 15f., 18f., 84, 299

mudzimu (pl. midzimu) 200, 206, 209, 221, 245, 297

mukoma 26

Mukombwe 11

mukuwasha 37, 41

munhu 200, 205

munun'una 26

murder, in chiefly families 107; by n'anga 163; and angry spirit 243f.; by witchcraft 180, 182, 189, 207, 248

muroyi (pl. varoyi) 179, 181, 183

Musami 56f.

musha 57, 58

Musikavanhu 109, 264, 273, 277

Muslim 7, 9, 11

Mutangakugara 277

Mutapa 3, 10f., 18

Mutare (formerly Umtali) 18

Mutasa 106, 255

Mutendi, Bishop 303-5

Mutota 10, 104, 264, 263; cult of 254, 277; medium of 256, 279

mutupo (pl. mitupo) 24f.

muzukuru 26 *33-6*, 127, 210, 217, 227f.

mwana (pl. vana) 26, 34, 37, 60

Mwari 67, 205, 277f.; cult of 12, 14, 70, 109, 117, *278-71*, 307; name spread by missionaries 277, 279

mweya 221, 222

Nalatale 12

name, personal 27, 215f., 320; clan 24f., 55, 61, 104; praise 25, n'anga 88, *149-51*, 234f.; divination by 156; treatment by 160-3; becoming a n. 163-8; contrasted with lion spirit mediums 254f.; in modern life 166f., 247

nationalism, nationalists, and chiefs 113, 123; opposition to community development programme 120; in cults 275, 281; hostility to missions 291

natural causes of illness and death 149, 173, 205f.

Ndau 12, 14, *17f.*; kinship 34; spirits 109, 243

Ndebele 268, 274, 279f.; settlement, invasion 6, 8, 12, 14, 17; relations with Shona 14, 17; spirits 246

Nehanda 259, 274, 276

Nembire 255

ngozi 233, 235; cuase of illness and death 159, 190, 207; and witchcraft 175

Nguni 7, 13

ngwena 154

nhokwara 154

Njanja 13

Noedza 255

Nyadenga 277

Nyakusengwa xix
Nyanhehwe 11

old age, and chiefship 107; of labour migrants 90-2, 97; security from family 28f., 46, 248; security from land 68, 71; similarity to spirits 220; in urban situation 302, 303f.
oral tradition 4, 5f., 12.
owl 175, 184
ox 72, 73f., 89; in ritual 201, 265, 280

parliament 119, 327
Paseka 299, 301, 302
Pfungwe 272
poison, the tool of witchcraft 150, 159, 177, 180f., 186, 207; use by n'anga 178, 181, 190; physical p. as witchcraft 177, 182
polygamy 49, 84; and Christian churches 291, 305f.; in towns 49, 314, 327
pool 162, 165, 202
Portuguese 4, 11f., 15
prophets 298, 300, 306; as diviners and healers 140, 169, 303f.; seeing faults 300f.; borrowing from traditional religion 295, 304; and witchcraft 195f., 295f., 306
prostitution 55, 96, 316, 321
Protestant 293, 294
purchase land, area 67, 79, *81-86*

quarrel, as independent churches 300, 301; and spirits 27, 231, 233, 262; associated with witchcraft 174, 186

rape 189
rates 58f., 73, 88
Roman Catholic Church 294, 296, 300
roora 41, 133, see also bride-price
Rozvi 12, 17, 68, 106, 110f.
rupenyu 111
rutsambo 41, 43, 48, 133

sabhuku 58
Sabi Valley 13, 87
sacrifice, of dedicated beast 27, 32, 232; cattle in 77; kinship relationships in 35, 42, 217; to Mwari 280; to angry spirit 206f., 234; in settling the spirit, 209, 211
sahwira 61f., 192, 209
Saint Mary's 313, 326
saving 97
schools, church controlled 286; in relation to chiefs 114, 119; to councils 120-2, 287; expenses 89; shortage of places 99; in relation to spirits 69, 268, 271
scorpion 245
secret, grudge 204; knowledge 161, 179; medicines 163, 177, 256, 295; of diviner-healers 256, 318; of witchcraft 177f., 179, 182, 256
sekuru 26, 33, 57
Sena 11, 13

trade, pre-colonial 3, 7f., 12f., 62f., 71; position of women affected by t. 51, 53; licence to 144

trade unions 323f.

Tribal Trust Land Act 113

tsetse fly 6, 28, 83

Tsonga 7

tsvitsa 212

ukama hwokutamba 34

umboo utsva hwavaPostori 298

university 99

uroyi 182; see also witchcraft

vadiki 230

vamwene 38

Vapostori 292, 297f.

vatete 26, 31, 318

vatorwa 265

Venda 7

voluntary associations 322-5

wage employment, labour 87-9, 92, 95; and agriculture 74; effects on family relations 29, 30; on position of women 53

war 14, 123, 145, 273-6, 281, 321, 329

ward 105

water, drinking 78, 245; supply 9, 86, 90; in towns 97, 311, 329; symbolic use in ritual 68, 161, 203, 213, 215, 232, 260; for test of fertility 47; in legend 165; use by spirit mediums 244f., 268; consecrated, in independent churches 169, 195, 300, 304

Wedza 13, 279

whites: w. administration and law 138, 144f.; desire for w. affluence 95, 98, 286f.; cattle sold cheaply to 78; independent churches and w. culture 307; relations with chiefs 111, 119; dominion over land 67; inequality with 99. 291; moved off land by 17, 71, 76, 87; mediums and w. culture 242, 276; w. missionaries 279, 293, 296; and Mwari 277, 280; w. settlers, early administration 14-6, 71, 88; spirits of 242, 246, 247; in towns 95, 313, 324, 328; war against 273-6; and witchcraft 186, 192, 193

widow, responsibility of family for 29, 210; inheritance of 51, 213, 214f., 249, 291; in mourning 204, 208; sexual intercourse with 182, 210; status of 191; in town 317

wild fruit 69, 72, 132, 137

Witchcraft Suppression Act 194

worn 161, 219-22

Zaire 299

Zambezi 6, 10, 16, 271; Z. Valley 3, 10, 18, 28, 115, 274

Zambia 84, 92, 123, 299

Zanu 113

Zezuru *17f*; mediums 257, 259; rituals 35, 103, 199; Nehanda 274; village structure 58

Ziki 68

Zimbabwe state 8f.; Great Zimbabwe 3, 8f., 12; Z. culture 8f.

Zimbabwe African Traditional Healers' Association 168

Zion 292 Zulu 14

Zionist Christian Church 303

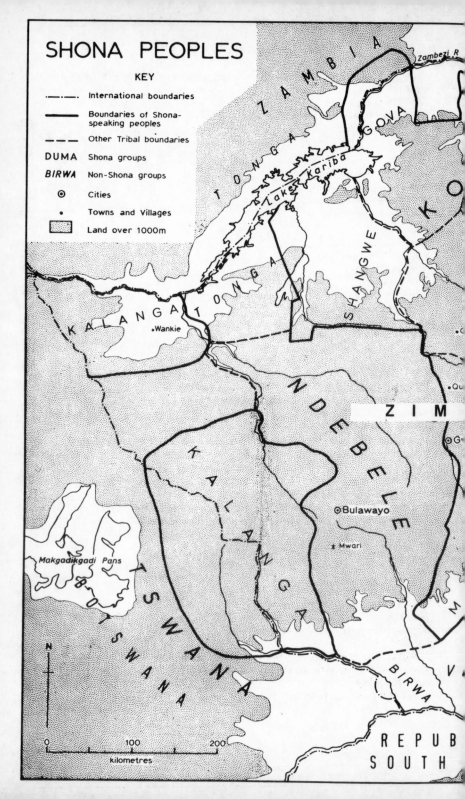

SHONA PEOPLES

KEY

‒ · ‒ · ‒ ·	International boundaries
——————	Boundaries of Shona-speaking peoples
– – – –	Other Tribal boundaries
DUMA	Shona groups
BIRWA	Non-Shona groups
⊙	Cities
·	Towns and Villages
▭	Land over 1000m

Zambezi R

ZAMBIA

GOVA

KO

TONGA

Lake Kariba

SHANGWE

KALANGA TONGA

·Wankie

·Qu

Z I M

N
D
E
B
E
L
E

·G

⊙Bulawayo

K
A
L
A
N
G
A

⋆ Mwari

Makgadikgadi Pans

B
O
T
S
W
A
N
A

M

BIRWA

V

N

0   100   200
kilometres

R E P U B
S O U T H

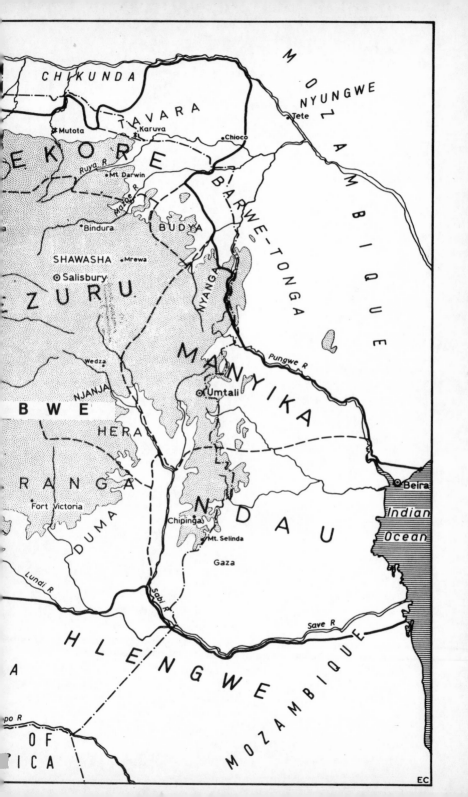